P9-BBO-616

THE GREAT AMERICAN ECONOMY

THE GREAT AMERICAN ECONOMY

HOW INEFFICIENCY BROKE IT AND WHAT WE CAN DO TO FIX IT

STEVE SLAVIN

59 John Glenn Drive
Amherst, New York 14228

Published 2017 by Prometheus Books

Inquiries should be addressed to
Prometheus Books
59 John Glenn Drive
Amherst, New York 14228
VOICE: 716–691–0133 • FAX: 716–691–0137
WWW.PROMETHEUSBOOKS.COM

21 20 19 18 17 5 4 3 2 1

Library of Congress Cataloging-in-Publication Data

Names: Slavin, Stephen L., author.
Title: The great American economy : how inefficiency broke it and what we can do to fix it / Steve Slavin.
Description: Amherst, New York : Prometheus Books, 2017. | Includes index.
Identifiers: LCCN 2016036582 (print) | LCCN 2016050164 (ebook) | ISBN 9781633883055 (hardcover) | ISBN 9781633883062 (ebook)
Subjects: LCSH: United States—Economic conditions—2009- | United States—Economic policy—2009- | United States--Social conditions—1980- | United States—Social policy—1993-
Classification: LCC HC106.84 .S59 2017 (print) | LCC HC106.84 (ebook) | DDC 330.973—dc23
LC record available at https://lccn.loc.gov/2016036582

Printed in the United States of America

CONTENTS

Introduction 13

PART I. LOSING OUR ECONOMIC BEARINGS 17

Chapter 1. Is Our Economy Fundamentally Sound? 19

Our Economic Fundamentals 19
Our Top Eight Fundamental Problems 20
Six Additional Problems 22
An Unsustainable Economic Course 22

Chapter 2. What Went Wrong? 25

No More Lean and Mean 25
Wasting Our Resources 26
Our Shrinking Manufacturing Base 29
The American Economic System 29

PART II. SIX CATACLYSMIC EVENTS 31

Chapter 3. Depression and War 33

The Great Depression 33
World War II 36
Employer-Based Healthcare Insurance 38
Summary and Conclusion 39

Chapter 4. Suburbanization 41

The Great Suburban Migration after World War II 42
Suburban Sprawl 43
Public Transportation in the Suburbs 45

Our Wasteful Suburban Lifestyle 46
The Consequences of Suburbanization 47
The Abandonment of Our Cities 48
Summary and Conclusion 49

Chapter 5. The Cold War 51

The Emerging Soviet Threat 51
Fighting World Communism 52
The Economic War 54
De-Escalation and Victory 55
The Cost of Victory 55
Summary and Conclusion 56

Chapter 6. Globalization and Global Warming 59

Globalization 59
Global Warming 64

PART III. THE DEINDUSTRIALIZATION OF AMERICA 71

Chapter 7. The Rise and Fall of American Industrial Power 73

The Rise of American Industrial Power 73
The Age of the Industrial Capitalist 74
From the Turn of the Century to the Great Depression 75
Wartime and Postwar Prosperity 75
The Fall of American Industrial Power 76
Last Word 79

Chapter 8. Innovation, Infrastructure, and Industrial Policy 81

How We Lost Our Innovative Edge 81
The Erosion of Our Innovative Capacity 82
The Growing Technical Proficiency of Our Global Competitors 87
Our Crumbling Infrastructure 89
Industrial Policy 91
Solutions 93

PART IV. JOBS, WAGES, AND THE JOB SHORTAGE 97

Chapter 9. Jobs and Wages 99

The Good Old Postwar Years 99
The Process of Creative Destruction 100
The Loss of Manufacturing Jobs 100
Measuring the Effect of Offshoring and Automation on the Loss of Manufacturing Jobs 101
The Next Ten Years 103
The Decline of Organized Labor 104
The Working-Class Job Squeeze 105
Is Wal-Mart Creating Bad Jobs and Destroying Good Ones? 105
The Two-Tier Wage System 107
Outsourcing vs. Offshoring 108
Offshoring and Wages 109
The Effects of Automation 110
Stagnation in Real Wages 111

Chapter 10. The Job Shortage 115

Jobs for High School Graduates 115
Jobs for College Graduates 116
Conclusion 117

PART V. WASTING OUR RESOURCES BY USING THEM INEFFICIENTLY 119

Chapter 11. Our Wasteful Transportation System 121

The Way We Were 121
The Shift from Public to Private Transportation 122
Bigger, but Not Better 125
The Advantages of Public Transportation 125
Cars, Trains, Planes, Buses, and Trucks 128
The Cost of Our Wasteful Transportation System 129
Solutions 130

Chapter 12. Our Failing Public Schools 133

What Are the Causes of Our Educational Decline? 133
Five Major Problems 135
Education and Poverty 142
Separate, but Still Unequal 143
Finding a Decent School for Your Child 144
Our Community Colleges and Career Schools 145
The Cost of Our Wasteful Public Education System 146
How Our Public Education System Can Be Fixed 147
Fixing What Doesn't Work 154

Chapter 13. Our Sick Healthcare System 159

Rising Healthcare Spending 159
Healthcare Financing 160
Seven Factors Pushing Up the Cost of Healthcare 163
The Affordable Care Act (ACA) of 2010 167
The Cost of Our Bloated Healthcare System 168
Solutions 168
A Comprehensive Solution 173

PART VI. WASTING OUR RESOURCES BY OVERPRODUCING 179

Chapter 14. The Military-Industrial Complex 181

The Economic Cost of Supporting a Huge Military Establishment 181
The All-Volunteer Army 182
Our Perpetual War Machine 183
The High Cost of Projecting American Military Power 184
Fighting the War on Terror 185
The Cost of Wasting Resources on Defense 186
Solutions 186

Chapter 15. The Criminal Justice Establishment 189

The Young Black and Hispanic Criminal 190
Incarcerating the Mentally Ill 191
Our Prison Population 191
The High Cost of Crime 193
Solutions 194
Summing Up 199

Chapter 16. Our Bloated Financial Sector 201

The Economic Role of Banking 201
Deregulation 203
The Financial Crisis of 2008 205
Dodd-Frank Wall Street Reform and Consumer Protection Act 207
The Financialization of the American Economy 208
The Economic Effects of Financialization 208
Financial Predators 210
The Real Estate Industry 211
The Insurance Industry 211
Summing Up 211
Solutions 212
Conclusion 214

PART VII. WASTING OUR RESOURCES BY PRODUCING USELESS GOODS AND SERVICES 217

Chapter 17. The Internal Revenue Code and the Tax Preparation Industry 219

The Cost of Compliance 219
Who Gains from a Complicated Tax Code? 220
Lower Tax Rates 222
The Cost of Complying with the Internal Revenue Code 223
Sharing the Tax Burden 223
Solutions 224

Chapter 18. Telemarketers, Ambulance Chasers, and Other Make-Work Occupations 225

Phone Work 226
The Healthcare Sector 227
Sales Reps 228
Our Best and Our Brightest 229
The Government Sector 230
Solutions 231

PART VIII. THE ECONOMIC, SOCIAL, AND POLITICAL CONSEQUENCES OF WASTING OUR RESOURCES 233

Chapter 19. The Economic Consequences of Wasting Our Resources 235

Our Wasteful Suburban Lifestyle 235
The Transportation Sector 235
The Public Education Sector 236
The Healthcare Sector 237
The Military-Industrial Complex 238
The Criminal Justice Sector 239
The Financial Sector 239
The Internal Revenue Code and the Make-Work Sector 240
Summing Up 240

Chapter 20. Our Twin Deficits 243

The Federal Budget Deficit 243
The Foreign Trade Deficit 246
Last Word: Cause and Effect 251

Chapter 21. Our Unraveling Social Contract 253

The New Deal 254
The Postwar Labor-Management Social Contract 254
The GI Bill of Rights 256
Making African Americans a Party to the Social Contract 256

The Great Society Program 257
The Unraveling of the Social Contract 258
Entitlement Spending 259
Cutting Entitlements 259
Cutting Government Subsidies 260
Conclusion 260

Chapter 22. Growing Income Inequality and the Shrinking Middle Class 261

The Great Compression and the Great Divergence 262
The Poor 264
The Middle Class 264
The Rich 266
Income Inequality Before and After Taxes and Government Spending 266
The Consequences of Income Inequality 268
Last Word 271

Chapter 23. Poverty and the Growing Permanent Underclass 273

The Urban Ghettoes before and after Suburbanization 274
Defining Poverty and Counting the Poor 274
Three Different Poverty Groups 275
The Growing Permanent American Underclass 275
Child Poverty 278
Last Word 278

PART IX. RESTORING THE AMERICAN ECONOMY 281

Chapter 24. How We Are Wasting Our Resources: The Big Picture 283

Our Top Eight Fundamental Economic Problems 284
A Holistic Approach: How Our Economic Problems Impact Upon Each Other 292

Chapter 25. Solving Our Economic Problems and Saving the American Economy 295

Solving Our Eight Fundamental Economic Problems 295
Last Word 306

Chapter 26. The Great Job Switch: Placing Tens of Millions of Americans in Useful Jobs 307

The Big Four 308
Other Major Economic Sectors 310
The Make-Work Sector 315
Private and Public Bureaucrats 317
Putting the Permanent Underclass Back to Work 317
My Personal Wish List of Jobs 318
Matching Job Applicants with Job Openings 319
Let's Do the Math 319
Getting People to Switch Jobs 320
War and Peace 321
A Word about Bernie Sanders's Presidential Campaign Platform 322

Chapter 27. A Long-Term Strategy to Save the American Economy 325

Ask the Experts 326
Presidential Commissions 326
BRAC 327
In Time of Economic Crisis 329
Shovel-Ready Projects 329
Summing Up Our Basic Economic Problem 330
Last Word 330

Acknowledgments 333

Notes 335

Index 389

INTRODUCTION

Make America great again.
—President Donald J. Trump's campaign slogan when he was a 2016 Republican presidential nominee

America already IS great!
—Hillary Rodham Clinton's response when she was a 2016 Democratic presidential nominee

To a large degree, Trump and Clinton were arguing about the state of the American economy. Trump won this very close election largely because tens of millions of his supporters believed the economy was not working for them.

Let's try to put aside our lingering feelings about the election and ask ourselves three very basic questions:

1. Was our economy *ever* great?
2. Is our economy great right now?
3. If not, how can we make it great again?

These three questions sum up what we'll be talking about in this book.

Back in 1941, Henry Luce, the most influential magazine publisher of his day, wrote an editorial in *Life* magazine entitled, "The American Century." Although the twentieth century was not yet half over, history has certainly proven him right.

By the turn of the twentieth century we had built the world's best transportation system, enabling people to travel quickly, comfortably, and cheaply, not just within urban areas but all the way across our vast country. Because we were the first nation to provide free universal public education, our well-trained and well-educated labor force gave us a huge competitive advantage in the emerging global economy. And our mass-production and mass-market economy made us the world's leading industrial power.

That, in turn, enabled us to become the world's foremost military power. Not only had the combination of American soldiers and our nation's economic might been decisive in winning World Wars I and II, but we then contained world communism from the mid-1940s through the 1980s. With the collapse of the Soviet Union, we were the only military and economic superpower left standing.

There is a widely held belief in American exceptionalism, perhaps best expressed by the line from our national hymn, "America the Beautiful"— "God shed his grace on thee." If you close your eyes, can't you just picture those "amber waves of grain"? And those "purple mountain majesties"?

We are a nation of great individualists. This powerful trait drove the pioneers to set out in covered wagons, traveling across the continent to settle on the free land they had been promised. Individualism also drove tens of millions of Americans to start their own businesses, helping to build the United States into an economic colossus.

Each generation has enjoyed a higher standard of living than its parents' generation. We have always been a nation of dreamers and a land of seemingly unlimited opportunity. As such, we have been a beacon of hope and a magnet for generations of immigrants hoping to better their own lives and the lives of their children.

As you must have surmised from this book's title, I believe that our economy is in very serious trouble. Ten or fifteen years from now, the standard of living of our average citizen may actually be lower than it is today. Large swaths of the suburbs will be slums, and tens of millions of Americans will have joined the permanent underclass. There will be three separate Americas—the rich and near rich, an economically downscaled middle and working class, and a very large poor population.

Our present and our future are being shaped by events that took place sixty, seventy, and even eighty years ago. Throughout this book we'll trace the effects of five cataclysmic events:

- The Great Depression
- World War II
- Our postwar suburbanization
- The Cold War
- Globalization

These events—and how we dealt with them—set off our long-term economic decline. But that decline has been imperceptible to the general public and even to the practitioners of the most dismal of sciences—my fellow economists. Still, once you've examined all the evidence, I think you will agree that our nation is in economic decline.

Long before the financial crisis and the Great Recession, there were clear indications that there was something rotten in the state of the American economy. For example, John J. Sweeney, who headed the AFL-CIO from 1995 to 2009, was fond of proclaiming, "America needs a raise."[1] He was referring not just to union members but to all nonsupervisory workers—some 80 percent of our workforce. He was right: the average hourly wage rate for these workers (adjusted for inflation) had not increased since the early 1970s.[2]

It is said that a nation should be judged by how well it treats its children. You probably remember the words to a song written and performed by Michael Jackson in 1985: "We Are the World." The song's title is repeated in each of its choruses. Do you remember the next line?

The next line says, in other words, that the children *are* our world! And yet in America, one of the world's richest nations, more than one out of five children is growing up in poverty.[3] Indeed, among all wealthy nations, we have one of the highest child poverty rates.[4]

Despite periodic recessions and occasional depressions, total employment always grew from one decade to the next. But during the first decade of the new millennium, for the first time in our nation's history, total employment did not grow.

Perhaps the most persuasive indicator of our nation's economic decline is that millennials are on track to be the first generation in our nation's history to be poorer than its parents' generation. In January 2017, CNBC reported,

> With a median household income of $40,581, millennials earn 20 percent less than boomers did at the same stage of life, despite being better educated, according to a new analysis of Federal Reserve data by the advocacy group Young Invincibles.[5]

These are just a few of the symptoms of our nation's long-term economic decline. But my purpose in writing this book is not to grieve over these symptoms, but to examine their causes. Why did the world's greatest economy become so much less efficient?

While economists agree about almost nothing, we are unanimous in believing that a nation must use its resources as efficiently as possible. Or, as the popular aphorism goes, "Waste not, want not." Increasingly, the American economy has been wasting its resources.

Ask yourself why we spend almost twice as much per capita on healthcare as most other rich countries, but Americans are no healthier than the citizens of these other countries. Or why half the entering freshmen at our colleges need to take remedial courses. Or why we account for nearly 40 percent of the world's military spending.[6]

No economy, no matter how large or how rich, can afford to use its resources as inefficiently as we have during recent decades. While some of our global competitors face similar problems, none must deal with so many.

Over the course of this book we shall answer three questions:

1. How do we explain our growing inefficiency?
2. What are our most serious economic problems?
3. How can we solve them?

Francis Bacon observed, "A prudent question is one-half of wisdom." While no one knows all the answers, one can at least try to ask the right questions. By writing this book, I hope to start a national discussion about what needs to be done.

Part I

LOSING OUR ECONOMIC BEARINGS

Political leaders from President Herbert Hoover to Sen. John McCain have proclaimed our economy fundamentally sound. But if our economy were *indeed* all that sound, then why would it be necessary to state the obvious?

In chapter 1, we shall enumerate our top eight fundamental economic problems. No economy with so many serious problems can be considered sound.

Then, in chapter 2, we shall describe how, in just a few decades, we managed to transform ourselves from the world's greatest economy into a declining economic power. What are we doing wrong? We are wasting a lot of our precious resources by using them inefficiently and by producing goods and services that don't raise our standard of living.

Chapter 1

IS OUR ECONOMY FUNDAMENTALLY SOUND?

The economy is fundamentally sound.

—President Herbert Hoover, 1931

Because our poor economic performance has been such a hot topic, there is no shortage of books explaining what went wrong and how it can be fixed. Each author believes that if we can solve just one or two problems, we can get our economy back on course. It has long been part of our can-do national psyche that there is a simple solution to almost every problem—from curing bad breath or erectile dysfunction to bad credit or body odor. So common sense tells us that there must also be a simple solution for our bad economy.

Most Americans agree that our economic troubles stem from just one or two basic causes. On the political right, Tea Party supporters think that if we drastically reduce federal government spending, taxation, and regulation, we could restore our economic state of grace. And those on the political left want to raise taxes levied on the rich and on highly profitable corporations and to redistribute the proceeds to the middle class, the working class, and the poor.

OUR ECONOMIC FUNDAMENTALS

Donald Trump's 2016 presidential campaign slogan was "Make America great again." He observed that while some people were very prosperous, tens of millions of Americans had been left far behind. How would he fix our economy? Mainly by cutting taxes, government spending and regulation, bringing back manufacturing jobs that had been shifted to other countries, and negotiating more advantageous trade treaties.

He also proposed repealing and replacing the Affordable Care Act (aka Obamacare), raising military spending, spending one trillion dollars to rebuild our crumbling infrastructure, and building a wall on our border with Mexico to keep out illegal immigrants.

Because President Trump was in office for just one hundred days before this book went to print, it was far too soon to know whether Congress would pass the legislation necessary to put his proposals into effect. Indeed, with the exceptions of a $54 billion defense spending increase for fiscal year 2018 and a strong effort to repeal and replace the Affordable Care Act (Obamacare), the Trump administration provided few other economic policy specifics until April 26, 2017, when Trump released his tax plan, which called for rate cuts in the corporate income and personal income taxes and the elimination of the inheritance tax.[1]

During his first one hundred days in office, President Trump did not have any notable legislative triumphs, but he did sustain a major setback. Although he spent weeks negotiating with Republican Congress members over a bill authored by House Speaker Paul Ryan to repeal and replace Obamacare, the bill was withdrawn when it became apparent that it would not be passed.

OUR TOP EIGHT FUNDAMENTAL PROBLEMS

Whenever Sen. John McCain looks back at the 2008 presidential campaign, he will probably never forget the day he may have lost the election. It was September 15 when he proclaimed, "The fundamentals of the economy are strong."[2] In politics, as in stand-up comedy, it's all in the timing. So when Lehman Brothers filed for the largest bankruptcy in US history just hours later, McCain appeared very much out of touch.

But was he *wrong*? Before answering, please look at the list of our top eight fundamental problems shown below.

1. Our inefficient transportation system: because we go almost everywhere by car, Americans spend twice as much on transportation as the citizens of most other rich nations.[3]
2. Our failing schools: just half of our eighteen-year-olds can function at an eighth-grade level.[4]
3. Our sick healthcare system: healthcare costs nearly twice as much per capita in the United States than it does in most other economically advanced nations.[5]
4. The military-industrial complex: we account for nearly 40 percent of the world's military spending.[6]

5. The criminal justice establishment: we have, by far, the highest incarceration rate among economically advanced nations.[7]
6. Our bloated financial sector: this sector is diverting increasing amounts of savings from productive investments into speculative activities.[8]
7. Our huge and growing make-work sector: more than fifteen million Americans hold jobs that do not produce any useful goods or services.[9]
8. Our shrinking manufacturing base: much of what had once been "Made in the USA" is now made in Japan, China, South Korea, Mexico, and other nations.[10]

Let's consider the first two items on this list.

One very important factor in our rise to economic power was the world-class public transportation system we had built by the turn of the twentieth century. Since the 1930s it has been almost completely destroyed as we became increasingly dependent on automobile transportation. Nearly all our global economic competitors have far better public transportation systems.

By 1900 we had built the world's first free, universal public education system, providing our nation with a well-trained and well-educated labor force. Now, just half of our eighteen-year-olds can function at an eighth-grade level.[11] On international examinations, our students usually rank below those from other economically advanced nations.

During the last eight decades, we have managed to turn some of our economic strengths into weaknesses. Are you old enough to remember the old Charles Atlas cartoon ad showing a beach bully kicking sand into the faces of a skinny guy and his girlfriend? That weakling took the Charles Atlas bodybuilding course, which soon enabled him to beat up the bully. Our nation seems to have taken a Charles Atlas course in reverse. We are well on our way to converting ourselves from an economic colossus into a ninety-seven-pound economic weakling.

Clearly then, many of the fundamentals of our economy are *not* strong. Henry Clay, a three-time presidential candidate, once remarked, "I'd rather be right than president." John McCain, sadly, was neither right *nor* president.

SIX ADDITIONAL PROBLEMS

We cannot reverse our economic decline without solving these eight fundamental problems. But even *that* would not be enough. These problems are largely responsible for six additional problems, which must also be addressed:

- There is a great shortage of decent jobs.[12]
- The average hourly wage rate (adjusted for inflation) for nonsupervisory workers has not increased since 1973.[13]
- Our income distribution is becoming increasingly unequal.[14]
- Our growing permanent underclass perpetuates itself from one generation to the next.[15]
- Our huge federal budget deficits are unsustainable.[16]
- Because we are running large trade deficits, we must borrow more than $1 billion a day from foreigners.[17]

Much of the debate about our economy has focused on these six problems. Indeed, the first three were central issues during the 2016 presidential election. Still, if we are to reverse our decline and once again become the world's greatest economy, we shall need to concentrate mainly on our top eight fundamental economic problems. Once they are solved, it will be much easier to deal with these six additional problems.

AN UNSUSTAINABLE ECONOMIC COURSE

Sixty years ago the United States was almost self-sufficient: we produced what we consumed and ran a trade surplus with the rest of the world. Today our nation consumes more than it produces, spends more than it earns, and needs to borrow large amounts of money from foreigners to finance its huge trade deficits. Wouldn't it be great if we could identify our problem, fix it, and then move on? But we can't point to any single cause, nor is there a magic bullet we can use to make it all better.

Our two most recent former Federal Reserve chairmen, Alan Greenspan and Ben Bernanke, have both observed that our current economic course is unsustainable. Perhaps they were thinking of Stein's Law, which was invoked by Herbert Stein, who had served as President Nixon's chief economic advisor: "If something cannot go on forever, it will stop."

Our top eight fundamental problems did not materialize overnight. The origins of some problems can be traced back to the Great Depression of the 1930s. During these last eighty years we sowed the seeds of our economic destruction. No longer the lean and mean industrial machine of the 1940s and 1950s, we are well down the road to long-term economic decline. To see how all of this happened, we need to look at the record.

Chapter 2

WHAT WENT WRONG?

We have met the enemy and he is us.

—*Pogo* comic strip, August 1970

What gave us our economic edge, and how did we lose it? Through most of the last century, we were the world's largest and most efficient producer of industrial goods. Anything you could make, we could make better—and cheaper. We did this by combining great technical know-how and a highly skilled labor force with the world's largest and most technologically advanced stock of plant and equipment. But today, much of the world's manufacturing has shifted to East Asia where multinational corporations have combined capital and the latest technology with highly motivated, well-educated, low-wage workers.

NO MORE LEAN AND MEAN

America limps along, a superpower that, like a star high-school athlete grown middle-aged, ate too much but didn't exercise.

—Anna Quindlen

Our economy, once the envy of the world, has grown quite flabby and inefficient. Like the old high school athlete, we keep eating as if we were in training, but we're no longer burning off all those calories. Still world-class consumers, but no longer world-class producers, we manage to keep up our consumption by borrowing over $1 billion a day from foreigners.[1]

How do we explain our astounding about-face from economic colossus to economic also-ran? To sum up all our problems in one sentence: *we are not using our resources as efficiently as our global competitors are using theirs.*

Two of the most important words in an economist's vocabulary are "efficiency" and "scarcity." They are always included in the definition of economics that can be found in any introductory economics textbook.

Here's the one you'll find in my *own* text: *economics is the efficient allocation of the scarce means of production toward satisfaction of human wants.* Using our scarce land, labor, and capital efficiently, we produce a large and growing amount of goods and services to meet the needs of our people.

While economists rarely agree, all of us believe that wasting resources is just about the worst thing that we can do. Our top eight fundamental problems illustrate how we are wasting our scarce resources. We are doing so either by using them inefficiently or by producing goods and services that don't improve our standard of living.

Let's look at the operations of two hypothetical pizzerias to show how we can compare their relative efficiencies. It costs the Leaning Tower of Pizza five dollars to produce a large pie, and it costs pi r Square Pizza seven dollars to produce an identical pie. Clearly, the Leaning Tower of Pizza is the more efficient pizza maker.

So, one way of comparing efficiency is by measuring cost. A second way is by comparing the amount of labor that is used. If it takes two people an hour to bake eleven large pies at the Leaning Tower of Pizza and it takes three people an hour to bake eleven large pies at pi r Square Pizza, then the Leaning Tower of Pizza is the more efficient pizza maker.

Until the 1930s we were still building what was, by far, the world's most efficient economy. We were able to turn out a wide array of goods and services more efficiently than any other nation on earth. But since then, we have allowed more and more inefficiencies to develop. Before we can even begin to set things right, we need to understand how this happened.

WASTING OUR RESOURCES

Every nation uses its resources—its land, labor, and capital—to produce the goods and services that its citizens consume. Until the 1960s we *did* use them more efficiently than any other nation. But since then we have been wasting increasing amounts of our resources—especially our labor.

Today we employ tens of millions of people who don't produce any useful goods or services. All of their work is utterly wasted. This happens three ways: (1) by using our labor inefficiently, (2) by producing much more output in some economic sectors than we need, and (3) by producing some goods and services that we don't need at all. We'll consider each in turn.

Wasting Our Resources by Using Them Inefficiently

How can we tell when resources are being used inefficiently? If a business owner's costs are much higher than those of her competitors, she knows she's using her resources inefficiently. Similarly, if it costs a lot more to produce a good or service in *one* country than in other countries, the high-cost country is using its resources much less efficiently. Let's compare our cost of production in three major economic sectors—transportation, education, and healthcare—with the production costs in other wealthy nations.

Over a period of about thirty years—from the 1930s through the 1950s—we managed to replace a world-class public transportation system with one based on extremely inefficient and costly private automobile travel. Today, transportation costs the average American family about twice as much as the average family in nearly every other wealthy nation.[2]

Our public education system is another prime example of using our labor inefficiently. Half of our eighteen-year-olds cannot read, write, or do arithmetic at an eighth-grade level. And over half of all incoming college freshmen are placed in remedial courses where they are taught elementary and middle school English and math.[3] We spend much more per capita on education than virtually every other nation, but we get a lot less for our money.

Now let's look at healthcare, which now accounts for 18 percent of our gross domestic product—our annual output of goods and services.[4] Per capita healthcare spending is almost twice that of other economically advanced nations, but the health of Americans is no better than the health of the citizens of the other nations.[5]

Wasting Our Resources by Overproducing in Some Economic Sectors

In three major economic sectors—defense, criminal justice, and financial services—we produce a much greater output of goods and services than we need. Do we really have to spend over $700 billion a year to defend our country, considering that the Cold War ended in 1989, and that our long-time adversary, the Soviet Union, no longer exists?[6] Our defense spending is driven largely by the military-industrial complex—a consortium of our major defense contractors, leading members of the House and Senate Armed Services Committees, high-ranking military officers, and Defense Department officials.

Because we imprison so many nonviolent offenders, our per capita incarceration rate is at least five times as high as that of nearly every other economically advanced nation.[7] Our entire criminal justice system—the police, courts, and prisons—consumes vast amounts of our resources. And yet, our rates of violent crime are the highest in the industrial world.

Now let's look at our huge financial sector, whose share of our GDP has doubled since 1970 to 9 percent.[8] Fifty years ago, financial institutions occupied themselves by channeling the savings of tens of millions of Americans into business investments in plant and equipment, and into the construction of railroads, canals, and the rest of our infrastructure. But since around 1970, the focus of the financial sector has been directed increasingly into speculative activities, eventually leading to the 2008 financial crisis.

Wasting Our Resources by Producing Goods and Services That We Don't Need

More than fifteen million Americans—most of whom work very hard—actually produce no useful goods or services. No other economically advanced nation employs such a large fraction of its labor force in make-work jobs.

Our byzantine Internal Revenue Code has resulted in the employment of three million people whose labors result in nothing that contributes to our economic well-being. And what useful services are provided by telemarketers, ambulance chasers, and the bureaucrats employed by overlapping government agencies, such as federal, state, and local departments of education, health, and environmental protection?

Now please consider this: huge armies of employees working for hospitals, doctors, and other medical practitioners spend most of their workday attempting to get reimbursement from insurance companies, while opposing armies of insurance company employees spend *their* days trying to either deny these claims or to reduce them. Basically, these forces cancel each other out, so their net contribution to our healthcare is zero.

We have just seen that our economy wastes vast amounts of our resources by using them inefficiently, by overproducing in some sectors, and by producing goods and services that we don't need. When we add up all the sectors wasting these resources, they account for three-fifths of our national output. Just imagine how much higher our living standard would be if our economy operated more efficiently.

OUR SHRINKING MANUFACTURING BASE

The clearest sign of our economic demise is the loss of most of our manufacturing base. Since the late 1940s, when we produced nearly half the world's manufactured goods, our share has fallen to just one-sixth, as foreign competitors have picked off one industry after another.[9] Today Americans often complain that "We don't make anything anymore." While a gross exaggeration, this statement does reflect the decimation of our steel, ship-building, home appliance, textile, apparel, TV, PC, and consumer electronics industries. In 2010 China surpassed us as the world's largest manufacturer, and it now produces twice as many cars and eight times as much steel as we do.[10] If current trends continue, in about ten years China's manufacturing output will be double ours.

THE AMERICAN ECONOMIC SYSTEM

Back in 1776, when Adam Smith completed his magisterial *The Wealth of Nations*, capitalism was in its infancy. His basic tenet was that business owners, seeking to maximize their profits, were driven to run their firms very efficiently. Not only would these entrepreneurs grow rich, but nations would use their resources very efficiently and would grow rich.

Throughout the entire nineteenth century, and well into the twentieth, we built the world's greatest economy by closely following Smith's private enterprise capitalist model. The defining characteristic of capitalism is the private ownership of the means of production. Despite the disappointing performance of our economy in recent decades, none of our political leaders—not even Bernie Sanders—has suggested that we abandon the capitalist model (see box: "We Can't Afford Everything"). In fact, the political debate has been confined largely to the levels of taxes and government spending, and the degree to which the government should regulate our economy. While some might call our economy socialistic, it doesn't even come close. The overwhelming majority of the means of production is firmly in the hands of private owners.

We Can't Afford Everything

As very young children, we learn that we can't afford to buy certain things. Even the children of relatively well-to-do families are told that certain luxury goods are just too expensive. Poor children learn that even an inexpensive toy or a new pair of shoes is unaffordable.

In his recent book, *Our Revolution*, Bernie Sanders asked why the United States does not provide for some of the basic needs of its citizens, while virtually every other country meets the needs of its own population. Why don't we provide paid medical leave after the birth of a child, universal childcare, medical insurance for all, and free college tuition?[11]

During the 2016 presidential campaign, his opponent for the Democratic nomination, and virtually every Republican candidate asked a very reasonable question: How will you *pay* for all of this? After all, it will cost trillions of dollars a year. How could even the "Great American Economy" afford to spend such great sums?

And yet, as Sanders repeatedly pointed out, *other* rich nations could afford to do all of this. So how come *they* could afford it, while we can't?

We can't because our economy has grown too inefficient to provide for most of these needs. Throughout this book, you'll learn how this happened—and what we'll need to do to turn things around.

Like most of my fellow economists, I am a strong believer in the efficient workings of a free-enterprise economy. As we proceed through this book, the question we seek to answer is how we can make our capitalist economy operate much more efficiently.

But before we can fix our economy, we need to know what went wrong. In part II we'll learn how our nation was overtaken by five cataclysmic events, and how a sixth may pose the greatest threat of all.

Part II

SIX CATACLYSMIC EVENTS

The Great Depression was, by far, the worst period in our entire economic history. Recovery did not fully set in until Congress, at the behest of President Franklin Roosevelt, began to ramp up military spending in anticipation of our entry into World War II. What followed were three decades of unparalleled prosperity. But during this period, we were also sowing the seeds of our subsequent economic decline.

Just as the onset of World War II brought an end to the Great Depression, soon after the war's end we were overtaken by two more cataclysmic events—the advent of the Cold War and the suburbanization of our nation. The Cold War, which would continue for the next four and a half decades, pitted the United States and its allies against the forces of worldwide Communist expansion. By the end of the 1980s the Cold War was winding down and the process of suburbanization had been almost completed. But again, the ways that our nation had met these challenges would contribute to our economic decline.

Globalization was the fifth event that would dramatically affect our economy and, in the long run, be part of the process of our economic self-destruction. The shrinkage of our manufacturing base, the leveling off of wage increases, and the downsizing of the great American middle class were all very damaging consequences of this process. When economic historians look back at the twentieth century to understand how the greatest economy in the history of the world could so rapidly self-destruct, they will point to these five cataclysmic events.

Each of these events contributed to our economic self-destruction. Now we are beginning to feel the effects of global warming, our sixth cataclysmic event. We have already begun to feel its economic effects, most notably in Hurricane Katrina, which struck the Gulf Coast in 2005, bringing death and vast damage in its wake, followed in 2012 by Hurricane Sandy, which struck a large swath of the East Coast, bringing still more death and destruction.

Chapter 3
DEPRESSION AND WAR

For Americans who came of age in the 1930s, the two defining events of their lives were the Great Depression and World War II. Both posed existential challenges to our nation that forced the federal government to take extraordinary measures to meet them. The good news was that these challenges were met successfully. The bad news was that in meeting them, we created conditions that would lead to the long-run decline of our economy.

THE GREAT DEPRESSION

If you think our economic performance was the main issue debated in the 2016 election, then you can just imagine how much more important it was in the election of 1932, during the depths of the Great Depression. Today, many Americans believe the economic role of the federal government is too *big*, while eighty years ago, most people were demanding that the government do much, much *more*.

Transportation

When President Franklin Roosevelt took office in 1933, one out of every four Americans was officially unemployed, and millions more had simply given up looking for work.[1] The main way to create millions of jobs was for the government to set up huge public works projects, which included building hydroelectric dams, airports, bridges, highways, schools, post offices, and other government buildings. About 80 percent of Roosevelt's New Deal's total spending was on construction.[2]

Of the two million construction workers hired, nearly half were employed on street or highway projects.[3] During the decade of the 1930s our surfaced road mileage doubled to nearly 1.4 million miles.[4] Killing two birds with one stone, we put a lot of people back to work, while creating more and better roads and highways. Without this tremendous investment, our postwar suburbanization could not have been based on automobile transportation.

Even in retrospect, would it be fair to blame the Roosevelt administration and Congress for lack of foresight in creating some of the conditions necessary for the postwar suburbanization? During the Depression, the number one priority was putting huge numbers of people back to work. Was doubling the mileage of paved roads and highways such a terrible thing? Who could have foreseen that this would facilitate the abandonment of our cities? Or even the shift in freight hauling from trains to trucks?

At the same time we were building roads and highways, we were allowing our world-class public transportation system to be sold off, or to fall into disrepair. The main villain of the piece was General Motors, and its role is described by Jane Holtz Kay:

> In 1932, General Motors, the manufacturer of buses . . . formed a consortium of tire, oil, and highway men to buy and shut down America's streetcar systems. Attacking the trolley mile by mile, the syndicate of General Motors, Firestone, Standard Oil, and Mack Truck, allied as National City Lines, cajoled and bought off local officials. . . . Between 1932 and 1949 they would help persuade 100 electric systems in more than forty-five cities to scrap their street rails. . . . By 1940 total public transportation ridership had shrunk by 2 billion. The magnificent rail lines fell, taking with them the private rights-of-way, the street corridors, that had insured their fast passage.[5]

Housing

Every month during the Great Depression tens of thousands of families were defaulting on their mortgages and losing their homes. Under the National Housing Act of 1934, the Federal Housing Administration (FHA) was created to insure mortgage loans by banks and other private lenders. Over time, this agency was a great success, enabling hundreds of thousands of families to keep their homes and millions more to buy new ones, primarily in the suburbs.

The FHA also had the Home Owners' Loan Corporation establish guidelines in 239 cities for the types of neighborhoods in which it would or would not insure mortgages. The most desirable areas were generally relatively well-to-do white neighborhoods in the suburbs; the least desirable areas were relatively poor, predominately African American neighborhoods in the cities. These neighborhoods were literally redlined on maps maintained by banks and other mortgage lenders. A redlined neighborhood was denied mortgage loans based on racial or ethnic composition without regard to the residents' qualifications or creditworthiness. FHA publications implied that different races should not share neighborhoods and repeatedly listed neighborhood characteristics like "inharmonious racial or nationality groups" alongside such noxious disseminates as "smoke, odors, and fog."[6]

Black families were effectively barred from receiving federally insured mortgage loans. If they tried to buy a home in a predominately black neighborhood, they found that this area was redlined, and therefore ineligible for federal mortgage insurance. Basically, the only way to buy a home there would be to pay cash, which few families could afford. And if a black family attempted to buy a house in a predominately *white* neighborhood—one that was *not* redlined—real estate brokers would refuse to show them any houses and homeowners would refuse to sell. And even if they *were* willing to sell to a black family, restrictive neighborhood racial covenants legally forbid the sale of homes to black families.[7]

African Americans were basically confined to what became known as inner-city neighborhoods, almost entirely as renters. Eventually, in the 1950s and 1960s, as millions of working-class, middle-class, and well-to-do black families were able to move out of these neighborhoods, most of those left behind soon became charter members of our growing permanent underclass.

The strong preference of the FHA for insuring mainly suburban homes set the stage for the post–World War II suburbanization of the country. This policy, along with that of the Veterans Administration to provide mortgage loans solely to white war veterans, ensured that the first wave of suburbanites would be white, while urban blacks were confined largely to the cities.

Because of the terrible economic conditions, by the late 1930s, the nation's birthrate fell by about 20 percent from its rate in the late 1920s.[8] It would not rise again until after World War II. Similarly, home construction fell dramatically during the Depression, as millions of families lost their homes through foreclosure.

Within a year after the war ended, some twelve million men and several hundred thousand women returned home to their civilian lives. Very little housing had been built during the war and the preceding depressed period, so most veterans came back to overcrowded houses and apartments, often with three generations under one roof. The first thing the veterans wanted was new housing. And next on their list was having more children. Couples had been forced to put off having children, not just because of the war, but in the years before that because of the Depression.

And so, the Depression and the war created a tremendous pent-up demand for new housing and for larger families. To accommodate these needs, our nation rapidly suburbanized.

Federal Budget Deficits

When our economy became depressed in the early 1930s, the federal government began running substantial budget deficits. Tax receipts fell, and the Hoover administration spent a few billion dollars in an effort to stimulate the economy. Indeed, it was quite ironic that Franklin Roosevelt, during his 1932 presidential campaign against Herbert Hoover, criticized the president for not balancing the budget.

Roosevelt, of course, upon ascending to the presidency, immediately forgot his implicit pledge and began running substantial deficits. In fact, for virtually all of the 1930s, the federal budget was in deficit. Not only was this an all-time record, but it was the first time we had large deficits during peacetime.

While nearly all economists would agree that during times of high unemployment the federal government *should* be running substantial deficits, we have since gone through long periods of running large deficits—in the 1970s, the 1980s, the first half of the 1990s, and the early years of the new millennium—when unemployment was relatively low.

And so, Roosevelt's legacy of deficits was both good and bad. The good part is that during periods of high unemployment, deficits promote economic growth and help create jobs. The bad part of that legacy was that they legitimatized the mega deficits we have had almost annually since the early 1980s.

WORLD WAR II

Federal Budget Deficits

Since the birth of our nation we have fought four all-out wars—the American Revolution, the Civil War, World War I, and World War II. These wars were financed by running large deficits and printing money. Although deficits were widely believed to be bad for our economy, nearly everyone accepted them as a necessary evil during wartime.

During World War II, however, our federal budget deficits dwarfed those we ran during the Depression. By 1944 our deficit was just over one quarter of our GDP.[9] The alternative to such huge deficits, of course, was the risk of losing the war.

Defense Spending

Our nation has not had to fight an all-out war since the end of World War II, but we have continued to devote about 5 percent of our GDP to military spending.[10] This high spending, in turn, has been largely responsible for the deficits we have run since the mid-1940s. But the precedent set by the war has been used to justify this continued high level of military spending.

Control of the world's oil supply was a major determinant of the outcome of World War II because oil was essential to the movement of planes, ships, and tanks. Germany and Japan, the prime aggressors, were both oil-poor nations desperately seeking oil to fuel their armed forces.

After conquering nearly all of Western Europe, Germany turned on its nominal ally, the Soviet Union, which sat astride huge oil fields. The German armies were halted by the Soviets not far from those oil fields. A major factor leading to its ultimate defeat was Germany's growing shortage of oil.

In a surprise attack on December 7, 1941, carrier-based Japanese planes destroyed nearly all of our Pacific fleet, which was stationed at Pearl Harbor, leaving the oil fields of Indonesia defenseless. But even after their conquest of Indonesia, the Japanese were still short of oil. In the meantime, the United States, which was, by far, the world's leading oil producer, had sufficient fuel to fight wars in the Atlantic and the Pacific theaters. Indeed, of the seven billion barrels used by the Allies—primarily the United States, the United Kingdom, and the Soviet Union—six billion were produced in the United States.[11]

As "the arsenal of democracy," we harnessed our industrial might to turn out hundreds of thousands of planes, ships, tanks, and artillery pieces, as well as huge quantities of munitions and other war materiel. Our entire economy was placed on a wartime footing; factories were converted from producing cars, refrigerators, radios, small appliances, and furniture to making whatever was needed to fight the war. Business was extremely good, and everyone who wanted to work could find a job. Finally, after ten long years of the Depression, prosperity had returned with a vengeance.

The lessons of World War II were not lost on us. Two which stood out were (1) always be prepared in the event of a foreign attack and (2) an abundant supply of oil is vital to our national survival.

So while we mothballed most of our naval and air fleets and discharged 90 percent of our service personnel in the immediate postwar period, we would spend an average of 5 percent of our GDP on defense over the next seventy years. And we would never again let down our guard. That is—at least until 9/11.

We would also go to great lengths to protect our oil supply, especially as we became increasingly dependent on foreign suppliers. In part III we'll discuss these issues in considerable detail.

EMPLOYER-BASED HEALTHCARE INSURANCE

Another economic legacy from World War II is our employer-based healthcare insurance system. With so many men in the service and the economy expanding rapidly, our unemployment rate fell below 2 percent in 1943.[12] Normally employers would simply raise wages to attract more workers, but the federal government, in an effort to prevent inflation, had imposed very strict wage and price controls. Casting about for a way around this restriction, many employers offered their workers free or very low-cost healthcare insurance. Adding icing to the cake, the federal government declared that this fringe benefit would not count as wages, nor would it be subject to the federal income tax.

In the years after the war, many large corporations agreed to extend health insurance benefits to their employees, and by the 1960s, two-thirds of all workers were insured by their employers.[13] Over time this system of providing healthcare has become extremely inefficient; today our healthcare costs are almost twice as much per capita as those in most other economically advanced nations. Later in the book we'll spend an entire chapter talking about our grossly inefficient healthcare system.

SUMMARY AND CONCLUSION

From the early 1930s through the end of the 1950s, Presidents Franklin Roosevelt, Harry Truman, and Dwight Eisenhower presided over federal policies that would shape our nation's economy for decades to come. Roosevelt led us through the Great Depression to the closing months of World War II. Truman and Eisenhower saw us through the first fifteen years of the Cold War and of our nation's suburbanization.

The Depression, World War II, and the Cold War were existential challenges that needed to be met with a huge expenditure of our nation's resources. Not only did our nation survive these challenges but through the entire twentieth century we were the world's largest economy, and one of the most prosperous as well. But we have also seen that the economic policies and programs undertaken during the administrations of Presidents Roosevelt, Truman, and Eisenhower would lead to our economic demise decades later. Let us now summarize the destructive by-products of our nation's efforts to meet the challenges of the Great Depression and World War II.

1. **Transportation:** During the 1930s our paved road mileage was doubled, making the postwar suburbanization possible.[14] But very little government money was spent on public transportation.

   A consortium of large oil, highway building, and transportation corporations headed by General Motors bought up and shut down one hundred electric streetcar systems.[15] With our public transportation system largely destroyed, Americans would need cars to get almost anywhere. This need, in turn, would eventually make us very dependent on foreign oil.
2. **Home Mortgages:** In the late 1930s the Federal Housing Administration authorized the redlining of relatively poor, largely black urban neighborhoods, making it impossible for home buyers to obtain mortgages. This policy, which extended well into the 1960s, strongly encouraged home building in the suburbs, leaving housing in the inner cities to decay. After World War II, the Veterans Administration—as well as the Federal Housing Administration—refused to extend home mortgages to returning black veterans.[16]
3. **New Home Construction:** During the Depression and the war, very little housing was built. Consequently, when twelve million veterans returned immediately after the war, the nation was faced

with a severe housing shortage that could not be relieved without rapid suburbanization.

4. **Birthrate:** Relatively low birthrates during the Depression and the war set off a baby boom in the postwar years. This, in turn, created still more demand for new housing, which would be created almost entirely in the suburbs.
5. **Federal Budget Deficits:** In the past, we had run large budget deficits during our major wars, but almost never during peacetime. Our large deficits during the Depression and the even larger ones during the war established the precedent of the United States running deficits almost every year since the early 1970s.
6. **Defense Spending:** The massive defense budgets during World War II set the precedent of continuing to support a huge defense establishment since then. We would never again be caught unprepared. Even after the demise of our archenemy—the Soviet Union seemed to obviate the need for such huge defense budgets—we still accounted for almost 40 percent of the world's military spending.[17]
7. **Oil:** The crucial importance of oil established during World War II led to our devoting as much as one-third of our defense spending to safeguarding the flow of oil to ourselves and our allies.[18] Although we had been a major oil exporter until the close of World War II, our rapid suburbanization made us increasingly dependent on foreign oil. Former city dwellers, who had used only public transportation, became increasingly dependent on their cars.
8. **Healthcare:** Because of government-imposed wage and price controls during the war, employers, desperate to retain current employees and attract new ones in an extremely tight labor market, offered free or low-cost healthcare insurance. This set a precedent for an employer-based healthcare insurance system that most large corporations followed during the postwar period. This way of paying for healthcare led to our grossly inefficient healthcare system.

Chapter 4

SUBURBANIZATION

In Houston, a person walking is somebody on his way to his car.
—Anthony Downs, economist

America is a very different place from the way it was at the close of World War II. Perhaps the largest change has been where most of us live. For most of our history the large majority of our population lived either in rural areas or in cities. But today, most Americans live in the suburbs.[1] We have truly become a suburban nation.

Although it is widely accepted that the suburbanization of America began at the close of World War II, the process actually began almost four centuries ago in Boston, New York, Philadelphia, Charleston (South Carolina), and other growing settlements along the Eastern Seaboard.[2] During the seventeenth century, since almost everyone needed to walk to work, few people lived more than a couple of miles from the downtown business district.

What made the suburbanization process possible were the great advances in public transportation—from horse-drawn wagons and trams to electric streetcars and commuter trains. In fact, soon after the turn of the twentieth century, these newest modes of transportation enabled the cities to expand at an accelerated rate.

For centuries, as the population of a city grew, it would annex neighboring towns and villages. These localities were happy to partake of the city's services and be part of its tax base as well. Most importantly, this development was planned and supervised by each of the cities.

Our cities were magnets, not just for immigrants but for migrants from farms and rural towns, hoping to earn better livelihoods. They found jobs in factories, stores, or in construction or domestic work. Most were eventually able to move to larger apartments, or even buy their own homes, often in the city's outlying suburban neighborhoods. The cities provided an economic ladder that enabled generations from poor economic backgrounds to attain what was called the "American Dream"—a comfortable living, a nice home, and an even better future for their children.

THE GREAT SUBURBAN MIGRATION AFTER WORLD WAR II

Immediately after the war, millions of servicemen and servicewomen came home, hoping to pick up their lives where they had left off years before. Very little housing had been built during the war or during the depressed decade that preceded it. Most veterans returned to live in overcrowded houses and apartments, often with three generations under one roof. The first thing veterans wanted was new housing.

During the Great Depression and the war years, the birthrate was very low. Making up for lost time, the veterans set off a baby boom that lasted for the next eighteen years. And so, a whole lot of housing was needed in a hurry.

The federal government obligingly facilitated the construction of new homes by providing Veterans Administration (VA) mortgages at about 1 percent interest and nothing down to returning veterans. The Federal Housing Administration (FHA) supplemented the VA program with FHA mortgages to millions of other Americans. Reflecting the racist views of the country at that time, virtually none of these mortgages went to black families.[3] Black veterans were offered apartments in low-income projects that were then being constructed.

To further facilitate suburbanization, the federal government embarked on a massive highway-building program, providing 90 percent of the funding, requiring the states in which highways were built to come up with just 10 percent.[4] To add icing to the cake, homeowners were permitted to deduct their mortgage interest payments on their federal income tax returns—a subsidy that totaled $77 billion in 2016.[5]

Because so little land was available in the cities, new housing developments sprung up in the nearby suburbs. Tens of millions of white middle- and working-class families moved beyond the city limits into different tax jurisdictions.[6] Their places in the cities were taken largely by poor blacks and, to a smaller degree, by Hispanic Americans, who migrated from rural areas.

When suburbanization resumed after World War II, few of the towns and villages surrounding the cities wished to be annexed. Consequently, the zoning authority for suburbanization passed from a few dozen cities to tens of thousands of much smaller localities. Instead of planning development along established or new public transportation routes, the local zoning authorities allowed private developers to scatter housing, shopping, schools, offices, and factories all across the suburban landscape. Because of relatively low population densities, public transportation was no longer economically feasible—with the occasional exception of a single rail line that took commuters to the nearest city.

Little or no consideration was given to how people would get to work, where they would shop, or even how their children would get to school. While most housing in the cities had been built near some form of public transportation, private developers and zoning authorities made the implicit assumption that people would drive everywhere.

Another radical departure in the postwar suburbanization process was the nearly total exclusion of blacks and Hispanic Americans from the new housing developments.[7] While America's cities—North *and* South—had long been segregated by neighborhood, now a new pattern was established. Consequently, our poor minority population was penned up in the large cities, while most entry-level jobs were being moved to the suburbs. It was just a matter of time before large swaths of the cities would become urban slums.

Unlike the cities, the new suburbs were not welcoming to the poor, to black people, or to most immigrants. Local zoning, mortgage redlining, and the racially discriminatory policies of the FHA, the VA, bankers, and developers ensured that the suburbs would remain *lily white* working class and middle class. And as millions of entry-level jobs were moved from the cities to the suburbs, the centuries-old ladder of economic opportunity was yanked away.

From the late 1940s through the mid-1950s, the prime motivation for middle- and working-class whites moving to the suburbs was owning an affordable brand-new home. But as poor blacks and Hispanic Americans flooded into their old neighborhoods, millions of additional white families fled to the suburbs.

SUBURBAN SPRAWL

> *L.A.: 72 suburbs in search of a city.*
>
> —Dorothy Parker

One of the great things about moving from a crowded city apartment to the suburbs was that your family had a lot more space. Now you had your own detached house on your own plot of land, and your subdivision had hundreds of other houses on *their* plots of land. It was almost as though you were living out in the country.

But urbanologists were soon criticizing the configuration of suburban development, derogatorily referring to it as "sprawl." And they were blaming sprawl for pollution, congestion, our dependence on foreign oil, global warming, and even the decline of the great American cities.

In their very provocative book, *Suburban Nation: The Rise of Sprawl and the Decline of the American Dream*, Andres Duany, Elizabeth Plater-Zyberk, and Jeff Speck enumerate the five components of sprawl: (1) housing subdivisions, (2) shopping centers, (3) office parks, (4) civic institutions, and (5) roadways.[8] Let's look more closely at each of these components.

1. housing subdivisions: Often called villages or neighborhoods by their developers, they are actually neither. While villages and neighborhoods have stores, schools, medical offices, and provide a sizeable number of jobs, the subdivisions are exclusively residential. In addition, city neighborhoods as well as many villages are served by public transportation, but subdivision residents are totally dependent on their cars.
2. shopping centers: These range from corner convenience stores and shopping strips to large malls. Suburban shopping centers are distinguished from traditional main streets in three ways. Almost no one walks there, they are bordered by huge parking lots, and they contain no housing or office space.
3 office parks: These places are only for work and usually consist of boxes standing in parking lots—not that I'm criticizing.
4. civic institutions: Public buildings such as town halls, courts, schools, sports stadiums, as well as museums and houses of worship are surrounded by parking lots, and accessible only by car. In traditional neighborhoods, nearly all children walk to school and most of them know each other.
5. roadways: These, of course, are central to suburban life, and here is how Duany, Plater-Zyberk, and Speck describe their function and, more generally, the consequences of sprawl:

> The fifth component of sprawl consists of the miles of pavement that are necessary to connect the other four disassociated components. Since each piece of suburbia serves only one type of activity, and since daily life involves a wide variety of activities, the residents of suburbia spend an unprecedented amount of time and money moving from one place to the next. Since most of this motion takes place in singly occupied automobiles, even a sparsely populated area can generate the traffic of a much larger traditional town.[9]

Who is responsible for this single-use development, which separates residential housing, shopping, work, and civic institutions from one another? The folks responsible are the local zoning authorities in the tens of thousands of suburban villages and towns across America. As Duany, Plater-Zyberk, and Speck observe, "A typical contemporary zoning code has several dozen land-use designations; not only is housing separated from industry, but low-density housing is separated from medium density housing, which is separated from high-density housing."[10] The obvious purpose is to protect property values and to keep the less affluent—as well as minorities—out of specific subdivisions.

PUBLIC TRANSPORTATION IN THE SUBURBS

Let's start with the typical suburban home, sitting by itself on one-sixth of an acre of land. Multiply this by the thousands of homes in each suburb. It is not economically feasible to have any kind of mass transit—even express bus service during peak travel times—unless there's a minimum population density of eight families per acre. So the typical suburban family is completely dependent on its cars to go virtually anywhere.

Workplaces, once concentrated in the downtowns of large cities, are now scattered all over the suburbs. Even in the rare instances where reliable mass transit is available, the chances are very slim that many commuters can use it getting to work and back home. Very few suburbanites lived within walking distance of a bus or train that would take them to within walking distance of their jobs.

Before suburbanization, 75 percent of the workers in large cities got to work by train, streetcar, or bus.[11] Today, just 5 percent of all Americans—city dwellers and suburbanites—use mass transit to get to their jobs.[12]

Office parks, factories, and shopping malls are rarely located near any form of mass transit. So they must surround themselves with huge parking lots.

Clearly, when the suburbs were built, no one was looking out for the public interest. Private developers and local zoning officials did not worry about our consequent dependency on automobile and truck transportation, and certainly could not have imagined that this would someday lead to our growing dependency on foreign oil.

OUR WASTEFUL SUBURBAN LIFESTYLE

We buy our cars to go to work and then we work to buy our cars.
—Elliott Sclar, economist

Suburban development was subject to a wide array of different zoning codes in tens of thousands of towns and villages. Although the federal government heavily subsidized mortgages and highway construction, suburbanization had no overall development planning on a national, state, or regional basis. Consequently, housing developments, strip malls, factories, office parks, and—later—shopping malls were scattered almost at random across the suburban landscape.

Initially, these largely former city dwellers were very happy to be able to afford their own little homes on small plots of land. Emblematic of the early developments was Levittown, a community of two thousand homes built on Long Island, within easy commuting distance from New York City. Each home was just eight hundred square feet.[13]

Today the median size of a new home is about 2,500 square feet.[14] Considering that our suburbanization was driven by the baby boom, it was understandable that larger houses would be needed for growing families. But even after 1964, when the baby boom ended, and our nation's birthrate went into a long-term decline, we continued building larger and larger homes in the suburbs and in the more remote areas known as "the exurbs."

The term "McMansion" was coined sometime in the 1980s, as the building of huge homes began to pick up again. According to *Wikipedia*, "*McMansion* is a pejorative for a type of large, new luxury house which is judged to be oversized for the parcel or incongruous for its neighborhood." Or alternatively, it "can be a large, new house in a subdivision of similarly large houses, which all seem mass-produced and lacking in distinguishing characteristics."[15] Bottom line: much too much space for too few people.

Initially most families had just one car, which the wife would use to drop off her husband at the commuter railroad station. She would then do her errands, chauffeur her children to their various destinations, and, just before dinner, pick up her husband at the station. But as more and more jobs were relocated to the suburbs, most husbands were no longer commuting into the city. Finding jobs in the suburbs, they needed their own cars. And when their teenagers came of age, they also needed cars to get around.

As the suburban lifestyle grew in affluence, the old family station wagon gave way to the minivan, along with two or three smaller cars.

Families traded up two or three times from starter homes to more elegant manses. And why not? After all, they were entitled.

Flying into Los Angeles, Phoenix, San Diego, or any other Sunbelt city, you may notice all the little blue dots—each one a backyard pool. You might even notice huge, unoccupied front lawns. Is this the most efficient use that can be found for all of this land?

Some families own not just one or two homes but multiple homes. Asked during his 2008 presidential campaign how many homes he and his wife owned, Sen. John McCain admitted that he did not know. Earth to McCain: the answer is eight.[16] Who needs eight homes? Well, before he was deposed, Iraqi dictator Saddam Hussein *did* own dozens of palaces.

Mitt Romney's lifestyle also came under observation during his 2012 presidential run. While he and his wife own just six homes, some observers considered it rather ostentatious that the San Diego home had an elevator for their cars. *New York Times* columnist David Brooks quipped, "This is not entirely fair. Romney owns many homes without garage elevators and the cars have to take the stairs."[17]

Think of all the underutilized resources that support our wasteful suburban lifestyle—the McMansions; the multiple homes, each occupied for just a few months each year; the huge lawns that are rarely used and the swimming pools in so many backyards. Then consider the 260 million privately owned motor vehicles—more than one for each licensed driver—and all of the land devoted just to parking.[18] Given all of our nation's economic problems, this is a lifestyle we can no longer afford.

THE CONSEQUENCES OF SUBURBANIZATION

The suburbanization of the United States was a much greater success in the short run than in the long run. While it provided desperately needed housing for millions of World War II veterans and their families, and for tens of millions of other families that followed them, it also contributed to some very serious long-term problems that have plagued our country for decades. The most obvious are traffic congestion, air pollution, and our dependence on foreign oil. But the most profound consequence of suburbanization was the abandonment of the nation's cities.

The downtowns of the cities lost millions of jobs as factories were shut down, corporate offices were moved, and people stopped going downtown to shop and to be entertained. Suburban shopping malls anchored by department stores, and later by a proliferation of big-box stores like Wal-Mart, Target, Home Depot, and Costco, basically destroyed the main streets of hundreds of cities—large, medium, and small.

THE ABANDONMENT OF OUR CITIES

For more than a century the cities provided generations of immigrants with the first couple of steps up the ladder to success in America. A young man or woman would be met at the boat by a relative and, the next day, taken to a job in a garment factory, in a store, or maybe on a construction site. Within a few years, the whole family had been sent for, the children had learned English in school, and they were well on their way to attaining the American Dream.

In the years immediately after World War II, when most poor African Americans were forced to leave the South after the mechanization of agriculture, they flocked to the cities in the hope of finding well-paying factory jobs. Their hope, like that of so many European immigrants before them, was that they too would be able to attain the American Dream. But that dream would soon be turning into an urban nightmare.

The white middle- and working-class families were followed to the suburbs by most of the entry-level factory jobs. A move to the suburbs by manufacturers made a lot of sense. Why deal with the congestion and with an aging factory when a much larger one could be constructed on relatively cheap suburban land? As the federally subsidized interstate highway network was being completed, trucking supplanted rail transportation, making suburban factory locations much more convenient. And then, too, a large and growing labor force was now living out in the suburbs.

The disappearance of millions of entry-level factory jobs left most of the urban poor without the means by which to climb out of poverty. Consequently, husbands left wives so their families could get welfare benefits. Teenage pregnancies increased. Crime and drug abuse soared, and nurtured by a welfare system that kept them alive, but did not raise them out of poverty, a permanent underclass perpetuated itself from one generation to the next.[19]

By the late 1960s most of the well-to-do, middle-class, and working-class black families had fled the central city ghettos, leaving behind mainly the poor underclass. Crime and drugs dominated these neighborhoods, while learning largely ceased at what once had been decent neighborhood schools. Within just one generation the inner cities had been transformed from ladders to economic success into holding pens for the permanent underclass.

With suburbanization came the decline and decay of the central shopping districts of the large- and medium-sized cities. As giant shopping malls, and later, big box stores, began attracting not just suburban residents but city dwellers as well, the cities' downtowns became ghost towns. Why shop in a decrepit downtown with little or no parking when you can drive out to a nice new mall?

SUMMARY AND CONCLUSION

Our postwar suburbanization was a huge short-term success, relieving an acute housing shortage and enabling tens of millions of families to buy their own homes. But in the long run, suburbanization was an abject failure. Not only did it make us very dependent on foreign oil and contribute to the destruction of our world-class public transportation system, but it led to the abandonment of our nation's cities.

The suburbanization process was based largely on the implicit assumption that we could always count on a cheap and reliable supply of oil. But because of the configuration of its development, suburbanites became completely dependent on automobile transportation. This made our nation more dependent on foreign oil, a development that had far-reaching consequences, including, increasingly, global warming.

As millions of white working-class and middle-class families moved to the suburbs, their places were taken by millions of poor black and Hispanic families who moved to the cities, sometimes termed "the Promised Land," hoping to find decent jobs. For more than a century the cities provided generations of immigrants with the first couple of steps up the ladder to success in America. But in the wake of the white exodus, millions of factory and construction jobs, as well as jobs in department stores and small businesses, also moved to the suburbs.[20] The disappearance of these jobs left most of the urban poor without the means by which to climb out of poverty, and quickly led to social disintegration, the breakup of families, rising crime and drug use, and deteriorating public school systems.

Throughout this book we shall talk about how we have been wasting our resources and mismanaging our economy. Here are six ways that our postwar suburbanization has contributed to that waste and mismanagement.

1. *Because our transportation system is based almost entirely on automobile travel, it is extremely inefficient.* By the end of World War II, our

public transportation system, while still heavily used, was in long-term decline. But if we had continued following the traditional suburbanization model, planning new development along existing streetcar, bus, and commuter rail lines, it is likely that our declining public transportation ridership would never have occurred. Instead, however, the postwar suburbanization model decreed the automobile to be virtually the only means of transportation.

2. *We need to import about one-third of the oil we use.* Until the end of World War II, we were, by far, the world's leading exporter of oil. By 1948 we had become an oil importer, and today we need to import about one-third of our oil.[21] Had our postwar suburban development continued along existing public transportation lines, we would not be so dependent on automobile transportation and would need to import little, if any, of the oil we use.
3. *We account for almost 40 percent of the world's military appending.*[22] As our need for foreign oil grew, our navy began patrolling the shipping lanes, especially those in the Middle East, and we eventually got into two wars with Iraq. About one-third of our defense spending is dedicated to ensuring an uninterrupted supply of imported oil.
4. *Our growing permanent underclass perpetuates itself from one generation to the next.* The postwar suburbanization was, by far, the most important cause of our large and growing permanent underclass. For centuries the cities had provided people from rural areas as well as generations of immigrants with a chance at entry-level jobs and the path to a better life. But the loss of millions of these jobs to the suburbs left millions of poor families trapped in our inner cities. White flight to the suburbs as well as the eventual exodus of the black middle- and working-class families led to the further isolation of the permanent underclass.[23]
5. *We are running huge trade deficits and must borrow more than $1 billion a day from foreigners.*[24] As we've noted, our postwar suburbanization quickly converted us from the world's largest oil exporter to the largest oil importer. These imports account for one-third to as much as one-half of our trade deficit.[25]
6. *Our humongous federal budget deficits are unsustainable.* Suburbanization has added to our deficits in two ways. First, by increasing our defense expenditures to protect our oil imports. And second, by adding over $100 billion a year in highway construction and maintenance costs.[26]

Chapter 5

THE COLD WAR

When the Japanese surrendered in August 1945, our nation looked forward to years of peace and prosperity. And for the next five years we did get to enjoy both. But the world was a very different place from the one that had existed before the war, and the economic and military roles that we were playing now involved us intimately with events all over the globe.

In the last chapter we described how America had quickly become a suburban middle-class nation. Had we been able to ignore what was happening in the rest of the world, that would have suited us just fine. But it was not to be; the Cold War with the Soviet Union had already begun. The world was changing, and we would be changing *with* it—whether we liked it or not.

If you're old enough to have lived through the Cold War, two memories may stand out. One is the Cuban Missile Crisis in 1962, when it seemed likely that the United States and the Soviet Union would go to war. The other memory was the school shelter drills when we scrambled under our desks and placed our hands over our eyes, protecting ourselves from an atomic attack.

The Cold War period also produced two "hot wars"—in Korea during the early 1950s, and in Vietnam from the mid-1960s through the early 1970s. Despite our large military expenditures, the Cold War did not have nearly the immediate economic impact of World War II. And yet, over forty-five years, the long-run economic effects of the Cold War far outweighed those of World War II.

THE EMERGING SOVIET THREAT

The defeat of Germany left a huge military power vacuum in Europe. The triumphant Soviet Union, our wartime ally, occupied Eastern Europe as well as what became known as East Germany. As the Americans demobilized and withdrew most of their forces, the Red Army appeared poised to march into Western Europe, giving the Soviets control of the entire continent.

That would have been utterly unacceptable to the United States, and to most Western Europeans as well. The two wartime allies had quickly become bitter adversaries. For the administration of President Harry Truman, who had taken office after the death of Franklin Roosevelt in 1945, the big question was, how could we stop Soviet Communist expansion without having to go to war?

The answer was provided by George Kennan, a high-ranking career diplomat. It could be summed up in just one word: containment. Believing that the Soviet threat was more political than military, Kennan proposed that the United States oppose any Soviet expansion into any major industrial country.[1] In Italy and France, for example, as much as one-third of the voters supported the Communist Party.[2] This posed the very real threat that the Communists might soon be voted into office and then take their marching orders from Moscow.

The economies of Western Europe as well as that of the western two-thirds of Germany that was occupied by American, British, and French troops had been largely destroyed by the war. So the Truman Administration created "the Marshall Plan," named for its author, General George C. Marshall, who was currently secretary of state. Providing hundreds of billions of dollars in economic aid (in today's dollars), we succeeded in getting these nations back on their feet.[3] And by doing so, we made free enterprise a much more attractive economic alternative to Communism.

FIGHTING WORLD COMMUNISM

The goal of winning the Cold War certainly trumped any other long-term economic considerations. After all, we were in a life-and-death struggle with world Communism—a struggle we could not afford to lose. While sending massive aid to the devastated nations of Western Europe, we also provided a strong helping hand to the leading Japanese industrialists whose factories had been destroyed by our wartime bombing. Later in this chapter we'll talk about how we were paid back.

While these acts were certainly not entirely selfless—since one clear objective was to thwart Communist expansion—their main effect was to enable our potential economic rivals to reenter world markets much sooner than they would have been able to on their own. By accelerating the forces of globalization, we ensured our own economic demise.

In the early 1950s the focus of our containment policy had shifted from Europe to Asia. What had really shaken us up was the Communist takeover of the Chinese mainland in the late 1940s, forcing President Chiang Kai-shek to flee with remnants of his army to Taiwan, an island about one hundred miles off the China coast. Quickly following the loss of China was the invasion of South Korea by the Soviet Communist client state of North Korea. We immediately intervened on the side of South Korea, and just months later the Chinese Communist army entered the war on the side of North Korea. Over the next two years, the war was fought to a standstill, leaving the Korean peninsula still divided between the Communist North and the non-Communist South, which would remain allied with the United States to this day.

After the fall of China and after the Korean War, the only question was which country would be next. The falling domino theory gained a considerable following. If the Communists could take over one country, its neighbors would fall next. The next major Communist target was Vietnam. During the early 1960s we were increasingly drawn into this conflict, and by 1965 President Lyndon Johnson had committed hundreds of thousands of troops in an effort to win this war. But despite all our efforts, we lost. Most importantly, this would be the last major "shooting war" our nation would be involved in until the1990–91 Gulf War with Iraq. By then the threat of Communist expansion had disappeared.

The Cold War was also fought on the economic front. The Soviets proclaimed that their own economic system was far superior to ours. Nikita Khrushchev, the Soviet leader from the mid-1950s through the late 1960s, famously predicted the outcome of this economic competition: "We will bury you."[4]

Over time it became increasingly evident that Communism could not provide people with the living standards enjoyed by Western Europeans, Americans, or the citizens of Japan, South Korea, Taiwan, or of other rapidly industrializing nations. Indeed, since the 1980s, China—for decades the bastion of Communist orthodoxy—has been evolving into a primarily capitalist nation.

THE ECONOMIC WAR

By the late 1940s it had become imperative for the United States to bolster the economies of Western Europe, Japan, and several other nations in Southeast Asia. At the same time, by tying their economies to ours, we hoped to ensure their continued loyalty in the worldwide struggle against Communist expansion. This policy proved to be a great success, but in the process we may have given away the store.

Our problems began when Japanese manufacturers targeted the huge American market, while keeping their much smaller home market largely closed to American imports. In the mid-1950s a cartel of Japanese TV makers plotted to take over the industry. At the time, General Electric, Westinghouse, and RCA produced the world's state-of-the-art TVs. Because the cartel excluded the sale of American TV sets in Japan, these companies licensed and then transferred their technology to members of the cartel. Foolishly, the American companies accepted short-term gains in exchange for much greater long-term losses.

Soon the American market was inundated with Japanese television sets sold well below cost. To subsidize this venture, the Japanese consumer was charged double what Americans paid. Using our own technology and flooding the huge American market with TVs sold below cost, the Japanese eventually were able to drive all the American manufacturers out of business.[5]

Since the early 1950s, Taiwan—technically still a province of China—had been rapidly industrializing. Wishing to make it into a showcase of capitalistic development, a succession of American presidential administrations undertook extraordinary measures to help Taiwan. According to Barry Lynn,

> U.S. officials . . . structured trade agreements to promote imports from the island, funded efforts to lure American companies to invest in Taiwan, and arranged for the transfer to Taiwanese electronics firms of radar, avionics, and other advanced technologies, and paid to educate thousands of Taiwanese engineers and scientists at American Universities.[6]

Our Cold War aid to Western Europe, Japan, Taiwan, and other Asians nations—along with very significant technological transfers—bolstered their economies and positioned them to eventually become our fierce global competitors.

DE-ESCALATION AND VICTORY

In the early 1970s, President Richard Nixon was a pivotal figure in de-escalating the Cold War. While he was winding down our involvement in the Vietnam War, he stunned the world by making a trip to our arch-enemy, "Red China." Before leaving office, he had normalized relations with that country, opening it to trade, and paving the way for its subsequent rapid industrialization. In addition, Nixon also worked with Soviet leader Leonid Brezhnev to de-escalate the nuclear arms race between the world's two military superpowers.

Although few outsiders seemed to notice, economic conditions within the Soviet Union had begun deteriorating in the 1970s. And then President Ronald Reagan, who served through most of the 1980s, renewed the arms race, doubling our defense spending. In response, the Soviet Union also vastly increased its own defense spending, but the effort largely bankrupted its tottering economy.[7] In short order the Soviet Union was swept into what Karl Marx had termed "the dustbin of history." And with its demise, the Cold War was finally over.

THE COST OF VICTORY

At long last we had finally won. But at what cost? Historians note that the British, while major partners on the winning sides during World Wars I and II, were so weakened by the effort that they soon had to give up their empire.[8] At the end of the Cold War we were the last military and economic superpower left standing. Still, the question of what our triumph cost us has never really been asked—let alone answered. Perhaps, that is, until now.

One cost *can* be calculated—our defense spending. Over this forty-five-year period we devoted an average of 7 percent of our gross domestic product (GDP) to defense—a figure surpassed only by the Soviet Union.[9] And interestingly, its enormous defense spending was largely responsible for bankrupting that nation.

So it would be reasonable to ask this question: What effect did all that defense spending have on our *own* economy? To what other uses could we have devoted those trillions of dollars' worth of resources?

During most of the Cold War years our allies—few of whom spent as much as 2 percent of their GDP on defense—were investing larger proportions of their GDP than we were on new plant and equipment, infrastructure, and research and development.[10] Had we also spent less on defense, then we too would have been able to invest more productively. When we tote up the true economic cost of the Cold War, we should include the trillions of dollars in resources that were not put to more productive use.

And so, while we footed most of the bill, our allies got an almost free ride. While we protected them against Communist expansion, they were able to devote more of their resources to building and improving their economies, so that over time they could become our rivals in the global economy. This was another major cost of fighting the Cold War.

Still one more profound and lasting effect of the Cold War was the establishment of our permanent military-industrial complex. This institution consists of the Defense Department, the armed services (the army, navy, air force, marines, and coast guard), the sixteen or seventeen spy agencies, the House and Senate Armed Services Committees, and the five major defense contractors and their thousands of subcontractors.

There are two salient facts we should know about the military-industrial complex: (1) it is responsible for us spending hundreds of billions of dollars a year, primarily on weapons systems; and (2) it has a vested interest to see that our nation is perpetually at war, or under the threat of war.[11]

After World War II, when we demobilized most of our armed forces, there did not seem to be much justification for continued high defense spending. Indeed, that spending was cut from 37 percent of the GDP in 1945 to under 4 percent in 1948.[12] But with the emergence of the Cold War—and the very real military threat posed by the Soviet Union—the growing power of the military-industrial complex became necessary for our national survival.

For nearly all of our four-and-a-half-decade battle against the expansion of world Communism, we spent hundreds of billions of dollars a year (in today's dollars) to contain what President Reagan called "the Evil Empire." While the Cold War ended more than twenty-five years ago, its legacy of huge military spending lives on.[13]

SUMMARY AND CONCLUSION

Fighting and winning the forty-five-year Cold War came at an extremely high economic cost. Although we emerged as the world's sole economic and military superpower, we had lost much of our manufacturing base.

Let us now summarize the destructive by-products of our nation's effort to meet the challenges of the Cold War.

1. **High Defense Spending:** Fighting the Cold War cost us trillions of dollars, created the powerful military-industrial complex, and made huge federal budget deficits commonplace. Even after the breakup of our archenemy, the Soviet Union—largely because of the great influence of the military-industrial complex—we have continued to devote 5 percent of our GDP to defense.[14]
2. **The Economic Effect of High Defense Spending:** While we were spending 7 percent of our GDP on defense during the Cold War, few of our allies devoted as much as 2 percent.[15] Consequently they were able to spend considerably more on plant and equipment, infrastructure, and research and development. This gave our erstwhile allies a leg up when they became our global economic competitors.
3. **The Marshall Plan:** To help thwart Soviet Communist expansion while helping the nations of Western Europe get back on their feet, the United States provided hundreds of billions of dollars in economic aid. This not only hastened their recovery from the wartime devastation, but enabled our economic rivals to reenter world markets much sooner than they would have been able to on their own.
4. **Television Production:** In the 1950s, when American manufacturers produced 90 percent of the world's TVs, the Japanese market was closed to them.[16] These companies then licensed the production of TV sets to be made in Japan to a cartel of Japanese firms who then used our technology to make TVs and sell them in the American market at prices below cost, eventually driving their American rivals out of business. This strategy was successfully repeated, until by the new millennium, American firms were no longer producing color TVs, video tape players, or DVD players.
5. **Taiwanese Electronics:** By funding American investment in Taiwan, providing new technologies and paying to educate Taiwanese engineering and science students at American universities, our government enabled that country to develop a world-class electronics industry. By the late 1990s, Taiwanese firms, having invested heavily in electronics production in Mainland China, had driven most American firms out of the industry.

Chapter 6

GLOBALIZATION AND GLOBAL WARMING

We'll take up globalization in the first part of this chapter and global warming in the second part. Globalization has already had a great economic effect, but Hurricanes Katrina and Sandy were mere dress rehearsals for what we can expect in the coming years.

GLOBALIZATION

At the beginning of chapter 4 we observed that the suburbanization of the United States began in colonial times four centuries ago. The process of globalization has also been evolving for just as long.

The British considered their thirteen American colonies primarily a supplier of raw materials and a market for their manufactured goods. But trade was very limited since cargo ships were relatively small and took two months to cross the Atlantic. The pace of globalization accelerated rapidly during the nineteenth century with the advent of relatively fast clipper ships, and then by still-faster steamships. By the turn of the twentieth century, ocean freight could be shipped nearly anywhere at relatively low prices.

Worldwide trade expanded until the Great Depression, but the United States continued to be largely self-sufficient. We fed and clothed ourselves and made almost everything we consumed. And when we went to war, we supplied our main allies—Great Britain and the Soviet Union—with most of the oil and much of the food and other military and consumer goods that they needed.

In the years immediately after World War II, the United States was producing nearly half the world's manufactured goods. Most of Europe, as well as Japan, had been devastated, and it took a good fifteen years for these nations to build new factories and begin turning out large quantities of manufactured goods. Well into the 1960s, "Made in the USA" was considered a sign of unsurpassed quality, while a product stamped "Made in Japan" was often greeted with derision. But as Bob Dylan wrote back then in his song, "The Times They Are A-Changin'."

The Fall of American Industrial Power

It was during the postwar period when everything began to change. Most Americans just wanted to get on with their lives and maybe even move to the suburbs and live the American Dream. Tens of millions of families were able to do this, but the world around them was rapidly changing. And like it or not, we were an integral part of that world. We found ourselves in a Cold War with the Soviet Union.

In the last chapter we saw how the pressures of the Cold War induced us to share critical technology with the Japanese and the Taiwanese. *Think* about it: until 1945, Japan was our mortal enemy, and both sides committed unspeakable atrocities against the other. But in the early years of the Cold War, there was great fear that these countries—as well as those of Western Europe—would fall victim to Communist expansion. We never considered the long-run consequences of our great largesse.

The Japanese takeover of our television industry was just the first salvo in a trade war between the two countries. The next major battle was over the automobile industry. Beginning in the late 1960s, Japan began exporting increasing numbers of compact cars, quickly capturing about one-tenth of the vast American market.[1] Only American import quotas were able to successfully limit imports, and induced several Japanese firms to begin assembling cars in the United States.

The Taiwanese not only developed a world-class electronics industry, but more significantly, in the 1980s they began investing heavily in electronics production in Mainland China. Having the dual advantage of sharing a nationality and language, the Taiwanese constructed a veritable export platform along the South China coast, enabling China to become the world's newest industrial colossus.

It had taken the United States and Western Europe over two centuries to develop the technology that enabled them to industrialize and to generate steadily increasing living standards, while creating the blueprint that was followed by much of the developing world since the end of World War II. It was no longer necessary for these nations to create the needed technology since it had become readily available to any nation that had the necessary capital to apply it.

During the 1980s and 1990s China was able to attain double-digit growth by turning out huge quantities of shoes, textiles, apparel, toys, and consumer electronics—all of which were manufactured goods requiring the application of relatively low-level technology. But by the new millennium the nation's political leaders had determined that if China were to continue growing at a double-digit rate, it would need to convert much more quickly from low-end manufacturing to high-end, high-tech industries. So they made it the nation's official economic policy to aggressively appropriate the world's most advanced technology by all possible means. These included buying foreign companies, encouraging multinational corporations to set up research and development facilities in China, and, increasingly, to force firms doing business in China to take on Chinese partners.[2]

Buying another company is a widely accepted way of acquiring its technology. Similarly, when a multinational corporation sets up a research and development operation in another country, it would not be unreasonable for the host country to expect to share at least some of the technology that is developed. But China goes far beyond these means of obtaining cutting-edge technology. Essentially, it forces companies wishing to do business in China to share its technology.

Because China is the world's largest market for cars, wind turbines, mobile phones, high-speed railroad lines, and electricity-generating plants, few companies producing these goods can afford *not* to be in China, even if it *does* require transferring its technology.[3]

Each company must make a Faustian bargain—share its technology or lose out on a profitable contract. And it faces this choicc knowing that if it does not agree to China's terms, at least one of its rivals will.

To gain access to this market, to be considered for procurement by the Chinese government, or to benefit from Chinese subsidies and from tax cuts, foreign companies are often forced to form joint ventures with Chinese firms—virtually all of which are large, state-owned enterprises—frequently requiring the transferring of the latest technology.

The Offshoring of Jobs

For a century we were, by far, the world's leading manufacturing power.[4] By the new millennium, however, we had lost most of our lead. Having literally given away our technology to potential competitors and having opened the huge American market to our trade rivals, shouldn't we blame ourselves for frittering away our lead? Or was it inevitable that, one way or another, much of our manufacturing base would be eroded by foreign competition?

There is no question that our government and our corporate leaders hastened these losses. But the spreading globalization of world production and trade since the end of World War II ensured that eventually our dominance in manufacturing would diminish, if not disappear entirely. As Taiwanese manufacturers moved production to Mainland China in the 1980s, and with the spread of capitalism in the lands of the former Soviet empire in the 1990s, thousands of multinational corporations were able to harness the labor of hundreds of millions of literate, highly motivated workers with their world-class capital and technology.

Business firms, both large and small, have almost always tried to maximize their profits. This drive, intensified in recent decades by the forces of globalization, has compelled these companies to search the world in an effort to minimize their costs. Consequently, many have shifted at least some of their operations abroad.

As late as the 1970s, mainly because they used the best available capital and technology, American workers were the most productive. But today, with the same capital and technology available throughout much of the world, hundreds of millions of other workers can be just as productive. And better yet, most of them are quite willing to work for a dollar an hour. So if you were a manufacturer, where would *you* set up shop?

If your business can hire workers who are able to do their jobs as well or better than your American employees—*and* are willing to work for a fraction of their pay—would *you* think twice about shifting your operations to another country? Besides, just ask yourself where the smart money is going. This process is described by Ron and Anil Hira in their book, *Outsourcing America*:

> The cost savings have been so great that Silicon Valley venture capitalists—companies that provide seed funding for the most advanced start-up technology companies in exchange for an equity stake and some managerial control—are requiring their fledgling organizations to have an offshore outsourcing plan before the venture capitalists hand out the next round of funding. So, even with start-up companies, generally with small staffs, offshore outsourcing is becoming an imperative.[5]

Offshoring and Wages

How has the offshoring of jobs affected American wages? As whole industries were downsized, or completely disappeared, what effect did this have on wages in other blue-collar occupations? *Think* about it. What's your gut reaction?

If you think that the offshoring of these jobs pushed down wages, you'd be right! When the workers in these industries lost their jobs, they were forced to look for other work. Generally they looked for similar jobs in other industries. With the entry of all these unemployed workers—many of whom were willing to work for less than the prevailing wage rate—there was a downward pressure on the wage rate.

According to some studies conducted since the early 1980s, most workers laid off due to offshoring who later found jobs took an average pay cut of 25 percent.[6] Many were unemployed for more than a year. Perhaps 35 to 40 percent of the displaced workers actually did find new jobs at equal pay. Think of the outcomes of these layoffs like those of this coin toss—heads you lose and tails you break even.[7]

Clyde Prestowitz notes that so far only 15 to 20 percent of our workforce has been directly affected by the offshoring of jobs, and yet American wages have been stagnant since 1973.[8] Imagine, then, the future effect of the offshoring of our service sector jobs, affecting up to 80 percent of our labor force.

Over the last three decades, as well-paying blue-collar jobs have disappeared, millions of workers have been pushed into the labor market, eventually willing to settle for almost *any* type of work. The forces of supply and demand explain why thousands of people line up for applications whenever Wal-Mart opens a new store. What accounts for the huge supply of workers hoping to land jobs that pay poverty-level wages? A large contributing factor is the offshoring of so many jobs.

But offshoring plays an even more pernicious role in holding down wages. It provides hundreds of thousands of employers with a Sword of Damocles to hold over the heads of their workers: we can always move this business to Mexico, Indonesia, Thailand, Malaysia, or wherever else there are people willing to work for much less than we're paying you. This is a faithful replay of Karl Marx's "reserve army of the unemployed." If a worker objected to being paid starvation wages, his employer would ask him to look out the window at the factory gate where hundreds of people stood waiting for a chance to have his job.

To sum up, offshoring has had two pernicious effects:

1. **Offshoring manufacturing jobs:** Since 1979 employment in manufacturing fell from a peak of twenty million to just twelve million today.[9] Capital and technology have been shifting from the older and richer industrial nations to the newly industrializing nations

where highly skilled, educated, and motivated workers are willing to work for a dollar an hour. Multinational corporations, driven by fierce competition, must operate in low-wage nations or be forced out of business.

2. **Offshoring and wages:** How has the offshoring of millions of manufacturing jobs affected the hourly wage rates paid on the remaining jobs? Those who lost their jobs competed for other jobs, tending to bid down wage rates. Since 1973, the (inflation adjusted) hourly wage rate paid to nonmanagerial workers—80 percent of our labor force—has remained about the same.[10] Employers often succeed in holding down wage rates by threatening to move their businesses to low-wage countries.

Conclusion

How well has our nation dealt with globalization? Quite well, actually, until the 1950s. By then, we were engaged in a life-and-death struggle with Communist expansion. By providing a huge amount of economic aid to our allies and opening up the vast American market to their exports, we bolstered their ability to complete with us in the global marketplace. Had the Cold War never happened, perhaps we might have been able to continue riding the rising wave of globalization.

GLOBAL WARMING

> *Treat the earth well. It was not given to you by your parents. It was loaned to you by your children.*
>
> —Native American proverb

Unlike the five catastrophic events we've described, the effects of climate change have only just begun to be felt. But by midcentury global warming may have done as much to harm our economy as any of the other five events.

What Is Global Warming?

The temperature of our planet's surface is determined mainly by our distance from the sun. That distance, 93 million miles, is ideal. Mercury, which is much closer to the sun, is too hot to support human life, while Jupiter and Saturn, both much farther from the sun, are far too cold.

A second factor enabling human life on Earth is our atmosphere, which also regulates our planet's temperature. Unlike Earth, our moon, which is just a quarter of a million miles from us, has no atmosphere to moderate its temperatures. During sunlight hours the moon's temperature can reach 212 degrees Fahrenheit—the boiling point of water.[11] And during nighttime it can fall below -270 degrees. These are well beyond the most extreme temperatures recorded on Earth.

One main reason Earth has been able to sustain human life is because it has stayed within a very compatible temperature range. This is enabled by greenhouse gases in the atmosphere, especially carbon dioxide. These gases act like a blanket, keeping Earth warm by preventing some of the sun's energy from being reradiated back into space. But as the amount of carbon dioxide that has accumulated in the atmosphere has increased since the beginning of the Industrial Revolution in the mid-eighteenth century, its effect has been similar to adding to our layer of blankets and retaining more and more heat arriving from the sun.

Scientists have determined that the amount of carbon dioxide in the air has increased by more than 40 percent over the last 150 years.[12] They have concluded that man-made carbon dioxide is the major cause of global warming. Two others are methane and nitrous oxide.[13]

We have been burning increasing amounts of oil, coal, gas, and other fossil fuels. This has produced vast quantities of carbon dioxide, methane, and nitrous oxide, which have risen into the atmosphere. And as a direct consequence, over the last few decades land and ocean temperatures have been rising.

All of this is "settled science"; these findings are supported by virtually all climate scientists. They further maintain that even if we stopped burning fossil fuels today, global temperatures will keep rising through the midcentury. The polar ice caps will continue to melt, sea levels will keep rising, coastal areas will be in increasing danger of being flooded, and our weather will grow more erratic.

Carbon dioxide remains in the atmosphere for thousands of years. There is nothing we can do right now to reduce its level. Indeed, as we continue burning fossil fuels, the level will keep rising, and with it global temperatures.

Global warming is of course not just our problem, but a worldwide problem as well. Rising temperatures and ocean levels affect not just us, but every nation on Earth. Indeed, in the long run the very survival of the human race is at stake. In another few pages, when we talk about solving this problem, we shall need to take into account the actions of other nations as well as our own.

The Economic Consequences of Global Warming

The most costly economic consequence of global warming will be the flooding of the East and Gulf Coasts as the oceans continue to rise. Perhaps the most vulnerable area will be lower Manhattan, which experienced major flooding during Hurricane Sandy in 2012 (see accompanying box).

Damage to New York City Subway System by Hurricane Sandy

The coastal areas of New York and New Jersey were especially hit hard by Hurricane Sandy in 2012. These states suffered more fatalities than the rest of the states that were hit, as well as tens of billions of dollars in property damage.[14] And still greater economic damage was very narrowly averted.

Manhattan is connected to Brooklyn, Queens, the Bronx, as well as to Northern New Jersey by a series of subway tunnels. Millions of commuters get to work each day by subway. During the hurricane, salt water from New York Harbor poured into one of the subway stations and, from there, into a tunnel connecting Manhattan and Brooklyn. After three years of repairs, the tunnel was finally reopened.

One can only imagine what would have happened if more tunnels had flooded. As sea levels rise, the probability will increase that New York, Boston, Philadelphia, Washington, DC, San Francisco, and other coastal cities with subway lines will become even more vulnerable.

Climate Warming Deniers and Skeptics

> *Yes, Donald Trump did call climate change a Chinese hoax.*
> —Louis Jacobson, *PolitiFact*, June 3, 2016

Although man-made climate warming is now "settled science," according to a 2014 Pew Research Center poll, "35 percent of Americans say there is not enough solid evidence to suggest mankind is warming the Earth while another 18 percent says the world has warmed due to 'natural patterns' and not human activity."[15]

Perhaps some of the skeptics and deniers just need to see more scientific evidence before they can support measures to deal with climate warming. But to lend some perspective to the science backgrounds of the American public, please consider this unsettling fact:

> A survey of 2,200 people in the United States was conducted by the National Science Foundation in 2012. . . . To the question "Does the Earth go around the Sun, or does the Sun go around the Earth," 26 percent of those surveyed answered incorrectly.[16]

Solutions

What can be done about global warming? Let's consider first how we can mitigate some of its effects. And then we'll talk about what we can do in the long run to stabilize, or even lower, the level of carbon dioxide in the atmosphere.

Mitigating the effects of global warming in the short run

Having already experienced the effects of Hurricane Katrina in 2005 and Hurricane Sandy in 2012, we know all too well how much more damage we may be in for in the coming years. And as sea levels continue to rise, the best we can do is to hold the damage to low-lying coastal areas to a minimum.

It will require the building of sand berms, sea walls, levees, and other barriers to hold back rising flood waters. Vulnerable buildings can be placed on stilts. Some homes can be moved farther inland. New building along the water's edge can be restricted. To do this we will need to spend tens of billions of dollars a year while employing millions of people.

Combatting global warming in the long run

Right now we cannot do anything about the carbon dioxide that is already in the atmosphere. But we can take immediate steps to curb emissions by placing a high tax on all fossil fuels. This would help in three ways. First, the tax would discourage some consumption of these fuels, particularly gasoline. Second, the added tax revenue could be used to finance the development of alternate energy sources. And third, raising the price of fossil fuels would make wind, solar, and nuclear power more affordable.

We also should invest heavily in scientific research to develop new energy sources and to find ways of removing carbon dioxide from the atmosphere and then storing it. Although actually doing this may be at least ten years away, we need to be working on this now so that decades down the road we may actually be able to reverse global warming.

In this effort, all nations must be willing to share their research findings. This would lead to much faster progress than if each nation kept this knowledge to itself (see box: "The Paris Agreement").

Despite widespread ignorance about the degree of global warming, here is one indisputable fact: since the 1880s, when we began to record annual global temperatures, the three highest were in 2014, 2015, and 2016. In fact, 2016 was the highest, 2015 the second highest, and 2014 the third highest. According to a *New York Times* article, "Of the 17 hottest years on record, 16 have occurred since 2000."[17]

The Paris Agreement

In December 2015, 195 nations hammered out what may prove to be the most significant international agreement in the history of the planet. The world's two largest greenhouse gas producers, China and the United States, were the two most important signatories.

The goal is to decrease the world's dependency on oil, coal, and other fossil fuels to the point where greenhouse emissions will level off. Helen Briggs of the BBC News reported that it was hoped that we shall achieve "a balance between output of man-made greenhouse gases and absorption—by forests or the oceans—by the second half of the century."[18]

To help the poorer nations switch to renewable energy, the richer nations have agreed to provide as much as $100 billion per year in "climate finance."[19]

Given the political opposition to actually doing anything about global warming, we will need a powerful campaign to educate the public about this gathering danger. We will also need to persuade some members of Congress that not every tax increase is ill-advised, especially if it is needed to save our planet.

Part III

THE DEINDUSTRIALIZATION OF AMERICA

As late as the 1960s we were a largely self-sufficient industrial superpower, able to generate millions of well-paying manufacturing jobs. But since 1979, when manufacturing employment peaked, we have lost more than 40 percent of those jobs.[1] And now, increasing numbers of service sector jobs are being offshored to low-wage countries. The big question we need to ask is this: Is the United States facing a future with a declining number of decent jobs, while evolving into a low-wage nation of Wal-Mart greeters, McDonald's hamburger flippers, and Starbucks baristas?

As our nation transforms itself from being the world's dominant industrial power into one of several postindustrial economies, many of our best jobs are being moved to developing countries, where workers are willing and able to perform them at a fraction of what American workers earn. How did all of this happen, and what does our future hold?

More than anything, what enabled us to build our economy was our ability to churn out a steady stream of outstanding innovations. But in recent years we have lost most of our lead to other countries, especially to the rising economies of Asia. These nations, drawing on a store of technology developed over the last two centuries, have managed to catch up in just a few generations and are now competing with us in the global marketplace.

Still another factor that fostered our economic development was our rapidly growing and improving infrastructure of roads, bridges, pipelines, water mains, electrical power grids, seaports, airports, and railroads. But over the last four decades our infrastructure has fallen into disrepair.

For more than two centuries the federal government has spent huge amounts of money to help build our infrastructure, finance research and development, and provide aid to selected industries. But we have never had a true industrial policy—a national strategy to leverage existing resources within companies, universities, the labor force, and the public sector. Indeed, while many of our economic rivals have very successful industrial policies, we have not even made a start on developing one.

Chapter 7

THE RISE AND FALL OF AMERICAN INDUSTRIAL POWER

The Industrial Revolution began in England around 1750, and that country soon became the world's first manufacturing power. Its colonies supplied England with raw materials and were important markets for the country's manufactured goods. One of the sources of conflict with the thirteen American colonies was their outright prohibition of the manufacture of many products that were made in England.

Then came the American Revolution. You may recall the suffering of the ragtag American army through the frigid winter of 1776–77 at Valley Forge, when nearly a quarter of General George Washington's troops died from cold, disease, and hunger. As Washington's top aide, Alexander Hamilton learned firsthand how the troops lacked for warm clothing, boots, gun powder, muskets, and other basics. Thirteen years later, as America's first secretary of the treasury, Hamilton noted in his *Report on Manufactures* that manufacturing was the key to America's "independence and security."[1]

THE RISE OF AMERICAN INDUSTRIAL POWER

When George Washington took his oath of office as the nation's first president in 1789, nine of every ten Americans were farmers.[2] Our third president, Thomas Jefferson, believed we would continue to be a nation of small farmers. But even during the rest of Jefferson's lifetime, textile mills, iron foundries, and other small manufacturing enterprises were springing up, especially in the North and the Midwest. It would take us the rest of the century to surpass England and become the world's largest industrial power.

THE AGE OF THE INDUSTRIAL CAPITALIST

Nothing is particularly hard if you divide it into small pieces.
—Henry Ford

The last quarter of the nineteenth century was the age of the industrial capitalist. The great empire builders—Carnegie (steel), DuPont (chemicals), Swift (meat packing), McCormick (farm equipment), and Rockefeller (oil) dominated this era. In 1872, just before Andrew Carnegie opened the Edgar Thompson works, the United States produced less than 100,000 tons of steel.[3] Twenty-five years later Carnegie alone was turning out 4 million tons, almost half of the total American production.[4]

Pioneered by American industrial capitalists, mass production became the standard mode of manufacturing. Mass production was possible only if there was also mass consumption. In the late nineteenth century, once the national railway network enabled manufacturers to sell their products all over the country, and even beyond our shores, it became economically feasible to invest in heavy machinery and to turn out volume production, which, in turn, meant lower prices. Lower prices, of course, pushed up sales, which encouraged further investment and created more jobs. At the same time, productivity, or output per hour, was rising, which justified companies paying higher wages, and a high-wage workforce could easily afford all the new low-priced products.

Henry Ford personified the symbiotic relationship between mass production and mass consumption. Selling millions of cars at a small profit per unit allowed Ford to keep prices low and wages high—the perfect formula for mass consumption. His great contribution was the emphasis he placed on an expert combination of accuracy, continuity, the moving assembly line, and speed, through careful timing of manufacturing, materials, handling, and assembly. The assembly line speeded up work by breaking down the auto-making process into a series of simple, repetitive operations.

By the turn of the twentieth century the United States was among the world's leaders in the production of steel, coal, steamships, textiles, apparel, chemicals, and agricultural machinery. We were able to mass produce hundreds of manufactured goods very cheaply and sell them in the world's first mass market. Our technological talent, a large agricultural surplus, the world's first universal public education system, and the entrepreneurial abilities of our great industrialists combined to enable the

United States to emerge as the world's leading industrial power by the beginning of the twentieth century. And then we *really* got going.

FROM THE TURN OF THE CENTURY TO THE GREAT DEPRESSION

The chief business of the American people is business.
—Calvin Coolidge

During the first two decades of the twentieth century, we dramatically increased our lead in the production and consumption of goods and services. Better yet, our great innovators and inventors—Henry Ford, Thomas Edison, the Wright brothers, Peter Cooper Hewitt, Willis Carrier, Robert H. Goddard, among others—were on the technological cutting edge, putting forth a stream of new products that further increased our lead.

The decade of the 1920s—known as "the Roaring Twenties"—was one of almost unparalleled expansion driven largely by the automobile industry. Another important development was the spreading use of electricity. During this decade electric power production doubled.[5] Not only was industrial use growing, but by 1929 two out of every three homes in America had been wired and were now using electrical appliances.[6] The telephone, the radio, the toaster, the refrigerator, the vacuum cleaner, the phonograph, and other conveniences became commonplace during the 1920s.

As you well know, the party came to an end with the stock market crash in 1929 and the subsequent Great Depression. It was not until our mobilization for World War II, accompanied by massive defense spending, that our industrial labor force was once again fully employed and our nation's factories were humming.

WARTIME AND POSTWAR PROSPERITY

As "the arsenal of democracy," we harnessed our industrial might to turn out hundreds of thousands of planes, ships, tanks, and artillery pieces, munitions, as well as huge quantities of other war materiel. Our entire economy was placed on a wartime footing; factories were converted from producing cars, refrigerators, radios, small appliances, and furniture to making whatever was needed to fight the war. Business was extremely good, and everyone who wanted to work could find a job. Finally, after ten long years of the Depression, prosperity had returned with a vengeance.

THE FALL OF AMERICAN INDUSTRIAL POWER

America, which had been turning out nearly half the world's manufactured goods immediately after the war, saw its share fall to just over one-third by the early 1950s.[7] Still, this was to be expected. Our manufacturers continued to dominate the vast and wealthy American market and most of the world markets as well. Few of our rivals could compete on the basis of price or quality.

As our industrial rivals—most notably Japan—once again began to compete with us, American manufacturers did not take them seriously. Rather than demand protection from our government because of "unfair competition," since these competitors were paying much lower wages, our manufacturers did not believe that any foreigner could actually compete with the great American industrial machine. We were, by far, the best in the world—and everybody knew it!

Our political leaders did as well, welcoming the economic recovery of our Cold War allies—even those like Germany, Italy, and Japan—who had so recently been our bitter enemies during World War II. Their growing economic strength would prove a sturdy defense against worldwide communist expansion.[8] Indeed, through the decade of the 1950s, and well into the 1960s, our growingly powerful economic rivals were no great threat to the seemingly invincible American industrial machine.

The first real sign of trouble became apparent when Japanese TV manufacturers targeted the huge American market, while keeping their much smaller home market almost completely closed to American imports. The market for TVs had been extremely important in the 1950s. At the beginning of the decade just one American family in ten owned a TV, because a "large-screen" seventeen-inch black-and-white set cost well over two weeks' pay.[9] By the end of the decade TVs had become much more affordable—and larger—and nine out of ten families owned at least one set.[10]

The Japanese TV manufacturers, backed by their government, made the leading American manufacturers—GE, Westinghouse, RCA, and Sylvania among them—a seemingly attractive offer: license your technology to us, and we'll pay you a handsome royalty for each TV we produce.[11] Unable to restrain themselves from accepting a large, short-term profit in exchange for this huge technology transfer, these firms enabled their Japanese counterparts to utilize a technology that had taken more than two decades to develop.

Taking advantage of its nation's low-wage labor force, the Japanese were soon able to produce TV sets at relatively low cost. They sold them in Japan at very high prices—about twice what they charged to American consumers—since they had a monopoly in Japan. Taking advantage of the economies of scale, they were able to mass produce TVs at a low cost and ship millions of sets each year to the United States and to other relatively wealthy nations, selling their TVs below cost.

And so, using our own technology, and subsidized by the Japanese consumer, Japanese TV manufacturers were soon able to capture most of the lucrative American market by underselling the very firms from whom they had licensed their technology. Talk about biting the hand that feeds you.

What did we learn from this experience? In the famous words of the great philosopher George Santayana, "Those who cannot remember the past are condemned to repeat it." Using the same tactics of licensing our technology for color TVs, VCRs, and DVD players, Japanese manufacturers drove American manufacturers completely out of business. Indeed, by the mid-1990s, Asian firms had pushed us almost entirely out of producing consumer electronics.

Another Cold War ally upon which we showered economic aid was Taiwan, which lies just one hundred miles off the coast of what had become, in the late 1940s, Red China. In a very successful effort to turn Taiwan into a free-market economic showcase, we paid to educate tens of thousands of Taiwanese engineers and scientists at American universities. And US officials arranged for the transfer to Taiwanese electronics firms of radar, avionics, and other advanced technologies.[12] Within a decade Taiwanese consumer electronics firms were competing with American firms. Then, adding insult to injury, in the early 1980s, these firms set up shop in Mainland China.

They were joined by thousands of multinational corporations based in Japan, South Korea, Western Europe, and the United States. As more and more of our manufacturing operations were shifted to China and other developing countries, our employment in manufacturing shrank from a peak of twenty million workers in 1979 to less than twelve million today.[13] In 1979 over 20 percent of our labor force was employed in manufacturing; today less than 10 percent have jobs in manufacturing.[14]

All of our presidents from Harry Truman in the late 1940s through

Ronald Reagan in the 1980s were complicit in shoring up the economies of our allies, even though that resulted in the erosion of our manufacturing base. Barry Lynn summed up the long-term effect:

> In a sense, the postwar economic system set into motion by Harry Truman was a radical inversion of Hamilton's doctrine. Rather than seek security through industrial *independence from* other nations, America would now seek security through industrial *interdependence with* other nations.[15]

Traditionally, large manufacturers were located close to their markets. They could most easily design their products to meet the tastes and needs of their customers. And then too, shipping costs were held down—especially for bulky products like steel, automobiles, and major household appliances. The vast American market enabled manufacturers to mass produce low-cost consumer goods.

But increasingly, foreign markets are becoming more important than what had been the Great American Market. More cars, cell phones, TVs, and other consumer electronics are sold in China than in the United States. Back in the 1980s the Big Three Japanese automobile firms—Toyota, Honda, and Nissan—set up assembly line plants in the United States. Today, GM, Ford, and Chrysler have built plants in China and in other emerging mass consumption markets.

Who is to blame for the deindustrialization of America? Surely our ungrateful Cold War allies. And the greedy multinational corporations who laid off millions of loyal American employees, while moving their operations to low-wage nations like China, Vietnam, Bangladesh, Mexico, and the Philippines. But we have not yet mentioned the name of the company that may be most responsible for the loss of millions of manufacturing jobs—Wal-Mart.

By far the nation's largest retailer, Wal-Mart has played a central role in the migration of manufacturing from the United States to China and other low-wage countries. By using its vast market power to relentlessly lower the prices it paid to its suppliers, Wal-Mart forced hundreds of major manufacturers to lower their cost by moving their factories offshore. So many manufacturers had become so dependent on Wal-Mart—and, to a lesser degree, other big-box retailers such as Target and Costco—that they had to move operations offshore just to survive. Hedrick Smith called this Wal-Mart's "Move offshore or die" message.[16]

It may be hard to believe that a single retail store would have so much power. For more than a century, from the post–Civil War period until the rise of Wal-Mart in the 1980s, the dominating American firms were the great industrial corporations—GM, GE, US Steel, Ford, DuPont, and IBM. Each was a manufacturer. Back in the 1950s, when GM president Charles Wilson declared that what was good for General Motors was good for the country, he was telling it just like it was. But increasingly, in recent decades, it is Wal-Mart and other giant retailers who are calling the shots.

If all this were not enough, we have managed to further damage our manufacturing sector by pushing up the healthcare premiums paid by employers and by making our large corporations pay a very high corporate income tax rate.

Because most employers pay part or all of their employees' healthcare insurance premiums, this very large expense is added to the cost of the goods and services they sell. This has put our manufacturers—especially our automobile companies—at a great disadvantage when competing against foreign companies whose governments provide health insurance. (In chapter 13 we'll discuss this issue much more extensively.)

Among industrialized nations, the United States has the highest corporate income tax rate—35 percent of net profit.[17] Most of our major global competitors have rates of about 20 to 25 percent.[18]

This relatively high tax rate has adversely affected our manufacturing base in two ways. First, it raises our cost of doing business, since our competitors pay less tax. And second, it encourages our multinational corporations to do increasing amounts of business abroad to avoid our high corporate income tax rate. This issue came to a head in 2014 when some large American pharmaceutical companies began buying foreign competitors and then nominally shifting their operations to the United Kingdom, Ireland, the Netherlands, and other relatively low-tax nations in order to pay much lower corporate income taxes.[19]

LAST WORD

For a century we were, by far, the world's leading manufacturing power. By the new millennium, however, we had lost most of our lead. Having literally given away our technology to potential competitors and having opened the huge American market to our trade rivals, shouldn't we blame ourselves for frittering away our lead? Or was it inevitable that, one way or another, much of our manufacturing base would be eroded by foreign competition?

There is no question that our government and our corporate leaders hastened these losses. But the spreading globalization of world production and trade since the end of World War II ensured that eventually our dominance in manufacturing would diminish, if not disappear entirely. As Taiwanese manufacturers moved production to Mainland China in the 1980s, and with the spread of capitalism in the lands of the former Soviet empire in the 1990s, thousands of multinational corporations were able to harness the labor of hundreds of millions of literate, highly motivated workers with their world-class capital and technology.

Survival in the global marketplace dictates that these firms scour the world for the cheapest ways of producing every good they manufacture. As late as the 1970s, mainly because they used the best available capital and technology, American workers were the most productive. But today, with the same capital and technology available throughout much of the world, hundreds of millions of other workers can be just as productive. And better yet, most of them are quite willing to work for just one or two dollars an hour.[20] So if you were a manufacturer, where would *you* set up shop?

Since the 1950s we have lost most or all of our steel, apparel, textile, and consumer electronics industries. But still, the Big Three American automobile companies—General Motors, Ford, and Chrysler—managed to hang on, albeit with growing foreign competition. Over the last thirty years, several Japanese companies have been building cars here, and since 2009 the Big Three have been making less than half the motor vehicles sold in America.[21] And of the more than one billion cell phones produced each year, not one is made in the USA.[22]

In 2010 China overtook us as the world's largest manufacturing power.[23] Still, there is some hope for us. As the world's technological leader, perhaps we can regain our lead. In the next chapter we'll look at our prospects.

Chapter 8

INNOVATION, INFRASTRUCTURE, AND INDUSTRIAL POLICY

More than anything, what enabled us to build the greatest economy in history was our amazing ability to churn out a steady stream of outstanding innovations. Although we continue to do so, other nations have not just caught up but have even begun to surpass us. In the first part of this chapter we'll discuss how we have been losing our innovative edge. Then we'll examine our crumbling infrastructure of bridges, highways, railroads, airports, pipelines, and other major supporting pillars that enable our economy to function. In the last part of the chapter we'll talk about industrial policy. We shall see why this much-maligned economic strategy—disparagingly referred to as "picking winners"—is very much needed today to help us regain our technological lead.

HOW WE LOST OUR INNOVATIVE EDGE

For close to two hundred years America led the world in technological innovation, from the telegraph and the telephone, the automobile and the airplane, radio and TV, to the personal computer and the Internet. Many of us have an abiding faith that American ingenuity can continue to keep turning out "the next best thing." Apple, Amazon, Google, Microsoft, IBM, Facebook, and Intel head a world-class roster of high-tech companies.

Today, by most measures, the United States has lost its technological lead. We have given away a large portion of our technology to emerging industrial nations that have since become our economic rivals. And increasingly, our multinational corporations are setting up their research and development facilities in China, India, and other nations in Asia and Eastern Europe where they can hire very well-educated employees who are willing to work for just a fraction of the wages earned by their American counterparts. Indeed, American employees are often forced to train their replacements.

A key indicator of innovation is the number of patents that a nation's individuals, business firms, and universities are awarded. There has been a very disturbing downward trend in the number of patents awarded to Americans by the United States Patent Office. By 2009, 51 percent of those patents went to foreign firms.[1]

Today we are importing more than half our machine tools, aircraft and motor vehicle engines and parts, printed circuits, optical instruments and lenses, telephone switching apparatus, machines that mold plastics, and broadcasting equipment used for radio, television, and wireless transmission. And all of our personal computers, TVs, and cell phones.[2]

We have already lost a range of newer high-tech industries—from solar panels, compact fluorescent light bulbs, and desktop and notebook PCs to advanced batteries and liquid crystal displays (LCDs). It is becoming more and more apparent that many of "the next best things" will not just be manufactured abroad, but they will be thought up, researched, developed, and designed abroad.

We need to ask ourselves, "What went wrong—and how can we set things right?" There are two underlying causes to our long-term decline in technological competitiveness. First, largely because of the loss of much of our manufacturing base, we began losing our technological edge. And second, other nations—most notably Japan, China, South Korea, and Taiwan—have grown increasingly technologically proficient.

THE EROSION OF OUR INNOVATIVE CAPACITY

The largest contributor to this decline is the loss of most of our manufacturing base. Another important factor has been our failing educational system, which we will discuss in chapter 12. Later in this chapter we shall also consider our lagging support for research and development.

Manufacturing and Technological Innovation

America has long been on the cutting edge of new technology. The steamboat, sewing machine, telegraph, telephone, electric light bulb, phonograph, computer, motion pictures, television, and most video players were invented by Americans. Technological innovation and the manufacturing process have a strong symbiotic relationship. Involvement in the manufacturing process stimulates innovation, while innovation constantly improves the manufacturing process. As we continue losing large chunks of our manufacturing base, we are also losing our opportunities to innovate.

Can we smoothly evolve from a manufacturing economy into a high-tech, information-based, service-oriented, post-industrial economy? Stephen S. Cohen and John Zysman are strong proponents of the view that manufacturing does indeed matter and that if our manufacturing base continues to shrink, our high-tech service sector will shrink along with it:

> The reason is clear and simple, involving what we call direct linkages. A substantial core of service employment is tightly tied to manufacturing. It is a complement, not a substitute or successor, to manufacturing. Lose manufacturing and we will lose—not develop—high-wage service jobs.[3]

Cohen and Zysman's view is seconded by Franklyn J. Vargo, a vice president of the National Association of Manufacturers:

> If manufacturing production declines in the United States, at some point we will go below critical mass and then the center of innovation will shift outside the country and that will really begin a decline in our living standards.[4]

Research and Development and the Manufacturing Base: The Breaking Link

As our manufacturers moved their factories abroad, they also began off-shoring their research and development facilities as well. Texas Instruments, General Electric, Microsoft, Intel, and IBM—as well as hundreds of other American corporations—have set up major research and development facilities in India, China, and other countries in Asia and Eastern Europe that provide them with well-educated—and, of course, relatively low-paid—labor forces.

When we boast about our giant high-tech firms employing millions of Americans, we are talking about household names like General Electric (GE), IBM, Hewlett-Packard (HP), and Dell. The table in Fig. 8.1 lists the number of employees of our largest high-tech firms both in the United States and abroad. I'd like you to focus on the number of jobs held by Americans.

2015 Employment in Thousands	in America	Abroad	Total
General Electric	144	189	333
IBM	62	316	378
Hewlett-Packard	120	167	287
Intel	51	57	108
Dell	37	65	102
Cisco	37	35	72

Fig. 8.1. Employment totals of downsizing American high-tech firms. These firms are primarily manufacturers who have off-shored not just their manufacturing operations but much of their research and development as well. Source: statistica.com.

The six firms listed in Fig. 8.1 are among the ten largest American high-tech employers—the other four, Microsoft, Apple, Oracle, and Google, are listed in Fig. 8.2. You can't miss the pattern in Fig. 8.1: each company except Cisco has more employees stationed abroad than in the United States. And since they've been downsizing for years, we can't look to any of them to generate growth in high-tech jobs. But it *can* be argued that other rapidly growing high-tech firms provide more hope for job growth in the United States. Each of the firms listed in the table in Fig. 8.2 except Oracle employs a substantial majority of its employees in the United States.[5]

2015 Total Employment	
Amazon	231,000
Oracle	135,000
Microsoft	118,000
Apple	115,000
Google	57,000
Facebook	13,000
eBay	12,000
Symantec	11,000
Twitter	4,000

Fig. 8.2. Employment totals of rapidly growing American high-tech firms.[6] Amazon is primarily a retailer, selling a wide range of goods. Most of its employees are low-paid warehouse workers. Unlike the other firms listed here, which are all primarily software producers, Apple not only produces software but is also a major manufacturer of hardware such as the iPhone, iPad, iPod, and iMac. The hundreds of contractors hired to manufacture these products employ well over one million workers. So while, technically, Apple has just 115,000 employees—76,000 of whom work in the United States—in actuality, these employees represent less than one-tenth of the people who produce Apple products.[7] Finally, most Apple employees are relatively low-paid retail associates.[8] Full disclosure: I own Apple stock.

In the foreseeable future, can we expect much employment growth from the firms listed in Fig. 8.2? The answers are yes and no.

Yes, we can probably expect Twitter and Facebook to become multiples of their current sizes, and each of the others will likely continue adding employees. But, no, the total number of employees of the nine companies shown in Fig. 8.2 was just over 400,000, perhaps 250,000 of whom worked in the United States. So these growing firms—along with dozens of other high-tech start-ups (many of which have not yet even been formed)—are unlikely, in the foreseeable future, to create enough high-tech jobs to employ more than another one or two million Americans.

In a 2004 report, the President's Council of Advisors on Science and Technology detailed how the erosion of our manufacturing base adversely affected research and development. The "research to manufacturing process is not sequential in a single direction, but results from an R&D–manufacturing ecosystem consisting of basic R&D, pre-competitive development, prototyping, product development and manufacturing," all operate in such a way that "new ideas can be tested and discussed with those working on the ground."[9] There is a link, then, between the research lab and the factory floor. Neither can survive without the other.

The federal government, itself, is complicit in our lagging R&D. Among all industrial powers, our government devotes a smaller percent of our GDP than nearly all of its competitors.[10]

Our Failing Education System

By the turn of the twentieth century we had created the world's first free universal public education system, providing our rapidly growing industrial machine with a well-educated and highly skilled labor force. Our vaunted American know-how enabled us to turn out one technological innovation after another, building the greatest economy in the history of the world.

Chapter 12 provides an account of how, over the last five decades, we allowed what had been, by far, the best public education system in the world to descend into a state of mediocrity. Half of our eighteen-year-olds cannot function at an eighth-grade level, making many of them virtually unemployable as they are increasingly forced to compete against better educated workers across the globe—most of whom are willing to work for much lower pay.[11]

Adding to our difficulties, our best and our brightest college students are no longer majoring in what is called the STEM subjects—science, technology, engineering, and mathematics. About 60 percent of our undergraduate and graduate engineering majors are foreigners—as are nearly 75 percent of our PhD students in the sciences—most of whom will be returning home after graduation.[12] All told, our colleges and universities train just a fraction of the STEM students trained in India and in China.

Our Lagging Support for Research and Development

By far, the most productive of our corporate R&D facilities was Bell Labs, which was a part of AT&T. From the 1920s into the early 1980s it produced an amazing stream of extremely useful innovations. Perhaps foremost was the transistor, invented in 1947, which became the building block of all digital products. Jon Gertner, an expert on Bell Labs, has explained the transistor's importance:

> These tiny devices can accomplish a multitude of tasks. The most basic is the amplification of an electric signal. But with small bursts of electricity, transistors can be switched on and off, and effectively be made to represent a "bit" of information, which is digitally expressed as a 1 or 0. Billions of transistors now reside on the chips that power our phones and computers.[13]

Here's a list of ten other significant innovations produced by Bell Labs:

1. silicon solar cell
2. first patent for a laser
3. the communications satellite
4. first fiber-optic cable
5. first long-distance television transmission
6. UNIX operating system and C programming language
7. first cellular telephone system
8. first long-distance computing
9. first FAX service
10. first binary digital computer

What happened to Bell Labs since the early 1980s? After the breakup of AT&T in 1982 it was downsized and eventually entirely phased out. In the meanwhile many other major R&D operations have been downsized also or were shipped abroad.

Technological progress is vitally dependent on an adequate level of research and development spending, which has long been supplied by both large corporations and by the federal government. But since the 1980s, support from both sources has been lagging.

Making matters still worse, IBM, Hewlett-Packard, Motorola, General Electric, Intel, Microsoft, and other huge, American-based multinational corporations have been building research facilities in China, India, Eastern Europe, and other places where they can find a very well-educated workforce—one that is willing to work at a fraction of the wages paid to their American counterparts.

THE GROWING TECHNICAL PROFICIENCY OF OUR GLOBAL COMPETITORS

At the mid-twentieth century few economic historians would have forecast the decline of the American economy. Nor would many have predicted the economic rise of Asia. The most important factor contributing to growing parity between the economies of the East and the West has been the spreading use of the world's most advanced technologies.

How the East Caught Up with the West

It took two and a half centuries to develop the technology that enabled older industrialized nations like the United States, the United Kingdom, France, and Germany to raise their standards of living to their current levels. More recently developed nations like South Korea, Singapore, and Taiwan have been able to raise their living standards to Western levels within just a couple of generations. And since the early 1980s, China, which had been one of the world's poorest nations, has been doubling its national output every seven years—the highest sustained rate of economic growth ever recorded.[14]

Clearly then, it has been the ability of these recently developing nations to draw upon this vast store of technology that has enabled their rapid growth. The problem *we* have with all their good economic fortune is that they are now competing with us in the global marketplace. And to a large degree, China in particular is using its vast economic power to coopt much of our cutting-edge technology.

The Chinese Challenge

China cannot continue to grow at a double-digit rate if it keeps producing just relatively low-tech consumer products such as toys, shoes, apparel, and consumer electronics. Wage rates have been rising rapidly, and multinational corporations are increasingly shifting their production to even lower-wage countries such as Bangladesh and Vietnam. China's leaders have determined that their nation's future lies in high-tech manufacturing, which can create tens of millions of higher-paying jobs for its well-educated and well-trained workers.

In 2011 China announced its innovation goals to be reached by 2020. They are summarized by Robert Atkinson and Stephen Ezell:

> The country plans to invest $1.5 trillion on seven strategic emerging industries—(1) energy saving and environmental protection; (2) new generation of information technology; (3) biotechnology; (4) high-end equipment manufacturing; (5) new energy; 6) new materials; and (7) new energy vehicles.[15]

Unlike any other developing nation, China—the world's most populous nation and the second-largest economy—has a vast and rapidly expanding consumer market. Virtually every multinational corporation is almost compelled to set up operations there to more easily tap into this market as well as to take advantage of government subsidies, tax breaks, and a well-educated, relatively low-paid, and compliant labor force. And then too, a physical presence is a very necessary requisite to doing business in China—rather than communication by fax, phone, or e-mail.

But setting up manufacturing operations in China may also incur one extremely high cost—the forced transfer of a company's most advanced technology.[16] Atkinson and Ezell explain the terms of this Faustian bargain:

> China's government unabashedly forces multinational companies in technology-based industries—including IT, air transportation, power generation, high-speed rail, agricultural sciences, and electric automobiles—to share their technologies with Chinese state-owned or influenced enterprises as a condition of operating in the country. For example, Chinese officials normally force multinational companies to form joint ventures with its national champions and transfer the latest technology in exchange for business opportunities. Companies that resist are simply excluded from projects and refused permission to invest.[17]

Why do foreign companies continue to capitulate to these onerous terms? It's because they really don't have good choices. They lose if they hand over their technology. But if they refuse these terms, then they cede the great Chinese market to their global competitors who *are* willing to give up their technology.

Having acquired all of this foreign technology, the Chinese have very quickly and skillfully used it to build their own industries, and then competed in the global market. A prime example is the high-speed rail system. China had required foreign companies bidding on what was to become the world's largest high-speed rail system to form joint ventures with CNR and CSR, two state-owned equipment makers. In addition, they had to offer their latest designs, and to have 70 percent of the work done locally. The winning bidder, Kawasaki, of Japan, agreed to train Chinese engineers and develop a local supply chain for 70 percent of the components.[18] Today, not only is China building its own railroad systems, but it is bidding against Kawasaki and other competitors around the globe.

OUR CRUMBLING INFRASTRUCTURE

At the dawn of the twentieth century our nation was tied together by its navigable rivers, its systems of canals, its railroads, telegraph and telephone lines, and increasingly by its electric grids. Our rapidly growing and improving infrastructure was the underpinning of our world-class economy, affording us the highest standard of living in history.

Every advanced economy is supported by a strong infrastructure that includes the following:

- water mains and sewer networks
- gas and oil pipelines
- electrical power grids
- local streets and roads
- highways and Interstates
- power dams
- levees
- canals and waterways
- seaports
- airports
- railroads
- public transportation systems

Until the early 1970s our infrastructure was in very good repair. The only major problem was our rapidly disappearing public transportation systems. But since then, because public and private spending reductions led to deferred maintenance, much of our infrastructure has been deteriorating.

In a landmark study of our failing infrastructure, *Too Big to Fall*, Barry B. LePatner reported that of our transportation system's 600,000 bridges, one-quarter "are deemed to be either 'structurally deficient' or 'functionally obsolete.'"[19] The failure of one such bridge is described in the accompanying box.

The Collapse of the I-35W Bridge

The I-35W bridge in Minneapolis "shuddered, buckled, and collapsed during the evening rush hour on Wednesday, August 1, 2007, plunging 111 vehicles into the Mississippi River and sending thirteen people to their deaths."[20] The bridge, which was opened in 1967, had been intended to carry 60,000 cars a day, and "was designed as fracture-critical, meaning that the failure of any one of its supporting structural members could result in the collapse of the whole bridge."[21]

By 2007, the bridge, which had not been well maintained, had 160,000 cars and trucks passing over it each day. And suddenly, with no warning, the bridge collapsed. Over the years there have been several other collapses resulting in the loss of lives.

Since the 1980s, nationwide engineering design specifications made these collapses much less likely. LePatner noted that "bridges now had to be designed so that if one structural support failed, the load could be distributed among other supports in order to prevent a sudden, catastrophic collapse." But there are still nearly 19,000 fracture-critical bridges in use today.[22]

The Department of Transportation has estimated that obsolete road designs and poor road conditions have been factors in about 14,000 highway deaths each year.[23]

Our nation has an infrastructure deficit of clogged roads and highways, antiquated air traffic systems, and outdated levees built more than fifty years ago to protect crops, but now protect communities. We have inefficient electrical power grids, leaking water and sewer mains, aging railroad systems, and clogged seaports.

Our rail network has such bad bottlenecks that it can take hours just to get through some of them. Our air traffic systems are so outdated and overloaded that the Federal Aviation Administration predicts that it will reach total gridlock within just another year or two.[24] And the US Chamber of Commerce estimates that our decaying infrastructure costs us $1 trillion each year in lost economic growth.[25]

The 2013 Report Card put out by the American Society of Civil Engineers gave our overall infrastructure a grade of "D+."[26] Estimates of bringing our deteriorating bridges and tunnels, airports, power grids, roads and highways up to acceptable standards by 2020 reach a staggering $3.6 trillion.[27] Indeed our current annual spending of just $400 billion a year—about 2.5 percent of our GDP—leaves us falling further and further behind.[28] Our global economic competitors—most notably, China—spend two or three times as much of GDP on infrastructure.[29] Once a competitive advantage, our once top-notch infrastructure is becoming a growing liability.

Our nation's spending on infrastructure has averaged just 2.4 percent of our GDP since the mid-1950s.[30] If we don't invest in a substantial upgrade, the cost to our nation will be considerably higher. The next report card is due in 2017.

INDUSTRIAL POLICY

Industrial policy is commonly defined as the government's picking industrial winners—such as clean energy, consumer electronics, or motor vehicles. But a true industrial policy is a national strategy to leverage existing resources within companies, universities, the labor force, and the public sector.

Industrial policy should support entire industries—not specific firms. Atkinson and Ezell recommend "placing strategic bets to support potentially breakthrough nascent technologies (such as . . . nanotechnology, human genome mapping, robotics, or advanced batteries) and industries . . . (such as broadband telecommunications, life sciences, software, and clean energy)."[31]

Not only does the United States *not* have an industrial policy, but we have not even made a start on developing one. Occasionally the federal government *has* made an effort to provide substantial aid to particular industries—semiconductors and motor vehicles under the Reagan administration in the 1980s, and, more recently, to clean energy and motor vehicles under the Obama administration. Whatever their degree of success, these were just ad hoc efforts, not part of an overall industrial policy.

The most successful practice of industrial policy was the formation of SEMATECH (short for Semiconductor Manufacturing Technology)—a consortium of fourteen American chip makers and DARPA (the Defense Department's Defense Advanced Research Projects Agency)—which would gain everlasting fame as the developer of the Internet. Under the aegis of the Reagan administration, such high-tech companies as Texas Instruments, Intel, IBM, and AT&T joined together to meet the growing threat of Japanese firms taking control of the semiconductor industry. Not only were semiconductors vital to consumer electronics, computers, and many other consumer products, but they were a major component of the weapons systems that were the backbone of our national defense.

The members contributed $100 million a year, a sum that was matched by DARPA. In addition, SEMATECH was staffed by hundreds of employees drawn from the member companies. All fourteen members of the consortium were chip makers, and their prime objectives were to build and run a chip plant, provide research grants to equipment suppliers, and to buy their equipment for testing.[32]

Japan, South Korea, Taiwan, Germany, and, most recently, China have very successfully used industrial policy to outstrip us in one industry after another. This has given each of these nations a great advantage in the global marketplace.

Germany, whose industrial workers earn about 40 percent more than their American counterparts, is arguably the world leader in high-tech manufacturing.[33] Largely responsible is the government's support of corporate applied research that translates into high-tech products.

While we have never had an overall industrial policy, there have been instances when the federal government went well beyond just "picking winners." In chapter 14 we shall talk about the military-industrial complex, composed of the Defense Department, the armed services, the large defense contractors, and the House and Senate Armed Services Committees. Into this one sector of the economy, the federal government pours hundreds of billions of dollars a year, the large part of which is paid to the major contractors. The armed services got the weapons systems that they wanted, while the Armed Service Committee members were able to steer much of this spending into their own states and congressional districts.

Most of the federal support for research and development went to defense contractors and to several large research universities. And best of all, our defense establishment is a closed system. Although top secret documents are occasionally stolen—most notoriously the plans for building atomic bombs in the mid-1940s—we basically ran a closed system. All of the research and development and manufacturing was done in the United States, and very little of our technology was ever made available to other nations.

SOLUTIONS

Bolstering research and development, repairing our crumbling infrastructure, and formulating an industrial policy need to be among our top national priorities. As a nation, however, we are barely aware of these problems—let alone ready to provide all the resources needed to solve them. But if we don't quickly at least make a start, we will fall further and further behind as a world-class technological innovator.

Bolstering Research and Development

To regain our place as the world's leading high-tech innovator, we need to spend much more on basic research and on applied research. Our nation's federal, corporate, and university labs will need tens of billions of dollars more each year. We must ask how we can recreate not just one Bell Labs but perhaps a dozen. And we need to once again induce many more of our best and brightest college students to major in the sciences, technology, engineering, and math. The strongest inducement would be the prospect of a good job in their chosen field.

Without a world-class labor force, we can no longer be a world-class economy. At this juncture it should be a no-brainer—forgive the pun—that we must drastically improve our public schools to be able to compete in the global marketplace. In chapter 12 we'll outline what needs to be done to rebuild what had been the world's best educational system.

During the financial crisis and the accompanying Great Recession, the federal government very reluctantly invested hundreds of billions of dollars to buy huge chunks of GM and Chrysler, and of AIG, Citicorp, and several other large financial corporations. Not only did this great infusion of cash prevent these firms from going bankrupt, but within just a few years the government was paid back almost in full. Indeed, in most cases, it even made a nice profit.

Using this model of government investment in private firms, why can't the federal government buy the stock of promising high-tech companies? To do this systematically, the government could staff an advisory board with experienced venture capitalists who would decide in which new firms to invest. This would create an efficient way of providing needed capital to firms willing to invest heavily in research and development. And who knows: maybe the federal government will end up making a large profit.

Nearly all the venture capital firms, which finance promising high-tech start-ups, are privately held. This arrangement deprives the public from investing in tiny companies, which might become the next Apple, Facebook, Amazon, or Microsoft. The federal government could provide the seed money to set up dozens of publicly held venture capital firms, and then sell stock to the public. If people are willing to invest in the future earnings of professional athletes, then they surely would be happy to buy into a future Google or eBay.

Publicly held venture capital firms would have four advantages: they would (1) allow small investors to put their money into high-tech start-ups, (2) offer the start-ups a reliable source of funding, (3) encourage innovation, and (4) boost employment in the high-tech sector.

Repairing Our Crumbling Infrastructure

An ounce of prevention is worth a pound of cure.

—Benjamin Franklin

If there is one economic sector to which this adage best applies, it's our infrastructure. Surely the loss of life—not to mention the huge repair costs—caused by the collapse of the I-35W bridge was a whole lot greater than the preventive maintenance costs that had been deferred.

Repairing and modernizing our crumbling infrastructure will actually kill not just *two* birds with one stone but *three*:

1. We can save of lot of lives and money in future years.
2. Our economy will operate much more efficiently.
3. We can put millions of people back to work.

On the downside, this massive effort will cost perhaps an additional $100 billion a year beyond what we are currently spending. That's a lot of money. But if we used it to pay previously unemployed people to do most of the work, then that would minimize the cost in actual resources. Lawrence Summers, a former US treasury secretary, has observed that the ideal time to begin large construction projects is during a recession and the subsequent recovery, when unemployment is high and when the government could borrow at very low interest rates. After all, we must fix our infrastructure *some*time, so why not when we have all these idle resources? The period from 2008 through 2016 was such a time.

When President Obama's economic advisors were compiling a list of "shovel-ready" public works projects to be provided with economic stimulus money in early 2009, they basically needed to start from scratch. Even though they would soon have nearly $900 billion at their disposal, there was no master list of needed projects available—let alone detailed blueprints.[34] So let us learn from this experience—which, incidentally, was similar to that of the incoming administration of President Franklin Roosevelt during the depths of the Great Depression. In both 1933 and in 2009, the federal government embarked on a course of investing in large public works projects on a completely ad hoc basis.

Today we need state and local governments to compile lists of needed infrastructure projects to be funded on the same 90 to 10 percent basis, like the federal highway program. The states, which would pay 10 percent of the costs, could list these projects in order of priority. From these, a master list could be compiled, and we could immediately begin to work our way down the list.

During his presidential campaign, Donald Trump proposed a $1 trillion upgrade of our highways, bridges, tunnels, airports, and other components of our nation's infrastructure.[35] Of course, it's one thing for the president to propose, but quite another for the Congress to dispose. We shall return to this proposal in chapter 27—the book's last chapter.

Formulating an Industrial Policy

> *Insanity: doing the same thing over and over again and expecting different results.*
>
> —Albert Einstein

As we cast about for ways to deal with the loss of our technological leadership, we would do well to take heed of Einstein's implicit advice. If you hope for different results, then try something new. That new something should be the formulation of an industrial policy.

SEMATECH saved our semiconductor industry. Clearly, then, it was an industrial policy that worked, and it should be applied to other industries. The Obama administration has made a few attempts, most notably in clean energy. But it has also made the fatal mistake of trying to pick winners. Solyndra, a solar panel manufacturer, managed to go through over $500 million in government loans before going bankrupt in 2011.[36] Perhaps the best approach would be for a presidential commission to come up with a list of industries that might profit from following the SEMATECH model, and then to see if the leading firms in those industries would be willing to form consortiums that might pool research and development and manufacturing costs.

All of our global competitors—most notably China, Japan, and the European Union—heavily subsidize major industries. Our own best model for industrial policy is our massive defense spending, which subsidizes our major weapons programs. As part of our industrial policy, the federal government should determine which industries we cannot afford to lose, as well as which new industries we can help grow. Each of them could be subsidized, if necessary. These subsidies would help finance the hiring of millions of employees, ranging from blue-collar and white-collar workers to people working in research and development and other high-tech jobs.

The most promising approach in recent years was a bill submitted by Senators Sherrod Brown (D-OH) and Roy Blunt (R-MS) in 2013.[37] It would have established a national network of manufacturing innovation hubs.

The basic idea is to create consortiums of research universities, community colleges, business firms, nonprofit organizations, and government agencies. They would accelerate manufacturing innovations in technologies into commercial applications. Research and development conducted at universities is rarely commercialized because it lacks not just the needed funding, but also the entrepreneurship of private businesses. Senator Brown has estimated that it would take $600 million of private and public funds to get dozens of hubs off the ground. Perhaps one day Congress will act on this initiative.

Part IV

JOBS, WAGES, AND THE JOB SHORTAGE

Forty or fifty years ago a blue-collar factory worker could support his family while his wife stayed home with the kids. They lived in a new suburban home and could even afford to send their children to college. The chances were, his employer not only paid his health insurance premiums but also provided a generous pension. And almost each year his wages rose faster than the rate of inflation.

But over the last forty years those jobs have been disappearing. Today two-thirds of all women with young children must hold down jobs, and even two salaries seem to go no further than one did four or five decades ago.[1]

The real hourly wage rate for the average nonsupervisory worker is no higher than it was in 1973.[2] In recent years only the relatively well-to-do have enjoyed substantial income increases. For millennials who have been entering the labor force, the big question is whether their generation will be able to live as well as their parents' generation.

Tens of millions of Americans hold make-work jobs. They range from low-paid telemarketers to accountants, attorneys, and hedge fund operators. What they all have in common is that they don't produce any useful goods or services.

There are a variety of reasons why make-work is so deeply embedded in our economy. Among the villains are our Internal Revenue Code, our healthcare insurance system, and even the way our laws are written.

Throughout our history, waves of immigrants have enhanced our labor force, started their own businesses, and assimilated into our society. But since the 1920s we have severely restricted their numbers, and during the last few years illegal immigration has become a very controversial political issue. Another major question is the degree to which we want to increase the immigration of well-educated and highly skilled foreigners.

Chapter 9

JOBS AND WAGES

America needs a raise.

—John J. Sweeney, president of the AFL-CIO

The problem millions of Americans are faced with is not finding a *decent* job—but *any* job. In this chapter we'll be looking at how this terrible jobs situation developed—and what we can do about it.

THE GOOD OLD POSTWAR YEARS

We look back at the period from the late 1940s through the 1960s as the years of post–World War II prosperity, and indeed they were. But one can argue that even *then* our nation was hardly in a state of economic grace. Systemic employment discrimination against African Americans, women, and other populations groups resulted in the underemployment of more than half our labor force. Our nation's largest firms—among them the Fortune 500 largest industrial corporations, our largest financial institutions, public utilities, law firms, and retail chains—had virtually no women or African Americans even among the lower ranks of their management positions.[1] In other words, these companies seemingly could not find qualified African Americans or women to fill more than two hundred of these three or four million positions.

Think of the vast waste of talent that employment discrimination imposed on our economy. Instead of being permitted to work at jobs for which they were highly qualified, tens of millions of Americans were shunted into much lower-paying positions for which they were greatly overqualified. Over recent decades, thanks largely to the civil rights and women's rights movements, employment discrimination has been greatly diminished. That's the *good* news. The *bad* news is that the employment prospects of millennials are substantially worse than they were for preceding generations.

THE PROCESS OF CREATIVE DESTRUCTION

Over the long term, some industries rise and others fall. Before the 1920s, the primary modes of private transportation were the horse-drawn carriage and the horse-and-buggy. Think of all the carriage and buggy makers thrown out of work in that decade when tens of millions of Americans switched to cars. Or think of the typewriter manufacturers who lost virtually all of their business to the makers of word processors, and then personal computers.

Our economy is in a perpetual state of what the noted economist Joseph Schumpeter termed "creative destruction." The government must not interfere with this process of industries rising and falling over time, because in the long run, economic evolution dictates that only the fittest firms and industries will survive. And this process, however painful in the short run, ensures that our economy keeps growing and, with it, our standard of living.[2]

Were Schumpeter alive today, he would agree with our government policy of sitting back and letting our large corporations downsize and ship millions of manufacturing jobs abroad. It's all just part of the creative destruction process that will help the economy grow in the long run, as new industries replace the dying ones, and eventually reemploy the workers who have been laid off.

THE LOSS OF MANUFACTURING JOBS

> *Here you are standing in an employment line at my age. Nobody wants you no more. You're left out. You're not American no more.*
>
> —James Hash, who had lost his job at Carrier when the firm moved its manufacturing operations from Tennessee to Mexico.[3]

For most of us, we *are* what we do. Take that away from us and what have we got left? Not having a decent job means there's something very deficient about us. And that has been happening to tens of millions of Americans.

For a century, from the time of the Civil War until the early 1960s, our economy added manufacturing jobs most years. In 1979 our manufacturing employment peaked at twenty million jobs.[4] Since then manufacturing employment has fallen nearly every year, and now totals less than twelve million.[5] There are two primary reasons for this decline. First, because of technological advances, we have been able to more than triple our output of manufactured goods with less than two-thirds the number of workers. And second, much of what we had been producing here is now produced abroad. So our loss of manufacturing jobs is due to technological advance (or automation) and offshoring.

Competition—whether among American manufacturers, or between American manufacturers and their foreign competitors—forces everyone to cut costs to the bone. If you can produce more cheaply by laying off your employees, whether through automation or offshoring, you rarely hesitate. Your goal is always to protect your bottom line. If you don't, then you'll be driven out of business. The corporations that laid off their loyal employees would very likely have gone bankrupt if they tried to be nice guys. As legendary baseball manager Leo "the Lip" Durocher famously put it, "Nice guys finish last."

Still, economic theory predicts that those who are laid off will, at least in the long run, be able to find well-paying jobs in expanding industries. Let's look at the record.

According to some studies conducted since the early 1980s, most workers laid off due to offshoring who did find jobs took an average pay cut of 25 percent. Many were unemployed for more than a year. Perhaps 35 to 40 percent of the displaced workers actually did find new jobs at equal pay. Think of the outcomes of these layoffs like those of this coin toss—heads you lose and tails you break even.[6]

Clyde Prestowitz notes that so far only 15 to 20 percent of our workforce has been directly affected by the offshoring of jobs, and yet American wages have been stagnant since 1973.[7] Imagine the future effect of the offshoring of our service sector jobs, affecting up to 80 percent of our labor force.

MEASURING THE EFFECT OF OFFSHORING AND AUTOMATION ON THE LOSS OF MANUFACTURING JOBS

Measuring the effect of offshoring on employment is relatively easy in comparison to the effect of automation. For example, when the Carrier division of United Technology announced a plant closing in Indiana, we knew that two thousand American workers would be replaced by two thousand workers in Mexico. In November 2016, President-Elect Donald

Trump was able to save several hundred of those jobs by securing an agreement between the company and the state of Indiana, which provided $7 million in tax credits.[8]

On the much broader scale, a study by the Economic Policy Institute determined that during the period from 2001 to 2013, 3.2 million jobs—two-thirds in manufacturing—had been moved from the United States to China.[9]

When an American company closes a plant in the United States and opens one in Vietnam, we can easily count the number of jobs that have been offshored. But what if that company continues opening new factories in Vietnam, Bangladesh, the Philippines, and Indonesia? We can't classify the resulting jobs as offshored since no American jobs were destroyed. But the effect is almost the same, since those jobs might otherwise have been filled by Americans.

So what we *can* say is this: over the last four decades, American-owned international corporations have shifted much of their production of manufactured goods offshore. This has resulted in the loss of perhaps as many as ten million factory jobs that Americans might have otherwise held.

Now, let's shift gears and consider how the process of automation has affected the number of manufacturing jobs held by Americans.

Automation is a major part of technological change. But instead of creating *new* goods and services, it creates more efficient ways of producing the *same* goods and services. In fact, the effects of automation on manufacturing employment can ostensibly be measured by making this comparison. As mentioned before, since 1979, manufacturing employment fell from twenty million to about twelve million. And yet, our output of manufactured goods nearly tripled.[10]

So it would appear that automation caused a huge drop in manufacturing employment. One might even argue that it was the process of automation, rather than the offshoring of jobs, that caused most of the decline in manufacturing employment. This would partially invalidate the argument presented by Donald Trump during the 2016 presidential campaign that by renegotiating our trade treaties, we can bring back millions of manufacturing jobs.[11]

On the other hand, if we look at the role of automation over the last century, there is no evidence that it lowered *total* employment. Consider, for instance, the introduction of ATMs in the 1980s and 1990s. This greatly reduced the need for tellers in each bank branch. But ATMs also stimulated banking activity, ultimately increasing the number of bank employees.[12]

Still, maybe automation *has* caused some unemployment in recent years. After all, during the first decade of this century, there was no increase in total employment. But since the end of the Great Recession of 2007–2009, the unemployment rate fell steadily, and since mid-2015 it has hovered around 5 percent—which is considered full employment.[13]

MIT professor David Rotman, who has long studied the economic effects of technological change, has concluded that rather than affecting total employment, it has polarized the workforce and caused a "hollowing out" of the middle class. It has created many higher-paying jobs requiring creativity and problem-solving skills, while eliminating many more lower-skilled office and manufacturing jobs.[14]

Two other MIT professors have a much more pessimistic view. Erik Brynjolfsson and Andrew McAfee "believe that rapid technological change has been destroying jobs faster than it is creating them, contributing to the stagnation of median income and the growth of inequality in the United States." Brynjolfsson adds, "People are falling behind because technology is advancing so fast and our skills and organizations aren't keeping up."[15]

To sum up: in recent years, technological change may be causing *some* net loss of jobs. Clearly, more jobs paying middle-class incomes are being destroyed than very well-paying jobs are being created. The millions of displaced workers are left to do relatively low-paying, unskilled work. And in the process, the middle class is being hollowed out.

THE NEXT TEN YEARS

After seeing so many jobs offshored in recent decades, let's consider what will be happening over the next ten years. The authors of two recent books believe that many of us will soon be competing with billions of foreign workers. *Three Billion Capitalists* by Clyde Prestowitz and *The World Is Flat* by Thomas Friedman both contend that newly laid intercontinental broadband cable and the spread of the Internet have brought three billion more people into the global economy. Many of these people, almost all of whom live in developing countries, are just beginning to compete with Americans for jobs. To the degree that work can be digitalized, tens of millions of American workers in the service sector may soon be competing with people who are willing and able to do their jobs for a fraction of their wages.

Although we are losing our manufacturing base, Prestowitz believes that Americans will continue spinning out great inventions. But he asks how these inventions can be commercialized in the United States to create high-wage employment:

> Surely there will always be the next new thing waiting somewhere in the wings. But it won't necessarily be waiting in America, and even if it is, it almost certainly won't be commercialized in America and won't provide jobs for ordinary Americans. Intel's [Craig] Barrett captured the situation perfectly when he commented that "Intel will be okay no matter what. We can adjust to do our R&D and manufacturing wherever it is most economically advantageous to do so. But in addition to being chairman of Intel, I am also a grandfather, and I wonder what my grandchildren are going to do."[16]

THE DECLINE OF ORGANIZED LABOR

In the mid-1950s one out of three American workers was in a labor union. By 2016 just one in ten was a union member.[17] Much of this decline was due to the precipitous fall in manufacturing jobs. As we've seen, those lost jobs, on average, were much better paying than the jobs that the laid-off workers ultimately found. Obviously then, the loss of manufacturing jobs pushed down wages, especially since the early 1970s.

The wages of unionized workers are about 20 percent higher than non-unionized workers in the same industry.[18] So wage rates took a one-two punch these last four decades with the decline of both manufacturing jobs *and* unionized jobs.

Relatively high-paying jobs in the steel mills, auto plants, as well as somewhat lower-paying jobs in textiles, apparel, furniture making, and consumer electronics were sent offshore. The service economy, which now employs four out of every five American workers, has been much harder to unionize than manufacturing.[19] Wal-Mart, Target, Costco, and McDonald's, for example, are completely free of unions.

The diminished economic role of labor unions is described by Jeremy Rifkin:

> Trade unions . . . have served as the counterweight to management, forcing companies to share the fruits of productivity gains broadly among the workers, in the form of increased wages, shorter working hours, and improved working conditions and benefits. But . . . unions have been weakened by the forces of globalization and especially by the ability of management to move capital and plants elsewhere and play the game of "beggar thy neighbor."[20]

The unions have long relied on the one weapon at their disposal to exact gains—the ability to withhold their labor through the strike. Strikes, however, become less effective when management can simply shift production to plants in other countries or outsource to anonymous subcontractors. Moreover, with increasing automation of factories and offices, management can often continue to run production and maintain services—at least for the short run—with skeleton crews.[21]

THE WORKING-CLASS JOB SQUEEZE

Two or three generations ago, many of the girls who got commercial diplomas were hired as tellers, typists, and telephone operators—the three t's. But today most tellers have been replaced by ATMs, most typists have been superseded by PCs, and nearly all telephone operators have been replaced by telephone answering machines, direct dialing, and voice simulators more or less capable of carrying on conversations.

Today thousands of people line up outside newly built Wal-Marts, hoping to land one of the few hundred nine-dollar-an-hour part-time jobs. McDonald's, Kentucky Fried Chicken, and 7-Eleven are hiring. The American working class has been reduced largely to hamburger flippers, parking lot attendants, telemarketers, bedpan orderlies, retail clerks, gas pumpers, supermarket checkers, medical assistants, waiters, and waitresses. Where have all the good jobs gone?

IS WAL-MART CREATING BAD JOBS AND DESTROYING GOOD ONES?

In the last chapter we described how Wal-Mart forced scores of manufacturers to move production to China and other low-wage countries to cut costs. Now we shall examine how else this giant retailer has affected jobs and wages.

Wal-Mart is perhaps the nation's most controversial firm, a company that is loved by tens of millions of Americans, and hated by many others. Let's start out with some basic facts about this company.

- It is the nation's largest employer with over 1.5 million employees.[22]
- Its average full-time employee earns just over ten dollars an hour.[23]
- It is, by far, our largest retailer.

- It has successfully kept unions from organizing its workers.[24]
- When a new store opens, thousands of people line up for applications.

So what could be so bad? For *one* thing, Wal-Mart may well be the reason why many of its job applicants are out of work in the first place. By driving smaller retailers out of business, Wal-Mart and other big-box retailers have been responsible not just for the loss of hundreds of thousands—or possibly millions—of jobs, but for the demise of downtown shopping areas in towns and cities across America.

For *another*, every year since 2013, Wal-Mart has imported more than $50 billion of manufactured goods from China and additional tens of billions from other countries.[25] Had the store bought more goods made in the USA, we would not have lost so many manufacturing jobs these last few decades. On the *other* hand, if Wal-Mart tried harder to buy American, it would not be able to charge such low prices.

So here is Wal-Mart's message: We may be responsible for your losing your job; or, if you happen to work for us, we admit that we are paying you rock-bottom wages. But because we pay such low wages and we buy low-cost goods overseas, we charge low enough prices so that even *you* can afford to shop at our store.

In 2006 the Chicago Board of Aldermen passed a bill mandating that Wal-Mart and other big-box retailers pay their workers at least ten dollars an hour, but Mayor Richard Daley promptly vetoed the bill.[26] As much as he would have liked his constituents to have earned decent wages, he said that relatively low-paying jobs were better than no jobs at all. A few months later, when Chicago's first Wal-Mart opened in a very poor neighborhood, some 25,000 job applicants lined up in the hopes of getting one of the 425 available positions.[27]

Does the opening of a large retail store create jobs and help economic development? Greg LeRoy provides *this* answer:

> To measure the ripple effects of a new business, you look "upstream" to see how many supplier jobs the region would gain, and then you look "downstream" to see how many jobs would be created by the buying power of the people who work at the business. The upstream of a big-box store does not create many jobs for the local economy (think of all those goods made in China), and the downstream ripple effects are terrible because retail jobs are overwhelmingly part-time and poverty-wage, with no healthcare. That means most retail workers have very small disposable incomes; after paying for bare necessities, they have nothing left with which to stimulate the local economy.[28]

LeRoy sums up that "you and I do not have more money in our pockets because we have more places to shop. Building new retail space just moves sales and lousy jobs around."[29] To carry his argument to its logical conclusion, imagine if *all* our jobs were in retailing. And that all we did all day was shop. If current trends persist, we will eventually become a nation of shoppers—and the low-paid workers who wait on us.

Wal-Mart is certainly more the product of globalization than one of its architects. But if Wal-Mart is the future of America, at least with respect to the job outlook, that future is frightening indeed. We may all soon need to memorize the line, "How may I help you?"

THE TWO-TIER WAGE SYSTEM

It took the civil rights revolution of the 1960s and the women's liberation movement of the 1970s to firmly establish the principle—not always honored in practice—of equal pay for equal work. Men and women, blacks and whites—and, in effect, all Americans, performing the same jobs—are now legally entitled to the same earnings.

But sadly, we have been drifting away from this principle. Millions of Americans, whether working as part-timers, temps, or for labor contractors, are paid much less than the full-time, regularly employed work force. Jeremy Rifkin describes the trend toward hiring increasing numbers of "disposable workers":

> Temporary workers and outsourcing make up the bulk of today's contingent workforce—millions of Americans whose labor can be used and discarded at a moment's notice and at a fraction of the cost of maintaining a permanent workforce. Their very existence acts to drive wages down for the remaining full-time workers. Employers are increasingly using the threat of temp hiring and outsourcing to win wage and benefit concessions from unions—a trend that is likely to accelerate.[30]

Wal-Mart, United Parcel Service, and many other large employers pay their part-time employees considerably less than those who work full-time. But now many companies are formalizing a two-tier wage system by paying newly hired employees as little as half of what long-term employees are earning. Here are some examples:

- Under a contract between the International Longshoreman's Association and waterfront management, new workers are paid sixteen dollars an hour, while long-term workers are paid twenty-eight dollars an hour.[31]
- The United Automobile Workers (UAW) union accepted an identical pact with General Motors.[32]
- Similar wage structures have been established at Ford, Chrysler, and Dana Corporation and Delphi, auto parts manufacturers. In 2015, General Motors and the UAW reached an agreement to phase out the two-tier wage arrangement by 2024.[33]
- New workers at Caterpillar earn fifteen dollars an hour, compared to twenty-five dollars an hour paid to long-term workers.[34]

Hedrick Smith describes how the two-tier system has worked in other industries:

> Airline pilots pushed into feeder airlines have had to accept de facto demotions at lower pay for similar work. Ticket clerks, back office workers, and bank cashiers as well as factory workers have been pushed out of full-time jobs and then hired back by the old company as theoretically "independent contractors" at lower pay as temporary or part-time workers with few or no benefits.[35]

In a front-page *New York Times* article, Louis Uchetelle described the two-tier system set up by three large Wisconsin manufacturers—Harley-Davidson, Mercury Marine, and Kohler. Faced with plant closings, the unions representing workers at each of these companies agreed to a two-tier system of wages. Second-tier workers now earn five to ten dollars an hour less than those in the first tier. Laid-off or furloughed workers at Harley-Davidson and Mercury Marine who were rehired would return as second-tier employees—at substantially reduced wages.[36]

OUTSOURCING VS. OFFSHORING

Many companies contract out some of their jobs to other firms. For example, Wal-Mart hires local janitorial firms to clean their stores at night. Magazine and newspaper subscriptions are sold by telemarketers who are employed by companies that specialize in telephone soliciting. Briefs for law firms may be typed by people in the West Indies.

All of these jobs are outsourced. But if they are performed abroad, then they are also offshored. When a company shuts down a textile mill in South Carolina and then imports its textiles from China, those jobs are not just outsourced but offshored as well.

As long as outsourced jobs remain in the United States, one American's job loss is another American's job gain. But when a job is offshored, our employment goes down by one. While most of those whose jobs are offshored eventually find other work, it may take them months or even years to do so, and then the new job will usually pay less than the job that was lost.

In our nation's entire history, our employment has always risen from one decade to the next. But total employment actually fell slightly between 2000 and 2010.[37] What happened? Well, we *did* suffer from the worst economic downturn since the Great Depression. But to make matters still worse, our large multinational corporations added 2.4 million employees to their overseas workforces, while cutting 2.9 million workers in the United States.[38]

OFFSHORING AND WAGES

Over the last three decades, as well-paying blue-collar jobs have disappeared, millions of workers were pushed into the labor market, and most were eventually willing to settle for almost *any* type of work. The forces of supply and demand explain why thousands of people line up for applications whenever Wal-Mart opens a new store. What accounts for the huge supply of workers hoping to land jobs that pay poverty-level wages? A large contributing factor is the offshoring of so many jobs.

But offshoring plays an even more pernicious role in holding down wages. It provides hundreds of thousands of employers with a Sword of Damocles to hold over the heads of their workers. We can always move this business to Mexico, Indonesia, Thailand, Malaysia, or wherever else there are people willing to work for just a fraction of what we're paying you.

THE EFFECTS OF AUTOMATION

We have seen that offshoring was widely blamed for the loss of millions of factory jobs—as well as a rapidly growing number of jobs in the service sector—during the last three decades of the twentieth century. But increasingly, the continued job losses, especially since the new millennium, are being blamed on automation.

The process of automation may be described as the use of machines and technology to enable workers to be more productive. For example, one typist using a word processor might have replaced five typists using typewriters.

Was the process of automation ushered in by the advent of computers and industrial robots? Perhaps the first economist to describe automation was Adam Smith, who is considered by many to be the founding father of modern economics. Back in 1776, he described the operations of a British pin factory.

One worker, said Smith, "could scarce, perhaps, with his utmost industry, make one pin a day, and certainly could not make twenty." He then described how pin-making had become specialized. "One man draws out the wire, another straightens it, a third cuts it, a fourth points it, a fifth grinds it at the top for receiving the head."[39]

Ten pin workers, working on their own, could turn out at most a total of two hundred pins. Smith estimated that ten people working together in a factory could produce forty-eight thousand pins a day by using the automated process he described.

Over the next two centuries, manufacturing throughout the workplace remained highly labor intensive. But the introduction of computers and, increasingly, industrial robots has vastly expanded the processor of automation throughout the industrialized world. Because of rapidly rising labor productivity in the United States since 1980, we have been able to almost triple our output of manufactured goods with about 40 percent fewer workers.

According to a study by Michael J. Hicks and Srikant Devaraj of Ball State University in Indiana, between 1980 and 2012, 13 percent of manufacturing job losses were due to trade imbalances and 87 percent were attributable to productivity growth—or, in a word, automation.[40]

One might get the impression that nearly all of the job losses in manufacturing before the new millennium were caused by the offshoring of jobs and that, since then, the large majority of job losses was caused by automation. But a more accurate conclusion is that *most* of the job losses were due to offshoring before the new millennium, and *most* of the job losses since then were due to automation.

What can we say about the coming years? Lawrence Katz, a Harvard economist who studies labor and technological change, has summed up our prospects: "Over the long haul, clearly automation's been much more important—it's not even close."[41]

While automation has clearly been costing us millions of manufacturing jobs, in other economic sectors it may actually be expanding employment. Let's consider the effect on employment at urban banks during the period from 1988 to 2004, when they installed tens of thousands of automatic teller machines (ATMs).

As it might have been expected, the average number of tellers fell from twenty per bank branch in 1988 to just thirteen in 2004. But the introduction of the ATMs greatly reduced operating costs, allowing the banks to open more branches in response to greater demand for bank services. By 2004, bank employment was up substantially, as former tellers shifted to work in sales and customer service.[42]

To sum up, for centuries, automation has clearly displaced hundreds of millions of workers, but it has greatly enhanced worker productivity. It has, in the long run, created even more jobs than it destroyed. That said, there is no guarantee that it will continue to do so. Furthermore, in a growingly global economy, it is quite conceivable that losses caused by automation in one nation might result in job gains in another. In an international race based on technological prowess, we may well be falling behind.

STAGNATION IN REAL WAGES

> *We have thousands and thousands of people working on full-time jobs, with part-time incomes.*
>
> —Martin Luther King Jr.

Let's distinguish between real wages and money wages. By real wages, economists mean what you can actually buy with your wages. Money wages are what you're paid in dollars and cents. If the rate of inflation were 10 percent a year, you'd need a 10 percent pay raise each year (in other words, your money wages would need to rise by 10 percent a year), just to maintain your standard of living.

If we go all the way back to the 1820s, we'd find that real wages increased every decade until the 1970s. And then they stopped increasing. Real wages—what you can actually buy with your pay—began to fall in 1973. The table in Fig. 9.1 shows the record of real wages earned by 80 percent of all American wage earners between 1945 and the present. As you can see, real hourly wages reached a peak in 1973, and are now about the same as they were in that year.

Year	Real Hourly Wage Rate
1947	$5.35
1973	$9.26
2015	$9.07

Fig. 9.1. Real hourly wage rate, 1947, 1973, and 2015 (in 1982–1984 dollars). Source: Bureau of Labor Statistics, *Monthly Labor Review*, December 2016.

Between 1947 and 1973 real wages almost doubled. Why? Because as workers' output rose, their employers compensated them accordingly (see Fig. 9.2).

	Real Average Hourly	
Period	**Wage Rate Increase**	**Productivity Increase**
1947–1973	73%	95%
1973–2015	-3%	109%

Fig. 9.2. Real average hourly wage rate and hourly productivity increases, 1947–1973 and 1973–2015. Source: Bureau of Labor Statistics, *Monthly Labor Review*, December 2016.

In 2015 output per hour was more than double what it had been in 1973. So we would expect that real wages to have approximately doubled. But they didn't. They actually declined slightly.

How could this have happened? Earlier in this chapter we discussed the factors that depressed real wages:

- The loss of more than 40 percent of our manufacturing jobs since 1979.

- The decline in union membership from one-third of the labor force in the mid-1950s to one-tenth today.
- The offshoring of millions of manufacturing jobs, and the increased offshoring of service sector jobs.
- The threat by employers to offshore still more jobs when employees demand higher wages.
- The process of automation has displaced millions of workers.

Two additional factors have held down real wages. First, because the rise in healthcare costs has far outpaced the overall inflation rate, employers, burdened by their employees' rapidly rising healthcare premiums, grew increasingly reluctant to grant wage increases as well. We'll talk about healthcare in chapter 13. And second, over the last four decades, there has been a massive shift of income from the poor, the working class, and the middle class to the rich. Growing income inequality will be discussed in chapter 22.

Chapter 10

THE JOB SHORTAGE

The rate of unemployment is 100 percent if it's you who is unemployed.

—David L. Kurtz

As she was leaving a fancy restaurant, a woman was asked by the owner how she enjoyed her meal. She replied, "The food was like poison . . . and such small portions!"

This anecdote could serve as a metaphor for our job market. The available jobs often pay the minimum wage or a bit more, provide almost no benefits, and—there are so *few* of them.

JOBS FOR HIGH SCHOOL GRADUATES

Back in 1979 the US automobile industry employed 600,000 workers, and perhaps another 500,000 more worked for their suppliers.[1] Today just 200,000 work in the industry, and that total includes not just General Motors (GM), Ford, and Chrysler, but also about a dozen Japanese, German, and Korean automakers.[2]

In the 1980s and 1990s I taught at Union County College, a northern New Jersey community college, whose student body was drawn mainly from working-class families. Most had friends or family members who worked at the local GM assembly plant—or once had. On the first day of class I would ask this question: If GM were hiring today, how many of you would quit school if you got a job there? Usually more than three-quarters of my students raised their hands.

Writing in the *New York Times* back in 1990, Anna Quindlen noted how much the job prospects had changed for working-class boys:

> Life was easier a generation ago. They graduated from high school, or maybe they didn't. It didn't really matter, because someone from the family or the neighborhood could get them into the union or the

civil service, could find them a job working construction or picking up trash.[3]

What kinds of jobs are now available to high school graduates and community college dropouts? Maybe a career at Wal-Mart or McDonalds? Perhaps pumping gas or bussing tables? If you have a good phone voice, you might even be able to find work as a telemarketer.

The US Department of Labor is very bullish on job prospects in health-care. In 2014 there were 1,768,000 people who were employed as personal care aides; by 2024 their ranks are expected to swell to 2,227,000. The median annual pay is just under $21,000.[4]

In 2014, there were 914,000 people working as home health aides at a median annual wage of almost $22,000. By 2024 their ranks are expected to grow to 1,262,000. These are among the fastest-growing jobs in America. If you're worried about job security, you might want to look into *those* promising careers.[5]

JOBS FOR COLLEGE GRADUATES

It's not just the children of the poor and the working class who are worried about finding decent jobs. Growing numbers of college students are wondering what will happen to them after graduation. Hundreds of thousands of recent graduates have settled for unpaid internships, hopeful that these would not just provide valuable on-the-job training but eventually lead to a paying job in that field. Most of these unpaid internships lead nowhere, and many turn out to be nothing more than an excuse to use free labor.

Over half of our recent graduates have jobs that don't require a college degree.[6] And many of the jobs that *do* require a degree could be performed by those with less impressive academic credentials. Their employers reason that if they can get a college graduate to do clerical work at relatively low wages, why not hire her rather than a community college dropout?

A college diploma, once the ticket to a well-paying job, is now, at best, just a minimum requirement. Millions of teenagers are wondering if it still pays to invest four years of their lives and tens of thousands of dollars in a college education—and then be left with a high student debt and a low-paying job.

CONCLUSION

A decent job is central to our identity, our welfare, and the welfare of our families. To tens of millions of Americans, our main economic problem is that there aren't enough decent jobs.

In mid-2017, eight years after the end of the Great Recession, seven million Americans were still officially unemployed, another ten million had dropped out of the labor force, and an additional six million part-time workers wanted full-time jobs.[7] It would be fair to say, then, that our economy needs to provide more than twenty million jobs if we are to put everyone back to work. But we have a much more serious employment problem.

Tens of millions of Americans hold jobs that require them to work hard, put in long hours, and yet produce goods and services that add little or nothing to our material well-being. These jobs will be described in the next three parts of this book:

Part V: Wasting Our Resources by Using Them Inefficiently
Part VI: Wasting Our Resources by Overproducing
Part VII: Wasting Our Resources by Producing Useless Goods and Services

We have an extremely serious job shortage—a lot more serious than just needing to find jobs for the seventeen million Americans who are out of work. We also need to create perhaps another forty million jobs for the workers who should be shifted from the production of virtually useless goods and services to much more useful work.

As we shall see, at least one-quarter of our labor force is engaged in virtually useless work. If we are to have an efficiently operating economy—one that minimizes the waste of its resources—then these tens of millions of workers need to be shifted into jobs in which they can produce the goods and services we need to help create a higher living standard and to promote a greater economic well-being for the American people. Toward the end of this book we'll talk about how this can be done. Right now, let's see how we are wasting our scarce resources—especially our labor.

Part V

WASTING OUR RESOURCES BY USING THEM INEFFICIENTLY

The easiest way to measure efficiency is by looking at the cost of producing a good or service. If you can grow a bushel of wheat at a cost of two dollars, but it costs me four dollars to grow that much wheat, then you produce wheat about twice as efficiently as I do.

Now let's consider these two facts:

1. The average American family spends almost twice as much of its income on transportation as the average family in most other wealthy nations.[1]
2. We spend almost twice as much per capita on healthcare as do most other wealthy nations.[2]

And so, it would be fair to say that our transportation and healthcare sectors are about half as efficient as those of most other wealthy nations.

Another way we can measure efficiency in an economic sector is by looking at the results of our spending. Again, please consider two facts:

1. Half of our eighteen-year-olds cannot read and do math at an eighth-grade level.[3]
2. Half of our college freshmen are placed in at least one remedial course.[4]

So do you think that in these three economic sectors—transportation, healthcare, and education—we are using our resources efficiently? If you do, then perhaps—as an almost lifelong resident of Brooklyn—I could interest you in buying a bridge.

Chapter 11

OUR WASTEFUL TRANSPORTATION SYSTEM

Any urban economist will tell you that ours is one of the most inefficient transportation systems in the economically developed world. We are completely dependent on our cars to get almost *any*where. And we spend more per capita on transportation than any other nation.[1]

Transportation accounts for one-third of the energy we use, and two-thirds of our oil consumption.[2] With the exception of Canada, no other developed country uses nearly so much oil per capita.[3] Our dependency on oil is due mainly to the suburbanization of our country over the last six decades.

THE WAY WE WERE

You would have to be well into your seventies to remember the streetcars. Unless, of course, you live in Portland (Oregon), San Diego, San Francisco, New Orleans, or some other city in which they are enjoying something of a revival. But until the 1930s, streetcars were our primary form of transportation. Not only did they carry millions of passengers along the streets of every city, but interurban lines connected entire urban regions. It was possible, for instance, to go from New York to Boston by streetcar. Of course you had to change many times, and the fare came to just over two dollars, all in nickels and dimes.

By the late 1920s the nation was served by nearly four thousand different electric trolley and interurban streetcar lines. Not only were there dozens of lines in each of our major cities, but even many smaller cities such as Fort Wayne and Gary, Indiana; Allentown, Lancaster, Scranton, and Wilkes-Barre, Pennsylvania; Rochester and Syracuse, New York; and Toledo, Ohio, had more than a dozen lines.[4]

Why did this mode of public transportation, which served us so well, almost disappear by the early 1950s? The main villain of the piece is General Motors, and its role is described in a book by Jane Holtz Kay, entitled *Asphalt Nation*.

> In 1932, General Motors, the manufacturer of buses . . . formed a consortium of tire, oil, and highway men to buy and shut down America's streetcar systems. Attacking the trolley mile by mile, the syndicate of General Motors, Firestone, Standard Oil, and Mack Truck, allied as National City Lines, cajoled and bought off local officials. . . . Between 1932 and 1949, they would help persuade 100 electric systems in more than forty-five cities to scrap their street rails. . . . By 1940 total public transportation ridership had shrunk by 2 billion. The magnificent rail lines fell, taking with them the private rights-of-way, the street corridors that had insured their fast passage.[5]

THE SHIFT FROM PUBLIC TO PRIVATE TRANSPORTATION

Let's look at a few numbers in the table in Fig. 11.1. In 1949, just as suburbanization was taking root across the nation, public transportation ridership peaked at 23.5 billion rides. But only seven years later it had fallen to just 10.7 billion rides. So it's not hard to detect a cause and effect relationship: rapid suburbanization caused tens of millions of Americans to abandon public transportation for automobile travel.

Year	Billions of Trips
1949	23.5
1956	10.7
1995	7.8
2015	10.6

Fig. 11.1. Number of trips taken by Americans using public transportation. Source: American Public Transportation Association, press release, March 10, 2014, APTA.com (accessed October 8, 2016).

For the next forty years, public transportation ridership continued to decline, reaching an all-time low of just 7.8 billion riders in 1995. But then, finally, things began turning around, and by 2015, we were back up to 10.6 billion rides, a level not seen since 1956. But before we congratulate ourselves on this great comeback, let us consider two additional facts. First, our nation's population has nearly doubled since 1956.[6] And second, the number of mass transit trips we took in 2013 was still less than half of those taken in 1949.

Until the late 1940s we had an efficiently run mass transportation system that got people where they needed to go quickly, safely, and cheaply. The General Motors syndicate saw to the destruction of many electric trolley systems, but it was the federal government during the decades of the 1930s, 1940s, and 1950s that got most Americans to shift from public to private transportation.

The Origins of the Federal Highway System

> *If you pave it, they will come.*
>
> —Jane Holtz Kay, author of *Asphalt Nation*

Do you remember the line in the Kevin Costner movie *Field of Dreams*, "If you build it, they will come"?[7] Then you'll understand how the federal highway building program that began under President Franklin Roosevelt's New Deal engendered the immense automobile and truck traffic we have today. To create jobs for nearly one million unemployed men, the Roosevelt administration put them to work building streets and highways. During the decade of the 1930s our surfaced road mileage doubled.[8]

For every dollar the federal government spent on building streets and highways, only a dime was spent on building or improving mass transit.[9] But that was just the beginning. Immediately after World War II our national highway building program shifted into high gear, enabling not just the suburbanization of the country, but the eventual completion of the national highway network. Heavily subsidized by the highway trust fund—public transportation received a small fraction of government funding—the automobile became the primary mode of travel, while the truck replaced the freight train as the main way of hauling freight.

Growing Traffic Congestion

Probably no one was more responsible for the way our nation suburbanized than Robert Moses, New York's great highway builder. During his more than four decades as the most powerful nonelected public official in the state, if not the country, Moses literally paved over much of New York State. He believed that the most efficient way to travel was by car, and the way to cut down on traffic congestion was to build more highways.[10]

On Long Island alone, Moses built eleven expressways, but he fought off any attempt to incorporate mass transit rights-of-way into them. He did this knowing that if provisions for tracks were made in the original highway design, their cost would be one-tenth of providing them later.

Widely considered a visionary, Robert Moses set the standard for American urban development in the second half of the twentieth century. Public officials from all over the country journeyed to New York to learn from the master builder. The lesson they learned was to make Moses's highways the model for their own localities. Within decades they had succeeded in paving over most of urban America.

Robert Caro's largely critical biography of Moses describes how he operated:

> Watching Moses open the Triborough Bridge to ease congestion on the Queensborough Bridge, open the Bronx-Whitestone Bridge to ease congestion on the Triborough Bridge and then watching traffic counts on all three bridges mount until all three were as congested as one had been before, planners could hardly avoid the conclusion that "traffic generation" was no longer a theory but a proven fact: the more highways were built to alleviate congestion, the more automobiles would pour onto them.[11]

Like Robert Moses, most of us truly believe that if we could just build more highways or add lanes to existing highways, we would eliminate traffic congestion. But adding more highway capacity makes longer commutes less burdensome, so as a result, people are willing to live farther and farther from their workplace. As increasing numbers of people move out to the exurbs, the long-distance commute grows crowded as the commuters living closer to the cities clamor for additional lanes, and the cycle repeats itself. An aphorism popular among traffic engineers sums this all up: "Trying to cure traffic congestion by adding more capacity is like trying to cure obesity by loosening your belt."[12]

Perhaps the worst aspect of Moses's legacy was that his highways eviscerated entire neighborhoods. The Cross Bronx Expressway, for example, is credited with destroying that borough.[13] Picture a bulldozer a hundred feet wide leveling everything in its path. Large swaths of housing on both sides of the expressway were abandoned, as hundreds of thousands of people just picked up and moved. Within just a few years, a borough that had been the home of hundreds of thousands of working-class families living in close-knit neighborhoods was transformed into a huge slum.

Moses created the national template for building expressways through urban neighborhoods. From the late 1940s through the 1970s hundreds of viable neighborhoods were destroyed in New York, Chicago, Los Angeles, and in nearly every other large and middle-size city.[14]

Today close to half of urban America's land is dedicated to the driving and parking of vehicles. In Los Angeles that ratio jumps to two-thirds, while Houston provides the equivalent of thirty asphalt parking spaces per resident.[15]

BIGGER, BUT NOT BETTER

Since the onset of the baby boom in 1946, Americans needed to buy large motor vehicles to accommodate their growing families. General Motors, Ford, and Chrysler—which would soon be making nine out of ten cars sold in the United States—built only large vehicles.[16] After all, their top executives declared, these were the cars that American families wanted and needed. Of course, the fact that the profit margin on large cars was much greater than that on smaller vehicles had nothing to do with their production decisions. Only when German and Japanese automobile companies began shipping growing numbers of compact and subcompact cars to our shores in the late 1960s did the Big Three even begin to *consider* making smaller cars.

Unlike drivers in nearly every other wealthy country, Americans are adamant about owning SUVs and other relatively large and heavy motor vehicles that are classified as light trucks. Even though the median American household now averages just two people, we still insist on driving these gas-guzzling monsters. Indeed, more than half of all new passenger motor vehicles sold today are light trucks.[17]

Perhaps the best explanation why Americans drive large vehicles is "because we can." In fact, we're *entitled*. Federal mileage standards are much lower in the United States than they are in the European Union, Japan, and other economically advanced nations—a factor we'll return to near the end of the chapter when we discuss solutions to our transportation problems.

THE ADVANTAGES OF PUBLIC TRANSPORTATION

Every urban economist will tell you that we need to get peak hour commuters out of their cars and into trains, trolleys, and buses for their trip to and from work. Doing so would kill five birds with the same stone. It would reduce:

- our dependency on foreign oil.
- air pollution.
- traffic congestion.
- the need to keep building more highways.
- global warming.

A bus carries up to sixty passengers in the space occupied by two cars. Eight-car trains can comfortably carry up to forty thousand persons per hour past a given point. By contrast, a lane of freeway has a carrying capacity of just two thousand cars per hour—or about three thousand people.[18]

To induce more people to use mass transit, we need to make it relatively cheap and convenient. For it to be economically feasible, we need to be able to quickly move large numbers of people to their jobs and back home again. They must be convinced that they are better off using mass transit than spending hours sitting in traffic.

The tabloid the *New York Daily News* is noted for its catchy headlines. This one is not so catchy as thought-provoking:

FOR MASS TRANSIT NEED MASS

You can't have mass transit, then, unless you have a lot of people riding the buses, trains, and trolleys. Here's how Jane Holtz Kay explains the headline:

> [T]he average rider will walk no more than eight or ten minutes to his or her transit stop. This truism of transportation and humanity means that collecting enough riders to fill the trolley or bus depends on collecting passengers who live nearby. . . . [T]he more people dwelling in a smaller radius around the fare box, the bigger the ridership.[19]

Transportation expert Jeffrey M. Zupan supplies precise figures needed to make public transportation feasible:

> To get an hourly bus in the residential district, you have to have one house per quarter acre. . . . To get one every half hour, it's seven an acre, and for every ten minutes, it's fifteen an acre.[20]

Very few suburbs have as many as four houses per acre, so they don't have the population density needed to support even an hourly bus.

Because housing is so spread out, mass transit is just not economically feasible.

While the typical American family devotes almost 20 percent of its budget to transportation, Japanese and European families spend less than 10 percent.[21] A well-run public transportation system can move people faster—and at a much lower cost.

Our Dependency on Foreign Oil

> *Hey, you mean we're going to walk from the car to the living room? My feet haven't touched pavement since we reached Los Angeles.*
>
> —from the movie *Annie Hall*[22]

In the years after World War II, as the world's leading producer, we needed to import no more than 10 percent of our oil.[23] But American production peaked in 1970, and as our need for oil grew rapidly with suburbanization, we had to import more and more.

In the 1970s we went through two oil crises when our imports from the Middle East were partially cut off. Those crises were illustrated vividly by gas lines that often extended for many blocks. As our dependency on oil imports grew, one of the main jobs of our armed forces, particularly the navy, was to ensure that there was an uninterrupted flow of oil to our shores. In recent years our oil production has risen substantially, but we will continue to depend on large foreign oil imports in the foreseeable future.

Air Pollution

We know that automobile and truck emissions contribute substantially to air pollution and global warming. These emissions have more than quintupled since suburbanization began in earnest after World War II. Every second of every day our cars and trucks travel another eighty thousand miles, use up four thousand gallons of fuel, and add eighty thousand pounds of carbon dioxide to the atmosphere.[24] Although we've still got a lot to learn about the effects of all that driving on global warming, it is clear that there are consequences, and these consequences will drastically affect the lives of our children and grandchildren.

CARS, TRAINS, PLANES, BUSES, AND TRUCKS

Back in the 1940s, we had the world's greatest railroad network. You could go from New York to San Francisco by train in just under three days. Commercial air travel was still in its infancy, and fear of flying was quite common. Today, of course, almost no one goes across the country by train. In fact very few will take a train ride of more than a few hundred miles. Why bother when a plane will get you there in just a couple of hours and cost about the same?

The shorter the trip, the more likely that people who fly will spend more time getting to and from the airport than in the air. While most major foreign cities have fast rail connections to the downtown, most American cities do not. If you've ever been stuck in traffic around Kennedy, O'Hare, or LAX, you know exactly what I'm talking about.

Our national railway system has grown shabby, and year by year we cut routes, run fewer trains, and carry fewer passengers. The 20th Century Limited made its last run across America more than thirty years ago. Meanwhile the Japanese bullet trains and the ultramodern Eurorail system speed millions of passengers a day all across the landscape.[25] While our economic rivals have improved and expanded their own railway networks, we have allowed a priceless national asset to deteriorate over the last six decades. Without world-class railroads, we cannot be a world-class economic competitor.

Intercity trains in Europe, China, and Japan cruise along at average speeds exceeding 140 miles per hour, while our fastest passenger trains, the New York to Washington and New York to Boston metroliners, cover the 240-mile distance in about three and a half hours, making four or five stops.[26] Our real problem is the condition of the road beds, which rarely allows speeds of more than one hundred miles per hour.

Former Speaker of the House of Representatives Newt Gingrich notes,

> By contrast, in France, high-speed rail captures half of the market share on journeys of four and a half hours or less. On routes with two hours or less of train travel time, it wins 90 percent of market share. Of course, the French have made substantial investments in creating high-speed rail corridors. The Japanese have made similar investments in what they call bullet trains.[27]

The closest we've come to building a high-speed line is an Amtrak project linking Chicago and St. Louis along the existing right-of-way. It will eventually enable trains to hit top speeds of 110 mph. Whoopee!!! In late 2016, the 284-mile trip is completed in five and a half hours.[28]

Today America remains virtually the only economically advanced nation without high-speed rail transportation. It is truly astounding that the world's largest and richest economy has neither the will nor the means to build even one high-speed line. China, with a per capita income just one-eighth of ours, has been able to launch twenty systems, but we can barely afford even one?[29] Perhaps, more than anything, this failure symbolizes our nation's economic decline.

Just stop for a minute to think of how much oil we consume transporting people by car and by plane, while the people living in most other economically advanced nations make those trips at least as quickly by train. If we invested about three hundred billion dollars to build a first-class rail system—like the one we enjoyed through the 1940s—we could cut tens of billions from our oil annual bill for imported oil.

One of the most promising developments in intercity public transportation is the advent of very low-priced private bus lines. Pioneered by the "Chinese buses" based in New York's Chinatown, these companies speed riders to Boston and Washington for just ten or fifteen dollars—about a tenth of the price charged by Amtrak. The largest of these bus companies is Megabus, serving more than one hundred cities, and carrying more than ten million passengers in 2015.[30]

Trucking has replaced the railroads as our nation's primary way of moving freight. Even though trucks consume fifteen times the fuel for the equivalent job, two-thirds of our freight is moved by truck.[31] So how did trucking become so dominant? First, it is much more convenient than rail transportation to deliver goods to so many scattered suburban sites, and second, the government pays an annual subsidy of tens of billions of dollars to truckers, largely to repair the damage they do to our highways.[32]

THE COST OF OUR WASTEFUL TRANSPORTATION SYSTEM

In the first sentence of this chapter, I stated that ours is one of the most inefficient transportation systems in the developed world. Let's very briefly summarize our three main inefficiencies:

1. We have gone from a highly efficient public transportation system to extremely inefficient in automobile travel.
2. Most of our trips of just a few hundred miles are by plane rather than by train.

3. Trucking has replaced the railroads as our primary mode of hauling freight.

Beyond the huge inefficiencies of our transportation, we must also factor in the hundreds of billions of dollars of additional costs incurred each year to pay for our vast network of gas stations, service stations, auto insurance brokers, highway construction contractors, as well, of course, as our automobile companies and their dealerships, marketers, and advertisers.[33]

The average American family spends close to 20 percent of its income on transportation, about double the percentage spent by families in most other wealthy nations. The American Automobile Association (AAA) has calculated that it costs an average of $8,588 to own and operate a medium-sized car in 2016.[34]

Our entire transportation bill comes to approximately $3 trillion—about 17 percent of our GDP.[35] No other nation on earth devotes such a huge percentage of its output to transportation. Were our transportation system as efficient as those of France, Germany, Japan, and China, our costs would be about one-third lower. In other words, one third of the $3 trillion we now spend on transportation is wasted.

SOLUTIONS

Are you ready for a pop quiz? How much federal, state, and local taxes do you pay for a gallon of gasoline? . . . Okay, is that your final answer? The average in the United States in September 2016 was just forty-eight cents a gallon.[36] Which is why gas is so cheap here compared to other wealthy countries. British and German drivers are paying over four dollars a gallon in taxes; French and Italian drivers are not far behind.[37]

The first order of business—and this would be political suicide—is for Congress to raise the federal tax on gasoline, currently just 18.4 cents per gallon, to at least three dollars. For most drivers this would discourage all but the most necessary automobile trips, induce people to switch to more fuel-efficient cars, or maybe even to move to communities where public transportation is available. Most Europeans quite willingly pay high gas taxes, but then again, most Europeans do not share the average American's sense of entitlement.

Would Americans *ever* be willing to pay an extra two or three bucks a gallon? Never! Even if it meant we'd be able to cut our foreign energy dependency in half and our trade deficit by one-quarter? Still no! Hey, there are priorities around here, buddy. And nobody messes with American priorities. We love to drive and expect our gasoline to be cheap. No matter *who* has to pay for it in the long run.

In 2008 Congress finally passed the first increase in highway mileage standards in twenty years, mandating that the nation's fleet of new vehicles increase its efficiency from its current average of twenty-five miles per gallon to thirty-five miles per gallon by 2020.[38] In 2009 the Obama administration required that for the model year 2011 fuel economy for passenger cars attain 30.2 mpg and light trucks 24.1 mpg. And in 2011 it announced new fuel efficiency standards that require an average of about forty-three miles per gallon for new vehicles in 2025—about the average of what new vehicles in most other economically advanced nations have already attained.[39]

We could also place a luxury tax on SUVs, pickup trucks, and other gas guzzlers. And maybe reinstitute the fifty-five-mile-per-hour speed limit, which would force us to drive at more fuel efficient speeds.

Another incentive to drive is free parking, which is provided by virtually every suburban office park, shopping mall, and strip mall. These facilities are surrounded by parking lots—not the most efficient use of this relatively expensive real estate. The more that is charged for parking, the more people will car pool, use public transportation, walk, or bike to these destinations.

Express lanes dedicated to buses have become increasingly popular in urban areas. To further encourage people not to drive, there needs to be a lot more congestion time toll increases. And more park and ride facilities as well.

Still another development that should be encouraged is the advent of electric cars. But widespread use will continue to be very limited until either the creation of longer-lasting battery charges or of a nationwide system of stations where batteries could be quickly exchanged or recharged.

Our next move should be to very heavily subsidize not just mass transit systems, but our national railroad network as well. Cheap, reliable, and convenient buses and trains will draw tens of millions of Americans out of their cars. Why pay six or seven dollars a gallon and then sit in traffic, when you can get there faster and much more cheaply by taking public transportation?

The nations of Western Europe as well as Japan and China put most of their transportation funds into public transportation. The results are readily apparent. They have first-class rail systems, while the American railroads continue to deteriorate. Their commuters are sped to work by efficiently operating mass transit systems, while Americans are left to fight rush hour traffic to and from work every day.

Denver, Charlotte, Phoenix, Salt Lake City, Houston, Seattle, and Cincinnati are among the cities that have recently introduced or are planning to introduce streetcars. Portland, Oregon, which built the nation's first modern streetcar system in 2001, has integrated it with its light rail system. Dozens of other cities may follow suit. But regretfully, few suburban areas have sufficient population density to support trolley transportation.

Public transportation ridership has been steadily inching up since the mid-1990s. But just a dozen large metropolitan areas have decent systems, and the New York area alone accounts for over one-third of the nation's total ridership.[40] Three out of four Americans live in areas that provide no public transportation whatsoever.[41]

It's fine to pay for such government services as education, police protection, and national defense, but it's somehow a bad idea to subsidize public transportation. Joe Vranich, the former head of the High Speed Rail Association, put it this way: "We 'invest' in airports. We 'invest' in highways. But we 'subsidize' mass transit."[42]

Until the 1960s, the federal government spent tens of billions of dollars (of 2017 purchasing power) on highways, but virtually nothing on public transportation.[43] Since then, federal spending on public transportation has been increased, and now amounts to 20 percent of federal transportation spending.[44]

As the only major economic power without a network of high-speed rail lines—let alone even one—we will have an increasingly difficult time competing in the global economy. Instead of making excuses about why we *can't* do this, we need to begin building these lines immediately. Not so long ago we had the "can-do" spirit that created and sustained the world's greatest economy. Today we can begin once again by building a high-speed rail system.

What would it cost us to make our transportation much more efficient? If we charged people a lot more to drive, and then used that money to subsidize mass transit, the net cost might even be zero. But how likely is *that* going to happen? Getting the government to provide larger mass transportation subsidies, while not impossible, does not seem to be in our immediate political future. In the meanwhile, probably the best we can do is look to metropolitan areas, regions, and states to at least make a start at solving this problem.

Chapter 12

OUR FAILING PUBLIC SCHOOLS

Well over a century ago the United States became the first nation in history to provide free universal public education. While other industrializing nations educated just the children of the relatively well-to-do families, not only did our schools teach all students at least the three Rs—reading, 'riting, and 'rithmetic—but attendance was mandatory.

At the turn of the twentieth century, having by far the world's best educated workforce enabled us to become the leading industrial power. During the first half of the century, we increased our lead. But in the next few decades the public education systems of many other countries not only caught up, but far surpassed us.

Half of our high school graduates go on to college, but more than half of all college freshmen are placed in remedial courses.[1] Clearly, these students—who have not mastered even middle school subjects—are completely unprepared to do college work.

A nation's labor force is, by far, its greatest economic resource. And yet we are writing off half of our teenagers by the time they enter high school.

Whatever is wrong with our public education system, it is certainly not any lack of spending. Indeed, we spend more per student on education than any other nation on earth.[2]

What can be done? Because our problems have multiple causes, we shall need multiple solutions.

WHAT ARE THE CAUSES OF OUR EDUCATIONAL DECLINE?

If you think education is expensive, try ignorance.

—Derek Bok, former president of Harvard

Our public education system from kindergarten through high school provides a great example of just how inefficiently our economy has been using its resources. Although we spend more per pupil than virtually every other country, our eighteen-year-olds are among the most poorly educated students in the developed world.[3]

How bad *are* our schools? Here are just a few measurements:

- Some forty million adults cannot read, write, or calculate well enough to function effectively at work.[4]
- We are graduating students who lack the skills to do assembly line work, let alone sophisticated, high-tech jobs.
- Half of our math and science teachers are unqualified to teach those subjects; primary school teachers in math and science have degrees in these subjects.[5]
- Chinese students spend about twice as many hours doing homework as do their US peers.[6]
- Half of adults cannot read a book written at an eighth-grade level.[7]

It's hard to conceive of just how poorly educated we are. Few people believe me when I tell them about my basic mathematics textbook, which is used in community colleges. Here's a list of the first five chapters, which account for nearly two-thirds of the book:[8]

1. Addition and Subtraction of Whole Numbers
2. Multiplication and Division of Whole Numbers
3. Proper Fractions
4. Improper Fractions, Complex Fractions, and Mixed Numbers
5. Decimals

Can you believe that this is a college textbook? But it's quite appropriate, since more than 70 percent of all community college freshmen are placed in remedial courses where they learn reading, writing, and arithmetic.[9]

When we put all of these findings together, it is not surprising that half of our eighteen-year-olds cannot do eighth-grade work. This is very evident when we look at the extremely low academic success rate of community college students. Over 80 percent of entering freshmen say they wish to ultimately earn a bachelor's degree, but after six years only 12 percent actually do.[10] Having taught at a community college for nineteen years, I can personally vouch that most of the students drop out without having completed even their remedial courses in reading, writing, and arithmetic.

Nearly half of all American adults believe that human beings coexisted with dinosaurs.[11] Perhaps the middle schools and high schools they attended did not offer enough courses in "creationism." Equally amazing, more than one-quarter of all adults think that the sun revolves around the earth.[12]

Still sadder are the results of a 2011 study by the Detroit Regional Workforce, summarized by Thomas Friedman and Michael Mandelbaum:

> 47 percent of adult Detroit residents, or about 200,000 people, are functionally illiterate—which means that nearly half the adults in the city can't perform simple tasks such as reading an instruction book, reading labels on packages or machinery, or filling out a job application. Depressingly, about 100,000 of those functionally illiterate adults have either a high school diploma or the GED equivalent.[13]

Clyde Prestowitz, an international economist, observed that the longer students remain in school, the worse they do.

> International tests show U.S. fourth graders in the eighty-fifth percentile in science and the fifty-fifth percentile in math. By the twelfth grade, however, they have slipped to zero in science and the tenth percentile in math. But never mind, the same tests show that they rank first in students' assessment of their own performance—making Americans number one on the feel-good scale.[14]

FIVE MAJOR PROBLEMS

Our educational system would be great if not for five major problems—the parents, the students, the teachers, the teachers' unions, and the educational establishment.

The Parents

Each generation of parents does not seem to measure up to the previous generation. Part of the problem is that so many more children are being brought up by just one parent. Another is that both parents are busy at work.

And then too, there is a changing parental attitude toward education. Perhaps taking too literally the presidential slogan "no child left behind," parents often pressure teachers and school administrators to pass their children regardless of whether or not they are able to master the work.

Parents are much less likely—or able—to help their children with their homework than earlier generations of parents. Working and single parents have greater time constraints. Often their children bring home little or no homework. And when they have math homework, the so-called "new math" is virtually undecipherable to nearly all parents—and perhaps to most teachers as well.

In Japan, many mothers buy copies of their children's textbooks, help them every night with their homework, and send notes back and forth with their children's teachers.[15] Parental involvement is essential, and it's something that our society has largely lost over recent generations. Maybe teachers and parents could at least e-mail each other.

By the time children enter kindergarten, their educational careers have already been shaped by their parents. Learning does indeed begin at home (see box).

Learning Begins at Home

In the 1980s, two child psychologists at the University of Kansas, Betty Hart and Todd R. Risley, did an intensive study of forty-two families with newborn children, observing their interactions through the age of three. In a *New York Times* article, Paul Tough describes what they learned:

> They found, first, that vocabulary growth differed sharply by class and that the gap between the classes opened early. By age 3, children whose parents were professionals had vocabularies of about 1,100 words, and children whose parents were on welfare had vocabularies of about 525 words. The children's I.Q.s correlated closely to their vocabularies. The average I.Q. among the professional children was 117, and the welfare children had an average I.Q. of 79.[16]

What caused this huge IQ differential? It turns out that there was one simple explanatory factor—the number of words the parents spoke to their children. In the professional homes, "parents directed an average of 487 'utterances'—anything from a one-word command to a full soliloquy—to their children each hour. In welfare homes, the children heard 178 utterances per hour."[17]

Janice Goldfarb, a director of Jumpstart, a program that works with 100,000 preschoolers around the country, observed,

> Average preschoolers know about 20,000 words by the time they are old enough to start school. In low-income areas, by contrast, they can possess a vocabulary of as few as 5,000 words. They are two years behind their peers.[18]

Children from poor families entering kindergarten are, on average, one year behind children from the children of professionals.[19] Few will ever catch up.

The Students

Peer pressure militates against being labeled "a brain," "an egghead," "a bookworm," "a nerd," "a geek," "a dweeb," "an Einstein," or "a teacher's pet." If you volunteer too often and know too many answers, you're showing up your classmates. Maybe you've even done your homework. Bad form!

Unlike the children growing up before the 1950s, when television ownership became widespread, most children today just want to be entertained. Any information they have—and it's not a lot—comes from television or the computer. Reading? Get real! Who *reads* these days? Kids never see their parents pick up a book. Reading went out in prehistoric times.

Perhaps the most important cause of the demise of public education in our cities is the fleeing of the white middle- and working-class families to the suburbs—followed by the exodus of most of the black and Hispanic middle- and working-class families from inner-city neighborhoods. This left inner-city schools—and, to a somewhat lesser degree, the schools in the outlying neighborhoods—largely to the children from poor minority families.

A very high proportion of children attending inner-city schools begin at a tremendous educational disadvantage: they are simply not ready to sit quietly and learn. They're used to being entertained, and now they're expected to sit quietly. And then too, it's very frustrating when you can't keep up with what's being taught.

Consequently, most ghetto neighborhood schools no longer serve as educational institutions, but as holding pens for unruly youngsters. The teachers spend their days trying to maintain order, breaking up fights, and just hoping to survive until they accumulate enough seniority to be assigned to a better school. Many teachers view the children as "animals" and themselves as "zookeepers." But occasionally there's a success story, like the one in Paterson, New Jersey, where Joe Clark, the principal, maintained order by patrolling the halls wielding a baseball bat.[20]

Fewer than half of the poor children at the age of five are ready for school, as opposed to three-quarters of those from families with moderate or high incomes. But 86 percent of the children from families with incomes of over $100,000 can be termed "learning ready."[21]

Is it poverty per se that works against learning readiness, or is it accompanying family characteristics that are the determining factors? Mothers of poor children are much less likely to be married, to have a high school degree, to be supportive of their children, and to provide cognitive stimulation than mothers of children whose families are not poor.[22]

These are facts, and as the Israeli defense minister Moshe Dayan was fond of saying, "You can't argue with a fact."[23] Still, toward the end of this chapter, we'll consider what we can do to help the children from poor families to overcome the obstacles that have prevented them from learning.

The Teachers

A few years ago, Sir Michael Barbor, a senior educational advisor to Britain's prime minister Tony Blair was asked what all the world's great educational systems had in common. "They all select their teachers from the top third of the college graduates, whereas the United States selects its teachers from the bottom third."[24]

In an article written for *MoneyWatch,* Lynn O'Shaughnessy succinctly sums up the role of the education major in academia:

> Slackers wanting to earn the country's easiest college major, should major in education. . . .
>
> Research over the years has indicated that education majors, who enter college with the lowest average SAT scores, leave with the highest grades. Some of academic evidence documenting easy A's for future teachers goes back more than 50 years![25]

And the four years they spent in college did not help their standing. In a study conducted by the National Institute of Education of student performance on the LSATs, GMATs, and GREs, of "25 different study areas, students whose undergraduate major was education scored at the bottom, or at best, second from the bottom."[26]

The declining quality of our teachers can be traced back to the 1930s when teaching provided one of the best-paying and most secure jobs available to college graduates.[27] Most of the people who entered the teaching profession in those years *had* to be good, because local school boards had their pick of the best available applicants. The quality of teachers was also enhanced by almost universal employment discrimination against women, which forced the vast majority of female college graduates to apply for teaching jobs. Again, the more qualified among them were selected.

My father, who taught math in New York City high schools during the Great Depression, earned between sixty-five and seventy-five dollars a week, which was more than what most college graduates made—*if* they could find work.

Well through the 1940s, 1950s, and 1960s, our elementary, middle, and high schools were staffed mainly by bright, dedicated, and highly skilled teachers. But as they retired, most of the younger teachers replacing them did not share these qualities. Two things had changed. First, our brightest and most ambitious college graduates did not want to go into a profession that paid so poorly—and offered so little prestige. And second, in the wake of the women's liberation movement and affirmative action programs, employment discrimination against women declined substantially. As opportunities in other professions—most notably in law, medicine, finance, computer technology, and corporate management—became plentiful, fewer highly intelligent women became teachers.

So, who were left? Basically, the people who couldn't do anything else. To paraphrase George Bernard Shaw, those who can, do; those who can't, teach.

So, a major reason for the decline in public education has been the decline in the quality of teaching. Those choosing to major in education are consistently among the nation's poorest-performing students, based on SAT scores.[28] And those teaching education are the least brightest among the ranks of college professors. In fact, several people added to the words of Shaw: "Those who can, do; those who can't, teach; those who can't teach, teach teachers."

John Silber, the former president of Boston University, declared that the main business of college education departments is "certifying the uneducable to be educators" with a curriculum that amounts to "a two- or three-year negative intelligence test."[29]

This is not to say that all elementary, middle school, and high school teachers are not well educated. Of course there are many intelligent, talented, and dedicated teachers. Today, however, they are just a small fraction of the 3.2 million people who teach school.[30] Five decades ago, they were the large majority. Probably more than anything, this sea change in the quality of teaching has set back American public school education more than any other factor.

Also many education majors have never mastered the subject(s) that they teach. Just half of our math and science teachers are qualified to teach those subjects, and even many who *are* ostensibly qualified had managed to take education courses like math education or science education rather than actual math or science courses.[31]

The Teachers' Unions

The two very large and powerful teachers' unions—the National Educational Association (NEA) and the American Federation of Teachers (AFT)—have been consistent opponents of educational reform.[32] Teachers were very poorly paid and often treated shabbily by school administrators and local school boards until the 1960s, when the NEA and the AFT were able to organize most of the nation's elementary, middle, and high school teachers and secure steady pay increases and job security. But over the last five decades, while the unions have been great for the teachers, they have not been so great for the education of our children.

Union contracts have made it extremely difficult and time-consuming to fire incompetent teachers, institute merit pay, school choice, educational vouchers, and national testing.[33] Why? Because none of these is perceived to be in the interest of union members.

The Educational Establishment

Our public education system is weighted down by a plethora of local school boards, superintendents, assistant superintendents, learning consultants, curriculum advisors, principals, assistant principals, administrative assistants, deans, and supervisors, many of whom have not seen the inside of a classroom since *they* went to school. And let's not forget the municipal, state, and federal departments of education issuing a stream of mandates, goals and objectives, curriculum changes, guidelines, strategic plans, evaluations, and reports.

Those staffing the schools of education and all of the people teaching education courses are the "brains," so to speak, of the educational establishment. These folks have been sponsoring "progressive education" for decades. No longer do children have to memorize multiplication tables or engage in competition with their classmates. And so, almost everything learned in the first three or four grades is "virtually content free," said Diane Ravitch, a former US assistant secretary of education.[34] Sociologist Thomas Sowell has observed that professors of education rank just as low among college and university faculty members as education students do among other students. So it is not surprising to find these people easy prey to fads and harebrained educational schemes.[35]

The folks running the schools of education believe that instead of trying to spur children on by imposing high standards, teachers should invest their energies in making sure that slow learners do not come to think of themselves as failures.[36] So let's hold back the better students until the slower ones catch up. High self-esteem is much more important than actually learning anything. Consequently our high schools are graduating millions of illiterates and innumerates who feel quite good about themselves.

These leaders of education think that memorizing and rote learning is passé; it's much more important for students to understand *why* they are doing something. So students no longer really need to learn how to add, subtract, multiply, and divide as long as they can explain how they would go *about* carrying out these operations.[37] Tell us about the *method* you would use. Whether or not you get the right answer is secondary. Besides, that's what calculators are for. Kind of sounds like being able to pass your road test by just *telling* the driving inspector how you would parallel park and make a broken U-turn.

Indeed, since the widespread availability of cheap pocket calculators in the late 1970s, most children pretty much stopped learning math. Keeping right up with this trend, virtually all of these professional educators endorsed the regular use of pocket calculators by first graders.[38] This ensured that most American children would never properly learn math. Today, our high school graduates score at the bottom of the heap on math exams administered to students around the world.[39] But they rank first in their opinion of their math skills.

One of the most amazing ideas to come out of the educational establishment was that high school vocational education programs should be scrapped and that every child—regardless of ability or personal preference—should be required to pursue a college prep course. Millions of students who might have profited from meaningful vocational education programs that prepared them for lifelong careers are being set up for almost certain academic failure. "Meanwhile," as Joe Klein, the former reformist New York City education chancellor, has noted, "the U.S. has begun to run out of welders, glaziers and auto mechanics—the people who actually keep the place running."[40]

Finally, the schools of education, in cahoots with local school boards and state departments of education, have managed to impose onerous teaching certification requirements that ensure that the best and the brightest college graduates do not go into teaching.[41] Basically, you need to take a series of seemingly mind-dulling education courses. With the exception of a practical student teaching course, it has never been demonstrated that those who completed all of these other courses became better teachers. Indeed, there is ample evidence that most of those who submitted themselves to this process were considerably less intelligent than those who did not.[42]

Think about it. Our public education system has been getting progressively worse for fifty years. Does it make sense to leave the same folks in charge who presided over this decline? Albert Einstein defined insanity as "doing the same thing over and over again and expecting different results."

EDUCATION AND POVERTY

Is it really fair to place the blame for our educational failures on the doorstep of our schools? Writing in *Harper's Magazine*, Peter Schrag notes some of the difficulties faced by the schools:

> Because of the relative paucity of social services in this country—as opposed to the universal preschool, health care, and similar generous children's services provided in other developed nations—our schools are forced to serve as a fallback social-service system for millions of American children. In addition to teaching a far greater diversity of children than is the case in other nations, our educational workers must address countless medical, social, and family problems before they can even begin to think about teaching math, reading, or history.[43]

If the children of the very poor, especially those living in our impoverished inner cities, were the only ones Schrag was referring to, then perhaps if we concentrated our educational resources on those children, we could actually give most of them decent educations. But in the fifteen states of the South, 54 percent of the public school students come from low-income families. The figures for the West (47 percent), the Midwest (36 percent), and the Northeast (36 percent) are also quite high.[44] A 2007 report by the Southern Education Foundation defines low-income students as those who qualify for free or reduced-cost public school meals.[45]

By the time poor children reach kindergarten, after years of inadequate nutrition, limited reading and conversation at home, and little or no preschool experience, they are already at a disadvantage that is difficult to overcome. It's analogous to a race in which most children of the poor are asked to begin far behind the starting line.

Clearly there is no single factor that can explain why some children do well in school while others don't. But Richard Rothstein, a professor of education at UC Berkeley, provides this interesting perspective:

> The fact is that good teachers get bad results in poor zip codes and bad teachers get good results in wealthy zip codes. That should be the starting point for any debate about performance.[46]

SEPARATE, BUT STILL UNEQUAL

> *A mind is a terrible thing to waste.*
>
> —United Negro College Fund slogan

Six decades after the landmark *Brown v. the Topeka Board of Education* decision of the Supreme Court, over three-quarters of all black and white students attend racially segregated schools.[47] Nearly all large cities have four separate school systems. There's an elite private system for the children of the rich and upper middle class and another parochial private system, largely Catholic, for the children of middle-class and some working-class parents. Then there are the elite public schools, or public school programs for the gifted, nearly all of whom turn out to be children of upper-middle-class and wealthy parents. And finally, there are the regular public schools for the children of lower-middle-class, working-class, and poor families, most of whom just happen to be black or Hispanic.

There is something very, very wrong with an educational system that forces so many parents to desperately seek out decent public schools to educate their children. In nearly every large city most of the public schools are no longer viable educational institutions. Why should these parents pay taxes to support schools that their own children cannot attend?

One of the biggest educational handicaps facing minority and low-income students is that their schools generally attract the worst teachers. In virtually every school district, the most experienced teachers are free to choose where they work. And rarely do local school boards provide monetary incentives to entice the best teachers to work with the neediest students. The state of Illinois, for example, measures the quality of its teachers, dividing them into four quartiles. "In majority-white districts, just 11 percent of the teachers are in the lowest quartile." But in schools with few white students, "88 percent of the teachers are in the worst quartile. . . . At schools where more than 90 percent of the students are poor . . . just 1 percent of teachers are in the highest quartile."[48]

FINDING A DECENT SCHOOL FOR YOUR CHILD

Fifty years ago, students living in urban areas went to their neighborhood elementary school, then to their neighborhood middle school, and finally to the neighborhood or area high school. Most of these high schools turned out well-educated graduates, but most of today's graduates can barely read and write. Lousy students create lousy schools.

Is that a fair observation? Yes! Let's not sugarcoat it. There are two sets of victims. The parents and kids from middle-class and working-class families who are left with fewer viable educational options. But the main victims, of course, are the children from those poor families who never had a chance at a real educational opportunity because they were educationally damaged goods before they even set foot in a school.

In virtually all of our cities parents struggle to find schools with gifted programs or so-called "magnet schools" that promise a chance for a decent education. And if your child doesn't get into one of those schools, there may be a seat available in a charter school. And you've always got the option of sending your child to a private school for about $25,000 or $30,000 a year.

In the suburbs, desperate parents have bid up home prices in relatively safe neighborhoods located in "good" school districts. Indeed, most of the cost of their home is actually the cost of living in a good school district. Since the early 1970s, there has been a bidding war for housing in desirable suburban neighborhoods that drove up the price of housing by more than 80 percent after allowing for inflation.[49]

So much for every child having the right to a decent education. In

America today, just the children of the relatively well-to-do still have that right.

OUR COMMUNITY COLLEGES AND CAREER SCHOOLS

Virtually all of the nation's 1,200 community colleges—which enroll 40 percent of all college freshmen—and hundreds of four-year colleges have almost nonexistent admissions standards. You need to have either a high school diploma, a general equivalency degree (GED), or to have managed to live to your eighteenth birthday.[50] The fact that all the community colleges offer remedial courses in reading, writing, and arithmetic—I kid you not—tells us just who's coming to college these days. And, of course, the taxpayer gets a second chance to pay for these students' elementary and middle school educations.

There are two very different groups of students attending these schools. Those who are there solely because they could not afford to go to a four-year school and those who are there by default. In fact, nearly 70 percent of the incoming freshmen are placed in at least one remedial course, and perhaps two-thirds are placed in more than two or three. Of the latter group, no more than 1 percent will ever get a two-year degree.[51]

Please think about this: each day, hundreds of thousands of community college students attend classes in community colleges, where they are trying to learn elementary and middle school reading, writing, and arithmetic. Not only is that a sad commentary about our elementary schools and middle schools, but it's largely a waste of time for these students and a vast waste of resources for our nation. Ostensibly these courses provide a second chance at getting an education. But a dropout rate of 99 percent is hardly an indication of success (see box: "Lowering the Dropout Rate by Lowering Standards").

Our community colleges are all public institutions funded mainly by states and counties. There is also a parallel private system of so-called "career" colleges—among them, DeVry University, Corinthian, Stanley Kaplan University, and the University of Phoenix. These schools attract the same population of students as the community colleges—mainly individuals from poor and working-class families who did not do very well in high school. They are promised an education and training that will qualify them for great-paying jobs and job placement upon graduation. And there's no worry about paying tuition, because most of that

Lowering the Dropout Rate by Lowering Standards

Hundreds of thousands of community college students drop out of school because they are unable to get through remedial math.[52] For nearly all, a two-year degree—let alone one from a four-year school—becomes an impossible dream. Many ask, "Why do I need to learn how to do algebra if I'll never use it at a job?"[53]

College administrators are often very sympathetic. Why indeed *should* we require all of our students to take these courses? In many cases, they are willing to sign waivers, allowing students to skip them.[54] At some four-year colleges, students in many majors are excused from fulfilling *any* math requirements.[55]

If not every college student must be proficient in math, then where should the line be drawn? Should we demand that nearly *all* college graduates be able to do basic arithmetic and have some facility with numbers? Two mathematics professors at Worcester State University answer this question: if developmental math courses are eliminated, students who lack basic skills will be placed into courses for which they are ill-prepared. Such students will either fail to progress or will be passed through a dumbed-down version of the course.[56]

is paid by generous government loans. Sadly, the large majority of these students never graduate, and few of those who do are even placed in decently paying jobs.[57] But nearly all of them are saddled with student debts usually totaling tens of thousands of dollars. Although just one out of ten college students attends a for-profit career school, alumni from these schools account for nearly half of all student loan defaults.[58]

THE COST OF OUR WASTEFUL PUBLIC EDUCATION SYSTEM

Let's ask ourselves this question: How efficiently are we using our resources to educate our children? We spend more per child than virtually every other nation on earth.[59] And just look at our results.

Perhaps emblematic of our waste, the taxpayer gets to pay twice for the same elementary and middle school education of hundreds of thousands of community college students, who *still* end up barely able to read, write, and do simple arithmetic. And many can't even seem to manage that.

Many of our teachers are drawn from among the ranks of the poorest-performing college graduates, as are most of those who teach education, or serve in the armies of educational administrators.[60] Hundreds of thousands of these folks are drawing salaries, but seem to be doing little or nothing to actually educate our children.

Are we getting a decent return on our educational dollar? On international exams our students, at best, place in the middle of the pack. Students from many other nations, spending much less per pupil, consistently score higher than their American counterparts.[61]

Our public school systems, local school boards, our university schools of education, and our local, state, and federal departments of education spend over $600 billion a year—and just look at the results.[62] Perhaps as much as half of this money is completely wasted.[63]

HOW OUR PUBLIC EDUCATION SYSTEM CAN BE FIXED

There's a lot that needs to be done before our public schools will once again be turning out well-educated high school graduates. We have to take a hard look at our largely dysfunctional public education system to see what works and what doesn't. Then we should do more of what works and try to fix what doesn't.

Doing More of What Works

Provide universal preschool and childcare programs

Because nearly two-thirds of the mothers of children six and under are in the workforce, we need universal daycare and preschool programs.[64] It should be available in every locality from 7:00 a.m. to 7:00 p.m., and parents should be able to pay on a sliding scale, depending on their income level.

Today we remain one of the very few economically advanced nations that do not provide universal childcare and preschool. Just 40 percent of all three-year-olds attend preschool; the average of the rest of all the wealthy nations is 80 percent.[65] W. Steven Barnett and Donald J. Yarosz report that "true high quality is not the norm for the nation's preschool education programs."[66]

The strongest argument for a vastly expanded preschool program is this simple fact: increasing the vocabulary of a child before the age of five is the single highest correlate with later success.[67] By the time a child from an educationally deprived background arrives at kindergarten, it is already too late.

James Heckman, a Nobel laureate in economics, has long emphasized the importance of early education as a great equalizer of economic opportunity. He points out that high-quality early childhood programs "supplement the family lives of disadvantaged children by teaching consistent parenting and by giving children the mentoring, encouragement and support available to functioning middle-class families."[68] In other words, the learning environment so lacking in most poor families can be provided by good preschooling.

These programs would have still other salutary effects. They would substitute learning and playing experiences for some of the hours that children would otherwise be sitting in front of their television sets, computer screens, or PlayStations. And they would get inner-city children away from their crime- and drug-infested environments for most of their waking hours. Most important, they would place all children in a learning environment.

Of course, universal preschool would also enable parents—especially single mothers and fathers—to be better able to hold down jobs.

Oklahoma, Florida, Georgia, West Virginia, and Vermont are the only states providing every four-year-old with access to a year of high-quality pre-kindergarten, while younger children from disadvantaged homes often get access to full-day, year-round nursery school. Yet none of the other forty-six states is able to find the money to support universal preschool. But each ends up spending a lot more later on for remediation and for special education classes.[69]

Because of the lack of publicly supported preschool programs, Americans are forced to spend more than parents in every other country for private daycare centers, preschools, and nannies.[70] This money alone could pay for universal preschool.

Keep the schools open from 7:00 a.m. to 7:00 p.m. all year long

What are six-, seven-, and eight-year-olds supposed to do after three o'clock? After-school care could provide not just supervised recreation, but extended learning beyond the school day. Children could get extra help, get a start on their homework, and help each other with difficult lessons. Peer tutoring, or tutoring by older children, could also be arranged. After three o'clock the empty schools are just sitting there. Let's use them.

The biggest problem that working parents must deal with is finding safe, educationally enriching, and affordable daycare. Since very few working parents are off all summer, what are their kids supposed to do? Not everyone can afford to send their children to camp.

How much would all of this cost? Surprisingly little. The schools are already there, so the cost of just keeping them open these extra hours would be minimal. Many teachers would be happy to make a few extra bucks, and it would take just three or four teachers to run before-school and after-school programs. Unemployed teenagers and single mothers could also be hired to help out.

Create more schools for the gifted

We have some great private schools for gifted students and some even greater public schools. The only problem is that there are not nearly enough of them. Of our nation's more than 20,000 public schools, just 165 are devoted solely to the education of the gifted.[71] The only admission requirement is passing an extremely rigorous entrance exam.

Just 1 percent of our high school students attend these schools.[72] Depending on how we define "gifted," surely this 1 percent is only a fraction of our gifted students. If our children are our future, then we would do well to invest much, much more in the futures of our gifted children by establishing many more schools for them from kindergarten through high school.

Vocational and apprenticeship programs

Not everyone goes to college, and not everyone who does will graduate. In fact, fewer than one in three twenty-five-year-olds is a college graduate.[73]

So what happens to all of the people who don't have college degrees? Fifty years ago a man might have had a job on an automobile assembly line, in a steel mill, or as a policeman or a mailman. A woman would have been employed as a secretary, a telephone operator, or as a nurse. But today, just a small fraction of the folks without college degrees can find decent jobs.[74]

Until the 1970s, students not planning to attend college could learn a trade in high school. Most of the girls learned to type, while the boys took up vocational subjects like printing and automobile repair. When they graduated, they usually found jobs. But since then, it was considered more democratic if *everyone* took "college prep" subjects, whether they wanted to or not.

Finally, the pendulum has begun to swing the other way. Recognizing the great success of German apprentice programs, increasing numbers of companies—often in partnership with high schools, community colleges, and state governments—have been starting up their own apprentice programs.

Let's see how the German programs train teenagers for what are usually lifetime careers. While still in high school, the student takes vocational subjects one or two days a week and receives on-the-job training three or four days a week. She or he is paid around $1,000 a month and remains apprenticed for about three years. Half of all German high school graduates end up working as car mechanics, electricians, bakers, carpenters, doctor's assistants, construction workers, aircraft mechanics, or in other skilled jobs. Most other high school graduates go on to either four-year colleges or vocational colleges.[75]

The two keys to the success of the German apprenticeship programs are having the apprentice work alongside an experienced worker and having a virtual guarantee of a job upon the completion of the apprenticeship. Interestingly, just half of the apprentices end up working for the company that trained them.[76]

In the United States, the heaviest use of apprenticeship programs is in the construction industry. About sixty thousand apprentices participate in programs administered jointly by construction employers and construction labor unions.[77] They work up to forty hours a week under the supervision of an experienced electrician, plumber, iron worker, welder, or other craftsman, while getting a few additional hours of classroom training.

Toyota, Volkswagen, Siemens, and a few other foreign-owned companies have also begun apprentice programs. South Carolina, Kentucky, and a handful of other states have begun programs as well. Still, just a few hundred thousand young workers are receiving this training. Germany, a nation with just one-quarter of our population, trains 1.5 million people annually.[78]

Considering how long we need to wait for electricians, plumbers, and other folks we need to come to fix things in our homes, there's a substantial shortage of these workers. And in an increasingly high-tech economy, the demand for well-trained and highly skilled blue-collar workers will continue to grow.

One of the most promising vocational programs was initiated by IBM, which has opened more than two dozen STEM (science, technology, engineering, and mathematics) high schools in New York, Chicago, and a few other cities. The students graduate in six years with not just a high school diploma, but also an associate degree. What gives the students the incentive to stay the course is the guarantee of a job for which they are training with a salary in the neighborhood of $40,000 with IBM, or another high-tech employer.[79]

Charter schools

Charter schools have been touted as a better alternative to our traditional public schools. These are publicly funded schools freed from some of the rules and regulations that apply to other public schools. Growing rapidly since the early 1990s, they now enroll about 2 percent of all school children.[80] They have tended to attract mainly low-income, minority, and low-performing students, whose parents were seeking a better educational alternative for their children.

Many of the charter schools have drawn highly skilled and motivated teachers and administrators, as well as the children of ambitious and involved parents. They have usually managed to run streamlined organizations avoiding the bureaucratic waste of the traditional school systems often laden with employees holding political patronage jobs. Adding icing to the cake, they have received billions of dollars from philanthropic foundations.[81]

So what's *not* to like? Mainly, that the charters divert resources from neighboring traditional schools. As the children of the more motivated parents enroll in charter schools, those left behind are children whose needs are still greater. And as the better teachers and administrators move to charter schools, their less able counterparts remain at the neighborhood schools. And then too, the schools most in need receive the fewest dollars from philanthropies.

Some charter schools have been very successful, most notably the KIPP schools (see the accompanying box). Others have been abject failures. In general, have charter schools raised scores on statewide tests? No.

What we may conclude is that charter schools provide an alternative to our traditional public schools—an alternative that, freed from onerous

Knowledge Is Power Program (KIPP)

In 1994 two former Teach for America recruits, David Levin and Michael Feinberg, started their own school system, which they named, "Knowledge Is Power Program," or KIPP. Targeting low-income and minority students, they emphasized measurable results, offering an extended school day and school year, providing their students with 60 percent more time in school than most public school students receive. They encouraged two basic behavioral principles—"Work Hard" and "Be Nice."[82] Attracting millions of dollars in foundation money, the two hundred KIPP schools in twenty-two states served more than eighty thousand children in 2016.[83] Typically the teachers work sixty- and eighty-hour weeks, arriving at school at 7:00 a.m. and staying late to provide tutoring.

KIPP reports, "More than 87 percent of our students are from low-income families and eligible for the federal free or reduced-price meals program, and 95 percent are African American or Latino. Nationally, more than 90 percent of KIPP middle school students have graduated high school, and more than 80 percent of KIPP alumni have gone on to college."[84]

bureaucratic red tape, allows very useful experimentation. While it is far too soon to render a verdict, it does seem unlikely that these schools will greatly improve our public education system.

Teach for America

In a hugely successful effort to recruit brighter and more capable teachers, Wendy Kopp, a Princeton senior, dreamed up an organization she would call Teach for America (TFA). Starting in 1989, she persuaded corporate leaders to back her organization with donations totaling tens of millions of dollars a year. By 2012 over forty thousand college graduates—including over 10 percent of the seniors at several Ivy League schools—applied for 5,800 training slots.[85] After undergoing an intensive five-week course, the newly minted teachers were placed in hundreds of failing schools around the country. TFA has maintained its size since 2012.

TFA and KIPP are educational success stories. They have worked intensively with children from very poor households and helped many of them succeed at school. Both TFA and KIPP demonstrate that bright, dedicated teachers, willing to work sixty- and eighty-hour weeks can bring most kids—even those from educationally deprived home environments—up to acceptable educational levels.

Several foundations and a handful of philanthropic billionaires have been willing to provide seed money for demonstration projects, a few of which, like TFA and KIPP, have actually succeeded. They have shown that it *can* be done. If these two programs could be replicated on a much larger scale, would they significantly raise the educational level for most children from low-income and minority families? Yes, they would! But this would require an investment of tens of billions of dollars a year. In addition, teachers would need to work much longer hours.

The Khan Academy

Salman Khan, a thirty-five-year-old hedge fund manager with no experience as an educator has created about four thousand YouTube videos that are used in a growing number of schools throughout the world. Most are ten- or fifteen-minute lectures on topics ranging from elementary school subjects such as basic addition, fractions, and decimals to college courses like computer science, macroeconomics, and calculus. Backed by substantial help from foundations and wealthy individuals, the Khan Academy's videos are free.[86]

The traditional method of pedagogy calls for teachers to lecture while their students passively take notes, and maybe ask a few questions. Then they do their homework on their own. The Khan Academy reverses the learning process. Children watch videos at home, re-watching them until they understand the material. Then in class the children solve actual problems, with the teacher available to provide one-on-one help.

In an article in *Time,* Kayla Webley describes how Khan completely upends how students are taught:

> The traditional classroom model essentially forces educators to teach to the middle. High-achieving students aren't challenged, and low-achieving students are made to move on to the next concept before they've mastered the previous one. In the flipped classroom, proponents are fond of saying, the teacher shifts from being sage on the stage to being the guide on the side.[87]

As someone who has taught college economics for over thirty years, I can attest to how hard it is to gear a course to the widely varying abilities and academic backgrounds of my students. Khan's approach seems to hold great promise, and hopefully, it will be adopted by many school systems.

The Core Curriculum

Perhaps the most promising recent educational development is the introduction of the core curriculum, which, by early 2013, had been adopted by forty-five states.[88] It provides a uniform set of math and English standards to be met grade by grade, from kindergarten through high school. These standards, which are considerably higher than those that had been set by each state, are presenting a difficult challenge to teachers, students, and parents. Indeed, several states have since opted out, and many parents believe that their children are so stressed out by the difficulty to the initial testing that they have refused to allow them to take these tests.[89]

Still, much of the assault on the Common Core is based on the misunderstanding that it is a national curriculum foisted upon the states by the Obama administration. In reality, it is just an outline of what students should be learning at each grade level, leaving it up to local officials to select curricula that comply with the standards.

While the core curriculum presents excellent educational goals, and replaces a hodgepodge of largely very lax state standards, there are no accompanying means provided for the schools in each state to attain those goals. So the poor initial test results—and the consequent backlash—were easily predictable. Unless we can implement very radical changes in our failing public education system, the mere setting of goals—however excellent—cannot succeed.

FIXING WHAT DOESN'T WORK

Get Rid of Disruptive Students

Nearly every public school has some students who are chronically disruptive. By legally guaranteeing that they have the right to attend—and indeed *must* attend—we are effectively denying everyone else's right to an education.

I propose that when a student is habitually in trouble—he or she should be removed from school and placed in an alternative situation. Where? Perhaps a special school for disruptive students.

Deny College Admission to Anyone Who Can't Read, Write, or Do Simple Arithmetic

Why should we be asking the colleges to do the job that wasn't done in grade school? And why should the taxpayers foot the bill? If high school students knew they couldn't get into college without these minimal skills, they would have more of an incentive to acquire them.

More than 70 percent of the incoming freshmen at the community colleges are placed in at least one remedial course. Only an infinitesimal fraction of those placed in more than one remedial course ever get their two-year degree.[90] Admitting them to college sends out the false signal that, somehow, they are ready and able to do college-level work. Instead, they're given elementary school and middle school work, which the vast majority *still* cannot master.

Where should these students learn to do the basics? The obvious choice is in elementary school. So why not provide this needed help to six-, seven-, and eight-year-olds? Why wait until they're in community college?

Disband the Entire Educational Establishment

> *I didn't meet the bar. But I think truly and honestly it has no relevancy to what I do every day.*
>
> —Wilfredo Laboy, the school superintendent of Lawrence, MA, on failing a basic literacy test for the third time

If there were just one thing we could do to drastically improve our educational system, what would it be? My vote would be to abolish the entire educational bureaucracy from the federal Department of Education all the way down to the thirteen thousand local school boards. These entities, along with the schools and college departments of education, are mainly responsible for our largely dysfunctional public education system.

Raise the Pay of Teachers

You know the old adage: you get what you pay for. To some degree it holds true for teachers. Surely if we paid beginning teachers what we pay beginning lawyers and newly minted MBAs—well over $100,000 a year—we would certainly attract more of the best and the brightest.[91] My father, who was a high school math teacher for forty years, would frequently point out that "teachers are paid less than garbage men." A modern-day King Solomon might advise that we pay new teachers more than garbage men, but less than the beginning lawyers and MBAs.

Change the Teacher Certification Process

Taking a lot of mind-numbing, content-free education credits does not make someone a better teacher. This process not only discourages brighter individuals from becoming teachers, but it encourages the less able college students, because, in most of these courses, all you have to do is show up.[92]

I would shorten this process to one student teaching course that could be covered in as little as six weeks. For high school teachers, I would require a minimum number of credits in the subject or subjects they would be teaching. But not Mickey Mouse math education or science education courses.

In most states, over 90 percent of the applicants pass the certification exam.[93] So either we have a lot of very smart people taking the exam—or just maybe the exam is too easy. Say, *here's* an idea! Let's test them on what they'll actually be teaching. Don't know much about history? Then don't teach it.

Get Rid of Incompetent Teachers

One way to get rid of some of the more blatantly incompetent teachers would be to administer nationwide literacy tests for teachers. If you can't read at an eighth-grade level, then out you go. It would be very interesting to see how many teachers would fail this test.

Because the National Educational Association and the American Federation of Teachers have managed to negotiate contracts with most local school boards that provide tenure after just a few years of teaching, it is extremely difficult to fire even the most incompetent teachers. Not only does this process often take years, but less than 1 percent of all teachers are fired in any given year.[94] Surely this is not because the other 99 percent are all that competent.

Because union contracts are negotiated between local school boards and unions, it would be very difficult, at least on a state or national level, to have new contracts drawn up that would protect the needs of the nation's fifty million public school students.

Garbage In, Garbage Remains

There is something very wrong with how our nation selects the people who will teach our children. First, students who scored poorly on college entrance exams choose to take education courses so they can become teachers.[95] And taking the least challenging major makes it much easier for them to graduate. Having learned very little during their college years, they then take a ridiculously easy certification exam, and have little difficulty finding a job. A few years later they receive tenure and are set for life. And no matter how incompetent, they cannot be fired. We need to get rid of about half of our public school teachers and replace them with people who can actually teach.

Ban Pocket Calculators from Elementary Schools

Why are Americans so bad at math? Most of the blame lies with the widespread use of pocket calculators among elementary school students. Why bother to learn how to add, subtract, multiply, or divide when your calculator will save you the trouble? Indeed, why bother to do *any* arithmetic when all you need to do is press a couple of buttons and read the answer shown in the window? You know the expression, "use it or lose it"? Well, most Americans have *lost* it.

We need to get back to basics. By the end of the third grade, everyone should have learned the entire multiplication table—all the way up to ten times ten. If you haven't learned it, you stay in third-grade math until you do.

Why all this fuss about the multiplication table? If you don't know the table, you not only can't multiply, but you can't divide either—which forecloses learning algebra, trigonometry, calculus, as well as what we call the hard sciences. And all because of the pocket calculator.

Change How Math Is Taught and Who Teaches It

Because so many teachers, especially at the elementary school level, are not only untrained in mathematics, but are themselves math-phobic, the children need to be taught by math specialists, just as their music and art teachers have some training in those fields.[96] In addition, children need to be placed in homogeneous grouping by ability rather than age. A bored seven-year-old with a high math aptitude should not be doing second-grade addition and subtraction if she already knows how to multiply and divide. But under the lingering philosophy of "no child left behind," we hold back so many who should be moving ahead.

School Choice and Education Vouchers

> *Welcome to Lake Wobegon . . . where all the children are above average.*
>
> —Garrison Keillor

One provision of the No Child Left Behind Act was that children in failing schools would have the option of enrolling in better schools. Great! That will solve everything. We can just close up the failing schools as their students depart for better schools, and, to paraphrase Garrison Keillor, eventually all children will be attending better-than-average schools.

Let's ask a simple question: Why are those schools so bad in the first place? The main reason is that they have many students who perform far below grade level. So, in an effort to help those students, let's allow them to transfer to better schools. It doesn't take a genius to figure out what they will do to the better schools in very short order.

Moving right along, let's consider the logic of school vouchers. Suppose every child were assigned a voucher worth, say, $11,000, which is the average cost for one year's public school education.[97] No decent school, public or private, would accept the poorly prepared students. So yes, for the good students, a school voucher program would work. But what happens to the underperforming students, who, for good reason, no one wants?

Students who cannot keep up are usually placed in special education classes. Others are regularly promoted, and even manage to graduate from high school barely able to read and write. Probably the best solution is very early intervention, perhaps when the children are still toddlers. But that's just my guess. Clearly, there are plenty of experts who know a whole lot more than I do about educational reform.

Chapter 13

OUR SICK HEALTHCARE SYSTEM

We have the greatest health care system in the world.
—Sen. Richard Shelby (R-AL)

Our current system is the most expensive, bureaucratic, wasteful, and ineffective in the world.
—Sen. Bernie Sanders (D-VT)

America arguably has the best healthcare system in the world, and clearly the most expensive. More than one out of every six dollars of our national output is devoted to healthcare.[1] But are we getting the maximum bang for our healthcare buck? Not even close.

We rank at or near the bottom in terms of life expectancy, infant mortality, and overall medical coverage. Two-thirds of all American adults are overweight, and one-third is obese.[2] The World Health Organization (WHO) ranks the US healthcare system last among seventeen industrialized countries.[3] But we do lead the world in administrative costs and in the prescription of unneeded medical tests and procedures.

Not only do we spend much more per capita than any other country for healthcare, but we are the only developed country that doesn't provide universal healthcare. The healthcare reform law passed in 2010, known more formally as the Affordable Care Act, provided healthcare insurance to seventeen million previously uninsured people by early 2016.[4] Still, the act will leave us well short of universal coverage.

RISING HEALTHCARE SPENDING

- We have fewer doctors per capita than most other rich countries.[5]
- We spend almost twice as much per capita on healthcare as most other wealthy countries.[6]

- In 1950 our country spent $500 in today's dollars on the average person's medical care, compared to just over $10,000 in 2016.[7]
- In 2015 the average cost of insuring a family was $17,545.[8]

Since 1960 the percentage of our national output, or gross domestic product (GDP), devoted to healthcare has more than tripled (see Fig. 13.1). And it is expected to keep rising at a strong clip as more baby boomers enter their retirement years.

Year	Percentage
1960	5
1990	12
2015	18
2035	30 (projected)

Fig. 13.1. Healthcare spending as percentage of GDP, selected years.[9]

HEALTHCARE FINANCING

Our healthcare is financed by the federal, state, and local governments, employers, and individuals.

Employer-Sponsored Programs

Until the early 1940s, nine out of ten Americans paid their medical costs completely out of their own pockets.[10] If you could not afford needed medical care, you were just out of luck unless a doctor provided it free, at a very low cost, or let you pay him off over time. During World War II, as severe labor shortages were developing, the federal government imposed strict wage and price controls to curb inflation. And so, since they could not offer higher wages to attract workers, many employers offered their workers free or very low-cost healthcare insurance. This cost was tax deductible as a business expense, while the Internal Revenue Service ruled that healthcare insurance provided by employers was not taxable as employee income.[11]

In the years following the war, the United Auto Workers, the United Steel Workers, and other major unions negotiated contracts with very generous provisions for medical insurance—not only for current employees, but even for retirees. By the mid-1960s, nearly three-quarters of all American families had employer-sponsored medical insurance, generally with low deductibles and copayments for doctor visits and hospitalization.[12]

As insurance premiums began to rise rapidly in the 1970s and 1980s, most employers looked for ways to curb their spending. They began asking their employees to pay more of their insurance premiums, and some even stopped offering their employees any healthcare insurance at all. By 2015 just 57 percent of all Americans had insurance coverage at their workplace.[13]

Until the mid-1960s four large population groups remained uninsured—the poor, the disabled, the elderly, and those whose employers did not provide healthcare insurance. The purpose of the Medicare and Medicaid programs, both passed by Congress in 1965 at the behest of President Lyndon Johnson, was to help these first three groups.

Medicare

Medicare pays most of the medical costs of nearly everyone over sixty-five, as well as those of people between the ages of twenty-five and sixty-five who are disabled. These include doctor visits, lab tests, MRIs, CAT scans, X-rays, surgery, hospital stays, and prescription drugs. This system guarantees an escalating national medical bill. Lawrence Kotlikoff and Scott Burns show how Medicare is a virtual blueprint for abuse:

> [W]e have a system in which millions of old people can receive as much medical care as they'd like without having to pay a penny at the margin. . . . [I]f you have to see a doctor and the doctor's costs are covered by Medicare, why not see the best? Better yet, why not seek several expert opinions? And why not have the latest and most expensive medical tests performed? And why not encourage the medical equipment makers to come up with better and more expensive devices? And why not ask the government to pump billions into medical research to produce new procedures, tests, and therapies for you and your fellow oldsters to consume?[14]

The heart of the problem with the rapid growth in Medicare spending is the program's fee-for-service structure. Although capping the fees would appear to limit what doctors and hospitals can charge, they can always schedule more visits, run more tests, and change the classifications of the services they provide to ones for which they are allowed to charge higher fees.

Medicare has three separate programs, each with its own funding. Hospitalization is funded by a payroll tax of 2.9 percent, shared equally by employees and employers, on all wages and salaries.[15] Doctor visits, lab tests, and surgeries are funded by premiums paid by nearly the entire over-sixty-five population, who have Medicare as their primary medical insurance. And finally, the prescription drug program is funded mainly by federal government general tax revenues, and insurance premiums and out-of-pocket costs paid by the recipients.

Just like the Social Security trust fund, the Medicare trust fund is an accumulation of the surpluses paid into the Medicare hospital benefits account. It has already peaked, because hospital spending has surpassed Medicare payroll tax revenues. And the fund is expected to run out of reserves by 2030.[16] However, the Medicare fund that pays doctors' bills and outpatient treatments should remain adequately financed into the indefinite future.

Medicaid

The Medicaid program provides healthcare to the poor and, increasingly, to the elderly. Total spending for this program is almost as great as Medicare spending, but the federal government pays an average of about 60 percent, while the rest is picked up by the states. As Kotlikoff and Burns note, "Medicaid is not only helping bankrupt the federal government, it's the key cause of the burgeoning red ink in most state government budgets."[17]

Because the federal government reimburses fifty to seventy-five cents on every dollar it spends on health benefits for the poor, the states do not have a strong enough incentive to curb their Medicaid spending.[18] In addition, in most states it is run on a fee-for-service basis. And just like under Medicare, the participants are free to get the best available medical care with no worry about cost.

There is a widespread misconception that all poor people are eligible to receive Medicaid. But one-third of those without medical insurance are poor adults who are ineligible because they do not have any dependent children. Under the Affordable Care Act (which we'll discuss after the next section), most of these people will soon be eligible to receive Medicaid.

SEVEN FACTORS PUSHING UP THE COST OF HEALTHCARE

Why have healthcare costs been rising so rapidly? Let's look at seven major causes.

(1) Our Growing Senior Citizen Population

Old age is usually defined as beginning at sixty-five. Not only are people living considerably longer than previous generations, but as the baby boomers—those born between 1946 and 1964—continue to retire, the ranks of the aged will swell even more. Today 15 percent of our population is over sixty-five; by 2030 about 20 percent will be senior citizens.[19] The first generation to believe in its own almost unlimited entitlement, the boomers will expect to receive whatever medical care is needed to keep them going. And with little regard for the expense, since they won't be footing much of the bill.

Right now, the 15 percent of our population over sixty-five is responsible for over 40 percent of our medical bills. By 2030, that group may well account for more than two-thirds.[20] Keep in mind that boomers, despite all the hype about going to the gym, running, and dieting, will be the most obese group of retirees in history. Better medical care will keep them alive despite their high rates of diabetes, hypertension, and heart disease. But their increased longevity will come at a very high cost—much greater spending by Medicare, Medicaid, and private insurance providers. So our nation will need to devote an even larger slice of national output to keep them alive and reasonably healthy.

(2) The Provision of Unneeded Services

There are four main reasons why unneeded surgery is performed, unneeded lab tests are run, and unneeded drugs are prescribed. The first is medical errors due to poor record keeping. As medical records are computerized, the provision of unneeded medical services should fall sharply.

A second reason is the threat of malpractice suits, which has given rise to the costly practice of defensive medicine. Unnecessary lab tests as well as surgical procedures are undertaken to avert potential lawsuits. After all, these superfluous tests and procedures cost the patient nothing and the doctor is fully reimbursed by the insurance providers.

The third reason why doctors often provide unneeded medical services is that they are reimbursed for services performed, whether or not they are needed. So why not just drum up a little more business?

Finally, many patients with insurance plans that require low or no copayments consume medical services as they would consume food at an all-you-can-eat buffet. If it's free, then why should I limit what I consume? Even if a simply X-ray will do, I might as well go for an MRI. Why not? It's *free*, isn't it?

Alan Hubbard, who served as chairman of President George W. Bush's Council of Economic Advisors, wrote, "Health care is expensive because the vast majority of Americans consume it as if it were free. . . . To control health care costs, we must give consumers an incentive to spend money wisely."[21] So, just like eating at a buffet, we readily consume more expensive medical care if we don't have to pay for it.

(3) Vast Administrative Costs

As many as three million people are employed by healthcare providers and insurance companies to deal with two basic questions: Is this procedure covered, and how much will the insurance company pay?[22] Your doctor's employees and their counterparts at the insurance companies have diametrically opposed objectives. The former tries to get as much reimbursement as possible, while the latter tries to deny as many claims as it can. But we're all losers because these three million people add zilch to our national output.

Just imagine how unnecessarily difficult and complex medical billing has become. Employees of healthcare providers must deal with hundreds of different insurance companies, each with a different billing system, different forms, and different contact information.

Medical care used to be on a pay-as-you-go basis. Now, even a simple medical procedure unleashes a flood of paperwork and multiple phone calls. Dealing with insurance companies requires every medical office to put more people on the payroll and to rent more office space. Because of this huge overhead, doctors are driven to work much longer hours and to see more patients per hour.

(4) The Shift from Pay-as-You-Go to Insurance Payments

After studying data going back to the 1960s, Amy Finkelstein, an MIT economist, reached the conclusion that the massive expansion of medical insurance is the underlying cause of our rising national medical bill. Why, she asked, did doctors and hospitals adopt expensive new technologies so freely? They did so because medical insurance foots the bill. And if patients had to pay more for their medical care through high-deductible health plans, they would cut back substantially on their medical care.[23]

Writing in *Business Week*, Howard Gleckman seconds Finkelstein's view:

> Why is insurance so important? One obvious reason, Finkelstein believes, is that consumers opt for more care if someone else pays for it. But the more significant effect may be that insurance guarantees a steady source of revenue for hospitals and other health providers. Such ready cash encourages them to build new cardiac-care centers and stock up on the latest high-tech equipment, knowing it will be paid for.[24]

(5) The High Cost of Hospital Care

One-third of our nation's $3.4 trillion medical bill is accounted from by inpatient and outpatient hospital care.[25] An overnight stay—exclusive of any physicians' charges—costs an average of over $4,000, five times the average charge in most other developed nations.[26] That's the *average* cost; you can find some hospitals that charge over $12,000.

In defense of the grossly inflated billing of hospitals, we need to consider that these institutions are legally required to treat every patient who comes to their emergency rooms. Indeed, many uninsured poor people use the emergency room the way the rest of us use visits to our primary care physicians. Not only are emergency room visits much more costly than office visits, but the hospitals do not receive any insurance reimbursement, even if they incur thousands of dollars of expenses. Still, at most hospitals, the cost of treating the uninsured and underinsured comes to no more than 2 percent of their total costs.[27]

(6) The High Cost of Medical Procedures

The cost of medical procedures done in the United States is much higher than in other industrial countries.[28] In addition, the cost of such common procedures as hip and knee replacements, colonoscopies, and MRI scans can vary widely not just from one city to another, but within the cities as well.

You can undergo a colonoscopy for less than $1,000 in virtually every city, but the same procedure may cost some patients over $5,000 in New

York, Austin, San Antonio, Indianapolis, Detroit, Orlando, Los Angeles, and some other cities.[29] How do we explain this wide disparity of prices?

New York Times columnist Tina Rosenberg attributes this disparity to "price secrecy." Insured patients rarely even look at their medical bills and have little incentive to shop around as they would when making a major purchase like a new car or a home. For example, in California, where hip and knee replacements range in price from $15,000 to $110,000, patients have little incentive to search for the hospital charging the lowest price.[30]

Perhaps the most startling indictment of our medical practices comes from David Cutler, a health economist at Harvard who has argued that "a third of our health care dollars go to therapies that do not improve our health."[31]

(7) The High Cost of Prescription Drugs

After the cost of hospital care and physician care, prescription drugs are the third largest area of health expenditures, accounting for 10 percent of the total.[32] We spent about $1,400 per capita on prescription medications—considerably more than the citizens of any other nation.[33]

Why do pharmaceutical companies charge so much for their drugs? Because they can. While other nations regulate drug prices, Congress—virtually in the thrall of Big Pharma and its lobbyists—has fallen all over itself to give the drug manufacturers free reign. Indeed, when the Medicare Prescription Drug Improvement and Modernization Act of 2003 was passed, one of its main provisions was to prohibit the federal government from negotiating drug prices with the drug industry.

Prescription drugs—very often those manufactured in the United States—commonly cost one-half to one-third less abroad.[34]

Q: How do we explain why American pharmaceutical companies charge such high prices in the United States?

A: Because they can.

The main justification for the high prices charged by Big Pharma is that the proceeds are needed for drug research. But 50 percent of its spending is on marketing, and only about 20 percent is spent on drug research.[35]

THE AFFORDABLE CARE ACT (ACA) OF 2010

This law, which was passed without any Republican votes in the House or the Senate, has one main objective—to provide healthcare insurance for more than thirty million Americans.

The two ways the ACA provides additional insurance coverage is through a vast expansion of the Medicaid program and of privately insured individuals. On January 1, 2014, all children, parents, and childless adults who had not been entitled to Medicare and who had family incomes up to 133 percent of the poverty line—about $30,000 for a family of four—became eligible for Medicaid. Between 2014 and 2016 the federal government was paying 100 percent of the cost of covering newly eligible individuals. Then, between 2017 and 2020 the federal share of the cost will be gradually reduced to 90 percent.[36] About seventeen million of the poor—almost all adults—became eligible.

The ACA also helps as many as twenty million people to enroll in private insurance programs or enable them to retain their coverage by these three provisions:

1. Prohibits termination of health insurance policies.
2. Prohibits pre-existing condition exclusions for children.
3. Extends dependent coverage up to age twenty-six.

Also, annual and lifetime benefit limits are eliminated.

Questioning the constitutionality of the Affordable Care Act, twenty-six state attorneys general brought suit against the federal government. The case reached the Supreme Court in 2012, and the court announced its decision in June of that year. The big question was whether the court would uphold the entire act, just parts of the act, or find act unconstitutional in its entirety.[37]

A pivotal provision of the ACA is the personal mandate that requires all uninsured individuals to either take out a policy or pay a fine or "tax," as it was termed by Chief Justice John Roberts in his majority opinion, which upheld most of the ACA's requirements.[38] The mandate was aimed at healthy individuals who saw no need to pay for medical insurance, and would now have to either enroll in a healthcare insurance program or pay a fine or tax of up to about $2,000. Since the ACA prohibited insurance companies from dropping coverage or capping benefits of people requiring expensive medical care, they would recoup these funds with the premiums paid by the newly enrolled relatively healthy customers.

Chief Justice Roberts also wrote the majority opinion stipulating that the states were not required to expand their Medicare rolls even if the federal government were to pick up nearly the entire tab. Almost half the states, all led by Republican governors, are not participating.

Despite the disastrous rollout of the federal and state healthcare exchanges in the fall of 2013, about eight million Americans were added to the insurance rolls by the spring of 2015. The Affordable Care Act has reduced the ranks of the uninsured from over fifty million to thirty-two million by early 2016.[39] But it could hardly be termed "healthcare reform," since its main accomplishment will be to provide about twenty million more Americans with healthcare insurance in a system that delivers medical care at a cost that is almost double that of most other rich countries.

THE COST OF OUR BLOATED HEALTHCARE SYSTEM

While we devote 18 percent of our GDP to healthcare, not only is the health of Americans no better than the health of the citizens of other wealthy nations, but by some measures, it's markedly worse. Clearly then, we are not getting much bang from our healthcare buck.[40]

How much do administrative costs add to our national healthcare bill? Most estimates range from one-quarter to one-third of that bill—perhaps about $800 billion.[41]

We know that our high healthcare costs are due mainly to high administrative costs and to the overconsumption of medical care. If these two costs could be minimized, our healthcare costs would be cut almost in half. In sum, each year we waste close to $1.5 trillion in resources because of our grossly inefficient healthcare system.[42]

SOLUTIONS

Before we consider a comprehensive plan to make our healthcare system much more efficient, here are seven smaller steps we should take.

(1) Curb Malpractice Suits

Virtually everyone agrees that medical malpractice is a mess and needs to be fixed. Its costs include about $150 billion per year for tort litigation, defensive medicine, and malpractice insurance premiums.[43] The way things stand now, the only winners are the patients who are successful in their lawsuits, and their lawyers. But their winnings are much smaller than our society's losses. Not only do doctors waste tens of billions of dollars a year practicing defensive medicine, but some doctors are driven out of business by humongous malpractice insurance premiums—often exceeding $200,000 a year.[44] For example, many OB-GYNs have given up the OB part of their practices, which carries the most risk, or relocated to places where malpractice insurance premiums are cheaper, such as rural areas.

Richard Thaler, an economist at the University of Chicago School of Business, suggests a way to dispense with malpractice insurance premiums altogether:

> Those with a record of providing high-quality care at good value could apply to the government for a safe harbor from malpractice suits. Organizations that receive this status could require patients to waive their right to sue for adverse outcomes.[45]

Another alternative to having doctors buy malpractice insurance premiums would be for the federal government to set up a fund to be used to pay medical malpractice victims. The total paid would be four or five billion dollars a year, which is about how much the courts award in malpractice suits.[46] Then, instead of going through the courts, any patient claiming to be the victim of medical malpractice would go before a board of medical experts, which would determine how much money, if any, should be awarded in damages. An added benefit would be that doctors who were repeatedly called before the board could lose their licenses.

The most damage caused by the threat of malpractice suits is the consequent practice of defensive medicine. With the elimination of this threat, doctors would no longer have this incentive to prescribe unneeded lab tests, surgery, or drugs, saving tens of billions of dollars a year. These savings would be perhaps ten or twenty times the cost of setting up an alternative way of dealing with malpractice cases. The only losers would be the trial lawyers, a group that almost everyone loves to hate.

(2) Create a Standardized Medical Insurance Form

A *New York Times* editorial made this observation:

> Any doctor who has wrestled with multiple forms from different insurers, or patients who have tried to understand their own parade of statements, know that simplification ought to save money.[47]

A standardized form would enable automated processing and save tens of billions of dollars a year.

(3) Expand Population-Based Primary Care

Here is a proposal of Dr. Michael Fine, a physician who has written extensively about primary healthcare:

> Population-based primary care is that system of healthcare distribution that assigns every person in a geographical area to a primary care practice accessible to that geographic area, and makes every primary-care practice responsible for the primary care of every person in that defined area. . . . Population-based primary care looks more like public libraries, public schools, and local police stations than it does like the hodgepodge system of private practitioners stacked in medical office buildings that we have now. Each neighborhood, town, or village of 10,000–20,000 people would have a primary-care center, providing robust primary care that includes 90–95 percent of the medical services used by that community's inhabitants. . . . Primary care centers can be open 12 hours a day, eliminating the need for urgent care centers and limiting the need for hospital emergency rooms for all but life-threatening emergencies.[48]

What do *you* think of having a population-based primary care system? I think it's a great idea. In fact, we actually have such a system in place. During the administration of President George W. Bush (2001–2009), financing of community health centers in medically underserved areas was doubled. The program traces its origins to President Lyndon Johnson's war on poverty in the 1960s. Today there are about nine thousand sites serving more than twenty-two million patients, 70 percent of whom have incomes below the poverty line.[49]

Getting good primary medical care is not just a problem for the poor. Americans wait longer to see primary care physicians than patients in Britain, Germany, Australia, and New Zealand. *Newsweek* observed that "26 percent of Americans . . . reported being able to see their doctor on the day they called, compared with 60 percent in the Netherlands and 48 percent in Britain."[50]

(4) Alter the Pricing of Medical Procedures and Hospital Care

Because the prices of medical procedures vary so widely, it would be very helpful if the US Department of Health and Human Services posted the prices charged at all of the nation's hospitals. This would enable insurance providers and individual patients to shop around for the best deals. Because of the spreading knowledge of the widely varying cost of these procedures, competition would force those charging the highest prices to lower them, or lose their business to other hospitals.

Similarly, the prices charged by hospitals for inpatient and outpatient services, as well as daily room charges, should also be posted.

A substantial and rapidly growing number of medical facilities are providing highly discounted services, charging all-inclusive fees for such procedures as knee replacements, rotator cuff repairs, and MRIs. Often called direct pay facilities, these medical practices do not accept healthcare insurance payments. This virtually eliminates high administrative expenses, and these savings are passed on to patients in the form of much lower prices.[51]

Here are a few examples of these savings. A hysterectomy for which an insurance company is charged $54,000 costs just $11,000. The cost of a spinal fusion is reduced from $144,000 to $59,000. And a coronary bypass is provided for $51,000, rather than $253,000.[52]

(5) Lower the Cost of Prescription Medicines

The 2003 law that created the Medicare prescription benefit program expressly prohibited Medicare from either setting drug prices or even negotiating prices with pharmaceutical companies. If the law were amended to allow price-setting or negotiation, it would save insurers and individual patients tens of billions of dollars a year.

The federal government should also set price ceilings for prescription drugs and provide a directory listing the price and effectiveness of every drug.

(6) Eliminate Medically Unnecessary Drugs, Operations, and Procedures

In a *New Yorker* article entitled "Overkill," Dr. Atul Gawande reported that a study of more than one million Medicare patients disclosed many received tests and treatments that professional organizations had "consistently determined to have no benefit or to be outright harmful." He went on to say, "In just a single year, the researchers reported, twenty-five to forty-two percent of Medicare patients received at least one of twenty-six useless tests and treatments."[53]

Surely Medicare officials themselves are derelict in approving payment for these procedures—and the medical practitioners themselves are complicit in providing these useless services. Clearly, this very costly problem needs to be addressed.

(7) Improve Medical Care During the Last Year of Life

Over the next fifteen years the number of people who are sick, old, and frail will double. We also know that one's medical bills usually shoot up in the last year of life. In fact, about 30 percent of all Medicare dollars are spent in the last year of life.[54]

My father, who had lived independently until he was ninety-five, agreed to move to an assisted living residence, and then, finally, to a nursing home. He was painfully aware of his deteriorating mental capabilities and pleaded with every visitor to give him a gun and a bullet. Anyone who has ever visited a nursing home must wonder why terminally ill people are kept alive, often against their will, only to endure painfully imminent death.

Here are some examples of costly procedures and treatments that provide no benefits, but often cause discomfort or lower the quality of life:

- Feeding tubes, which can cause infection, nausea, and vomiting, but rarely prolong life.
- Hip replacements for people with advanced Alzheimer's disease.
- Abdominal and gall bladder surgery and joint replacements on the very frail, leading to complications, repeat hospital stays, and placement in nursing homes.
- Aggressive chemotherapy for ninety-year-olds with heart failure, diabetes, and cancer.
- Tight glycemic control for type 2 diabetes, which is intended to prevent blindness and kidney disease, and are not expected to occur for another eight or ten years.

In the absence of a patient's objections, the healthcare provider default position is to keep the patient alive. And if this effort requires several days in ICU or the use of expensive technology, then so be it—as long, of course, as everything is covered by the patient's insurance. "One of the things that frustrates us all is to see care being provided in an absolutely futile situation . . . and doctors and hospitals are not accountable but are also being rewarded (financially) for that (futile care)," says John Santa, medical director for the Center for Evidence-Based Policy, based in Portland, Oregon.[55]

A COMPREHENSIVE SOLUTION

What additional steps can we take to improve the efficiency with which we deliver healthcare? Clearly, we need a comprehensive solution that can come only on the national level. The Affordable Care Act, while certainly a step in the right direction, left intact a highly inefficient healthcare system.

Our nation's healthcare is now paid for by the federal, state, and local governments, individuals, employers, and by thousands of insurance companies. This has created an extremely costly administrative nightmare for our healthcare providers. But under our plan, they will deal with just a single payer of all medical bills.

If we could do just one thing to create a better healthcare system, what would it be? We've already identified what is, by far, the most important factor raising our national healthcare bill—extremely high administrative costs. So the eight-hundred-billion-dollar question is, how can we drastically cut these costs?

For decades, American healthcare experts have advocated switching to a single-payer system, like those in Australia, Canada, Denmark, Italy, Spain, Sweden, and the United Kingdom. Instead of relying on a jury-rigged system of thousands of private insurance companies—each with its own set of rules, procedures, reimbursement schedules, and forms—to pay the lion's share of our medical bills, why not relegate this job to a single organization with just one set of forms, rules, and procedures? This would obviate the need for healthcare providers to employ armies of workers to deal with all the insurance companies. And best of all, our nation's healthcare bill could be cut by about one-quarter.

Medicare posts an easy-to-use schedule of reimbursement payments for healthcare providers. There are no negotiations because virtually all medical treatments are preapproved. Medical assistants submit the bills, and Medicare provides automatic reimbursement.

Our plan is to extend Medicare—which is now limited primarily to people who are at least sixty-five—to all Americans who choose to join.[56] This will finally provide our nation with a single-payer, relatively low-cost system of universal healthcare. Everyone will be free to enroll, but no one will be forced to. Similarly, hospitals, physicians, and other healthcare providers will be encouraged to accept Medicare patients, but again—no one will be forced to.

Two very large groups of people will need to decide whether to join "Medicare for All." For individuals and families now paying their own healthcare insurance premiums, their decision will be relatively easy: Which will provide better coverage and lower costs?

For those whose medical insurance is paid in part or fully by their employers, the decision of whether or not to switch to Medicare could be more difficult. Since, under our plan, employers will no longer be able to deduct the cost of healthcare insurance premiums from their taxes, few will continue insuring their employees. Their employees will have to decide whether to join Medicare or take out private healthcare insurance. If a small minority of employers continue to pay some or all of their employees' premiums, some employees may choose not to join Medicare.

Medicare for All will not be free. After all, people now over sixty-five paid a Medicare tax equal to 1.45 percent of their wages for their entire working lives. This payment was matched by their employers. What seems likely is that under Medicare for All, the wages of everyone under sixty-five will be taxed at a rate of least 5 percent—a figure matched by their employers.

Medicare for All will be open to every American, but we know that one size does not fit all. Some people already have a better deal. Among the elderly, there are millions of veterans who receive free medical care from Veterans Affairs. Another group of people, largely drawn from the top 1 percent, enjoy so-called "Cadillac" healthcare plans paid for by their employers. As long as their employers are willing to pay for them, why switch to Medicare for All?

Some doctors and other medical providers refuse to accept Medicare payments. And there are a substantial number of individuals over sixty-five who are not on Medicare. Will anyone be required to join Medicare for All? *No!* Not one doctor or patient will be forced to join. Is Medicare for All a government takeover of healthcare? Again, *no*! Nearly all doctors and other healthcare practitioners will continue to work in the private sector.

A key part of our plan would be to no longer allow employers to deduct the business expense of paying for the healthcare insurance of their employees from their taxes. In this case, what the federal government will taketh away, it will more than give back by relieving employers of this massive expense, since nearly all their employees will now be covered by Medicare for All.

Although we will continue paying for our prescription drugs, their cost will plummet. Under current law, Medicare officials are actually prohibited from negotiating with pharmaceutical companies, resulting in much higher drug prices. Under Medicare for All they will be able to negotiate much lower prices in exchange for bulk purchases.

Many drugs, which are produced by American companies, are sold for five or ten times as much in *our* country than they are abroad. But there are legal barriers to reimporting these drugs to the United States, ostensibly because they may be "unsafe." This blatant rip-off will end.

What happens to the seventy-two million Americans currently receiving Medicaid and CHIP (Children's Health Insurance Plan)?[57] Under Medicare for All, all these patients will be shifted to Medicare (see accompanying box).

Medicaid Folded into Medicare for All

Under our plan, Medicaid and CHIP will be folded into Medicare. Doing this has three main advantages. First, it relieves the state and localities of a huge financial burden—about $100 billion, while eliminating layers of bureaucracy at the state and local levels.[58]

Second, since the passage of the Affordable Care Act in 2009, the expansion of Medicaid has become a political football. Nearly every Republican-controlled state has refused to expand its Medicaid program to all its eligible citizens, even though the federal government would be paying the entire cost. But once Medicaid becomes part of Medicare, this issue will no longer exist.

And finally, receiving Medicaid carries almost the same stigma as getting public assistance. Medicare is perceived as being for those who have earned it, while Medicaid is seen as just another unearned handout given to the poor. Why perpetuate this stigma?

Before we talk about who wins and who loses under Medicare for All, we need to address two major shortcomings of the current Medicare system. First, we shall need to do something to discourage patients from treating medical care as a free good. A second shortcoming is the widespread reimbursement of unnecessary medical procedures. Perhaps the most effective way of discouraging them would be for Medicare to deny reimbursement.

What we're proposing is a massive change in the way we deliver and pay for our healthcare. And while hundreds of millions of Americans will be much better off, and we will be able to deliver more and better healthcare for a much smaller cost, there will still be some people who will definitely not like our plan.

It would be virtually impossible to create a healthcare system that doesn't leave some people worse off than before. But we *can* create one that has far more winners than losers.

The biggest winners are the thirty-two million Americans who currently have no medical insurance.[59] Other big winners are all the people who will be able to secure much better medical care—often at greatly reduced cost. And then too, there are those healthcare providers who will no longer have to employ so many people just to deal with all the insurance companies.

Let's consider how our plan will affect the firms that are no longer insuring their employees. Today, healthcare insurance premiums account for as much as one-third of a business firm's total employee compensation.[60] Sharing this massive cost cut with their employees, most companies will now be able to afford large-wage increases.

Still another big winner will be the American economy. Relieved of the burden of our extremely inefficient healthcare system, we will be able to devote more of our resources to such pressing needs as rebuilding our manufacturing base and our crumbling infrastructure.

Now let's turn to the losers. By far, the two biggest losers will be the insurance companies and all the people who will lose their jobs, since their work will no longer be needed. Because there are so many jobs that need to be filled—from staffing nursing homes and childcare facilities to rebuilding our public transportation system and producing clean energy, we will find a decently paying job for every person who is ready, willing, and able to work. You can read all about it in chapter 26.

Many insurance companies will be put out of business, but won't that be in the great capitalist tradition of "creative destruction"?[61] And because the giant pharmaceutical firms will be charging a lot less for thousands of prescription drugs, their profits will decline sharply. Another group of losers are the people who don't join Medicare for All, but continue to pay the Medicare payroll tax. Still, it's *their* choice.

There will continue to be a substantial sector of our healthcare system not associated with Medicare for All. It will include mainly the doctors and patients who choose not to join. We will continue to pay for non-covered medical procedures such as tummy tucks, face-lifts, and various other bodily "enhancements." Also not included are dental care, nonprescription drugs, and visits to health spas.

Part VI

WASTING OUR RESOURCES BY OVERPRODUCING

We spend almost as much on defense as the rest of the world put together. Even though the Cold War ended more than twenty-five years ago, and we have been winding down our more recent military involvement in Iraq and Afghanistan, we are still spending over $700 billion a year on defense, homeland security, and our spy agencies.[1] These expenditures could probably be cut in half without compromising the defense of our country.

We shall be exploring how the military-industrial complex has succeeded for so long in keeping defense spending so high. And we'll also look at the economic effects of devoting so much of our resources to defense.

We imprison more of our citizens per capita than any other nation on earth. This is done at great cost to our economy as well as to our society. About one-quarter of those currently incarcerated are nonviolent drug offenders, and more than half imprisoned are mentally ill—both of whom could be better served by being sent to drug rehab facilities or mental hospitals.[2] This would not just save billions of dollars a year, but would be a much more efficient allocation of our resources.

For centuries the basic job of the financial sector has been to gather funds from small savers, bundle them into large loans to business firms, which would use the money to invest in plant, equipment, and inventory. For this work, it received about 4 percent of our GDP.[3] But since the 1950s, this share has more than doubled. In effect, the financial sector is sucking increasing amounts of resources out of the real economy, which produces useful goods and services.

Chapter 14

THE MILITARY-INDUSTRIAL COMPLEX

We must guard against the acquisition of unwarranted influence . . . by the military-industrial complex.

—President Dwight D. Eisenhower

Since the sneak attack by Japan on our Pacific fleet anchored in Pearl Harbor, we have resolved to never again let our defenses down. True to our resolve, we have built and maintained the world's most powerful armed forces. And even today, more than twenty-five years after the implosion of our long-term adversary, the Soviet Union, we continue to spend nearly as much on defense as the rest of the world put together.[1]

THE ECONOMIC COST OF SUPPORTING A HUGE MILITARY ESTABLISHMENT

He who defends everything defends nothing.

—Frederick the Great

President Ronald Reagan often railed against the "Evil Empire," referring to the Soviet Union and its East European satellites. He believed that the massive arms buildup he engineered was instrumental in bringing about the Soviet's collapse. And he may well have been right, since Soviet arms spending rose to match ours. But, to extend Reagan's logic, if massive arms spending wrecked *their* economy, it sure didn't help *ours*. In addition to being responsible for a massive misallocation of resources, this doubling of defense spending was largely responsible for creating a string of record federal budget deficits that extended well into the 1990s.

What is the economic cost of supporting a huge military establishment? Paul Kennedy's classic book *The Rise and Fall of Great Powers* claims that the great powers of the past—most notably the Spanish and British empires—expanded well beyond their means of defending their interests, and built military establishments that wasted too much of their resources.

"A large military establishment, like a great monument, looks imposing to the impressionable observer; but if it is not resting upon a firm foundation (in this case a productive economy), it runs the risk of a future collapse."[2]

Will we go the way of Spain in the early seventeenth century and England in the first half of the last century? The United States now runs the risk of indulging in what Paul Kennedy calls "imperial overstretch." "Decision makers in Washington must face the awkward and enduring fact that the sum total of the United States' global interests and obligations is nowadays far larger than the country's power to defend them all simultaneously."[3]

How do we avoid this eventuality? "Without a rough balance between these competing demands of defense, consumption, and investment, a Great Power is unlikely to preserve its status for long," says Kennedy.[4] This is a lesson that the leaders of the Soviet Union learned the hard way. And it's evidently a lesson that we have yet to learn.

Military spending, unlike investments in healthcare, education, infrastructure, or in plant and equipment, does not generate any future output or wealth. Once that money is spent—it's gone. It's not an investment in the future. It's current consumption. But unlike the consumption of food, clothes, of going to the movies or on a vacation, military spending provides us with no pleasure and does absolutely nothing for our standard of living.

THE ALL-VOLUNTEER ARMY

War is good for business; invest your son.

—sign on a New York City subway wall
during the Vietnam War

When the draft ended in 1975, we needed to attract enough volunteers to fully staff our armed forces. Although at least half the draft-age men used exemptions and deferments to avoid serving, the draft did ensure that the ranks of enlisted men included a large number of "college boys."

Today our armed forces are overwhelmingly staffed by poor and working-class men and women, while wealthier people, after graduating from high school, just get on with their lives, most often by going to college. Essentially, we have two parallel universes. And aside from the lip service our political leaders pay to the patriotism and bravery of those who are serving, most people don't seem to care about them. In fact, few among the relatively affluent even *know* anyone in the service. As Andrew

Bacevich put it, "Like mowing lawns and bussing tables, fighting and perhaps dying to sustain the American way of life became something that Americans pay others to do."[5] Back in 1956, 400 out of 750 in Princeton's graduating class went into the military. In contrast, in 2004, nine members of Princeton's graduation class joined up, and they still led the Ivy League in numbers![6] Once the draft was ended and we went to the volunteer armed services, we lost a great democratizing institution. This profound social change pushed us that much further toward two separate Americas.

Join the Army and Learn a Trade. Become a technician, a mechanic, get your high school equivalency diploma, and maybe pick up some college credits while you're at it. Wow! Where's the nearest recruitment office? Where do I sign up? Sure it's a good deal—if you don't have any better alternatives. The children of middle-class and wealthy parents don't have to give up three, four, or five years of their lives for the opportunity to get some education and training. These young people can get that without enlisting.

Just over half of our nation's eighteen- to twenty-four-year-olds have had some exposure to a college education.[7] But only 7 percent from that age group who joined the military as enlisted men and women (i.e., as non-officers) have had that exposure.[8] So, in the words of Stanford historian David M. Kennedy, our society "has in effect hired some of the least advantaged of our fellow citizens to conduct some of our most dangerous business."[9]

We've been recruiting a poor man's army—an army of young people who don't have a lot of other options. For the children of the poor, it's a lot better than nothing. But if we justify having large standing armed forces as a way of providing the poor with education and training, it would be a lot more efficient and a whole lot cheaper to just give out free training and education to whoever wanted it.

An observation by Andrew Bacevich aptly sums up how the American public's view of those who serve in the military makes it easier for us to go to war:

> A public disengaged from military service has lost an important check on Washington's inclination to use force, with the result that the troops professed to be held in high regard are repeatedly misused and abused.[10]

OUR PERPETUAL WAR MACHINE

Since the "day of infamy," when the Japanese attacked Pearl Harbor, we have devoted a huge part of our national output to armaments. Most of that money goes to defense contractors, who turn out not just tanks, planes, jeeps, rifles, bombs, missiles, bullets, and uniforms, but also multibillion-dollar weapons systems, and are still at work on a controversial "Star Wars" missile defense system. Surely these folks, as well as the millions of other Americans whose livelihoods come from our defense establishment, have a vested interest in the continued flow of funds from the federal government.

Let's look at the military-industrial complex about which President Eisenhower warned us more than fifty years ago. With the end of the Cold War in 1990, reduced defense spending left defense contractors with a great deal of excess capacity. Encouraged by the federal government, more than fifty major suppliers consolidated into just five dominant firms. In his book on the global power elite, David Rothkopf observed,

> The executives of Lockheed Martin themselves have said that the concentration of power among military contractors is more intense than in any other sector of business outside banking. Since the attacks of 9/11 and wars in Iraq and Afghanistan, business has been booming.[11]

Each of our top fifteen military contractors earns over $1 billion dollars a year from defense contracts.[12] Cutbacks on defense spending would cause layoffs all over the nation—and create such an outcry—that few members of Congress would go along with them.

New York Times columnist Bob Herbert believes that our major defense contractors have encouraged a steady beating of the war drums to keep those dollars flowing:

> The endless billions to be reaped from the horrors of war are a perennial incentive to invest in the war machine and to keep those wars a-coming. . . . The way you keep the wars coming is to keep the populace in a state of perpetual fear. That allows you to continue the insane feeding of the military-industrial complex at the expense of the rest of the nation's needs.[13]

THE HIGH COST OF PROJECTING AMERICAN MILITARY POWER

Because, until very recently, we needed to import almost half of our oil, and we happen to be the world's sole military superpower, it was logical that we used that power to ensure the uninterrupted flow of oil from the Middle East and elsewhere to the oil refineries of the United States.

Were we not so dependent on foreign oil, would we need to maintain such a large military establishment, especially our naval surface fleets and far-flung military bases? We have over one thousand military installations in 130 countries around the globe.[14] The cost of maintaining these bases is about $150 billion a year, and supplying the troops manning them is even higher.[15] Do we really need to maintain such a far-flung military presence?

FIGHTING THE WAR ON TERROR

How much we should spend to defend ourselves from the next terrorist attack is a completely arbitrary figure. Obviously the cost will be prohibitively high if we guard every bridge, tunnel, national monument, hospital, school, nuclear power plant, and every other large public and private edifice. As Cullen Murphy puts it, "[G]overnments can win only by defending everywhere; terrorists can win by succeeding anywhere."[16]

This is not to say that the war on terror could be fought on the cheap. Indeed, the Department of Homeland Security spends about $70 billion a year, and our sixteen or seventeen separate spy agencies spend about the same amount.[17] State and local governments spend perhaps another $10 billion, while private businesses spend tens of billions more to defend themselves against terrorist attacks.[18]

But our anti-terrorist bill also includes economic costs that cannot be toted up in dollars and cents. Gregg Easterbrook described some of those intangible costs:

> Extra security layers . . . burden the economy. Roadblocks slow the movement of goods; complex inspections of shipments add to processing costs; restricting entry to the United States of the 99.9999 percent of foreign citizens who mean no harm is bad for tourism, for movement of intellectual capital and other aspects of the economy. One reason America has prospered is that it invested heavily in removing friction from the economy by making trade, travel and transactions as convenient as possible. Since 9/11 "we've been putting the friction back in," Brian Michael Jenkins of the RAND Corporation has noted.[19]
>
> The main focus on the so-called "War on Terror" must be to prevent nuclear weapons from falling into the hands of terrorists. No red, yellow, or orange Homeland Security alerts will protect us against this threat. Nor will searches for suspicious packages on trains and buses. In fact, not one penny of the more than the $100 billion we're spending—publicly

and privately—on homeland security will help us avert a terrorist nuclear attack. Unless, of course, some alert citizen discovers a nuclear device left in the Topeka bus terminal.

THE COST OF WASTING RESOURCES ON DEFENSE

The United States accounts for almost 40 percent of the world's defense spending.[20] Stretching our armed forces around the globe comes at an extremely high price.

Since 2010, federal defense spending has averaged about $800 billion a year.[21] This figure includes veterans' pensions and benefits, the Defense Department's civilian retirement program, military aid to foreign governments, construction and other projects in Iraq and Afghanistan, and impact payments to communities that host military bases. But it does not include the cost of running our intelligence agencies, our homeland security apparatus, and business spending to thwart terror attacks. Altogether, we are spending more than $900 billion a year to defend our country, which comes to about 5 percent of our gross domestic product.[22]

SOLUTIONS

If we cut these expenditures substantially, would our enemies be more emboldened to attack us? A substantial part of our defense expenditures is devoted to ensuring a continuous flow of oil to meet our huge needs. Although we are a suburban nation heavily dependent on automobile transportation, there is surely a lot more we can do to reduce our need for oil. Energy conservation should head that list. In addition, the federal government needs to fund a new Manhattan Project to develop alternate energy sources, especially for fueling motor vehicles—just as we used our best scientific minds to build an atomic bomb during World War II.

Andrew Bacevich describes the impact on the military-industrial complex if we actually *were* to attain energy independence:

> Imagine the impact just on the Pentagon were this country to achieve anything approaching energy independence. U.S. Central Command would go out of business. Dozens of bases in and around the Middle East would close. The navy's Fifth Fleet would stand down. Weapons contracts worth tens of billions would risk being canceled.[23]

Since the 1940s we have been the world's police officer. That role should be performed, of course, by the United Nations. But the UN cannot act without sufficient troop contributions from its members, and those contributions have not been forthcoming. Before 1990, the Communists were a very real threat to our national security, but al Qaeda and other terrorist groups are not. By and large, they cannot be fought effectively by conventional military forces. We need to cooperate more fully with the intelligence agencies of the rest of the international community.

We need to ask whether the tail of terrorism is not wagging the dog of defense policy. Our armed services cannot defend us against terrorist attacks. How then can we deal with this very serious threat?

Terrorism can be defined as a willful act intended to strike fear in people. Obviously we can go back well before 9/11 to find acts of terrorism. Terrorists have been killing people for thousands of years, and they will undoubtedly continue doing so well into the future. John Mueller, who believes the terrorist threat is greatly overblown, suggests, "Terrorism should be treated essentially as a criminal problem calling mainly for the application of policing methods, particularly in the international sphere, not military ones."[24]

Terrorists are criminals. We are smart enough to know we can't prevent every violent crime. When will we begin to realize that we can't stop terrorists from killing Americans? What we *can* do is make sure that we minimize the number of deaths that they cause, just as we try to minimize the number of deaths that murderers cause.

Chapter 15

THE CRIMINAL JUSTICE ESTABLISHMENT

Violence is as American as cherry pie.

—H. Rap Brown, president of
Student Nonviolent Coordinating Committee,
a civil rights organization very active in the 1960s

Are the citizens of other nations more law-abiding than Americans? Does the fact that we have at least ten times more handgun deaths per capita than nearly every other economically developed nation have any particular significance?[1] Was H. Rap Brown correct? *Is* violence as American as cherry pie?

Please consider these facts:

- One out of every three young black men is in prison, on parole, or on probation.[2]
- Almost two-thirds of all prison inmates are black and Hispanic males.[3]
- 2.2 million Americans are incarcerated.[4]
- It costs $100,000 to build one prison cell.[5]
- It costs $35,000 to keep someone in prison for one year.[6]
- One-quarter of our prison inmates are serving time for drug-related offenses.[7]
- The main cause of death for black males aged fifteen to twenty-four is homicide.[8]
- Nearly two-thirds of those released from prison are back in again within three years.[9]
- One out of three black males born today can expect to serve time in prison.[10]
- High school dropouts account for 80 percent of state-prison inmates.[11]

THE YOUNG BLACK AND HISPANIC CRIMINAL

As mentioned above, about 67 percent of prison inmates are African American and Hispanic males. It doesn't take a rocket scientist to figure out that most of these young criminals come from poor, broken families, were subjected to parental abuse and neglect, and have grown up to be troubled. Their role models were drug dealers, pimps, petty criminals, and other lowlifes, and from the age of just seven or eight, many were pressured into joining violent youth gangs. When they reach adulthood, these young men are very severely emotionally damaged goods.

Growing up in this hopeless and violent environment, where gunfire and death are everyday occurrences, is it any wonder that so many ghetto youths join gangs and often commit crimes? For many, it may be the only way to survive—a rational response to an irrational world.

Over half of all young black men living in the urban ghettos do not have regular jobs.[12] An anthropologist, Marvin Harris, sees a clear connection between their lack of economic prospects and their high rates of criminality:

> It is my contention that hundreds of thousands of unemployed blacks choose violent crime as a solution in the chronic despair and envy that they must otherwise endure—especially young black men for whom failure looms as condemnation of manhood as well as a sentence to perpetual want.[13]

An often cited statistic is that one-third of all young black men are in prison, on parole, or on probation.[14] But within the urban ghettos, this fraction is much closer to one half. Not surprisingly, the leading cause of death among young black males is murder.[15]

Bruce Western reports, "Among black men born in the late 1960s who received no more than a high school education, 30 percent had served time in prison by their mid-thirties; 60 percent of high school dropouts had prison records."[16]

Here is what former House Speaker Newt Gingrich has observed about the culture of imprisonment:

> In some parts of the country we now see third- and fourth-generation prisoners. In some neighborhoods going to jail is a sign of status. . . . As a result of the "warehouse" prison model, we have created generations of hardened criminals who are comfortable in prison culture and aliens in law-abiding society.[17]

INCARCERATING THE MENTALLY ILL

The same society that abhorred the idea that we lock people up in mental hospitals, now locks people up in jails.

—Thomas Dart, Cook County (Illinois) sheriff

Decades ago, we discharged hundreds of thousands of people from mental institutions. Many of them subsequently committed crimes and ended up in prison. Some people actually commit a crime so that they can receive medical treatment in jail.

More than three times as many mentally ill people are housed in prisons or jails as in hospitals.[18] In 1955 there was one bed in a psychiatric ward for every three hundred Americans; now there is one for every three thousand Americans.[19]

Surely it would make a lot more sense for these people to be treated for their illnesses rather than imprisoned. And it would save billions of dollars. What can possibly justify imprisoning the nonviolent mentally ill?

OUR PRISON POPULATION

Either we're the most evil people on Earth or we're doing something wrong.

—Sen. James Webb (D-VA)

Of the 2.2 million Americans doing time, about two-thirds are in federal or state prison serving sentences of over one year.[20] The rest are in county or local jails, serving sentences of less than one year. Another five million people are under probation or parole supervision.[21] So our entire correctional population is over seven million.

No other nation incarcerates such a huge proportion of its citizens. More than one out of every one hundred adult Americans is behind bars, about five times the world's average.[22] In fact since 1980, when our prison population was half a million, it has more than quadrupled. There are three main reasons why we have been putting and keeping so many people in jail.

1. Our drug laws mandate jail sentences not just for major drug dealers, but for low-level pushers as well as for drug users. Con-

sequently, the number of people serving time for drug crimes shot up from just forty thousand in 1980 to nearly half a million today.[23]

2. "Three strikes and you're out" laws in California and several other states, which puts third-time offenders in jail for twenty-five years to life for often trivial third offenses. This results in the growing population of elderly inmates—a group that poses little threat of committing violent crimes.
3. Federal sentencing mandates, which take away judicial discretion, force judges to mete out long minimum sentences.

Especially hard hit by these measures have been young African Americans. The Anti-Drug Abuse Act, passed by Congress in 1986, "created a 100 to 1 sentencing disparity for crack vs. powder cocaine possession, which some people consider to be a racist law which discriminates against minorities, who are more likely to use crack than powder cocaine."[24] You would receive the same five-year sentence for possession of five grams of crack as you would for the possession of five hundred grams of cocaine.

A *Wikipedia* article also points out that while African Americans make up just 13 percent of our nation's drug users, they make up 35 percent of drug arrests, 55 percent of convictions, and 74 percent of people sent to prison for drug possession.[25] And nationwide, black men are sent to state prisons for drug offenses thirteen times more often than white men. Clearly the drug laws, policing, and the courts do not treat blacks and whites equally.

On any given day between 1925 and 1975, just one-tenth of 1 percent of the US population was locked up.[26] Today more than seven-tenths of 1 percent are in prison; virtually all economic rivals have less than one-tenth of 1 percent of their population incarcerated.[27] In other words, we are incarcerating more than seven times as many people per capita as are other economically advanced nations.

Let's take another look at who we're locking up. One out of four prisoners has violated a drug law and is most likely an addict.[28] In addition, more than half of prisoners are mentally ill.[29] Do *you* think prison life will cure either affliction?[30]

The less educated you are, the greater your chances of going to jail. And if you're a twenty- to forty-year-old black male high school dropout, then your odds of being behind bars on any given day are almost one out of three.[31] If you happen to be black, then your chances of being incarcerated are about five times greater than if you are white or Hispanic.[32] So if you want to stay out of jail in this country, don't be black and don't drop out of school. Instead of resorting to stop-and-frisk, the police should just ask to see a high school diploma.

Newsweek columnist Dahlia Lithwick summed up our criminal justice dilemma very succinctly: "We lock up more people, for less violent crime, at ever greater expense, breeding more dangerous criminals who often come out unemployable, violent and isolated."[33]

THE HIGH COST OF CRIME

How much does each criminal cost us? According to one estimate provided by First Focus, "Each young person who fails to finish high school and goes on to a life of crime costs the nation between $1.7 and $2.3 million."[34]

Since hundreds of thousands of teenagers—especially poor black and Hispanic males—drop out of school each year, our society is generating a steady supply of potential new recruits to its criminal population. Many will be living under the supervision of the criminal justice system well into their thirties and forties.

The criminal justice system consists of three main elements—policing, the courts, and what we euphemistically refer to as "corrections." Policing is done by local and state police officers, federal marshals, FBI agents, members of the Secret Service, agents of the Bureau of Alcohol, Tobacco, and Firearms, sheriffs, narcotics agents, and other government employees such as the postal police. Those employed directly or indirectly by the courts include judges, clerks, court officers, prosecutors, criminal defense attorneys, bail bondsmen, and city marshals.

Now we come to "corrections," which consists mainly of our far-flung system of local jails and state and federal prisons. Implied by its name, this system receives criminals and turns out people who have presumably have had their bad behavior "corrected." But only a miniscule fraction of prison budgets actually goes toward rehabilitation. Those employed in corrections include prison guards and other prison staff, and parole and probation officers. About two million people—directly or indirectly—earn their living from our criminal justice system. The annual bill for our criminal justice system is over one-quarter trillion dollars.[35]

Jim Dwyer, a *New York Times* columnist, describes our tax dollars at work when a young man is arrested for possession of one gram (one-thirtieth of an ounce) of marijuana:

> [H]is case absorbed the energy of two police officers, a desk sergeant, a clerk who processed his paperwork and fingerprints, a driver who transported him to booking, other officers to secure him in the pen awaiting his appearance, a Legal Aid Society lawyer, an assistant district attorney, a court clerk and a court reporter to transcribe the proceedings. Also, a judge, who instantly dismissed the case.[36]

SOLUTIONS

Crime and Poverty

> *We have a criminal-justice system that treats you better if you're rich and guilty than if you're poor and innocent.*
> —Bryon Stevenson, founder of Equal Justice Initiative

We need to get at the root causes of violent crime. Most violent criminals grew up in the slums, so clearly this type of upbringing has a lot to do with their subsequent antisocial behavior. Concentrated poverty and its attendant social breakdown breeds despair and crime. Young criminals grow into adult criminals. How do you break the cycle? You need to alleviate extreme poverty. Easier said than done. But if we're serious about substantially reducing violent crime, we need to lift millions of families out of poverty.

If young men living in the ghettos of our nation's cities were bigger stakeholders in their communities, they would be subject to greater social constraints and less likely to commit crimes. This view is summarized by Princeton sociologist Bruce Western:

> Steady jobs and good marriages build social bonds that keep would-be offenders in a daily routine. They enmesh men who are tempted by crime in a web of supportive social relationships. Strong family bonds and steady work restrict men's opportunities for antisocial behavior and offer them a stake in normal life. For persistent law-breakers, the adult roles of spouse and worker offer a pathway out of crime. Those who fail to secure the markers of adulthood are more likely to persist in criminal behavior.[37]

Putting teenagers in juvenile detention facilities and young men in prison, Western believes, is usually counterproductive because they "delay entry into the conventional adult roles of worker, spouse, and parent."[38]

If young men leave their ghetto environment to join the military, this, Western believes, often has a positive effect and serves as a "legitimate timeout." Indeed, military service may well provide a more positive environment than life in the ghetto. But time spent in prison often exacerbates criminal behavior, rather than deter it. Isn't it said that prisons provide the best schooling for criminals?

Punishing Violent Criminals and Nonviolent Criminals

Just a small fraction of those who appear before a judge have committed violent crimes. *The Economist* makes *this* observation: "If the book is thrown at the second lot and more leniency shown to the first, prison populations and crime rates could both fall. The intelligence lies in throwing the books correctly."[39]

I happen to be a segregationist. Violent criminals should not be allowed to live among the general population. They need to be placed in protective custody. That is—*we're* the ones being protected and *they're* the ones in custody.

My own preference is to quarantine the more violent-prone from the rest of society. Set them up in isolated areas, perhaps old military bases, provide them with support, and, if they are so inclined, some kind of work. Those who are threats to the public safety need to be living apart from the rest of us.

Should we also be locking up nonviolent criminals? Let's look at one startling fact: about one-quarter of those initially imprisoned for nonviolent crimes later return to prison for a violent offense.[40] We may conclude, then, that prison serves to transmit violent habits rather than reduce them. So we need to ask ourselves, if time in prison greatly increases the likelihood that a convict, upon release, will commit violent crimes, then surely we need a plan B.

Here's *my* plan B. Lock up all the criminals who have repeatedly committed violent crimes at least until they are too old to hurt anyone. Since we lock up a lot of people who have committed nonviolent crimes—why does Bernard Madoff's name spring to mind?—then put them in different prisons from those that house violent criminals.

Most nonviolent criminals could be sentenced to terms of community service instead of being sent to prison, and, in some cases, paying extremely large fines as well. For example, some of the people who engaged in insider trading could spend five days a week teaching reading or math to poor inner-city children. Or they could be working in nursing homes, shelters for the homeless, or cleaning public toilets.

Where would these nonviolent criminals live? Most could be placed in group homes, and the rest could live under house arrest. They would wear monitoring bracelets and live relatively restricted lives. Basically then, they would still be punished, but their punishment would cost society a lot less than incarceration, and they would be able to lead productive lives.

Ending Gang Violence

David Kennedy, a criminology professor at New York's John Jay College of Criminal Justice, has created a strategy called "Ceasefire" that has sharply reduced gang-related homicides in New York; Boston; Cincinnati; Stockton, California; High Point, North Carolina; and is now being tried in a few other cities. This is how he describes it:

> Ceasefire was basically simple—have law enforcement, community elders, and social-service providers sit down and talk with the gangs and drug crews that drove the shooting. The community said that the violence had to stop, the providers offered help, and the cops promised that the first gang that killed someone after the meeting was going to get all their attention.[41]

Newsweek writer Andrew Romano explains why Ceasefire succeeds:

> [W]henever the cops give these gangsters a choice between (a) shooting people and going to prison or (b) not shooting people and going on with their lives, they almost always choose the latter.[42]

Recidivism

Few prisoners have jobs waiting for them when they are released. And who would *want* to hire an ex-con? A majority of prisoners are functionally illiterate.[43] A literacy program would give some prisoners a better chance for gainful employment, but very few learn how to read and write while in jail. In Japan, convicts are not released until they are literate.[44]

Because almost two-thirds of those released from prison are rearrested within three years, we need to make a huge effort to smooth the readjustment process when prisoners are set free.[45] They usually need a job and a place to live. Otherwise, they'll most likely fall back into their old lives and resume the only trade they know—crime.

Ideally they would receive some vocational training in prison, with a job waiting for them on the outside. Considering the reluctance of most employers to hire ex-cons, the federal, state, and local governments need to set up job programs for the six hundred thousand people released each year.[46]

Each year just thirty thousand inmates are released during their last year of confinement to about two hundred halfway houses around the country.[47] These are meant to ease their transition back into society. Regretfully, many of these places are understaffed and not well prepared to do the job. Still, we need a vastly expanded network of fully staffed halfway houses that are well equipped to meet the needs of all inmates—especially those who are mentally ill, or are recovering drug addicts.

Dealing with Drug-Related Crime

Go into any impoverished inner-city neighborhood, and, if you know where to look, you'll see young men selling drugs on street corners. In Camden, New Jersey, one of the nation's poorest cities, they stand near highway exit ramps selling drugs to suburbanites.[48] To us, these guys are criminals who should be jailed. But as they see it, it's just a job—a day at the office.

Is what they're doing so sufficiently bad that they should be locked up? And do we want to keep building more jail cells and employing more prison guards to keep them incarcerated? Four out of five drug arrests are for drug possession, not sales.[49]

Since the 1970s, we've been throwing drug dealers—large and small—into prison for relatively long sentences. But the dealers are immediately replaced, so the net effect of putting these guys in jail is zero.

Dealing with drug-related crimes calls for entirely different solutions. As a first step, marijuana, which is relatively harmless, should be legalized across the country immediately. It should be sold the way cigarettes and alcoholic beverages are sold—subject to a fairly high tax, and not sold to minors. I'll leave it to the experts to figure out how to deal with the folks selling cocaine, heroin, crack, meth, and PCP.

Hundreds of thousands of addicts are on waiting lists for drug treatment programs.[50] It's nuts to put more cops on the street to arrest these guys, but not to make beds immediately available in treatment facilities for addicts requesting help. What are they supposed to do for the six or eight months while they're waiting?

Drug treatment is much more cost-effective than prison. It costs less than half as much to build and maintain a treatment facility than a prison.[51] And when we weigh the results, it's no contest. Well over 90 percent of the people who go to prison for drug-related crimes wind up back in prison.[52] In contrast, some of the better drug treatment programs—like Phoenix House—have a "cure" rate of over 70 percent.[53] Federal health officials have estimated that every dollar spent on substance-abuse treatment saves seven dollars that would be spent on prison, police, and courts.[54]

Jailed Until Proven Innocent

Of the 2.2 million people behind bars, almost 500,000 are not convicts; they are accused individuals awaiting trial.[55] A small fraction of these folks are too dangerous to be set free or are flight risks. But the vast majority cannot afford to pay their bail—even when it is set at less than $500. In fact, when it is set at $500 or less, just 15 percent of defendants are able to come up with the money to avoid jail.[56] Many, after having spent weeks or even months behind bars, will be found not guilty and set free.

When unable to make bail, most defendants agree to a plea deal to stay out of jail, even if they are not guilty. The courts would be overwhelmed if even a small fraction of these defendants asserted their right to a trial. Poor people are much more likely to plead guilty than those who can afford bail.[57] So much for equal justice in America.

Miami-Dade County, Florida, has cut costs associated with detention by supervising defendants outside of jail while they await trial.[58] The American Bar Association has endorsed this practice, and a few other jurisdictions are beginning to try it. Simple justice—not to mention huge cost savings—dictates that nearly all those awaiting trial should remain free.

New York Times columnist Nicholas Kristof asks, "Is it a crime to be poor?" Tens of thousands of poor people are sitting in jails today for not having paid various government fines or fees. In most cases, these payments have not been made because these people just don't have the money. One might ask how these people will ever be able to make these payments when they're sitting in jail instead of working?[59]

Dealing with Gun Violence

Guns don't kill people, people kill people.

—mantra of the pro-gun lobby

The United States has the highest rate of gun ownership in the world and the highest firearm homicide rate among economically developed nations.[60] In fact the firearm homicide rate in America is 5.5 times higher than in Italy, which has the next highest rate.[61]

The regular mass rampages, such as the one at Sandy Hook Elementary School in Newtown, Connecticut, which left twenty children and seven adults dead, seems to be a specifically American phenomenon. And so too does the bloodiest attack on American soil since 9/11, which left forty-nine dead in Orlando in June 2016.

We also know that gun deaths are lower in the states with the strictest gun control laws.[62] So it would seem logical that if we are going to lower the number of murders resulting from gun violence, then we need to impose much stricter gun control laws in every state. A lot fewer homicides would occur if guns were not so readily available.

Almost half of all US households have at least one gun, and very few people will voluntarily give them up.[63] The best we can do is to try to ban the sale of guns to the wrong people as well as ban the sale of assault weapons and large-capacity magazines. Even then, we will continue to lead the industrial world in gun deaths; somewhat minimizing that number may be the best we can do.

But the extremely powerful gun lobby, led by the National Rifle Association, opposes virtually *any* gun control law—even against the selling and possession of submachine guns. While it is understandable that hunters and people who shoot at targets want to own their own rifles, why would they want rapid-firing weapons holding huge magazines? The gun lobby also opposes universal background checks, which could deny guns to anyone who is mentally ill, or has a history of violent behavior.

SUMMING UP

Here's what we can do to minimize crime and minimize the cost of maintaining our criminal justice system.

1. Lock up all violent criminals at least until they are too old to be a threat.
2. Legalize marijuana across the nation, tightly regulate its sale, and impose high taxes on this drug.
3. Stop locking up people for most drug offenses.

4. Provide immediate drug treatment programs for addicts.
5. Place most mentally ill criminals in mental institutions.
6. Allow most nonviolent criminals to perform community service instead of being incarcerated.
7. Make vocational training and basic literacy courses available for all inmates.
8. Provide a job and a place to live to everyone released from prison.
9. Allow nonviolent defendants to await trial without putting up bail money.
10. Institute David Kennedy's strategy to lower gang-related homicides in more localities.
11. Vastly expand the network of well-staffed halfway houses.

Chapter 16
OUR BLOATED FINANCIAL SECTOR

The only thing useful banks have invented in 20 years is the ATM.
—Paul Volcker, former chairman of the Federal Reserve Board

The financial sector has three main components—banking, real estate, and insurance. Banking has, by far, the greatest influence on our economy, so in this chapter we shall concentrate on the economic role the banks have played.

THE ECONOMIC ROLE OF BANKING

A banker is a fellow who lends you his umbrella when the sun is shining, but wants it back the minute it begins to rain.
—Mark Twain

The main job of our banks is gathering our savings and then lending them primarily to large business firms. This process has a fancy technical name—intermediation. In simple English, our banks act as middlemen between savers and investors.

Since investors borrow huge sums of money—often tens of billions of dollars—our financial intermediaries need to bundle the savings of tens of millions of Americans and lend that money to large corporations. These firms, in turn, invest that money in plant, equipment, and software that is needed to produce goods and services. A second job of our banks is providing smaller loans to individuals for home mortgages and consumer spending—largely credit card loans. And finally, our financial services industry enables business to be conducted smoothly and safely.

How well are these jobs performed? By and large, from day to day, they are performed quite well. But from time to time, most notably from

1929 to 1933, and again in the middle of the last decade, our financial sector has failed us miserably.

The poor and the near poor are excluded from many of the services that banks provide, such as being able to open checking accounts, being issued credit and debit cards and granted access to bank ATMs. Their exclusion has left them to the mercy of check cashing services, finance companies, payday lenders, pawn brokers, and tax preparation firms. Stroll through nearly any poor neighborhood and you'll find a plentiful supply of these predatory institutions, but few, if any, bank branches or even bank ATMs.

From the 1860s on, the rapid growth of our manufacturing sector and the building of our canals, railroads, and the rest of our infrastructure was made possible by funding from the financial sector. It sustained the expansion of the textile, apparel, steel, and chemical industries, and helped make possible the electricity and automobile revolutions. In recent decades, however, finance has increasingly become a speculative activity. Today, rather than supply our economy with needed capital, the financial sector siphons off those funds for speculative purposes.

Until the 1970s the productive system—often termed "the real economy"—dominated the financial system. But by *the 1980s*, this balance of power was reversed: since then the tail has been wagging the dog.

Historically, our banks facilitated the flow of savings into investment, enabling our economy to grow rapidly throughout the nineteenth century, as well as through most of the first seven decades of the twentieth. Financial intermediation was provided at a cost of from 2 to 4 percent of our GDP. Today the financial sector accounts for 9 percent of our GDP—up from just 5 percent in 1980.[1]

Over nine million people are employed in finance—primarily in banks and insurance companies. Among them are managers of hedge funds and private investment funds, some of whom earn hundreds of millions of dollars a year.[2] Amazingly, most of the work in financial services consists of using computers to shift money from one bank account to another. If computers are doing most of the job, then why would over nine million employees be needed?

Our financial system is structured and functions very differently from how it did just forty years ago. Most of the change was due to the process of deregulation, which in turn was codified by two laws—one passed in 1980, and the other in 1999.

DEREGULATION

Economic historians will mark the 1970s and 1980s as decades of swift and significant change in American banking. During this period, the distinction between commercial banks and thrift institutions—savings banks, savings and loan associations, and credit unions—became blurred to the point where it was hard to tell what was a bank and what wasn't.

Until 1980 there was a clear legal line of demarcation between commercial banks and thrift institutions. Commercial banks could issue checking deposits, and the thrifts could not. But during the 1970s, the thrifts began creating savings accounts that provided check-writing privileges. In addition, they paid interest on these accounts, giving them a competitive advantage over the commercial banks, which were prohibited by Federal Reserve regulation from paying interest on their checking accounts. The commercial banks complained that the thrifts had an unfair advantage in attracting depositors by being able to pay interest. In response, Congress passed a law in 1980 that created a level playing field for the commercial banks and the thrifts.

The Depository Institutions Deregulation and Monetary Control Act of 1980

This law had two main provisions: (1) all depository institutions were now subject to the Federal Reserve legal reserve requirements and subject to its regulations and (2) all depository institutions were now legally authorized to issue checking deposits.

An extremely important consequence of the law was that by the end of the 1990s intense competition reduced the forty-thousand-plus financial institutions that existed at the beginning of the 1980s to just thirteen thousand today.[3] In fact, just a few dozen huge banks do most of the business.

The Banking Act of 1999

In 1980, the jurisdiction of the Federal Reserve had been extended to all commercial banks and thrift institutions. In 1999, it was further extended to insurance companies, pension funds, investment companies, securities brokers, and finance companies.

The new law repealed sections of the Glass-Steagall Act of 1933, which was based on the premise that America's financial house could best be restored if bankers and brokers stayed in separate rooms. It was thought that this could reduce the potential conflicts of interest between investment banking—the selling of new stock and new bonds for existing companies and the arrangement of corporate mergers—and commercial banking. Because thousands of banks had directly or indirectly invested their depositors' money in highly speculative stocks, when the stock market crashed in 1929, nearly all these banks failed, and their depositors lost all their money. Under Glass-Steagall, commercial banks could receive no more than 10 percent of their income from the securities markets, a limit so restrictive that most simply abandoned business on Wall Street selling stocks and bonds to their customers.

Over time federal judges and regulators chipped away at Glass-Steagall and other restrictions on cross-ownership of banks. The main purpose of the Banking Act of 1999 was to give all financial firms, including banks, the chance to sell all sorts of investments. In this way they would be similar to banks in other countries that already provided such services. The law allows banks, securities firms, and insurance companies to merge and to sell each other's products, and has enabled a wave of mergers as companies compete to build financial supermarkets offering all the services customers need under one roof.

What was wrong with allowing this? One main thing: during the Great Depression, the Federal Deposit Insurance Corporation had been created to prevent future bank runs by assuring depositors that their money was safe. At the same time, under Glass-Steagall, savings and commercial banks that held these deposits were prohibited from engaging in risky or speculative financial activities. Investment banks, however, were free to engage in speculative financial activities because, rather than accept deposits, they raised their capital largely by selling bonds. As Dean Baker, the cofounder of the Center for Economic Policy Research, summed it up, "The ending of Glass-Steagall removed the separation between investment banks and commercial banks, raising the possibility that banks would make risky investments with government guaranteed deposits."[4]

In sum, the repeal of Glass-Steagall enabled the emergence of big banks that would behave badly. Banks like Citigroup and Bank of America not only became "too big to fail"—a concept we'll explore near the end of the chapter—but their bad financial behavior led to the financial crisis of 2008. Without the banks providing financing to the mortgage brokers and Wall Street, while underwriting their own issues of toxic securities, the entire pyramid scheme would never have gotten off the ground.

THE FINANCIAL CRISIS OF 2008

Greed is good.

—Gordon Gekko,
leading character in the 1987 film *Wall Street*

Who was to blame for the financial crisis? There is certainly no shortage of villains. We can thank Congress for passing the Banking Act of 1980, signed by President Jimmy Carter, and for the Banking Act of 1999, signed by President Bill Clinton. Another contributor to the crisis was Federal Reserve chairman Alan Greenspan, who financed the real estate bubble, with an assist from his successor Ben Bernanke. And then too, there was President George W. Bush, who appeared almost unaware of the gathering crisis. While he was fond of describing himself as "the decider," he stood by idly as the financial situation grew increasingly grave. But perhaps the role of leading villain should be shared by all the folks at our financial institutions who profited so richly from the speculative frenzy they created. They did this largely by creating complicated financial products that few people really understood, but which were highly profitable. As the popular saying goes, "Never look a gift horse in the mouth."

The prime example of these financial products, the notorious collateralized debt obligations, or CDOs, is described in the accompanying box. This highly profitable financial product provided no useful economic service, but was largely responsible for the 2008 financial crisis.

Soon after the housing bubble burst and a large investment bank, Lehman Brothers, went belly up, it became more and more apparent that our entire financial structure might collapse. With our financial institutions holding trillions of dollars in CDOs as well as other securities of dubious value, they had no choice but to write down the value of what were now called "toxic assets." Because of the intertwined ownership of many of these securities, it was unclear who owed what to whom. There was a great danger that a large part of our financial sector would soon be toppled like falling dominos, possibly setting off a worldwide financial meltdown.

In October 2008, Congress passed the $700 billion Troubled Assets Relief Program (TARP), of which $475 billion would be used to help troubled banks and other financial institutions. But this effort was dwarfed by the approximately $17 trillion in direct and indirect financial obligations taken on by the Federal Reserve, the US Treasury, and the Federal Deposit

Collateralized Debt Obligations (CDOs)

Soon after the new millennium, real estate prices were rising rapidly, and interest rates on mortgage loans were very low, so it appeared a great time to buy a new home. Mortgage lenders, taking advantage of these conditions, vastly expanded the pool of home buyers by financing millions of subprime loans—which are at relatively high interest rates—to families that could not have otherwise qualified for home ownership. The borrowers, relatively poor people, would not have qualified either because their income was too low to meet the anticipated payments, or because of a bad credit history. Indeed, about 60 percent of subprime loans required either no income verification or only the most cursory check.[5]

After making the loans, mortgage companies usually sold them off to investment banks, which in turn, combined them into securities known as collateralized debt obligations (CDOs). The investment banks then paid Standard and Poor, Moody's, Fitch, and other credit agencies to rate these securities. Not surprisingly, they were usually rated AAA—the highest possible rating. Since investors thought the securities were virtually risk-free, the investment bankers were able to quickly unload these CDOs. Between 2001 and 2006, subprime loans rose from just $100 billion to almost $1 trillion.[6] With perfect hindsight, it was not hard to see the approaching train wreck. Two things would make this inevitable. First, hundreds of thousands of subprime borrowers would default on their mortgages, most of them losing their homes. And then too, real estate prices would not only stop rising but would begin to fall.

In the end, of course, the American taxpayer was stuck with the bill. None of the perpetuators of this massive fraud spent one day in jail. And when Congress took up financial reform, the financial establishment had the *chutzpah* to fight it tooth and nail, and managed to water down its key provisions.

The point I want to make here is that the CDOs were solely a financial vehicle used by the industry to make hundreds of billions in profits, but provided no useful financial service to the nation. It is just one of a whole array of financial "services" that wastes hundreds of billions of dollars of our precious resources.

Insurance Corporation.[7] In the wake of this massive bailout, our political leaders declared that never again should we allow such a serious financial crisis to occur. Their solution was Dodd-Frank.

DODD-FRANK WALL STREET REFORM AND CONSUMER PROTECTION ACT

Main Provisions

This law, which was passed in 2010, had several goals that included protecting consumers from unscrupulous lenders, curbing unsound mortgage-lending practices, restricting banks from making risky investments, and setting up an early warning system to detect potential trouble in the financial services market. Perhaps its most controversial provision was granting power to federal officials to break up banks whose failure would cause financial havoc—in other words, those banks that were too big to fail.

Too Big to Fail

If they're too big to fail they're too big.

—Alan Greenspan,
former chairman of the Federal Reserve

Some banks are so large and so integral to the economy that their failure would bring down our entire financial system. This was the rationale for the massive bailout in 2008 and 2009. But since then our biggest banks have grown much bigger. So the next bailout could be even more costly.

Perhaps the best measure of "bigness" is the concentration of financial assets. In 1990 the five largest banks held just 9.67 percent of the assets in the banking industry. By the end of 2013, the five biggest banks held 44 percent.[8]

The Dodd-Frank financial reform was supposed to ensure that the government would never again be faced with the choice of either bailing out our big banks or risking a financial meltdown. After this law was passed, President Obama declared that we would never again need to make that choice.

So far, Dodd-Frank has clearly done little to enforce the too-big-to-fail doctrine. Near the end of the chapter, we'll look at another major failing of the law—the fact that it did not reinstate Glass-Steagall.

THE FINANCIALIZATION OF THE AMERICAN ECONOMY

Financialization is a term used to describe the growing scale, profitability, and deregulation of the financial sector relative to the "real economy." It's a process that University of Massachusetts economist Gerald Epstein defines as "the increasing importance of financial markets, financial motives, financial institutions and financial elites in the operation of the economy and its governing institutions."[9]

Over the last forty years there has been a growing dichotomy between the financial sector and the real economy. For most of our history, the financial sector's primary role was to facilitate the growth of the real economy—the sector that produced the goods and services that enabled our rising standard of living. But in recent years, as we noted earlier in this chapter, the financial sector has become much more focused on speculative activities than on providing for the financial needs of the real economy.

Much of our financial system operates like a gambling casino. Instead of placing bets on the outcomes of playing cards, a roulette wheel, or a slot machine, the betting is on the movement in stock prices, bond prices, and other financial data. The total winnings are equal to the total losses—less a significant commission to stockbrokers and asset managers. Similar to casino gambling, financial gambling provides hundreds of thousands of people with their livelihoods. But their work does not result in any useful service—except, of course, a certain amount of entertainment to the gamblers.

By offering more and more complicated and highly sophisticated financial products and services, our financial intermediaries were able to capture an increasing share of the profits made by the entire corporate sector. Financial profits were 11 percent of corporate profits in 1947, the first year this data was compiled. But its share has climbed over the years, and since 2010 it has averaged about 40 percent.[10]

THE ECONOMIC EFFECTS OF FINANCIALIZATION

We need to ask one question: What are the economic effects of financialization? There are five primary effects, each of which impacts negatively on our economy.

1. *Because compensation in financial services is, on average, about 70 percent higher than in the rest of the economy, many of our best and our brightest college graduates are drawn to this field.*[11]

   Until the 2008 financial crisis, Wall Street was attracting about one-third of the graduates of the Ivy League and of other top colleges and universities, which deprived the productive sector of all this talent.[12] After a sharp drop-off, increasing numbers of our best and our brightest college grads are once again being drawn to high-paying jobs on Wall Street.
2. *As financialization rises, investment in the real sector declines.*

   The financial sector is sucking money out of the productive sector—the sector that creates the goods and services that we need. As Richard Eskow succinctly sums this up, "Never before has the manipulation of money counted for so much and the real-world economy of people and consumer goods counted for so little." He then goes on to say, "The money nowadays isn't in manufacturing or retail, or any of the other traditionally jobs-producing industries. The money now is in *money*."[13]
3. *It leads to a huge redistribution of income from the working class and the middle class to the rich.*

   The great American middle class, which came into its own by the early twentieth century, has provided the bulk of the consumer demand for our huge and growing output of goods and services. For decades the rich, who save a relatively high proportion of their income, have reaped an increasing share of our national income. Much of these gains have been due to growing profits of the financial sector. This huge redistribution of income has depressed demand for our economy's output of goods and services. The upper 1 percent earns a very disproportionate share of our national income, but it is the lower 99 percent that supplies nearly the entire demand for our nation's output.

   Between 1970 and 2012, financialization was largely responsible for a sharp decline in labor's share of our GDP. During this period, it sank from 59.3 percent to just 42.6 percent—the lowest on record over the entire eighty-eight years that this data has been gathered. Since 2012, labor compensation ticked up very slightly to 43.5 percent of the GDP.[14]
4. *The financial sector has grown increasingly inefficient.*

   The per unit cost of financial intermediation has more than

doubled since 1950.[15] More trading of financial assets has led to a doubling in the share of the financial sector as a percentage of the GDP.

5. *Much of the financial sector produces no useful services, but it generates a huge transfer of wealth.*

   The more we trade financial securities, the greater the generation of fees collected by financial institutions and the larger their share of our GDP. Finance has become primarily a speculative activity: investors are making bets on what other investors are doing rather than actually financing jobs and real investment.

FINANCIAL PREDATORS

We now come up to perhaps the worst of the worst, those who prey primarily upon the poor and the ill-informed. The most prominent are the payday lenders. Basically, you're getting a loan until payday. The only problem is that if you're strapped for cash in the first place, the chances are you won't be able to pay off your loan without taking out still another one. Once you're hooked, you'll be paying sky-high interest rates and falling deeper into debt.

Say you wanted to borrow $500 until payday, less than two weeks from now. No problem. Just write out a check for $575, which we promise not to cash until payday, and you'll walk out with $500 cash. That comes to an interest rate of over 390 percent, and that's just for starters. If you were short $500 two weeks before *this* payday, and you're starting out the *next* pay period $575 behind . . . well, you can see where this is going. Within weeks you'll be back for a bigger loan, and before long you'll owe thousands of dollars in interest on that original $500 loan you never really got out from under.

There are more than twenty thousand payday lenders, and as individual states either outlaw them or impose restrictions, a majority now operate online, where they are almost completely free of government regulation.[16]

Now let's talk about the nice folks who want to help you lower the exorbitant interest rates that you must pay on your home mortgage, credit cards, and student loan. They employ hundreds of thousands of telemarketers to call you, persuade you to give them your confidential financial information, charge you a hefty upfront fee and often a monthly fee as well, and then somehow don't manage to get your interest rates lowered at all.

THE REAL ESTATE INDUSTRY

From 1492, when Columbus "discovered" America, until the late nineteenth century, when our nation was largely settled, we managed quite well without the services of more than a handful of real estate brokers. But today, although it is just a fraction of our financial sector, our real estate industry is, by far, the largest in the world. Of the 1.5 million people on this planet who earn their living as real estate brokers or agents, almost half of them live in the United States.[17] When their supporting staff is added in, close to three million people earn their livelihoods in real estate.[18] Like the rest of our financial sector, we have far more people than we need working in real estate.

THE INSURANCE INDUSTRY

Some four million Americans work in the insurance industry.[19] It takes that many people to provide us with healthcare, life, auto, and property insurance. The work is extremely labor intensive. Hundreds of millions of claims—the large majority in healthcare—must be examined and reimbursement determined. This process often involves numerous e-mails, letters, phone conversations, and in-person meetings. For example, to settle a $2,000 claim when my eighteen-year-old car was destroyed by Hurricane Sandy in 2012, I spent about twenty hours on the phone with various representatives of the Hartford insurance agency. Incidentally, I was not disputing anything, but just responding to their questions.

SUMMING UP

More than nine million people work in finance, which includes banking, real estate, and insurance. Finance is central to our economy, but no other nation employs such a high proportion of its work force—about 7 percent—in its financial sector.[20] If all these other nations can deliver basic financial services with just of fraction of the workers that we employ, then why can't we?

SOLUTIONS

Like several other major sectors of our economy, finance is grossly inefficient and deeply entrenched. Perhaps worse yet, its major players—especially the giant banks—are well positioned to cause future financial crises. And adding the icing to the cake, these institutions are powerful enough to resist any meaningful change.

A Tax on Financial Transactions

The European Union has been considering the implementation of one-tenth of 1 percent tax on financial transactions between financial institutions. This comes to a one-dollar tax on a one-thousand-dollar transaction. It is expected to rise over $70 billion per year if implemented across the entire EU.[21]

Whether or not the EU proceeds with this tax, we should strongly consider such a tax ourselves. And rather than limit it to just transactions between financial institutions, why not broaden it to cover *all* financial transactions—such as the purchase of real estate, stocks, bonds, derivatives, and other financial instruments?

Such a tax would have four major advantages. First, it would raise several hundred billion dollars a year. Second, it would tax an economic sector that is far too large. Third, the tax would be paid by those who can most easily afford it. And fourth, the tax rate is so low, it would barely be noticed. After all, how much would *you* mind paying a one-dollar fee on a one-thousand-dollar stock purchase?

Higher Capital Requirements

Most business firms raise funds by either selling shares to investors or by reinvesting profits. Banks get nearly all their money from depositors. Because they are risking other peoples' money, bankers are much more inclined to take risks.

The eight largest American banks derive no more than 5 percent of their funding from shareholders, while the average equity financing for nonfinancial corporations is about 60 percent.[22] The solution would be to force bankers to put "more skin in the game." In other words, they need to risk more of their *own* money, and less of their depositors' money.[23]

The Dodd-Frank Wall Street Reform and Consumer Protection Act of 2010

This law, which was very successfully watered down by an army of lobbyists hired by the financial interests, has one basic goal—to prevent future financial crises. It *does* grant power to federal officials to break up huge banks whose failure would cause financial havoc. But it does little to address this central fact: our financial sector has grown much too big and powerful and is wasting far too much of our precious resources.

Reinstate Glass-Steagall

In July 2013, Senators Elizabeth Warren (D-MA), John McCain (R-AZ), Maria Cantwell (D-WA), and Angus King (I-ME) introduced a "21st Century Glass-Steagall Act." This bill proposed that deposit-taking institutions would not be permitted to buy or sell securities for profit, underwrite the issuance of stocks and bonds, or, in any other way, act like an investment bank.

The senators provided two reasons for passing this legislation. First, they asked why financial institutions should be allowed to engage in high-risk transactions using federally insured deposits. And second, they observed that splitting the relatively conservative depository banking functions from the investment bank functions would significantly downsize the nation's largest banks. That brings us back again to the issue of "too big to fail."

Break Up the Big Banks

While it is virtually unanimous that the failure of our largest banks would create a financial meltdown, there is little agreement about what can be done. Let's consider four broad options.

1. The most stringent option would be to place a limit on the size of a bank—perhaps a ceiling of $500 billion or $1 trillion in assets. A ceiling of $1 trillion would require the breakup of JPMorgan Chase, Bank of America, Citigroup, and Wells Fargo. If the ceiling were $500 billion, then Goldman Sachs, Morgan Stanley, American International Group (AIG), and General Electric Capital Group would have to be broken up.

To lend some perspective, when Lehman Brothers failed, setting off the 2008 financial crisis, it held assets of just over $600 billion—a substantial portion of which were of dubious value.[24] However appealing the imposition of a ceiling on assets might be in some quarters, there does not appear to be a great deal of support in Congress for this option.

2. A somewhat less draconian measure would be to place a tax of, say, 1 percent on a bank's assets of over $500 billion. Obviously, the effectiveness of this tax in curbing the size of large banks would depend on how high it was.
3. Former Federal Reserve chairman Paul Volcker would create a firewall between risky trading operations and government-insured savings that funds commercial lending. Although this so-called "Volcker Rule" was a stated goal of Dodd-Frank, the financial industry has managed to render this rule largely toothless.
4. Take no action until it appears that a bank may fail; at that point, the government would bail out the bank.

Despite the passage of Dodd-Frank, and all the proclamations by government officials that we must never be compelled to undertake another bailout, by default we appear to be left with just the fourth option.

CONCLUSION

We can make the same complaint about the financial sector that we did about the healthcare sector: its inefficient operation results in a tremendous waste of our scarce resources—namely our labor and capital. And just as healthcare's huge share of our GDP has more than doubled over the last forty-five years, so too has that of the financial sector.

But there is a very crucial difference between these two huge economic sectors. You'll probably remember the medical commandment, "First, do no harm." Regretfully, the 2008 financial crisis and our worst economic downturn since the Great Depression were direct results of the harmful actions of our financial sector.

Historically, our economy has managed quite well when we devoted just 4 percent of our GDP to financial services. Today that sector's share has grown to 9 percent, but with no discernible economic benefit.[25] So it would be fair to say that this sector is wasting resources equivalent to 4 percent of our GDP—more than $700 billion a year. Because those running our financial sector are so solidly entrenched and wield such great financial and political power, there does not appear to be an available means of reducing their economic role in the foreseeable future.

Part VII

WASTING OUR RESOURCES BY PRODUCING USELESS GOODS AND SERVICES

During the depths of the Great Depression, one out of every four Americans was officially unemployed, and many more had simply given up looking for work.[1] Under the New Deal, millions of the unemployed were put back to work. Along with their paychecks, they got back their dignity. They built highways, bridges, hydroelectric dams, schools, libraries, courthouses, and other public buildings. And while there *were* some make-work projects, they were vastly outnumbered by work that resulted in very useful goods and services.

Today, as we shall see, tens of millions of Americans hold down make-work jobs. Most are not, as generally supposed, government jobs, but rather are in the private sector. Most of these people work very hard, put in long hours, and are often quite well compensated. The only problem is that they do not produce any tangible goods or services—certainly nothing that adds to our standard of living.

Chapter 17

THE INTERNAL REVENUE CODE AND THE TAX PREPARATION INDUSTRY

The time for tax reform and tax simplification is now.
—Nina E. Olson, IRS national taxpayer advocate

You'd need to be a CPA to even begin to understand the Internal Revenue Code, and you'd have to be a world-class weight lifter to raise it just a few inches off the desk. The code has tripled in size since the new millennium, and it is now more than seventy thousand pages long. It's something only accountants and tax lawyers could love. After all, it's their bread and butter.

THE COST OF COMPLIANCE

Douglas Shulman, the Internal Revenue Service commissioner from 2009 to 2012, disclosed that because the tax code is so complicated, even *he* did not do his own taxes.[1] Like Mr. Shulman, six out of ten taxpayers need to pay someone else to do their taxes.[2] We manage to employ more accountants than the rest of the world put together.[3] The main task of our nation's 1.4 million accountants is to minimize the tax liabilities of their clients—small business firms, corporations of all sizes, and tens of millions of individuals.[4] Supplementing their efforts are 100,000 tax attorneys, 1.2 million workers at H&R Block, Jackson Hewlett, and tens of thousands of smaller tax preparation firms.[5]

Standing diametrically opposed to this formable array of tax minimizers are the 100,000 employees of the Internal Revenue Service (IRS). Their mission is to ensure that we pay all of the taxes that we owe.

Think about it. More than three million people—including support staff at the accounting and tax preparation firms—earn their livelihood either helping their clients avoid paying taxes or, in many cases, actually evading them. And trying to hold the fort against them is a vastly understaffed IRS that tries its best to collect as many tax dollars as it can.

We have to spend over six billion hours working on our taxes—the equivalent of almost four million unpaid people working full-time.[6] And most of us *still* have to pay someone else to complete our tax returns. Just imagine what it would be like to have a really simple tax code.

WHO GAINS FROM A COMPLICATED TAX CODE?

The hardest thing to understand in the world is the income tax.
—Albert Einstein

Everyone complains about our amazingly complex tax system, but no one *does* anything about it. Why not? Because some very powerful groups like it just the way it is.

Let's round up the usual suspects. First on our list are the accountants and tax lawyers, many of whom earn their livelihood by helping their clients find loopholes in the tax code so they can save lots of money. Next, there are the politicians, who amass hundreds of millions a year in campaign contributions from a variety of special interest groups.

But who *really* stands to benefit the most from our tax code? You were right if you said, "the rich." These folks save hundreds of billions of dollars a year on their taxes because that's exactly what our tax code is designed to do.

Accountants

We have 1.4 million accountants—more than the rest of the world put together.[7] Why do we need so many of them? Mainly to help business firms and individual taxpayers deal with the complexities of the Internal Revenue Code. And, of course, to minimize their taxes. In fact, if there *were* no Internal Revenue Code, we could probably get by with about one-tenth the number of accountants we currently employ.

Tax Attorneys

You don't hire a tax attorney primarily to prepare your income tax return. These folks do much more important work: they minimize your tax liability by utilizing all the tax breaks and loopholes they can find in the Internal Revenue Code. Only relatively large corporations and rich individuals can afford to hire them. But their fees, which may run over a thousand dollars an hour, may save you millions of dollars.

Tax Preparers

If you can't afford a tax attorney, or even a more modestly priced accountant, you can always go to one of the tens of thousands of tax preparation firms. Nearly all of them are located in store-front offices and usually promise "instant tax refunds." These "refunds" are, in effect, very high-interest, short-term loans that provide these firms with much of their profits.

Politicians

Congress writes our tax laws, and our Internal Revenue Code is its masterpiece. Virtually every loophole was placed there intentionally. All of these serve the interests of the big political donors—rich individuals and large corporate political action groups. Even though our convoluted Internal Revenue Code is wasting vast amounts of our nation's resources, it serves the interests of our elected representatives and their big contributors.

The Rich

> *For whosoever hath, to him shall be given, and he shall have abundance.*
>
> —Matthew 13:12

Because of the major loopholes in our Internal Revenue Code, the rich save hundreds of billions of dollars a year on their taxes. This is not to say that the rich don't pay a lot of taxes. In fact, as the *Wall Street Journal* editorial board often points out, the rich are paying a larger share of total federal income taxes than in the past.[8] How could this be if the top marginal tax rate is just over half of what it was thirty-five years ago?

Because the rich are making so much more than they had been back in the 1970s and 1980s, even though they are taxed at much lower rates, they *still* pay more taxes. Suppose that in 1980 you paid $5 million in taxes on your $10 million income, and in 2015 you paid $10 million in taxes on an income of $40 million. Your average tax rate fell from 50 percent to just 25 percent. But the amount of money you paid in taxes doubled—from $5 million to $10 million.

LOWER TAX RATES

Only the little people pay taxes.

—Leona Helmsley, billionaire who was sentenced to prison for four years for federal income tax evasion

Since 1981, the rich have benefited from a series of tax breaks. The first was the economic centerpiece of Ronald Reagan's presidency, when the top marginal federal income tax rate was lowered from 70 percent to just 50 percent. But the rich did even better in 1986, when Reagan signed another law that lowered the top marginal rate to just 28 percent. This extremely low rate was subsequently raised to 39.6 percent.[9]

But wait—that's not all, folks! Suppose you are *really* wealthy and get most of your income from stock market investments and higher property values. Instead of being taxed at the rate of 39.6 percent, because this income is considered capital gains, you need to pay just 20 percent.

Warren Buffett, who, in 2008, was the third-richest person in the world, pointed out the absurdity of the capital gains tax. That year he made $46 million, but had to pay only 17.7 percent of it in federal income tax. His secretary, who earned just $60,000, paid 30 percent of that in federal income tax and payroll tax.[10]

Using 1992 data from the tax returns of the four hundred people reporting the largest incomes, the IRS found that this group has aggregate taxable income of $16.9 billion, and paid federal taxes of 29.2 percent. By 2012 the aggregate taxable income of the top four hundred had soared to $111.1 billion, while their tax rate had fallen to 20.3 percent—considerably lower than the rate paid by the average American taxpayer.[11]

More than 90 percent of all working age Americans get at least 90 percent of their income from their wages or salaries.[12] The rich get most or all of their income from small business profits, interest, dividends, and capital gains.

Wages and salaries are subject to double, triple, and even quadruple taxation. New York City residents, for example, pay federal, state, and local income taxes, as well as federal payroll tax. The typical middle income wage-earning couple pays about 30 percent of their income in payroll and income tax.[13] But the multimillionaire investor pays just 20 percent of his capital gains in taxes.[14]

Still another tax break provided to the rich was a substantial lowering of the federal inheritance tax. The top rate, which had been 70 percent from the mid-1970s to 1981, was reduced to just 35 percent. Less than 1 percent of all heirs have to pay any tax on their inheritances.[15]

Very high inheritance taxes from the 1930s through the 1970s—on both the state and federal level—led to the decline of most of our nation's great family fortunes. Today few, if any, members of the Rockefeller, Ford, DuPont, Carnegie, Astor, Harriman, Kennedy, and Vanderbilt families have made the Forbes 400 list, which includes nearly all of our nation's billionaires.

But since the late 1970s things have been looking up for the super rich. The Walton family alone, heirs to the Wal-Mart fortune, has a net worth that is greater than that of the poorest 40 percent of all American families.[16]

Despite the widespread perception that the so-called "death tax" mainly targets the small family-owned businesses, it actually applies to just 5,300 very rich families each year.[17] So do you *still* think we should abolish the federal inheritance tax?

How do we explain this seismic shift from a relatively even distribution of income before the late 1970s to one that is increasingly unequal? Most of this shift is explained by the growing strength of the Republican Party, which has traditionally favored the well-to-do and the rich over the lesser folk. In fact, one can sum up its main economic policy prescription in just two words—cut taxes.

THE COST OF COMPLYING WITH THE INTERNAL REVENUE CODE

Think about it: more than three million people—including support staff at the accounting and tax preparation firms—earn their livelihood either helping their clients legally avoid paying taxes or, in many cases, actually illegally evading them. Just imagine what it would be like to have a really simple tax code. We have to spend over six billion hours working on our taxes, and most of us *still* have to pay someone else to complete our tax returns.

SHARING THE TAX BURDEN

Why has the Internal Revenue Code grown so large? A primary reason is the wide array of deductions, credits, write-offs, exclusions, and loopholes—technically labeled "tax expenditures"—that have been inserted into the tax code. These now total close to $1.5 trillion, and most of the savings goes to rich and relatively well-off taxpayers.[18] To take advantage of most of these tax expenditures, you would need to itemize your personal income tax deductions. But the large majority of less affluent taxpayers, rather than itemize, take the standard deduction.

Here are the main 2016 deductions aimed mostly at the rich:

- Exclusion for employer-provided health insurance (cost to Treasury: $216 billion).[19] While rank-and-file workers are asked to pay an increasing share of their insurance premiums, executives enjoy much more generous "gold-plated" policies.
- Mortgage deduction (cost to Treasury: $75 billion). The wealthy fifth of all families received more than four-fifths of this subsidy.[20]
- Exclusion for 401(k) contributions (cost to Treasury: $74 billion).[21]

SOLUTIONS

Some people would like to replace the federal personal income tax with a national sales tax. That would surely simplify our tax system, while freeing us from having to do our taxes every year. But it would be a regressive tax, falling disproportionately on the poor. That is because the poor spend all of their incomes, while the rich save a large part of theirs. Consequently the poor would pay a larger percentage of their income in sales tax than the rich.

Others think a flat personal income tax of, say, 15 percent would be a fine idea. Perhaps its greatest advocate is Steve Forbes, a two-time Republican presidential candidate, a billionaire who inherited his money—and who has the *chutzpah* to suggest ending the federal inheritance tax.[22] A flat personal income tax would, in effect, be regressive, since it is much harder for a poor family to pay 15 percent of its income than a rich family.

The best feature of our personal income tax is that it's progressive. Its burden is borne more heavily by the rich, since they have to pay—on average—a greater percentage of their income than the poor. It needs to be fixed, but not scrapped entirely. I would eliminate all the deductions and loopholes and tax on all income above a certain amount, with four or five different tax brackets. Best of all, nearly everyone could do their own taxes in about five minutes on a postcard-size tax form.

Perhaps in the not too distant future Congress will actually enact some kind of tax reform. And if it does its job the way it should, we could release three million people from their make-work jobs, while freeing the rest of us from six billion hours of time wasted in preparing our taxes.

Chapter 18

TELEMARKETERS, AMBULANCE CHASERS, AND OTHER MAKE-WORK OCCUPATIONS

People holding make-work jobs do not produce any useful goods or services. Suppose you invent a "cure" for baldness that you know does not grow even one hair. But you go ahead and hire hundreds of people to manufacture, advertise, and sell your magic formula, which you call "Hair Again"—and your competitors dub "Gone Tomorrow." Millions of people buy it. It takes a while until they realize it doesn't grow hair. In the meanwhile, you've created hundreds of jobs. By the time your customers catch on, you've sold your business to a large hair products company and have started another company that sells round trip tickets to Saturn and Jupiter.

Still, wasn't Hair Again good for our economy, since it *did* put hundreds of people to work? What do *you* think?

Okay, what if *all* the goods and services produced by an economy added nothing to our standard of living. What if our farmers grew food that was inedible, none of our consumer electronics worked, and none of our surgeons performed a successful operation? What if every employee just went through the motions of working, without producing any useful goods or services? You can just imagine what it would do to our standard of living.

In the last chapter, we talked about the three million people who owed their jobs to our convoluted Internal Revenue Code. In *this* chapter we'll talk about millions of other make-work jobs performed by the American labor force.

PHONE WORK

Telemarketers

These are the folks we all love to hate. They seem to have an uncanny sense of knowing just when we're sitting down to dinner, so they can read their prepared spiel about whatever it is that they're selling. Your phone rings, and when you say, "Hello?" there's a two- or three-second pause before some poor fool gets on the line and asks if this is Mr. or Ms. So and So, often managing to mispronounce your name. Never mind how many "Do not call" lists you're on: these folks just can't resist talking to you.

Now here's my question: What is the value of the work of these telemarketers? What useful service do they provide? If the millions of them who try to scratch out livings interrupting our dinners just walked off their jobs, what would be the loss to our economy? By how much would our output of useful goods and services decline? And—who knows?—many of them might even find jobs where they would actually be producing something useful.

Telephone Solicitors

One step above telemarketers are the folks who make calls on behalf of some worthy cause—whether the American Civil Liberties Union, Planned Parenthood, the American Heart Association, or your college's "development" office. At least they have *some* connection to you, and they are better educated and much more polite than most telemarketers. But again, what tangible good or service do they produce?

Attorneys

We have 1.3 million attorneys—far more than any other country in the world.[1] Because we are a nation of laws, we need lots of lawyers. Indeed, they are a large part of the price we pay to live in a democracy. But surely that price need not be nearly so high. Most other democracies manage to get by with a much lower number of lawyers per capita.

In the last chapter we talked about tax lawyers, whose job it is to reduce the tax bills of their clients. Back in chapter 15 we discussed the role of defense lawyers in our criminal justice system—which happens to be the largest in the world.

Divorce lawyers and personal injury lawyers make their livings solely from other peoples' misfortunes. Indeed, thousands of law firms advertise by telling potential clients to come in for a free consultation, with no money up front, and a fee of just one-third the damages award. So sue! What have you got to lose? (See box: "The Ambulance Chasers.")

In the 1987 film *Wall Street*, a character, Gordon Gekko, famously proclaimed, "Greed is good!"[2] Well, that greed *did* bring on our recent financial crisis. And the greed of the ambulance-chasing lawyers and their clients, who often think that they have hit the lottery, has driven up the costs of medical malpractice insurance and healthcare costs.

Finally, let's ask ourselves why so many of our laws need to be hundreds of pages long? Perhaps to take care of all the special interests? Or to create work for lawyers, since who else could even begin to understand these laws? After all, since lawyers write our laws, they have an incentive to make them as complicated as possible.

THE HEALTHCARE SECTOR

Healthcare is our largest economic sector, accounting for 18 percent of our GDP; in 1960 it was just 5 percent.[3] Did our nation's health improve *that* much?

The Ambulance Chasers

Attorneys specializing in medical malpractice are often referred to as "ambulance chasers." You can find their most blatant ads in your telephone Yellow Pages. Here are some taken from the Brooklyn Yellow Pages, where legal ads account for nearly 30 percent of the ads:

Injured? Get the Money You Deserve!
Accident Victims: Get Maximum CA$H Settlement.
Millions Won For Medical Malpractice & Accident Victims!
Multimillion-Dollar Awards for Injured Clients.
Hurt Bad? Get Justice!
Injured by a Construction Accident? Receive Money for Your Injuries.

Between one-quarter and one-third of healthcare spending is on administrative costs.[4] Millions of clerical workers employed by doctors and hospitals while away their hours negotiating with insurance company employees over reimbursement. In chapter 13 we talked about all the make-work and inefficiencies in this sector.

SALES REPS

You are, of course, familiar with the concept of the unpaid internship, which purports to give recent college graduates a chance to gain invaluable work experience, and possibly even a step or two up the career ladder. And indeed for some, things actually *do* work out. But long before anyone thought up the concept of the unpaid internship, hundreds of thousands of business firms hired sales reps on straight commission to "cold sell" their goods or services.

These jobs have always been relatively easy to get because the sales reps earned no money unless they sold something. In addition, since cold selling means you don't get any sales leads, it was left up to the new sales reps to find their own customers. This was almost always extremely time-consuming. Suppose one hundred brand-new sales reps are hired, given a day of training, and sent out into the field. Some get no sales and quit before the end of the week. That was my own experience selling burial plots for a cemetery. Others manage to get a few sales here and there, but their commissions do not provide them with even the minimum hourly wage. So they too soon quit. But the company still makes a profit on every sale.

After a couple of months, perhaps four or five reps are still on the job, and maybe two or three are actually making a decent living. So hiring one hundred new sales reps is basically a make-work project. You sink or swim. Those who sink have earned little or no money. But they sure got some great work experience.

Our large insurance companies have taken the unpaid sales trainee concept to its logical conclusion. Again, one hundred sales reps are hired, and provided with their own desks, phones, stationery, and training materials (for which they are often charged hundreds of dollars). Before they can legally sell insurance, they need to pass a state exam. Still, they do go out on sales calls with seasoned reps—an invaluable training tool. And just to put them at ease, they are encouraged to talk to their friends and family members about the wonders of life insurance and whatever other types of insurance might be useful.

But they are not allowed to actually *sell* insurance policies. Luckily, the seasoned rep they are working with *is* qualified to do that—*and*, of course, to receive the commission. And so, the company is making money on their trainees even before they receive their licenses. Again, of the one hundred trainees who start out, just a fortunate few last even six months. But the company still makes money on many of them, even if the new reps never see a penny in commissions.

In effect, then, the vast majority of the millions of sales reps hired each year end up quitting because they did not earn enough money to live on. Obviously, they were being exploited. And from the standpoint of our economy, these folks are superfluous to the process of producing useful goods and services. But they *do* play a major role in the make-work economy.

OUR BEST AND OUR BRIGHTEST

Over the course of the last six chapters we have established that we employ far too many sales reps, accountants, lawyers, tax preparers, real estate agents, insurance claims adjusters, educational administrators, bankers, financial advisors, stockbrokers, hedge fund operators, and other professionals. In effect, many among their ranks are basically engaged in make-work, because they are not producing any useful goods or services. This is not to say that these folks are not honest, hardworking people. It's just that their work does not produce anything that we actually need.

Perhaps no nation makes such poor use of its best and its brightest college graduates, not to mention the millions with advanced degrees. Writing more than thirty years ago, Robert Reich, who would later become President Clinton's secretary of labor, noted that our latest managerial innovations "have been based on tax avoidance, financial management, mergers, acquisitions, and litigation."[5]

Reich went on to observe,

> Paper entrepreneurialism relies on financial and legal virtuosity. Through shrewd maneuvering, accounting and tax rules can be finessed, and the numbers on balance sheets and tax returns manipulated, giving the appearance of greater or lesser earnings. Assets can be rearranged on paper to improve cash flow or to defer payments. And threatened law-

> suits or takeovers can be used to extract concessions from other players. Huge profits are generated by these ploys. . . . But they do not enlarge the economic pie; they merely reassign the slices.[6]

Reich seems to contradict what Adam Smith wrote two centuries before in his classic, *The Wealth of Nations,* when discussing the consequences of business owners who were motivated by self-interest: "By pursuing his own interest he frequently promotes that of the society more effectually than when he really intends to promote it."[7]

Smith argued that the owner of a small business, whose sole motivation was earning a large profit, provided his employees with jobs, and produced a good or service that customers were willing to buy. But Reich might ask whether the person who becomes a hedge fund operator helps society more than the person who becomes a social worker. Do we go for the MBA or the MSW?

Who was right—Reich or Smith? Actually, *both* were right. Reich was writing about people who chased the big bucks in the make-work economy, while Smith wrote about business entrepreneurs in the *real* economy—those who were engaged in producing useful goods and services. I would bet that if Smith were alive today, he would agree with Reich, and vice versa.

THE GOVERNMENT SECTOR

Do too many people hold government jobs? Of the 152 million Americans who are currently employed, how many work for the government?[8] Go ahead and take a guess.

The answer is twenty-two million.[9] Of those, how many work for the federal government (including the US Postal Service)?

Here's a surprise: it's just 2.8 million.[10] Of the rest of all government employees, over five million work for state governments and over fourteen million work for local governments.[11]

Do you think we have too many government employees? If yes, then which ones would you cut? Do we have too many air traffic controllers, teachers, building inspectors, police officers, firefighters, and school crossing guards?

Chances are you don't want to fire many of *these* folks. Almost half of all state and local employees work in education—although many are not teachers. There's definitely quite a bit of slack here. Also, we have parallel bureaucracies at the federal, state, and local levels for education, housing, labor, health, taxation, and public assistance.

A recurring theme at nearly every government agency is to look busy even when there is no work to do. Surely we don't want to see any of our civil servants reading a book, doing a crossword puzzle, playing a computer game, or making a personal phone call. But somehow it's okay to hire too many people in the first place, and then to demand that they look busy all of the time.

So I think it would be fair to say that there are perhaps a couple of million government employees who do little or nothing all day. The only problem is figuring out which ones they are. Maybe we could start with the ones who are napping.

SOLUTIONS

There are a number of things we could do to eliminate millions of make-work jobs. Drastically simplifying the Internal Revenue Code would not only make three million make-work jobs disappear, but it would save taxpayers six billion hours spent in tax preparation.[12] Meaningful healthcare reform would eliminate another three million make-work jobs. Reducing calls from telemarketers and telephone solicitors would also help a lot. And every new law should be no more than a few pages, and be written in clear English, so that a lawyer would not be needed to interpret it. Just doing that would eliminate the need for perhaps half of our lawyers.

How do we stop telemarketers from bothering us? The "Do not call" lists have had very limited effect. Maybe very high fines, criminal charges, or even a steep tax on each call would help curb this annoying activity. Also, there is a piece of technology called Nomorobo that blocks all telemarketing calls.[13] More than a million telemarketers might lose their jobs.

I would like to see the calls of telephone solicitors restricted—even those who call on behalf of worthy causes. Perhaps the best solution would be to confine their calls to a list of people who placed their numbers on a "Do call" list.

At this moment there are hundreds of thousands of newly hired sales reps who are working on straight commission, earning little or nothing, despite their best efforts. Knowing in advance that just 2 or 3 percent of these new hires would eventually be able to make a living in these jobs, their employers led them to believe that with hard work, they would succeed. To curb this practice, sales reps working on straight commission should be covered by the federal minimum wage law, currently $7.25 an hour.[14] That would discourage hiring sales reps for what are essentially make-work positions.

Still, make-work is very deeply embedded in our economy. On the positive side, the most promising strategy to get people to leave make-work positions would be to offer them higher-paying jobs producing useful goods and services. We shall come back to this topic in chapter 26.

Part VIII

THE ECONOMIC, SOCIAL, AND POLITICAL CONSEQUENCES OF WASTING OUR RESOURCES

So far we have seen how we have been wasting our resources in major sectors of our economy. This has had very substantial economic, social, and political consequences. But the bottom line is this: our standard of living is much lower than it would have been if we had used our resources more efficiently.

It's easy to mistake a consequence for a cause. Our huge budget deficit, for instance, is often blamed for our bad economy. But, as we shall see in chapter 20, it is a consequence of other problems, which, in turn, have resulted in a large waste of resources. Similarly, in chapter 22, we'll see that our increasingly unequal distribution of income, while a serious problem, is caused by still other major problems, which also resulted in wasted resources.

Chapter 19

THE ECONOMIC CONSEQUENCES OF WASTING OUR RESOURCES

Since the 1970s, our output of useful goods and services and our rate of economic growth have been increasingly depressed because of the eight fundamental economic problems we listed in chapter 1. They contributed to six additional problems—also listed in that chapter—which we shall now consider.

OUR WASTEFUL SUBURBAN LIFESTYLE

Our initial post–World War II suburban development consisted largely of modest homes on small plots of land. In Levittown, a New York City suburb, the houses were all eight hundred square feet.[1] But today, new suburban homes are three times that size, even though families are much smaller than they were during the postwar baby boom.[2]

Many of these homes have in-ground backyard pools and huge front lawns, which go largely unused. Homes are so spread apart that parents need to arrange "play dates" for their children. Richer families own multiple homes, some of which are dubbed "McMansions." Because most suburban families own several cars on which they depend for every trip away from home, about half of the suburbs are covered by roads and parking spots.[3]

Think of all the underutilized resources that support our wasteful suburban lifestyle. Imagine if these resources were devoted to producing goods and services that could actually raise our standard of living.

THE TRANSPORTATION SECTOR

As mentioned in previous chapters, between the 1930s and the 1960s our world-class public transportation system was replaced by automobile travel. Today the typical American family devotes almost 20 percent of its budget to transportation, while in the rest of the industrialized world, that figure is less than 10 percent.[4] Among other consequences of this shift, we have become very dependent on foreign oil, and to ensure an uninterrupted flow, we have been spending hundreds of billions of dollars a year maintaining a military presence around the world. For most of the last two decades our oil imports have accounted for about one-third of our trade deficit.[5]

For the last sixty years we have allowed our national railway network to deteriorate. In addition, today we are virtually the only economically advanced nation without a high-speed rail line. Without world-class railroads, we cannot be a world-class competitor.

Our entire transportation bill comes to approximately $3 trillion—about 17 percent of our GDP.[6] No other nation on earth devotes such a huge percentage of its output to transportation. Were our transportation system as efficient as those of our main economic rivals—the members of the European Union, China, Japan, Taiwan, and South Korea—our costs would be about one-third lower. In other words, one-third of the $3 trillion we now spend on transportation is wasted.

In the 1950s and 1960s, during the peak of the baby boom, it was certainly understandable for growing families to buy station wagons and other large passenger cars. But today, the median family size is just two persons, and more than one out of every two new cars sold is classified as a "light truck."[7] Furthermore, car ownership is now so widespread that there are more licensed motor vehicles than there are licensed drivers.[8] This self-indulgent excess comes at the cost of wasting a vast amount of our nation's resources.

Beyond the huge inefficiencies of our transportation system, we must also factor in the hundreds of billions of dollars of additional costs incurred each year to pay for our vast network of gas stations, service stations, auto insurance brokers, highway construction contractors, as well as for our automobile companies and their dealerships, marketers, and advertisers.

THE PUBLIC EDUCATION SECTOR

We have long prided ourselves on having the best educated workforce in the world, and until perhaps thirty years ago, that was certainly the case. But our public education system has been deteriorating since the 1960s, while those of our global competitors have not only caught up, but have now largely surpassed ours. Employers have been asking themselves why they should hire American workers when they can find better educated workers in India, China, and Eastern Europe who are willing to work for just a fraction of the pay their American counterparts are earning.

Two unpleasant truths about our public education system stand out. First, we are wasting hundreds of billions of dollars a year in a futile attempt to teach students who are unable or unwilling to learn. That outcome is further ensured by their being taught largely by people who are not that much better educated themselves.[9] And second, about half of our eighteen-year-olds are so poorly educated that most of them will never earn much more than the minimum wage.

This is our bottom line: without a well-trained and well-educated labor force, no nation can compete successfully in the global economy. So we have the worst of *both* worlds. We are wasting hundreds of billions of dollars each year, while *not* producing enough well-educated high school graduates.

THE HEALTHCARE SECTOR

The inefficiencies of our huge healthcare sector have two major economic consequences. They depress the wages and employment in the rest of the economy. And they require the employment of millions of people in make-work jobs.

The reduction of wages and employment are just two of the economic consequences of our system of having employers provide a major part of our medical insurance. Employee-based healthcare has had four additional adverse economic effects:

1. Through most of our history the average wage rate rose at about the same rate as productivity—or output per hour. But since 1973, although productivity continued to increase—generally between 2 and 3 percent each year—the average hourly wage paid to 80 percent of all American workers has remained about the same.[10] Most of this wage stagnation is explained by our rapidly rising healthcare costs.

   When employers determine how much they are willing to pay their employees, they consider the entire compensation package, which includes wages, health insurance premium payments, and retirement benefits. Since the early 1970s, rapidly rising healthcare insurance premium payments have accounted for virtually all employee compensation increases. In other words, the money that would have otherwise gone for wage increases went instead to paying for rising healthcare costs.

2. It discourages the hiring of more employees. Many businesses cite the cost of healthcare insurance as a factor in their decision not to hire.
3. When the unemployment rate shoots up, as it did during the Great Recession, millions of workers and their families lose their healthcare coverage—and some even fall into poverty.
4. It makes American goods and services less competitive in the global marketplace.

   For instance, American automobile makers have long maintained that healthcare insurance premiums add $1,500 to $2,000 to the cost of producing each car.[11]

Not only do the inefficiencies of the healthcare sector reduce employment and wages throughout our economy, but it also is responsible for the creation of about three million make-work jobs. These are filled by people employed by healthcare providers and by the insurance companies with whom they are in constant contact. Armies of clerical workers employed by doctors, hospitals, and other providers try to maximize insurance reimbursement, while the insurance claims adjusters seek to minimize it. Basically, their efforts cancel each other out, but their salaries, benefits, and the cost of the space they occupy and the equipment they use add hundreds of billions of dollars to our annual healthcare bill. Still more importantly, the labor of all these people is wasted on make-work, rather than expended on work that produces useful goods and services.

THE MILITARY-INDUSTRIAL COMPLEX

Unlike investment in health, education, infrastructure, or in plant and equipment, military spending does not generate any future wealth or output. Nor does it produce any useful goods or services that raise our standard of living.

The resources used to produce military goods and services might have otherwise been used to produce investment goods or consumer goods and services. If we can shift some of these resources to more productive uses, we can raise our standard of living. So the question comes down to this: How much can we cut down on our military spending without endangering the safety of our nation?

The argument against our extremely high military spending is not that this money is being spent inefficiently—the proverbial thousand-dollar toilet seats, multibillion-dollar missile systems, and huge cost overruns notwithstanding. I argue that we can defend ourselves perhaps just as well by spending half of what we are spending. In other words, we are wasting about $350 billion a year on unnecessary defense spending.

THE CRIMINAL JUSTICE SECTOR

The United States leads the world in imprisoning its citizens. One out of every one hundred adult Americans is behind bars, about five times the world's average.[12] Since 1980, when our prison population was half a million, it has more than quadrupled to 2.2 million.[13] Although this part of our criminal justice system is euphemistically called "corrections," almost two-thirds of those released from prison are back in again within three years.[14]

About half of our inmates are mentally ill or are drug addicts.[15] Both groups would be better served—and much more economically housed—in treatment facilities. Two-thirds of all prisoners are black and Hispanic males, the large majority of whom grew up poor and dropped out of school.[16] Many of them could be helped by vocational training in jobs programs, which would be a lot cheaper and economically useful than putting them in prison.

Close to two million people are directly employed in the criminal justice sector, and some seven million Americans are under its supervision either imprisoned, on probation, or on parole.[17] Few of them are producing any goods or services that enhance our standard of living.

How much does it cost to run our criminal justice sector? The annual bill comes to approximately $250 billion.[18] Once again we need to ask if our economy is getting a good return on this investment.

THE FINANCIAL SECTOR

The financial sector is sucking money out of the productive sector—the sector that creates the goods and services that we need. Finance has become primarily a speculative activity: investors are making bets on what other investors are doing rather than actually financing jobs and real investment. The financial sector, including banking and financial services, insurance, and real estate is much larger than its counterparts in the rest of the world. Consequently, it is wasting vast quantities of our scarce resources, especially labor and capital. These could have been put to use producing useful goods and services, which would have substantially increased our standard of living.

THE INTERNAL REVENUE CODE AND THE MAKE-WORK SECTOR

Our Internal Revenue Code is a blatant make-work project that wastes the labor of three million Americans who earn their living largely by helping taxpayers comply with it, while minimizing their tax liabilities. In addition, taxpayers are forced to put in another six billion hours a year in unpaid work—the equivalent of the labor of almost four million people working full-time for a year.[19]

Our relatively low capital gains tax rate enables the rich to pay an average of about 20 percent of their incomes, while many middle-class families are taxed at a higher rate.[20] This tends to redistribute income from the middle class to the rich, making our income distribution growingly unequal. Our low capital gains tax rate also encourages financial speculation over productive economic activity.

Tens of millions of Americans hold make-work jobs. Some, like tax attorneys and hedge fund operators, are extremely well compensated. Most others, like those who work in healthcare, tax preparation, and telemarketing earn much more modest incomes. And at the bottom of the barrel are the newly hired sales reps who work strictly on commission and earn absolutely nothing—or next to nothing. What all these folks have in common is that none of their hard work results in the production of any socially useful good or service. Their work is completely wasted.

SUMMING UP

In sector after sector of our economy we are wasting vast quantities of our labor and capital. Back in the 1940s, when America was a lean and mean industrial machine, we held that waste to a bare minimum. But over the years, we have become increasingly inefficient.

Until now, each generation enjoyed a higher standard of living than its parents' generation. But Americans coming of age today face a future in which the lifestyle their parents enjoy will be out of reach. More and more people in their middle and late twenties are still living with their parents—unable to afford their own apartments, let alone their own homes. Millions of college graduates are struggling to find decent jobs—or even unpaid internships. And those with no more than a high school education are fortunate if they can find jobs paying much more than the minimum wage of \$7.25 an hour.[21] Hopefully, the minimum wage will be substantially higher when you read these words.

Chapter 20

OUR TWIN DEFICITS

When we complain about "the deficit," we are obviously referring to the federal budget deficit. And when the deficit soared over $1 trillion in 2009 during the depths of the Great Recession, there certainly was a lot to complain about. But we actually have a second deficit—one that is just as worrisome and almost as big.

Our foreign trade deficit has averaged nearly $600 billion over the last ten years (see Fig. 20.2 later in this chapter). And while foreigners finance over *half* of our budget deficit, they finance *all* of our trade deficit.[1]

In this chapter we shall answer three questions:

1. What are the causes of our twin deficits?
2. What are their consequences?
3. How can they be reduced?

THE FEDERAL BUDGET DEFICIT

Deficits don't matter.

—Vice President Dick Cheney[2]

How big is the federal budget deficit? Let's look at the record. Fig. 20.1 lists our deficits (and surpluses) since 2000.

How did our deficits get to be so big, especially over the last few years? And what can be done to reduce them? Before we can answer those questions, let's get some political and historical perspective.

Fiscal Year	Deficit or Surplus
2000	+236
2001	+126
2002	-158
2003	-378
2004	-413
2005	-318
2006	-248
2007	-161
2008	-459
2009	-1,413
2010	-1,294
2011	-1,300
2012	-1,087
2013	-680
2014	-485
2015	-438
2016	-587
2017	-559*

Fig. 20.1. Federal budget deficits and surpluses, 2000–2017. Source: *Economic Report of the President: Together with the Annual Report of the Council of Economic Advisers* (Washington, DC: US Government Publishing Office, 2017).

*Congressional Budget Office estimate, April 2017.

Creating Deficits: The Democratic Way and the Republican Way

Former US secretary of commerce Pete Peterson, who served under President Reagan, observed that Democrats never met a spending program they didn't want to expand, nor did Republicans ever meet a tax they didn't want to cut.[3]

Since the time of President Franklin Roosevelt's New Deal during the Great Depression, the Democrats, according to Peterson, "turned the federal government into a massive entitlements vending machine which dispenses new benefits in return for organized political support, and defers costs as far as possible into the future."[4]

Traditionally, the Republicans have advocated small government, which meant low government spending and low taxes. But all that changed in 2001 when President George W. Bush entered the White House. Peterson, a life-long Republican, believes that Bush and the Republican congressional majority, actually outdid the Democrats:

> Big-government conservatives don't bother much about balanced budgets or the size of the rest of government. Abroad, they care about "national greatness" and national security. At home, they care about a powerful and popular government that can put together winning political coalitions. They will embrace big spending to outflank the Democrats and cement the loyalty of Americans whom they regard as their natural constituency—the employed, the affluent, the invested, and the retired.[5]

We're Entitled

Social Security, Medicare, and Medicaid are the big three of our government entitlement programs. By law, tens of millions of Americans are entitled to over $2 trillion dollars a year in benefits—primarily Social Security, Medicare, Medicaid, veteran's benefits, and federal government employee pensions. That comes to 11 percent of our GDP.[6] By 2020, unless Congress acts, that share will grow to almost 14 percent.

The most important characteristic of any entitlement program is having a powerful constituency. The fastest-growing part of our population, those over sixty, are much more likely to vote than younger Americans.[7] So it would be political suicide for anyone running for public office to even hint at trimming Social Security or Medicare benefits. And keep in mind that the baby boom generation—by far, the largest generation in our history—has been moving into retirement age.

Even Medicaid has a large, if not powerful, constituency—the poor—and, to a growing extent, the elderly. As our permanent underclass and senior population grow, so too will Medicaid spending.

High Defense Spending

In addition to huge entitlements, defense spending is the other big component of federal spending. During the first decade of the new millennium, defense spending doubled—even allowing for inflation. This was due almost entirely to President George W. Bush's "War on Terror," which he declared in the wake of the terrorist attacks on 9/11, and to our wars in

Afghanistan and Iraq. Even today, after ending our military involvement in Iraq, and winding down our involvement in Afghanistan, our military spending continues to be about $700 billion a year.[8]

From Surpluses to Mega Deficits

After nearly three decades of deficits, our federal budget finally began running surpluses in 1998. But in 2002 we returned again to deficits (see Fig. 20.1). In addition to rapidly climbing defense spending, tax receipts fell. This fall was precipitated by the lingering effects of a mild recession in 2001, as well as by a pair of fairly substantial tax cuts, the so-called "Bush tax cuts" of 2001 and 2003. Still, by today's standards, those deficits were not very large.

But then came the financial crisis and the accompanying Great Recession. Our deficit shot up from $161 billion in 2007 to $1,413 billion—a little over $1.4 trillion—just two years later (see Fig. 20.1). Every recession pushes up the federal budget deficit because tax receipts fall, while government spending on unemployment insurance benefits, public assistance, food stamps, Medicare, and other programs to aid the poor and the unemployed are ramped up. But the Great Recession of 2007–2009 necessitated a massive federal rescue package that totaled well over $1 trillion in tax cuts and additional spending. That, more than anything, is what drove the deficit up to $1.4 trillion.

Since the end of the recession in mid-2009, our deficit has come down by more than two-thirds. Still, we face deficits of about $400 billion a year for the foreseeable future. Here is a list of the main contributing factors:

- The continued retirement of the baby boomers driving up entitlement spending.
- Continued high defense spending.
- Rising healthcare costs driving up Medicare and Medicaid spending.
- The refusal by congressional Republicans to allow any tax increases.

THE FOREIGN TRADE DEFICIT

More and more of our imports come from overseas.

—President George W. Bush

America is being flooded with imports, and millions of workers are being thrown out of work. Americans are buying not just foreign-made cameras, cell phones, TVs, and tablets, but also foreign-made steel, textiles, apparel, personal computers, cars, and toys. But why worry? Since the world is now a global village, and we all buy from and sell to each other, why should we buy something from an American firm when we can get a better deal from a foreign firm? Why indeed?

I'll give you two good reasons why we need to worry about our foreign trade deficit: (1) as you can see from the table in Fig. 20.2, it's huge; and (2) we owe it all to foreigners.

Year	Deficit
2000	-380
2001	-369
2002	-425
2003	-501
2004	-615
2005	-714
2006	-762
2007	-705
2008	-709
2009	-384
2010	-495
2011	-548
2012	-537
2013	-476
2014	-505
2015	-500
2016	-502

Fig. 20.2. Foreign trade deficits, 2000–2016. Source: *Economic Report of the President: Together with the Annual Report of the Council of Economic Advisers* (Washington, DC: US Government Publishing Office, 2017).

From the beginning of the twentieth century until the 1970s we ran a small trade surplus virtually every year. Our nation was largely self-sufficient. We consumed what we produced, while enjoying the highest standard of living in the world. Foreign trade was relatively unimportant. But after World War II we exported substantial quantities of our manufactured goods to the Western European nations, still recovering from the wartime devastation.

The Great American Market

Consider the experience of Japan in the 1950s through the 1980s, and China since the early 1980s. Both countries hitched their growing, but relatively primitive economies to the huge economic engine provided by the United States. For more than a century, we have been not just the world's largest economy but also, by far, the largest consumer market.

In the mid-1950s, Japanese industrialists targeted the rich American market, flooding it with black-and-white TVs and, eventually, color TVs, cars, cameras, and other consumer goods. The Japanese home market was too small and too poor to absorb more than a fraction of what they produced. They undersold American producers—generally selling well below cost—and eventually driving them out of business.[9]

Starting in the early 1980s, the Chinese, following the Japanese model, also began selling in the huge American market. The Chinese home market was even smaller and poorer than Japan's had been. China made Hong Kong and the surrounding coastal provinces into a veritable export platform, shipping off low-end consumer electronics and, in time, TVs, microwave ovens, refrigerators, and now low-end automobiles.

Generally, trade is a two-way street, but in the case of Japan and China our exports were just a fraction of what we imported from them. This unbalanced exchange created a codependent relationship. We needed their goods, while they needed our market. When we didn't have the money to pay for these goods, Japan and China simply lent it to us.

Here's how this worked. We paid in dollars issued by the Federal Reserve. The Bank of Japan and the Bank of China ended up with these dollars, which they used to buy up US Treasury debt. In other words, they accepted our dollars as payment, and then recycled those dollars by lending them back to the US Treasury. In effect then, they lent us back our own money to buy their goods.

This worked out well for both sides. The American consumers got stuff they couldn't afford to pay for. And the United States was able to run huge budget deficits each year, which were financed mainly by the Banks of Japan and China.

So far, so good. There is no question that we will need to keep borrowing money to finance our trade and budget deficits. But will the Japanese and the Chinese continue to need the American market?

Our Manufacturing Base and High-Wage Jobs

Our only chance of surviving as a high-wage nation with a rising standard of living is to produce a lot of high-tech, high-value-added goods and services. The problem is that we have been losing our manufacturing base and that without it, we are also losing a lot of well-paying high-tech service jobs. Maintaining a high-tech manufacturing base is important for two reasons.

First, production is where the lion's share of value added is realized. It is where the "rent on innovation" is captured. If your company comes up with a great innovation—say, a much-improved cell phone—unless it can also manufacture that phone, it's not going to make a lot of money by just licensing the technology to another firm.

Second, unless research and development is tightly tied to the actual manufacturing of a continually improving product, your company will fall behind the cutting edge of incremental innovation. For example, by abandoning the production of TV sets, the US electronics industry quickly lost the know-how to design, develop, refine, and competitively produce subsequent generations of the VCR, the camcorder, and the DVD player.

It would be just great if we could all be software engineers, product designers, and research scientists, but we need a strong high-tech manufacturing base to support these activities. As that base continues to erode, we will lose more and more of those jobs. While many Americans will still find well-paid work, the rest of us may end up flipping burgers, pumping gas, waiting tables, and greeting customers at Wal-Mart.

Why Have We Been Running Huge Trade Deficits?

Until the early 1970s we basically consumed what we produced. Foreign trade was only of peripheral economic importance, and we ran a small, but positive trade balance every year. Since the mid-1970s, however, we have been running trade deficits. They have averaged about $565 billion over the last ten years (see Fig. 20.2).

Our huge trade deficit, while a very serious problem, is really a symptom of other more fundamental problems that were alluded to throughout this book. Let's consider the four main reasons why we have been running such large trade deficits.

1. **Our post–World War II suburban development**

   Back in part II we saw how our suburbs were built with the implicit assumption that we would always be able to count on a cheap and plentiful supply of oil. Consequently the suburban transportation system was based entirely on automobile travel, while most of our freight was shifted from rail to truck transportation. As a result, after American oil production peaked in 1970, we became increasingly dependent on foreign oil, and today must import about 40 percent of our oil.[10]
2. **The high cost of defense**

   We talked in part III about the need to safeguard our oil supply. This has necessitated the spending of hundreds of billions of dollars a year to maintain military bases all over the world and sending our navy to patrol the major shipping lanes. This effort has boosted our trade deficits by tens of billions of dollars, since we need to pay the expense of feeding and housing all these troops.
3. **High consumption and low savings**

   Our huge trade deficits are also caused by our extremely high national consumption rate and our consequent low savings rate. While the Chinese, who are much poorer, can save 40 percent of their incomes, the average American saves three or four.[11] Since much of what we buy is sold to us by foreigners, it follows that we would run up huge trade deficits.
4. **Our shrinking manufacturing base**

   We saw in chapters 7 and 8 that as our manufacturing base shrank over the last five decades, we became increasingly dependent on imported consumer goods. Thousands of American manufacturers have moved their factories to low-wage countries to lower their production costs. Not only have our imports soared, but our own manufactured goods have been losing their market share abroad.

LAST WORD: CAUSE AND EFFECT

Our federal budget deficit and our foreign trade deficit, while extremely serious problems, are really the result of many *other* problems. They are certainly not the causes of our national economic decline, but rather symptoms of it.

Still, it is necessary to acknowledge that both of these deficits are *themselves* very serious economic problems. How do we reduce—and ultimately eliminate—our budget and trade deficits? Only by solving the many problems that have created them. Our twin deficits are both consequences of the wasteful use of our resources.

We cannot continue to run such huge budget and trade deficits indefinitely. We cannot continue to go deeper and deeper into debt, especially when more and more of that debt is owed to foreign lenders—who, it happens, are also our global economic competitors. Eventually, even a nation as rich and powerful as the Unite States will run out of credit. And a nation that is in long-term economic decline will run out of credit even faster.

Chapter 21

OUR UNRAVELING SOCIAL CONTRACT

What's good for General Motors is good for the country.
—Charles Wilson, CEO of General Motors

After the traumas of the Great Depression and World War II, our leaders of government, business, and labor concluded that we needed a social safety net to ensure that the vast majority of Americans would have steady jobs, health insurance, and, in their retirement years, at least some minimal source of income. By the early 1950s this social safety net was fully in place.

An informal accord between our large labor unions and corporations ensured steady employment in exchange for labor peace. In addition, virtually all large employers provided their workers with free or low-cost health insurance, as well as private pensions upon their retirement. In 1938 the federal government inaugurated the Social Security system, which, a decade later, was providing retirees with a substantial part of their incomes. Then, in 1965, the Medicare and Medicaid programs were added, providing government-financed healthcare to the elderly, the disabled, and the poor.

For the first two and a half decades after the end of World War II, this system of publicly and privately provided pensions and health insurance worked quite well. But as well-paying manufacturing jobs began to disappear, our social safety net started to fray. No longer could large corporations guarantee virtual lifetime employment, nor could they continue to foot the entire bill for health insurance, which had become increasingly costly. By the 1990s, the social contract among government, labor, and business had unraveled.

We are a nation governed largely by contracts. Some are formal contracts, like agreements between labor unions and large corporations. And there are those codified by law, such as the federal minimum hourly wage and the payment of unemployment insurance and Social Security benefits.

THE NEW DEAL

Some major parts of our safety net were put in place under President Franklin Roosevelt's New Deal during the second half of the 1930s. The Social Security system provides retirees with some income. Unemployment insurance benefits enable many of those who are temporarily out of work to meet their minimum needs. Federal minimum wage legislation guarantees almost all workers a minimum hourly wage rate. And, of course, the Federal Deposit Insurance Corporation safeguards our bank deposits.

This contract with the American people provided a certain measure of economic security, and would be greatly strengthened by President Lyndon Johnson's Great Society program in the mid-1960s.

THE POSTWAR LABOR-MANAGEMENT SOCIAL CONTRACT

Worried about inflation, the federal government imposed wage and price controls during World War II, making it much harder for most employers to find enough help. Nearly every able-bodied man was in the armed forces, and the unemployment rate had fallen below 2 percent. As mentioned in chapter 13, to attract and retain employees, many large companies, looking for creative ways to give raises, provided pensions and health insurance. This development would soon differentiate our nation from all the world's other rich nations, whose governments provided universal health insurance and retirement pensions.

Most business owners prospered during the war, especially those with military contracts. Some were labeled "war profiteers," not exactly a term of endearment. Union leaders and their rank-and-file members felt that they had been shortchanged by their corporate employers during and immediately after the war. These workers, whose wages had been largely frozen by wartime controls, had not shared very much in the wartime prosperity, and now they were mad and were not going to take it anymore. So they made 1946 a great year for strikes. Some of the strikes caused considerable public inconvenience, and helped elect a Republican Congress. A year later the Taft-Harley Act was passed. Its main provision was to make it harder for labor unions to recruit new members.

But labor peace was soon at hand. By the early 1950s our large corporations and labor unions had informally agreed to a social contract. In return for the promise of labor peace, workers would share the gains in productivity. For the next twenty years, real wages grew by 2.5 to 3 percent a year, while benefits also improved.[1] (Real wages are defined as wages of constant purchasing power, after allowing for inflation.) Between 1950 and 1979 the number of workers covered under corporate pension plans rose from 10 percent to more than 55 percent.

This was a win-win situation. Corporate profits were high, and real wages rose enough to enable most blue- and white-collar workers to maintain secure middle-class lives. Dad supported the family while mom stayed home with the kids. They got to live the American Dream.

Also implicit was a guarantee of long-term, if not lifetime, employment, in exchange for the loyalty of the more senior employees of large corporations. Workers were not fired without cause, and those laid off during slack times had reasonable expectations of being rehired when business picked up again. During the postwar period there was enough prosperity to spread around. In the immortal words of Charlie Wilson, the head of General Motors, "What's good for General Motors is good for America."[2]

The federal government was also a party to this implicit social contract. By smoothing out the business cycle—ameliorating the extremes of inflation and recession—and refraining from interfering with workings of the free-enterprise market economy, the government enhanced the already prosperous postwar business climate. As Thomas Jefferson had put it, the government that governs best, governs least.

What had allowed this arrangement to work so well in the postwar years was that our economy had been an almost closed system based on mass production and mass consumption. We consumed nearly all of what we produced. Foreign trade was relatively unimportant. Americans built and drove American cars. Our clothing, consumer electronics, major appliances, and nearly everything else we bought were "Made in the USA." And the chances were that they were made by union members whose jobs paid good wages and provided excellent benefits.

But in the 1950s, as Japanese TVs began pouring into the humongous American market, soon followed by a flood of cars and other consumer goods from Europe and Asia, we began to hemorrhage manufacturing jobs. And with the loss of those jobs, the ranks of our great industrial unions fell precipitously. No longer was it in the interest of large corporations to offer lifetime employment, nor was it necessary to worry about the loyalty of their employees. And so, corporate leaders decided, why continue to shell out so much money for fringe benefits? Their employees were happy if they could just hang on to their jobs, while their labor-negotiating partners, the large unions, were losing members left and right.

THE GI BILL OF RIGHTS

In 1944 Congress passed the GI Bill of Rights, which not only offered veterans mortgage loans, as well as loans to start businesses, but also provided monthly stipends for those who wanted help with educational costs. By 1956, when the programs ended, 7.8 million veterans, about half of all who had served, had participated.[3] A total of 2.2 million went to college, 3.5 million to technical schools below the college level, and 700,000 to agricultural schools.[4] The GI Bill made college affordable to men from lower-middle-class, working-class, and even poorer backgrounds, and was almost entirely responsible for enrollments more than doubling between 1940 and 1949.[5]

Obtaining a college degree provided a means to get a good job and become a member of the emerging great American middle class. The GI Bill of Rights helped make us a much more egalitarian society.

MAKING AFRICAN AMERICANS A PARTY TO THE SOCIAL CONTRACT

Until the late 1940s African Americans were completely excluded from mainstream American life. They lived in segregated neighborhoods, their children attended separate schools, and they were almost never hired for any but the most menial, low-paying, dead-end jobs. Jim Crow laws in the South denied them not just the right to vote, but even dictated where they sat in restaurants and movie theaters, which water fountains they could drink from, and which hotels would put them up for the night. I can remember the tiny railroad station in Augusta, Georgia, back in 1961. There was a schoolyard fence that divided it into a section for "Whites" and for "Colored." And, of course, throughout the South blacks would ride at the back of the buses. To me, a kid from Brooklyn, it seemed like another country.

In the twenty years since the end of World War II, there were some major changes. President Harry Truman integrated the armed forces, while Brooklyn Dodger president Branch Rickey helped Jackie Robinson become the first black Major League Baseball player. And of course there was the 1954 Supreme Court decision that paved the way for school integration. But still, there was massive resistance throughout the South, and it took the passage of the landmark civil rights legislation of the mid-1960s to finally break the back of Jim Crow.

Until then, few African Americans had been a party to our social contract. Very few had been able to buy homes in the suburbs, find decent jobs, and, in the South, even register to vote. Now, at long last, African Americans finally had a good chance of attaining the American Dream. But as luck would have it, not long after they arrived, the party would begin to break up.

THE GREAT SOCIETY PROGRAM

The person most responsible for the passage of the civil rights legislation was President Lyndon Johnson. After he won the election of 1964 in a landslide, and carried with him very large Democratic congressional majorities, he used his considerable political skills to push through two monumental healthcare initiatives—Medicare and Medicaid. These were aimed at providing medical care for the elderly, the disabled, and the poor. Although Medicare and Medicaid became extremely costly and wasteful programs, they *did* enable tens of millions of Americans to obtain excellent healthcare.

President Johnson had proclaimed a "war on poverty," and his Great Society program was the most ambitious federal government initiative since the New Deal to end poverty and provide old-age security. After his landslide electoral victory over Sen. Barry Goldwater in 1964, the Democrats had very heavy majorities in both houses of Congress and were able to accede to the president's wishes.

Another very important addition to the social safety net at that time was the food stamp program, which provided the poor and near poor with the funds to meet the basic food necessities. The earned income tax credit, introduced in the 1970s, supplemented the incomes of the working poor families.

These were the last significant additions to the social safety net until President George W. Bush persuaded Congress to add a Medicare drug prescription plan that went into effect in 2005. There was, however, a significant subtraction made nine years earlier—the Welfare Reform Act of 1996, passed by a Republican Congress and signed by President Bill Clinton, a Democrat. What this law did was tell welfare mothers to get a job! But the enduring message was that the federal government would no longer promise to take care of the destitute.

THE UNRAVELING OF THE SOCIAL CONTRACT

A social contract depends on a shared sense of well-being. That sense lasted a good twenty-five years, but then things began to change. The oil price shocks of the 1970s, the beginnings of the shrinkage of our manufacturing base along with declining union membership, rapid technological change, and the renewed competition from the rebuilt economies of Japan and Western Europe were all contributing factors.

By the early 1980s layoffs of auto, steel, textile, and apparel workers became permanent as plants closed and jobs migrated to Mexico, Japan, Southeast Asia, and, more and more, to China. At first the federal government attempted to stave off these layoffs by imposing import quotas on cars, steel, textiles, apparel, and other manufactured goods. But at best, these measures just slowed the layoffs, postponing the inevitable shrinkage of our manufacturing base. American corporations, faced with strong and growing foreign competition, were able to cut costs drastically by shipping abroad most of their lower-skilled operations. Real wages, which had been steadily increasing since the end of the Great Depression, began to decline after 1973.[6] Union membership, which peaked in 1955, when it claimed 35 percent of the labor force, was in free fall.[7]

Jeff Faux sees globalization as the prime cause of the unraveling of the social contract:

> [T]o the extent that the economy is globalized, high wages, and the taxes needed to pay for social protections, put domestic firms at a cost disadvantage with firms in other countries. If you can manufacture your goods anywhere, you'll choose the economy with the lowest taxes and most desperate workers. The larger the international sector of the economy, the less power the government has to . . . maintain the social contract. . . . Social welfare programs, which must be paid for in taxes, add to the costs of production and appear increasingly "unaffordable."[8]

Steven Greenhouse, the *New York Times* labor reporter, wrote a book describing just how globalization has enabled large employers to squeeze its rank-and-file workers. This passage summarizes its effect:

> One of the least examined but most important trends taking place in the United States today is the broad decline in the status and treatment of American workers—white-collar and blue-collar workers, middle-class and low-end workers—that began nearly three decades ago, gradually

gathered momentum, and hit with full force soon after the turn of this century. A profound shift has left a broad swath of the American workforce on a lower plane than in decades past, with health coverage, pension benefits, job security, workloads, stress levels, and often wages growing worse for millions of workers.[9]

ENTITLEMENT SPENDING

As the baby boom generation (those born between 1946 and 1964) continue swelling the ranks of our retired senior citizens, they will keep pushing up federal government expenditures on the big three of our entitlement programs—Social Security, Medicare, and Medicaid. In the coming years we shall see growing political pressure, almost entirely from Republicans, to at least slow the rate of growth of these programs.

Opposition to the growth of these programs raises a much broader issue. Because of the widespread waste of our nation's resources, one may question whether our economy will be able to produce enough goods and services to continue supporting our senior citizens in the style to which most of them have grown accustomed. And a major part of that lifestyle is the level of healthcare provided by Medicare and Medicaid.

CUTTING ENTITLEMENTS

The great economic minds of our elected representatives in Congress are largely in agreement that since entitlements account for half of all federal spending, if the budget deficit is to continue to be reduced, we'll need to curb the continued rise of entitlement spending. And so, the running debate among Republicans and Democrats, and between the members of both parties as well, is how to do this. A large majority of Republicans want to make major cuts in the food stamp program, while most Democrats agree to making relatively small cuts. But a sizeable contingent of liberal Democrats demands that the food stamp program—which serves just the poor and the near poor—to not be cut at all.

Missing from this grand debate is any discussion about *why* it has become so necessary to make spending cuts, and, more broadly, *why* we have been running such large budget deficits in the first place. But, in fairness, how many Americans even have a clue about the underlying causes of our deficits?

As a result, we are fighting the wrong war. Instead of quarrelling over how our economic pie should be distributed, we need to be expending all of our efforts to bake a much larger pie. Again, because we continue wasting vast amounts of resources, we are ending up with a lot less useful goods and services. Instead of trying to cut down on this waste and producing *more* output, we are expending a great deal of time and energy fighting over the size of our shares.

CUTTING GOVERNMENT SUBSIDIES

Public libraries, public transportation, and the US Postal Service (USPS) are three very important services that are subsidized by the government. While there is a broad consensus that these services should be subsidized, there is widespread disagreement how large these subsidies should be. Those who would cut them argue that our nation just cannot afford to shell out billions of dollars a year to keep these institutions functioning.

I would ask how can we afford *not* to keep them functioning. In fact, I would substantially expand their subsidies. Our libraries should be kept open perhaps twelve hours a day, seven days a week. Our public transportation system should be serving the vast majority of Americans, instead of just a tiny fraction. And the USPS should receive enough money to hire perhaps 200,000 additional employees, so that customers would not have to wait on long lines. And—who knows?—maybe some of the post offices could even stay open after 5:00 p.m.

CONCLUSION

With the decline of unions, the shrinkage of our manufacturing base, and now the growing threat of the offshoring of service sector jobs, the social contract between management and labor is pretty much just a fading memory. Today corporate America calls the shots, while their employees are usually happy just to hold on to their jobs.

The generation that came of age during the Great Depression used to warn its children of the importance of finding secure jobs. These children, the baby boom generation, just laughed at this advice, since most jobs *were* quite secure. But now, as they watch their own children struggling with downsizing, layoffs, and the offshoring of jobs, these baby boomers have come to realize that their parents had gotten it right after all.

Chapter 22

GROWING INCOME INEQUALITY AND THE SHRINKING MIDDLE CLASS

The test of our progress is not whether we add more to the abundance of those who have much; it is whether we provide for those who have too little.

—President Franklin D. Roosevelt
in his second Inaugural Address, 1937

Since the stock market crash of 1929, there have been two very different trends in our nation's distribution of income. From the 1930s through the late 1970s, incomes became much more equal, as the middle class expanded. By the 1970s most families had attained the American Dream, which included a house, a car, a stay-at-home mom, and a dad who held a secure job that paid enough to support his family.

But since then that trend was reversed. As our income distribution grew less equal, the great American middle class began to shrink. The stereotypical suburban family supported by one wage-earner became less and less common. Well-paying jobs with benefits became harder to find. Long before the Great Recession, it had become clear that the middle class had suffered a great reversal of fortune.

We've already talked about the loss of most of our manufacturing base, the offshoring of millions of jobs, the decline of our labor unions, and the unraveling of our social safety net. Terms like downsizing, outsourcing, and offshoring have become part of our vocabularies.

From the 1930s through the early 1970s, the federal government introduced many programs to help the poor, the working class, and the middle class. The creation of government jobs, unemployment insurance, welfare benefits, food stamps, low-rent housing, Social Security, the GI Bill of Rights, Medicare, Medicaid, and the earned income tax credit all increased the living standards of the have-nots, and were funded largely by the haves. But since the mid-1970s, most of the new initiatives—especially with regard to tax cuts—were beneficial mainly to the rich.

As we shall see, the balance of political power these last three and a half decades has swung from Democratic dominance to a Democratic-Republican stalemate. Our elected officials, who have become extremely dependent on campaign contributions, are now much more responsive to the demands of those who give them the most money. One could say that we have the best government that money can buy.

We often hear that the middle class is being squeezed. More and more women with young children have had to join the labor force because their husbands were no longer earning enough to support their families, although many women with young children also joined the labor force because they simply wanted to work. And now, millions of recent college graduates have had to move back in with their parents. While most of our troubles are attributed to the Great Recession, they have been caused mainly by trends that have been going on for decades.

From the early 1940s through the early 1970s, the middle class expanded quite rapidly, while all income groups enjoyed steadily increasing incomes. But since the early 1970s, while the incomes of the rich grew still more rapidly, the incomes of almost everyone else stagnated, and for some, they even declined. Although the overwhelming majority of Americans consider themselves middle class, the actual size of this group has been in long-term decline. To sum up: the rich are getting richer, the poor are getting poorer, and the middle class is being squeezed.

THE GREAT COMPRESSION AND THE GREAT DIVERGENCE

The Great Compression and the Great Divergence were opposing trends in our nation's income distribution. During the Great Compression, which ran from the mid-1930s through the late 1970s, our income distribution became much more equal. But during the Great Divergence, which began at the end of the 1970s, and has continued since then, incomes became much less equal.

The Great Compression

Back in the 1930s and 1940s, the federal government imposed very high income and inheritance taxes on the rich, making it much harder to accumulate huge fortunes, and to pass them on from one generation to the next. This set the stage for an era of relative income equality in the decades following the close of World War II. The period was dubbed "the Great Compression" by economic historians Claudia Goldin and Robert Margo.[1]

In the 1930s, under the New Deal, there were four very important government initiatives that made incomes more equal—Social Security, public assistance, unemployment insurance, and the minimum hourly wage. Then in the 1960s, Medicare, Medicaid, and the food stamp program were added. And finally, in the 1975, the earned income tax credit was introduced.

The labor movement strongly boosted wages, not just of its own members, but of millions of other blue- and white-collar workers as well. Although the movement reached its zenith in the mid-1950s, it continued to strongly influence wage rates and fringe benefits for the next couple of decades.

The Great Divergence

There are two main explanations for this massive shift in income to the rich. First, since the late 1970s the incomes of the rich increased much faster than those of everyone else. And second, the rich have received much more favorable tax treatment in recent decades. First, let's look at the factors that enabled their incomes to rise so quickly.

There has been a steady increase in corporate power since the early 1970s. Much of it was due to globalization and the decline of labor unions. While the wages of most Americans have stagnated, after-tax corporate profits have soared, and along with them the earnings of the upper ranks of corporate management—not to mention those of the largest stockholders.

Back in the 1960s and 1970s, when women were largely barred from professional careers, doctors, lawyers, corporate executives, and other high-earning professionals would marry women who earned much less. Soon after marriage, the women would drop out of the labor force, staying at home to raise their children. Since then, vast numbers of college-educated women have entered the relatively higher-paying professions, married similarly high-earning professional men, and continued working after getting married. As Timothy Noah observed, "These two trends meant that a significant number of women were able to double their husbands' family income the moment they said, 'I do.'"[2]

Now let's turn to the tax treatment received by the rich since the early 1930s. Like other taxpayers, the rich are subject to the personal income tax, but they are taxed at relatively high rates. The federal capital gains tax and the inheritance tax are both paid mainly by the very rich.

The top marginal tax rate on the personal income tax was relatively low—except during World War I—until 1932, when it shot up from 25 to 63 percent.[3] It continued rising, reaching 94 percent during World War II.[4] It was reduced to about 70 percent from the mid-1960s until the early 1980s, when it was lowered to 50 percent.[5] Since 1987 it has generally been between 30 and 40 percent, and it is currently about 39.6 percent.[6]

Capital gains—profits from the sale of stock, bonds, real estate, and other assets held for more than one year—have generally been taxed at a lower rate than salaries and wages. The maximum tax rate on capital gains was just 12.5 percent from 1922 through 1933.[7] Between 1934 and 1967 the maximum rate was usually 25 or 30 percent.[8] It then drifted upward, reaching 40 percent in the late 1970s.[9] Then it began to trend, falling to a low of 15 percent in 2010.[10] It was raised to 20 percent in 2013.[11]

Now let's take a closer look at how the poor, the middle class, and the rich did during the Great Compression and the Great Divergence.

THE POOR

The basic problem faced by the poor is a lack of decent jobs that pay well enough to support their families. Those trapped in our inner-city, suburban, and rural slums are almost completely outside the social and economic mainstream. But as bad as their economic prospects have been, the federal government has managed to make things still worse.

The working poor have jobs that pay at or a little above the federal minimum wage rate—currently $7.25 an hour.[12] When the minimum wage rate was initially set at twenty-five cents an hour in 1938, it was not high enough to support a family. And although this rate has been raised occasionally, it has not nearly kept up with the rate of inflation.

In recent decades the federal government has actually been cutting its support of the poor. In the next chapter, we'll examine how a lack of decent jobs, cuts in federal antipoverty programs, and the effects of other forces have hurt the poorest Americans.

THE MIDDLE CLASS

Because the middle class depends almost entirely on wages and salaries for its livelihood, let's see what has happened to the average hourly wage, adjusted for inflation. And then we'll learn how the middle class has coped since the early 1970s.

Rising Productivity and Stagnant Wages

Our rising standard of living has been made possible by rising productivity—our output per hour. Historically, workers' pay has been closely tied to their productivity. During the period from 1945 to 1973 the productivity of our labor force doubled, as did the average hourly wage rate and median family income (both adjusted for inflation).[13]

The median family real income in 1973 (in 2015 dollars) was $50,000.[14] Half of all American families had incomes of more than $50,000, and half had incomes of less than $50,000.

Then things changed: between 1973 and 2015 productivity rose by 115 percent, while the median family income (allowing for inflation) rose by just 11 percent.[15] And that increase was due solely to the huge rise in the employment of women, most of them mothers of young children. Indeed, hourly pay, adjusted for inflation, has not risen since 1973.[16]

Rising Consumption and Stagnant Wages

Between 1973 and 2007 the average middle-class family more than doubled its consumption expenditures.[17] How were they ever able to do this when the average hourly wage did not increase?

Most importantly, tens of millions of women—many of them with young children—entered the labor force. Today, nearly as many women as men are holding down jobs.

A second way of keeping up was that people worked much longer hours.

They cut their savings rate from over 10 percent of personal income to less than 2 percent.[18]

And finally, families went further and further into debt by borrowing on their homes and by running up their credit card balances.

In 2007 we hit a wall. Nearly all the women who could join the labor force had done so. Few people were willing and able to work still-longer hours. And the housing bubble finally burst. Within short order we had a financial crisis, a huge recession, and a painfully slow economic recovery. The bottom line was that Americans could no longer keep increasing their spending.

The End of the American Dream

The American dream—the good life in exchange for hard work—is no longer guaranteed.

The dream of a steady job providing good pay and benefits, and the hope that one's children will enjoy a better future, has been slowly dying. And as it dies, the great American middle class is disappearing.

THE RICH

The rich are different from you and me.
—F. Scott Fitzgerald

Yes, they are different. They have more money.
—Ernest Hemingway

There are the rich, and then there are the rest of us. So what's the dividing line? Some would say that the rich are those who earn over a million dollars a year, while others would set the bar still higher. While there is no precise definition, a few years ago, a group calling itself "Occupy Wall Street" provided perhaps the most widely used definition—the 1 percent, as opposed to the other 99 percent (see box).

INCOME INEQUALITY BEFORE AND AFTER TAXES AND GOVERNMENT SPENDING

We've seen incomes grow increasingly unequal since the 1970s. But does the federal government play the role of Robin Hood, heavily taxing the rich and distributing that money to the poor? Yes, it does. The only problem is that the governments of nearly every other wealthy nation redistribute a much larger share of the incomes of the rich to government programs helping the poor.

Steven Rattner, who has earned a large fortune on Wall Street, explains how this can be:

> [O]ur taxes, while progressive, are low by international standards and our social welfare programs—ranging from unemployment benefits

The 1 Percent and the 99 Percent

Let's begin by stating six important facts:

- Between 1928 and 1970, the income share of the top 1 percent fell from 24 percent to 9 percent; from 1970 to 2007 it rose to nearly 24 percent.[19]
- The top 1 percent pulled in 22.5 percent of total income in 2012, their biggest share in more than one hundred years.[20] Their share fell to 20.2 percent in 2014.[21]
- The top 1 percent owns 40 percent of our country's wealth.[22]
- In terms of income, the top 1 percent earns more than the bottom 50 percent.[23]
- The Walton family—heirs of Wal-Mart founder Sam Walton—owns more wealth than the poorest 40 percent of all Americans.[24]
- The top 0.1 percent receives half of all capital gains in the United States.[25]

Are you in the top 1 percent? You would qualify if you earned at least $429,000 in 2013 (the last year this measurement was done).[26]

You would also be in the top 1 percent if you had a net worth (your assets minus your liabilities) of at least $8.4 million in 2012.[27]

Hedge fund operators and other financial market speculators make hundreds of millions—and in some cases billions—of dollars a year, while the middle class, the working class, and the poor try to get by on stagnant or shrinking incomes.

The chief executive officers (CEOs) of large corporations have been doing particularly well. In the mid-1960s, the average CEO earned about twenty-five times the earnings of a typical employee at his company. In the first decade of the new millennium, that ratio had shot up to over three hundred.[28] During much more hopeful economic times, President John Kennedy proclaimed, "A rising tide lifts all boats." Today, even when the tide is rising, a few boats are lifted a lot, while most of the other boats are not being lifted much at all.

> to disability insurance to retirement payments—are consequently less generous.[29]

Rattner concludes that because our nation collects so little in taxes, it cannot afford to pay for generous social welfare benefits, like those enjoyed by the citizens of most other wealthy nations. This, of course, exacerbates the effect of our growingly unequal income distribution.

THE CONSEQUENCES OF INCOME INEQUALITY

What are the consequences of how unequally our income is distributed? First we'll look at the economic consequences, and then the social and political consequences.

The Economic Consequences of Income Inequality

If everyone received the same income, that would almost entirely destroy the incentive to work hard. If no matter how hard you worked, you'd still earn the same income, then why bother? On this point the lazy and the industrious would agree.

In addition, the poor, the working class, and most of the middle class consume most or all of their income. The rich, however, save a large part of theirs, and that money is channeled into needed investments in new plant, equipment, and software. Without that savings and investment, our economy would not be able to grow.

The United States has one of the least equal distributions of income in the economically developed world.[30] To the degree that hard work is rewarded by income, a substantial amount of income inequality could be a good thing. But if income were extremely unequally distributed, then we would have millions of people starving to death.

So the real question is, how equally should income be distributed? There is, of course, no correct answer, so understandably there is widespread disagreement among economists and laymen as to whether our income distribution is too unequal, just about right, or even not unequal enough.

Still, there is a large body of research showing that rising income inequality slows economic growth. The definitive study was done by two International Monetary Fund economists, Andrew Berg and Jonathan Ostry, who calculated that a 10 percent decrease in income inequality increased the expected length of a period of economic growth by 50 percent.[31] Basically, more income inequality, they concluded, leads to slower economic growth.

Berg and Ostry also made this observation about the linkage between growing income inequality and financial crises:

> [T]he increase in U.S. income inequality in recent decades is strikingly similar to the increase that occurred in the 1920s. In both cases there was a boom in the financial sector, poor people borrowed a lot, and a huge financial crisis ensued.[32]

Walter Isaacson believes that our growingly unequal income distribution goes against our national identity:

> The fundamental creed of America is that if you work hard and play by the rules, you can support your family with dignity and believe that your children will have an even better future. But that is being lost as the middle class continues to be hallowed out and the poor get left further behind.[33]

The Social Consequences of Inequality

More than twenty years ago Christopher Lash perceived how much the rich had already removed themselves from the American socio-economic mainstream: "Many of them have ceased to think of themselves as Americans in any important sense, implicated in America's destiny for better or worse. Their ties to an international culture of work and leisure . . . make many of them deeply indifferent to the prospect of American national decline."[34]

In *Richistan,* Cornell economist Robert Frank observed that the rich have created "their own country within a country, their own society within a society, and their own economy within an economy."[35]

Frank described a separation that has been taking place in recent decades—the privately policed gated communities, the private clubs and schools, the social networks, corporate boards, and other meeting places set aside exclusively for the rich.

To sum up, the rich and the near rich are separating themselves from the rest of America in four ways:

1. They are lowering their legal obligation to support expensive social programs by inducing Congress to lower their tax rates and to gut these programs.
2. No longer bound by the social contract, they are moving millions of well-paying jobs abroad.
3. They are isolating themselves physically and socially from the other 95 percent of all Americans.
4. They are thinking of themselves increasingly as rich people, having much more in common with other rich people—foreigners and Americans—than with the rest of their fellow citizens.

The Political Consequences of Income Inequality

The great British historian Arnold Toynbee wrote about the causes of the rise and fall of civilizations. Invoking Toynbee, Hedrick Smith observed that the recent shift in economic and political power reflects a time in our own civilization

> when the business and political leadership class changes from acting as "the creative minority" that inspires and leads the rise and flowering of a civilization, into becoming "the dominant minority" of "exploiters" focused primarily on sustaining and expanding their wealth and power. . . . This shift . . . he contends, is a major cause of the schisms in the body politic that contribute to the disintegration of a civilization.[36]

Does our growing income inequality pose a danger to our democratic form of government? As defined by President Abraham Lincoln in his Gettysburg Address, democracy is a government "of the people, by the people, for the people." But today, while a rich person and a poor person each has one vote, our elected representatives are much more likely to listen to the large contributor than to the rank-and-file voter.

The rich, and their corporate allies, pour huge amounts of money into the reelection campaigns of their favorite members of Congress. They would not be spending all this money unless they were getting a good return on their investment.

As our income distribution grows increasingly unequal, what will happen to our democratic form of government? Let me tell you about a change you can believe in. We shall soon be able to replace the word *democracy* with a more appropriate word—*plutocracy*. Before you know it, we shall have a government *of* the rich, *by* the rich, and *for* the rich. And it will be a very good government. It will be the best government that money can buy.

LAST WORD

"The greatest generation," forged by the Great Depression and World War II, went on to shape our increasingly egalitarian postwar nation. People from all walks of life suffered through the Depression and then served together during the war. We were all Americans, and in the decades after the war, we had become a truly middle-class nation.

But the times have changed. The rich are withdrawing, the middle class is shrinking, and the permanent underclass is growing. Our increasingly unequal distribution of income is exacerbating these trends. We are well on our way to making a mockery of the bold words from our Declaration of Independence: all men are created equal.

Chapter 23

POVERTY AND THE GROWING PERMANENT UNDERCLASS

For the poor will never cease out of the land.

—Moses, Deuteronomy 15:11

For ye have the poor always with you.

—Jesus, Matthew 26:11

From the time of the Civil War to the late 1950s, our nation's economic activity was centered in the industrial cities of the North and Midwest. But as the post–World War II suburbanization proceeded, most of our factories, department stores, and offices moved to the suburbs. By the early 1970s our cities had been largely abandoned, not just by the white middle and working classes, but by most major employers as well.

As the white middle and working classes left the cities, their places were taken by poor African Americans from the rural South, Mexican Americans, Puerto Ricans, and, later, people from the West Indies. All hoped to find decently paying jobs and to live the American Dream. For two centuries the cities had provided a step or two up the economic ladder for European immigrants, so why should it be any different for native-born Americans seeking a better life? But for many of these new arrivals, that dream turned into a nightmare. The entry-level jobs were disappearing, and with them went any chance of a better future.

The abandonment of our cities led to widespread poverty, rising crime, and the economic and social marginalization of about one-third of our black and Hispanic population. In the long run, perhaps the most harmful legacy of suburbanization has been the creation of a large and growing permanent underclass occupying our inner cities.

THE URBAN GHETTOES BEFORE AND AFTER SUBURBANIZATION

Suburbanization did not create urban poverty. Every city had its share of poor people, but in the 1940s and into the 1950s, they were mainly what we now call "the working poor." Neighborhoods were racially segregated, so poor blacks tended to live near middle-class blacks, while poor and middle-class whites lived in the same neighborhoods.

Although the post–World War II suburbanization is not entirely responsible for the intense inner-city poverty that took hold in subsequent decades, that process was probably responsible for most of it. Keep in mind that until the Great Depression, the suburbanization process generally took place within city limits, and that it coincided with the economic and social integration of recently arrived immigrants. But after the war this process changed radically. Middle- and working-class whites poured into newly built housing subdivisions that were located beyond the city limits—housing from which black and Hispanic families were completely excluded. As the bulk of entry-level jobs also moved into the suburbs, these families were left high and dry.

Most inner-city neighborhoods today are areas of intense poverty so isolated from the rest of America that they could just as soon be in another country. The housing is substandard, the streets are unsafe, youth gangs roam freely, and dope dealers openly sell their wares. Just surviving is a challenge.

DEFINING POVERTY AND COUNTING THE POOR

God must love the poor—he made so many of them.

—Abraham Lincoln

The most widely used poverty standard in the United States is the official poverty line calculated each year by the US Department of Agriculture. In 2015 that line was set at $24,300 for a family of four.[1]

The poverty rate is the percentage of Americans who are poor. In 2015 it was 13.5 percent. There were 43.1 million Americans living below the poverty line.[2]

THREE DIFFERENT POVERTY GROUPS

Are the poor just like all the rest of us? Or do they live in a very different world? There are really three rather distinct populations among *the poor*. About one-third of the poor are mired in long-term poverty. Another third are *temporarily poor*. The last third are *intermittently poor*.

Who are *the chronically poor*? Millions are sick or disabled, or for some other reason cannot hold jobs. Many are illiterate, have poor work habits, live in dysfunctional families, or are alcoholics or drug addicts. Most of the disabled collect Social Security disability benefits.

Many poor families receive public assistance. Though these benefits are limited to five years, the states continue providing them to 20 percent of their recipients—families headed by single mothers who are virtually unemployable.[3]

The temporarily poor are mainly middle- and working-class people who have suddenly and unexpectedly fallen upon bad times—a separation or divorce, the loss of a job, an expensive medical problem, a failed business, or the loss of a home. These temporary setbacks are overcome, usually within a year. But in the meantime, these people are living below the poverty line.

Because family incomes and expenses may vary from year to year, millions of families slip into or out of poverty. These are *the intermittently poor*. Their incomes seldom rise that much above the poverty line that they can ever attain the economic security most middle-class families enjoy. These families have a lot more in common with the poor than with the middle class.

So let's lump together the chronically poor and the intermittently poor and call them the *permanent underclass*. Both groups are becoming increasingly divorced from the economic mainstream. Taking the family to dinner at McDonald's and then a movie would be an unaffordable luxury. These are folks who struggle to put food on the table, a roof over their heads, and clothes on their backs.

THE GROWING PERMANENT AMERICAN UNDERCLASS

> *I still have the audacity to believe that people everywhere can have three meals a day.*
>
> —Martin Luther King Jr.

Occupying the sub-basement of the permanent underclass are the 2.2 million Americans in jail, and the five million more currently on probation or parole.[4] Most of the latter rotate in and out of jail. In addition, there are another million or so ex-convicts no longer under probation or parole, whose criminal careers are not completely behind them, and may be back behind bars.[5] In general they have lower IQs and are less educated than the general population. Therefore, they don't have a whole lot of vocational alternatives to committing crimes.

Ranking just above the criminal class are the two to three million Americans who are officially and unofficially homeless.[6] The US Department of Health and Human Services estimates that one-third of the hardcore homeless are mentally ill and half of the homeless are alcoholics or drug addicts.[7] Rather than provide them with shelter and treatment, our society just lets them fend for themselves. Besides the familiar street people, those living in public and private shelters, and squatters living in abandoned houses and apartments, there are many more shuttling from friend to relative and rarely having a permanent address.

Just how large is the permanent underclass? Let's do the math. We'll start with the people currently under the supervision of the criminal justice system—in jail, on probation, on parole, or awaiting trial. That's well over seven million people.[8] Add to them the two to three million homeless (by my own estimate), and, allowing for some overlap, these two groups account for some nine million Americans.

What about the five million people on welfare and the eight million on Social Security disability, as well as the millions more whose welfare benefits have run out?[9] Or all the street peddlers, nannies, house cleaners, day laborers—many of whom are illegal immigrants—who work in the underground economy? Or the millions of people trying to support themselves, and often their families, on minimum wage or just above minimum wage jobs? What about some of the elderly, trying to get by on their Social Security checks, picking through garbage looking for soda cans they can turn in for their nickel deposits? And all the people who depend on soup kitchens and food pantries for most of their meals?

Then there are the "working poor," earning no more than ten or eleven dollars an hour, who cannot fully support themselves and their families. Millions of them are employed by fast-food chains, retail stores, nursing homes, and janitorial services.

How many people does that add up to? Thirty million? Thirty-five million? Our population is about 325 million, so perhaps 10 percent of all Americans are members of the permanent underclass. What are their chances of ever permanently rising above the poverty line? About the same as hitting the lottery.

What will happen to the millions of blue-collar families whose breadwinners have lost their factory jobs? And the millions of other families whose breadwinners' white-collar jobs were offshored? In the coming years we shall see many of them joining the ranks of the permanent underclass. By 2020, not only will the permanent underclass be much larger, but most of its new members will be white.[10]

New York Times columnist Nicholas D. Kristof sees a grim future for what he terms "the white underclass":

> Today, I fear we're facing a crisis in which a chunk of working-class America risks being calcified into an underclass, marked by drugs, despair, family decline, high incarceration rates and a diminishing role of jobs and education as escalators of upward mobility.[11]

Our permanent underclass imposes a tremendous burden on the rest of our society. They commit most of the violent crimes, their children have brought down the level of education in the school systems in most large cities, they have ruined entire neighborhoods, and nearly half of their men end up in prison.[12]

Let's cut to the chase: many poor families are basically dysfunctional. They consist largely of single mothers, often addicted to crack or some other drug, with a string of abusive boyfriends with long criminal records, who rotate in and out of jail. Their children are neglected, sometimes abused, attend failing schools, join gangs, and usually end up in jail.[13]

These characteristics, working in synergy, have created a culture of poverty, allowing the poor to stumble along, very separate from the rest of the country. They are geographically located in the United States, but they rarely function within our society.[14]

Let us say for the sake of argument that the millions of Americans mired in the culture of poverty could somehow be rehabilitated to the extent that they were ready, willing, and able to join the labor force. Would they then be able to find decent jobs that provided them with enough income to at least bring their families out of poverty? The answer is a resounding "no!"

So here's the obvious question: What is the point of making a monumental effort to help the members of the permanent underclass become employable if there are no decent jobs for them? And from their own perspective: Why bother making the effort if the best they can hope for is a job at McDonald's or Wal-Mart?

CHILD POVERTY

One out of five American children is poor.[15] Our social support system for poor children is, by far, the worst in the industrial world.[16] Unlike most of these other nations, most of which have universal preschool and childcare, most poor children—not to mention the children of the working class—do not attend preschool programs. And then, the public schools they attend, from elementary school through high school, are the worst in the nation. It is no surprise that poverty is perpetuated from generation to generation.

Now let's talk about extreme childhood poverty. A study by Kathryn J. Eden and H. Luke Shaefer found that three million American children—one out of every twenty-five children—live in households earning less than two dollars a day. These families do get food stamps and depend on whatever help they can get from private charities.[17]

These children would be considered extremely poor if they lived in one of the impoverished countries in sub-Saharan Africa, but they are living in our country. Perhaps more than anything else we have talked about, this may be the most shameful evidence of just how far our nation has fallen.[18]

LAST WORD

The lives of those in the permanent underclass are filled with hopelessness and despair. The lack of decent jobs put most of these families into this predicament, but three or four generations later, it will take much more than a jobs program to get them on their feet again.

Dr. David Rogers, president of the Robert Wood Johnson Foundation, remarked that "human misery is generally the result of, or accompanied by, a great untidy basketful of intertwined and interconnected circumstances and happenings" that need attention if a problem is to be solved.[19] This point was amplified by Lisbeth and Daniel Schorr in their landmark work, *Within Our Reach*:

> The mother who cannot respond appropriately to a child's evolving needs while simultaneously coping with unemployment, an abusive husband or boyfriend, an apartment without hot water, insufficient money for food, and her own memories of past neglect—even a mother who is stressed to the breaking point can be helped by a neighborhood agency that provides care, counseling, and the support that convinces her that she is not helpless and alone.[20]

What can we do to alleviate poverty in America? Poverty is largely a result of many other problems that we've talked about in this book. Even if we were to devote a great deal of our resources to alleviating poverty, we would still leave all of the other problems unsolved. So what do we do? In the next chapter, I've drawn up a very long list.

Part IX

RESTORING THE AMERICAN ECONOMY

Not only has our economy been operating with decreasing efficiency, but a growing amount of what we are producing is of little or no use. The healthcare, education, and defense sectors of our economy are prime examples.

Here's a medical analogy that describes our situation. After not feeling well for some time, you finally go to your doctor. She tells you that she has some good news and some bad news. You ask for the bad news first. She tells you that you may be terminally ill. And the *good* news? If you agree to a very aggressive course of treatment, you may be able to fully recover.

Chapter 24 sums up the arguments supporting the prime contention of this book—that our economy has been self-destructing for many decades. Chapter 25 outlines what we can do at the federal, state, and local levels to reverse our course of economic self-destruction.

Throughout this book I have argued that a fair amount of our labor force does work that does not produce any useful goods or services. In chapter 26 I explain how these people could be moved from their current jobs to new ones that will put their talents to good use. The federal government will need to finance a program that will create at least fifty million jobs to put all the underemployed and the unemployed into productive work.

Despite the very large role that will be played by the federal government, much can still be accomplished on the state and local levels. But given the political gridlock at the federal level, it will be almost impossible to obtain the hundreds of billions of dollars in annual financing needed to carry out my plan. Still, presidential commissions can create a blueprint that can be used when our nation is finally ready to act. These strategies are described in chapter 27.

Chapter 24

HOW WE ARE WASTING OUR RESOURCES: THE BIG PICTURE

From the beginning of the nineteenth century through the middle of the twentieth, we created the greatest economy in the history of the world. But over the last eight decades, we have allowed much of our economy to self-destruct. During this period, some of the same factors that had been responsible for our ascendancy have been contributing to our decline. For example, more than a century ago, we created the first free universal public education system. Our well-trained and well-educated labor force gave us a huge competitive advantage in the emerging global economy. But today, just half of our eighteen-year-olds can function at an eighth-grade level and our students score near the bottom on most internationally administered exams.[1]

Similarly, by the early twentieth century, we had built the world's most extensive and efficient national railroad system. In addition, our intercity and intra-city streetcar lines enabled most Americans to get where they needed to go safely, conveniently, and usually for no more than a nickel. Our transportation network facilitated the creation of the world's first mass-production and mass-market economy. But we allowed our public transportation system to deteriorate, and to be replaced by cars, trucks, and planes. Ours is now perhaps the most inefficient transportation system in the developed world.

In the late 1940s we produced nearly half of the world's industrial goods.[2] But our manufacturing base has eroded, and since 1970 manufacturing employment has fallen by nearly 40 percent.[3] We still have, by far, the world's largest mass market, but increasingly, the needs of that market are being met by foreign suppliers.

In sum, over the last eight decades, many of our greatest economic assets have become liabilities. We have stood by while the world's greatest economy has been self-destructing. What follows in this chapter is a summary of what we've covered earlier. Let's return once again to our top eight fundamental economic problems.

OUR TOP EIGHT FUNDAMENTAL ECONOMIC PROBLEMS

Let's take another look at each of these problems. We'll see how they impact on one another and why they will need to be solved simultaneously.

1. Our Inefficient Transportation System

Because we go almost everywhere by car, Americans spend almost twice as much on transportation as the citizens of other rich nations.

Americans rely almost exclusively on their cars for local trips, and on plane travel for trips of more than two hundred miles.[4] And trucks have replaced railroads as our primary mover of freight.

The effects of suburbanization

Our post–World War II suburbanization led to a huge misallocation of resources. By building single-family-home subdivisions isolated from schools, shopping, work, and entertainment, the developers ensured that the new suburbanites would be almost entirely dependent on their cars for transportation. Because of the configuration of housing, shopping malls, factories, and office parks, public transportation was not economically feasible.

In the cities, there were concentrated business districts that were easily served by rail transportation. But the new suburbs lacked this degree of concentration, necessitating that freight be delivered by truck. This method of delivery is much more labor intensive, and much less fuel efficient. Similarly, automobile transportation is not only less fuel efficient than mass transit, but it necessitates the building of millions of additional cars and thousands of miles of highways each year.

Trains and planes and cars and trucks

Very few Americans will take a train ride of more than a few hundred miles. Why bother when a plane will get you there in just a couple of hours and cost about the same?

Our national railway system has grown shabby, and for decades we cut routes, ran fewer trains, and carried less freight and passengers. Meanwhile the ultramodern Eurail system speeds millions of passengers a day all across the Continent, while Japanese bullet trains and Chinese high-speed trains do the same. While our economic rivals have improved and expanded their own railway networks, we have allowed a priceless national asset to deteriorate over the last eight decades. Without world-class railroads, we cannot be a world-class economic competitor.

Intercity trains in Europe, Japan, and China cruise along at average speeds of 140 miles per hour, while our fastest passenger trains, the New York to Washington and New York to Boston Acelas, cover the 240-mile distance in about three and a half hours, making four or five stops. Seventy years ago the Yankee Clipper took just half an hour longer to make the New York to Boston trip. Our biggest problem is the condition of the road beds, which prevents speeds of more than one hundred miles per hour.[5]

Trucking has replaced the railroads as our nation's primary way of moving freight. Even though trucks consume fifteen times the fuel for the equivalent job, almost two-thirds of our freight is moved by truck.[6] So how then did trucking become so dominant? First, it is much more convenient than rail transportation to deliver goods to so many scattered suburban sites, and second, the government provides an annual subsidy of nearly $100 billion to truckers, largely to repair the damage they do to our highways.[7]

2. Our Failing Schools

Just half of our eighteen-year-olds can function at an eighth-grade level.

How did the world's best public education system become one of the worst in the developed world? There's plenty of blame to spread around.

The five major problems of our public education system

1. The Parents

Each generation of parents does not seem to measure up to the previous generation. Part of the problem is that so many more children are being brought up by just one parent, or both parents are working.

Parents are much less likely—or able—to help their children with their homework than earlier generations of parents. Working and single parents have greater time constraints. Often their children bring home little or no homework. And when they have math homework, the so-called "new math" is virtually undecipherable to nearly all parents—and perhaps to most teachers as well.

2. The Students

Most children, who spend the bulk of their leisure time watching TV or playing computer or video games, do very little reading. To them, the outside world exists only as a source of entertainment. A very high proportion of children attending ghetto schools present an even greater educational challenge. They begin school at a tremendous educational disadvantage, and are simply not ready to sit quietly and learn.

3. The Teachers

A few years ago, Sir Michael Barbor, a senior educational advisor to Britain's prime minister Tony Blair, was asked what all the world's great educational systems had in common. "They all select their teachers from the top third of the college graduates, whereas the United States selects its teachers from the bottom third."[8]

Our brightest and most ambitious college graduates do not want to go into a profession that pays so poorly—and offers so little prestige. Those choosing to major in education are consistently among the nation's poorest-performing students, based on SAT scores.[9]

4. The Teachers' Unions

The National Educational Association and the American Federation of Teachers have raised teachers' salaries substantially and fiercely guarded their job security. But under provisions of the contracts they have negotiated, it is extremely difficult to fire incompetent teachers, and institute merit pay, school choice, educational vouchers, and national testing.

5. The Educational Establishment

These leaders of education think that memorizing and rote learning are passé: it's much more important for students to understand *why* they are doing something. So students no longer need to learn how to add, subtract, multiply, and divide, as long as they can explain how they would go *about* carrying out these operations. Tell us about the *method* you would use. Whether or not you get the right answer is secondary. Besides, that's what calculators are for.

Indeed, since the widespread availability of cheap pocket calculators in the late 1970s, most children pretty much stopped learning math. Keeping right up with this trend, virtually all of these professional educators endorse the regular use of pocket calculators by first graders.[10] This guarantees that most American children never properly learn math.

Finally, the schools of education, in cahoots with local school boards and state departments of education, have managed to impose onerous teaching certification requirements ensuring that the best and the brightest college graduates do not go into teaching. Basically, you need to take a series of "mind-dulling" education courses. With the exception of a practical student teaching course, it has never been demonstrated that those who completed all of these other courses became better teachers. Indeed, there is ample evidence that most of those who subject themselves to this process are considerably less intelligent than those who do not.[11]

The product of our education system

How well are our schools educating our children? Forty percent of our college freshmen enroll at community colleges, where about 75 percent are placed in remedial courses where they are taught reading, writing, and arithmetic. So, the taxpayer gets a second chance to pay for the elementary school education of these "students."

3. Our Sick Healthcare System

Healthcare costs nearly twice as much per capita in the United States as it does in most other economically advanced nations.

Why have healthcare costs been rising so rapidly? We'll consider, in turn, five major factors that have been pushing them up.

1. Our growing senior citizen population

Today 14 percent of our population is over sixty-five; by 2030, when the entire baby boom generation will have retired, about 25 percent will be senior citizens.[12] We know that among the older population, one's medical bills usually shoot up in the last year of life. Costly new medical advances—not to mention very labor-intensive care—have kept people alive who would otherwise have died. Right now our senior citizens are responsible for over 40 percent of our medical bills.[13] By 2030, that group may well account for more than two-thirds.

2. The threat of malpractice suits

A second reason for rising healthcare costs is the growing

threat of malpractice suits, which has given rise to the costly practice of defensive medicine. Unnecessary lab tests as well as surgical procedures are undertaken to avert potential lawsuits. Still, what could be bad if these sometimes superfluous tests and procedures cost the patient nothing and the doctor is fully reimbursed by the insurance providers?

3. The provision of unneeded services

Doctors are reimbursed for services performed, whether or not they believe they are needed. So why not just drum up a little more business?

Many patients with insurance plans that require low or no copayments consume medical services as they would food at an all-you-can-eat buffet. If it's free, then why should I limit my portions? Even if a simple X-ray will do, I might as well go for an MRI. Why *not*? It's *free*, isn't it?

4. Rising administrative costs

As many as three million people are employed by healthcare providers and insurance companies to deal mainly with two basic questions: Is this procedure or service covered? And how much will the insurance company pay? Your doctor's employees and their counterparts at the insurance companies have diametrically opposed objectives. The former tries to get as much reimbursement as possible, while the latter tries to deny as many claims as it can. But we're all losers because these three million people add zilch to our national output.

5. The shift from pay-as-you-go to insurance payments

Amy Finkelstein, an MIT economist, believes that the massive expansion of medical insurance is the underlying cause of our rising national medical bill. Why, she asks, do doctors and hospitals adopt expensive new technologies so freely? They do so because medical insurance foots the bill. And if patients had to pay more through high-deductible health plans, they would cut back substantially on their medical care.[14]

4. The Military-Industrial Complex

We account for almost 40 percent of the world's military spending.[15]

The military-industrial complex consists of the Department of Defense, high-ranking military officers, the armed services committees of the House and the Senate, and the defense contractors.

All of these folks have a vested interest in keeping the nation in a perpetual state of war—or at least under the constant threat of war.

Because we and our allies need to import much of our oil, and we happen to be the world's sole military superpower, it is logical that we use that power to ensure the uninterrupted flow of oil from the Middle East and elsewhere to the oil refineries of the United States and those of our allies. Were we not so dependent on foreign oil, would we need to maintain such a large military establishment, especially our naval surface fleets and far-flung military bases? And would we have gotten ourselves into Gulf Wars I and II?

Spending almost 5 percent of our GDP on defense has a very large impact on our economy.[16] Military spending, unlike investment in health, education, infrastructure, or in plant and equipment, does not generate any future output or wealth. It's not an investment in the future. It's current consumption. But unlike the consumption of food, clothing, or going to the movies or on a vacation, military spending provides us with no pleasure and does absolutely nothing for our standard of living.

5. The Criminal Justice Establishment

We have, by far, the highest incarceration rate among economically advanced nations.

Let's start out with three basic facts: (1) it costs $100,000 to build one prison cell, (2) it costs $35,000 to keep someone in prison for one year, and (3) our prison population now totals 2.2 million people.[17]

Every nation needs prisons, but we lock up more people per capita than any other country, with the possible exception of Russia.[18] Indeed, our prison population has more than quadrupled since 1980; about one-third of our inmates are serving time for drug-related offenses.[19]

More than five million Americans are employed to deal exclusively with crime, but they add absolutely nothing to our national economic well-being. Just imagine how much better off we all would be if these folks were productively employed.[20]

Nearly two-thirds of those released from prison are back in again within three years.[21] Every other economically advanced nation has a much smaller criminal justice establishment and locks up a much smaller percentage of its population. And yet we suffer from the highest rate of most categories of violent crime.[22]

6. Our Bloated Financial Sector

This sector is diverting increasing amounts of savings from productive investment into speculative activities.

Our financial system performs two very important jobs. It enables savings to be invested by business firms, and it facilitates payments for goods and services. Basically, it ensures that business is conducted smoothly and safely.

Our financial system employs a vast array of real estate agents, mortgage brokers, bank loan officers, insurance claims adjusters, financial planners, stockbrokers, and hedge fund operators. Indeed, some nine million people—about 7 percent of our labor force—work in this sector. This is double the percentage in most other wealthy nations.[23]

The inflation-adjusted per unit cost of financial services has more than doubled since 1950.[24] Finance has become primarily a speculative activity: investors are making bets on what other investors are doing rather than actually financing jobs and real investment. The financial sector has been diverting vast quantities of labor and capital from the "real economy," thereby lowering the production of useful goods and services.

7. Our Huge and Growing Make-Work Sector

More than fifteen million Americans hold jobs that don't produce any useful goods or services.

Some of these jobs are in the government sector, but most are in the private sector. The prime example is the tax preparation industry, which employs three million people.[25] Among them are tax attorneys, accountants, bookkeepers, tax preparers, as well as the hundred thousand folks at the Internal Revenue Service.

Why do we need so many people to work on our taxes? It's because the Internal Revenue Code is amazingly complex. If it were simplified so that it took the average taxpayer just a few minutes to fill out her tax return, then these three million people would be out of work.

Earlier we talked about the three million employees of insurance companies and healthcare providers who spend all their time negotiating reimbursement. While their salaries are included in our nation's healthcare bill, none provides any healthcare—or any other useful service.

Next come the telemarketers and telephone solicitors whose work arguably has negative value, since its primary product is the hundreds of millions of bothersome calls they make each day.

Millions more Americans are employed as sales reps, personal injury lawyers, bureaucrats, and in other make-work jobs. Most of them work long and hard, but produce no useful good or service.

8. Our Shrinking Manufacturing Base

Much of what had once been "Made in the USA" is now made in Japan, China, Taiwan, South Korea, Mexico, and other nations.

By the 1950s we had built what was, by far, the greatest industrial machine the world had ever known. The other industrial powers—Germany, Japan, and England—were still recovering from the devastation of World War II, which we had entirely escaped. While it was inevitable that we would be losing some of our lead, few Americans would have predicted how quickly much of the world would be catching up with us.

Because of the pressures of the Cold War with the Soviet Union and its satellite empire in Eastern Europe as well as with China—which had fallen to the Communists in the late 1940s—we were very anxious to provide economic aid to our allies in Western Europe and Asia. First came the Marshall Plan in the late 1940s, which helped England, France, Germany, Italy, and other Western European nations to rebuild their economies. These nations would eventually be competing with us in the global markets. Then we provided the Japanese with the technology to compete with us in the production of TVs and other consumer electronics, largely because we wanted to prevent them from being taken over by the Communists. And finally, we paid to educate tens of thousands of Taiwanese engineers and scientists in American universities, and arranged for the transfer of radar, avionics, and other advanced technologies to Taiwanese electronics firms.

How were we paid back? Beginning in the late 1950s, Japanese TV manufacturers, using our technology, had begun to drive American manufacturers out of business by selling TVs in the United States below cost. And the Taiwanese, in the early 1980s, set up consumer electronics manufacturing plants in Mainland China and began competing with American manufacturers, eventually driving most of them out of business.[26]

In 1970, manufacturing employment in the United States peaked at twenty million, and has since declined by almost 40 percent.[27] To a large degree, the forces of globalization would have eroded some of our manufacturing base, but unquestionably we were complicit in our own demise.

A HOLISTIC APPROACH: HOW OUR ECONOMIC PROBLEMS IMPACT UPON EACH OTHER

Let's begin with the disappearance of nearly our entire public transportation system, and the shift to car travel for shorter distances and to planes for longer trips. We also allowed our railroads to deteriorate as truck transportation became our primary way of moving freight. This too has added to our growing dependence on foreign oil, thereby pushing up defense spending, the federal budget deficit, and the trade deficit.

Spending so much on defense places us at a tremendous competitive disadvantage. Think of all the uses to which these resources could be put that would help our business firms to compete in global markets. Not only would our trade deficit be much smaller, and our manufacturing base much larger, but far fewer Americans would be poor.

The abandonment of our cities—a direct result of our postwar suburbanization—led to higher crime rates, deteriorating schools, and the formation of a permanent underclass in our inner cities. The growth of our permanent underclass has pushed up the federal budget deficit, as well as those of city and state governments.[28]

Our shrinking manufacturing base increased our trade deficit and forced millions of Americans into our growing permanent underclass. This development, in turn, has added to our problems with crime, education, and the federal budget deficit.

Every year our failing educational system turns out millions of semiliterate and innumerate teenagers, who are unqualified to hold down even relatively low-level jobs—let alone the growing number of high-tech jobs being created. Again, this has made it much harder to compete in global markets and has pushed up the trade deficit.

Our healthcare sector is riddled with inefficiencies. The fact that we spend nearly twice as much per capita for healthcare as most other economically advanced nations indicates that something is very rotten in this huge economic sector. The high administrative costs and all of the incentives to provide medically unnecessary tests, procedures, and operations result in almost half of the resources devoted to healthcare being wasted. Since this sector accounts for more than one out of every six dollars of our GDP, just imagine if we could devote these resources to more productive uses.[29]

Because employers are saddled with huge healthcare insurance premiums that push up their costs, they have had increasing difficulty competing in the global marketplace. Not only does this contribute to our trade deficit, but also to the offshoring of jobs and the shrinkage of our manufacturing base.

Finally, let's consider how running such an inefficient criminal justice system impacts on the rest of our economy. We lock up at least five times as many people per capita as nearly all other advanced nations, but we still have the highest rate of violent crime. We imprison people for petty drug offenses instead of placing them in much less costly drug rehabilitation programs. We do virtually nothing to help ex-convicts find jobs and places to live when they are released, and then, somehow, we are surprised that nearly two-thirds of them end up back in prison within three years after their release.[30] If we could run our criminal justice system more efficiently, not only would we have less crime, but we could free up valuable resources that could be used much more productively.

Because our fundamental problems are interconnected, we can't reverse our economic decline by solving just one or two of them. In the next chapter we'll consider the measures that we'll need to take.

Chapter 25

SOLVING OUR ECONOMIC PROBLEMS AND SAVING THE AMERICAN ECONOMY

We need to tackle most of our major problems simultaneously—a prodigious endeavor, which will require an all-out national effort. The only parallel in our experience has been our full-scale mobilization to win World War II, which required the total commitment of all our citizens. Not only did we turn out huge quantities of war materiel, but individual citizens saved up balls of tin foil and grew their own food in "victory gardens." Like people used to say back then, "What'sa matta, bub? Don't yuh know there's a *war* goin' on?"

We may quarrel over some of the details, but clearly it will take a tremendous national effort to solve our fundamental problems and to get our economy to operate more efficiently. So please consider my blueprint for change as just a starting point in a national discussion. Ideally, panels of experts would be selected to propose remedies for the inefficiencies in such sectors as education, transportation, healthcare, poverty, and criminal justice.

SOLVING OUR EIGHT FUNDAMENTAL ECONOMIC PROBLEMS

In the last chapter we summarized these problems, and now we'll summarize their solutions.

1. Our Inefficient Transportation System

How do we bring our transportation system into the twenty-first century? Nearly every other economically advanced nation has a system of high-speed railroad lines as well as heavily traveled urban mass transit systems. We are just beginning to *think* about building high-speed lines, while they are up and running in virtually all of the other nations. With the exception of New York; Washington, DC; Portland, Oregon; Chicago; Philadelphia;

Boston; San Francisco; and a handful of other cities, our urban mass transit systems are woefully inadequate. The fact that 85 percent of all Americans get to work by car provides glaring evidence of our failure.[1]

Not only do we need to drive practically everywhere, but we love to drive oversize cars. More than half of all new vehicles sold are classified as light trucks, and are usually gas guzzlers.[2] So not only do we drive more than the citizens of virtually every other economically advanced nation, but we get about ten or fifteen miles per gallon less than these other drivers. In 2011, the Obama administration announced that by 2025, new cars would need to attain an average of forty-three miles per gallon. But, you may ask, what are we supposed to do in the meanwhile?

Perhaps my most controversial tax proposal is a gasoline tax of three or four dollars a gallon. Again, most other industrialized countries have such a tax. Our federal tax is currently just 18.4 cents. This tax would greatly discourage driving, and encourage the use of more fuel efficient vehicles.

We could use the proceeds from the gasoline tax increase to build, equip, and run commuter rail, trolley, and bus lines. We must also make truckers pay for the nearly $100 billion of damages they do to our highways every year.[3]

The federal government should stop subsidizing highway building and put all of that funding—and a lot more—into urban mass transit and high-speed rail lines. If we don't take these measures, then we can pretty much write off our economic future. Without a world-class transportation system, we are well on our way toward becoming a third-rate economy.

I am proposing our nation's largest construction project since our post–World War II suburbanization and the completion of the interstate highway network—the building of high-speed rail lines in the most densely populated parts of the country. And how do we get millions of people to clear right-of-ways and lay track? It's simple: pay them decent wages, say about fifteen dollars an hour. You may remember the famous line in the movie, *Field of Dreams*—"Build it and they will come."[4] In *this* case, pay them and they will build it.

We must also refurbish our transcontinental railway system to haul freight more efficiently. This involves upgrading roadbeds, putting discontinued routes back in service, and building more transit reshipment hubs, where freight containers can be easily moved from trucks and ships to flatbed rail cars, and vice versa.

While all parties usually agree that high-speed rail lines are useful projects, the big question is where we will get the money to pay for them. I would suggest that we just apply the formula we've been using for over sixty years to pay for the construction of the Interstate Highway System. The federal government pays ninety cents on the dollar, and the states pay the rest. If a state will not provide even 10 percent of the funding, then just maybe that project is not that wonderful.

Because the commute to and from work accounts for much of our driving, let's ask what local and regional transportation planners can do to cut down on traffic. Basically, they need to do one thing: make public transportation more attractive than driving. Commuters want their trip to be safe, convenient, and cheap. Commuters enjoy the autonomy of driving to and from work—literally door-to-door—in their own cars. They can be persuaded to take public transportation only if it is at least as convenient as driving. How far must they walk to the bus stop, and how often do the buses run? Will I get to work at least as fast by public transportation as I can by driving?

Free parking—which is provided by virtually every suburban office park, shopping mall, and strip mall—provides a strong incentive to drive. The more that is charged for parking, the more people will car pool, use public transportation, walk, or bike to these destinations. Even more effective would be to limit available parking spaces. This can be done by taxing private parking spaces and limiting curbside parking spots or raising parking meter rates.

Every city, town, and village located on a major commuter rail or bus line should provide ample low-cost parking for all commuters—not just for those from that locality. And whenever possible, park and ride facilities should be built along major public transportation routes.

Express lanes dedicated to buses have become increasingly popular in urban areas. To further encourage people not to drive, there needs to be a lot more congestion time toll increases.

As highways become congested, what do we do? We build more highways, which, in turn, encourage still more driving. What we truly need is a moratorium on highway building, especially in urban areas.

2. Our Failing Schools

Traditionally, public education has been a service provided and paid for by localities, but increasingly the funding has come from the states and, to a lesser degree, from the federal government. First let's consider a very worthwhile federal initiative, and then we'll turn to state and local solutions to this problem.

Set up a national curriculum

We need a national curriculum, grade by grade. For example, children should be taught counting up to one hundred, simple addition, basic reading, and writing in the first grade, such and such in the second grade, and so forth. That way, a child whose family has moved would not find herself behind, nor have to repeat the same work. And even more important, if this curriculum were combined with nationwide testing, then we would ensure that no one would move on to the next grade without knowing a certain minimum amount of information and being able to perform at a certain level of skill.

The much-maligned core curriculum, which was initially adopted by nearly all states, is an excellent start. However, there is widespread misunderstanding about just what it is, and then too, it must also go far beyond the mere implementation of goals if it is to succeed.

There are many things we can do at the state and local levels to vastly improve our failing educational system. Most of these changes will cost very little to implement.

Keep the schools open from 7:00 a.m. to 7:00 p.m. all year long

What are six-, seven-, and eight-year-olds supposed to do after three o'clock? Or during the summer? Most parents work eight hours a day, and few are off for the summer. Schools can provide a safe and nurturing environment for young children. Let's make full use of them.

Get rid of incompetent teachers

In most lines of work, when you're not doing your job well, you get fired. But not in teaching. Once teachers have tenure, it often takes years to get rid of even the most incompetent. Protected by union contracts and civil service laws, teachers who show up for work every day, and refrain from committing any high crimes or misdemeanors, basically cannot be fired.[5]

Localities and states need to streamline their processes of firing incompetent teachers—and even taking the radical step of abolishing tenure. A still more effective measure would be to not hire so many incompetent teachers in the first place.

Change the teacher certification process

Let's shorten this process to one student-teaching course that could be covered in as little as six weeks. And then an eighth-grade reading test. For high school teachers, I would require a minimum number of college credits in the subject or subjects they would be teaching. But not Mickey Mouse math education or science education courses.

Raise the pay of teachers

You know the adage: you get what you pay for. To a large degree, it holds true for teachers. The salaries we pay our teachers do not attract our best and our brightest college graduates.

Get rid of disruptive students

Students who are frequently disruptive must be removed from the classroom. They should be placed elsewhere, where they won't interfere with the right of other students to learn. Forgive the pun, but this is a no-brainer.

Ban pocket calculators from elementary schools

Back in the good old days, before the widespread use of pocket calculators, almost all children actually learned arithmetic. Now about half of all eighteen-year-olds cannot add, subtract, multiply, or divide without the aid of a calculator.[6] It does not take a rocket scientist to recognize this cause and effect relationship.

Change how math is taught and who teaches it

Since so many elementary school teachers are innumerate and/or math phobic, the children should be taught by math specialists, just as they are taught music, art, and science.[7]

Deny college admission to anyone who can't read, write, or do simple arithmetic

If high school students knew they couldn't get into college without these minimal skills, they would have more of an incentive to acquire them. Elementary and middle school reading, writing, and arithmetic should not be taught in colleges.

Disband the entire educational establishment

If there were just one thing we could do to drastically improve our educational system, what would it be? My vote would be to abolish the entire educational bureaucracy from the federal Department of Education all the way down to the thirteen thousand local school boards. These entities, along with the schools and college departments of education, are largely responsible for our dysfunctional public education system.

3. Our sick Healthcare System

Two of the main reasons why our healthcare costs are so high are that doctors are paid on piece-work basis and patients treat their medical care as a free service. Because insurance pays the lion's share of medical bills, it provides doctors with a perverse incentive to overtreat patients, while patients have a perverse incentive to avail themselves of much more medical treatment than they need. Extremely high administrative costs also inflate our nation's medical bill.

Curb malpractice suits

Medical malpractice suits—or even just the threat of them—add about $150 billion to our healthcare bill in terms of tort litigation, defensive medicine, and malpractice insurance premiums.[8] Instead of having individual doctors paying for their malpractice insurance, state governments could set up funds to pay the victims of medical malpractice. The total paid out would be four or five billion dollars a year, which is about how much the courts award in malpractice suits. Those patients making claims would go before a board of medical experts that would determine the awards. Not only would this obviate the need of doctors to practice defensive medicine, but they would be relieved of paying onerous malpractice insurance premiums. And as an added bonus, doctors who are repeatedly called before these boards would have their licenses revoked.

The most damage caused by the threat of malpractice suits is the consequent practice of defensive medicine. With the elimination of this threat, doctors would no longer have this incentive to prescribe unneeded lab tests, surgery, or drugs, saving tens of billions of dollars a year. These savings would be perhaps ten or twenty times the cost of setting up an alternative way of dealing with malpractice cases. The only losers would be the trial lawyers, a group that almost everyone loves to hate.

Community primary care centers

Open twelve hours a day, these centers could provide for over 90 percent of the medical care needed in most poor and working-class urban and suburban neighborhoods as well as in many rural areas. Such centers now exist and need to be greatly expanded by local and state governments. Their presence would greatly reduce the need of the poor to rely on hospital emergency rooms for routine medical care.

A comprehensive solution: universal single-payer healthcare insurance

We already have such a system in place for nearly all Americans over sixty-five. Medicare is efficiently run, self-financing, and allows patients to see the doctors of their choice. Why limit Medicare just to people over sixty-five? Let's extend it to all Americans.

"Medicare for All" has two huge advantages over our current hodgepodge of individual and employer-provided insurance plans. Not only will this free individuals and employers from having to pay huge premiums, but it cuts administrative expenses by hundreds of billions of dollars a year.

This vast expansion of Medicare can be financed by tripling—or perhaps quadrupling—the 1.45 percent tax rate paid by employers and employees. Because employers would no longer be able to deduct the cost of their employees' healthcare insurance premiums, few would continue paying them. Freed of this expense, often totaling one-quarter to one-third of employees' wages, employers could easily afford to raise wages substantially and *still* come out ahead.[9] And individuals who had been paying for their own healthcare insurance will no longer have to do so.

Adding icing to the cake, healthcare providers would no longer have to employ vast armies of people to negotiate with insurance company employees over reimbursement. Millions of Americans could now be shifted to jobs producing useful goods and services.

Is this socialized medicine? Hardly. Doctors and other medical practitioners would continue to be privately employed. Those not willing to accept Medicare patients would be free to set up boutique medical practices, most of whose patients would come from the richest 1 percent, who would be willing to pay for the best medical care that money could buy. That could even include cosmetic surgery and other procedures not paid for by Medicare.

Why would nearly all doctors be willing to accept Medicare payments? Mainly because working with Medicare is virtually hassle-free. Which is why the large majority of doctors currently accept Medicare patients. So in one fell swoop, we could save individuals, employers, and healthcare providers hundreds of billions of dollars a year by switching to this single-payer system. To avoid a repetition of the disastrous rollout of the Affordable Care Act (Obamacare) and its nonfunctioning market exchange, Medicare for All could be phased in by expanding coverage first just to those sixty to sixty-four years old, and then to those fifty-five to fifty-nine years old, and so forth.

Would everybody be better off under Medicare for All? Perhaps 95 percent would be, while those who had previously enjoyed so-called "Cadillac insurance plans" paid for by their employers would now have to pay a higher "Medicare tax." But *all* Americans would now have fully paid medical and dental insurance covering doctor visits, hospital stays, medical procedures, prescriptions, and other healthcare costs.

4. The Military-Industrial Complex

Because we account for almost 40 percent of the world's military spending, surely we could cut this spending quite substantially without endangering American lives.[10] We just need to figure out how much spending we need to cut. Do we really need to spend nearly 5 percent of our gross domestic product (GDP) on defense? Our answer depends on how we answer three subsidiary questions:

1. Do we need to continue fighting long and costly wars in Afghanistan, Iraq, and Syria?
2. Do we need to station troops around the world and patrol the major shipping lanes to ensure an uninterrupted flow of oil to our shores?
3. Do we need to keep updating and adding to our weapons arsenal?

If your answer to each of these questions is no, then we could cut our defense spending very sharply without endangering our national security.

Today, the greatest foreign threat against Americans is terrorism. Terrorism should be treated essentially as a criminal problem calling mainly for the application of policing methods—not military ones. *Terrorists* are criminals. We are smart enough to know we can't prevent every violent crime. When will we begin to realize that we can't stop terrorists from killing Americans? What we *can* do is make sure that we minimize the number of deaths that they cause, just as we try to minimize the number of deaths that murderers cause.

Spending more on defense has done little to reduce the threat of terrorism. Despite the spectacular success of the US Navy SEAL team in collaboration with CIA operatives in finally killing Osama bin Laden ten years after the 9/11 attacks, we cannot justify the trillions that have been spent on the "War on Terror."

5. The Criminal Justice Establishment

First we must distinguish between those who commit violent crimes and those who commit nonviolent—and especially—victimless crimes. Violent criminals must be made to understand that they will receive swift and sure punishment. And those who make careers of violent crime need to be locked away permanently.

Most prisoners are functionally illiterate.[11] A literacy program would give some prisoners a better chance of gainful employment when they are released, but very few learn how to read and write while in jail.

Because almost two-thirds of the people released from prison are rearrested within three years, we need to make a huge effort to smooth the readjustment process when prisoners are set free. They usually need a job and a place to live. Otherwise, they'll probably fall back into their old lives and resume the only trade they know—crime.

Ideally they would receive some relevant job training in prison, with a job waiting for them on the outside. Considering the reluctance of most employers to hire ex-cons, the federal, state, and local governments would need to set up job programs for most of the six hundred thousand people released each year.

Drug treatment is much more cost-effective than prison. It costs half as much to build and maintain a treatment facility as a prison. And while over 90 percent of the people who go to prison for drug-related crimes wind up back in prison, some of the better drug treatment programs have a "cure" rate of over 70 percent.

Here's what we can do to minimize crime:

1. Lock up all violent criminals at least until they are too old to be a threat.
2. Legalize marijuana and impose high taxes on this drug.
3. Stop locking up people for most drug offenses.
4. Make vocational training and basic literacy courses available for all inmates.
5. Provide a job and a place to live to everyone released from prison.
6. Build and staff more drug treatment facilities to provide an alternative to prison.
7. Allow nearly all nonviolent defendants to await trial without putting up bail money.
8. Vastly expand the network of well-staffed halfway houses.

6. Our Bloated Financial Sector

What can be done to shrink our financial sector? Here are some of the proposals:

1. Break up the big banks.
2. Tax the deposits of large banks.
3. Prohibit financial institutions from doing both investment banking and taking deposits.
4. Impose a tax of one-tenth of 1 percent on all financial transactions.

Despite its responsibility for the recent financial crisis, the financial services industry and its powerful lobbyists have successfully opposed these and other proposals that would substantially curb the size and power of our biggest banks. Their huge expenditures on lobbying and on campaign contributions to members of Congress are evidently money well spent.

While our bloated financial sector continues to waste vast amounts of labor and capital and continues to pose a threat of causing another financial crisis, there does not appear to be any countervailing power strong enough to oppose it.

7. Our Huge and Growing Make-Work Sector

Our most obvious need is to simplify the Internal Revenue Code with respect to the personal income tax. I would eliminate all the deductions and loopholes and tax all income above a certain level, with four or five different tax brackets. Best of all, nearly everyone could do their own taxes in about five minutes on a postcard-size tax form.

Who would oppose such a great idea? Well, what about all the rich people who would end up paying more taxes? And, of course, the tax attorneys, accountants, and all the other folks in the tax preparation business.

What can be done to end most other make-work jobs? In many cases people can be persuaded to leave them if they get better job offers. We'll talk more about that in the next chapter.

The federal government can do a lot more than establish a "Do not call" list. It can impose heavy fines, and even put a steep tax for each call they make. It could also make robocalls illegal.

The government could also extend the minimum hourly wage law to cover anyone who works on commission. Companies hiring hundreds—or even thousands—of sales reps, few of whom have any chance of making a living, would be forced either to not hire nearly so many sales reps, or else to pay them at least the minimum hourly wage rate.

If we had single-payer healthcare provided by Medicare for All, we could cut out the middlemen—in this case the health insurance companies—and eliminate the negotiation of reimbursement and, along with it, the jobs of the three million people employed by the healthcare providers and the insurance companies who do all this make-work.

Finally, if we had far-going medical malpractice reform, then we could eliminate medical malpractice suits. This would put tens of thousands of ambulance-chasing personal injury lawyers out of business. And it would free doctors from preforming millions of unnecessary medical tests and procedures.

8. Our Shrinking Manufacturing Base

First, we need to understand that the manufacturing jobs that have been offshored are not coming back. Our workforce cannot compete with workers in developing nations who are earning just a dollar or two an hour when it comes to relatively low-skill, repetitive work.

Our best future lies in promoting the growth of our high-tech, high-value-producing economic sectors—and creating new ones. Still, there *are* a couple of things we can do right now for the millions of blue-collar factory workers who have lost their jobs.

First, we could cushion the blow by providing free retraining—with pay—for displaced workers. (There are government retraining programs on the books, but the assistance they provide is minimal.) Once these retrained workers find new jobs, the federal government could make up for any pay loss for, say, the next two or three years. While this would not solve the problem, it would at least minimize the pain.

And second, we could identify the types of jobs with little likelihood of being offshored—or becoming technologically obsolete—and provide tens of millions of teenagers and young adults with the education and training needed to fill these positions.

How can we stop our manufacturing base from hemorrhaging jobs? Despite my misgivings as an economist, perhaps we need to take a hard look at which economic sectors we can't afford to lose, and to provide them with subsidies. After all, we already *do* have two huge subsidy programs—agriculture and defense.

LAST WORD

Is there a single thing that we can do that would enable us to reverse our economic decline and enable us to use our resources much more efficiently?

The answer is *no*. As we've seen in this chapter, there are many things that we need to do in several major economic sectors. And yet there *is* one big thing we need to do, which, along with all of these other measures, will make possible this great economic transformation. I call it "the Great Jobs Switch."

Chapter 26

THE GREAT JOBS SWITCH: PLACING TENS OF MILLIONS OF AMERICANS IN USEFUL JOBS

Now we're ready to drastically reduce the systemic waste of our labor and to provide a productive job for every American who is ready, willing, and able to work.

There are more than fifteen million people who are officially unemployed, working part-time, but preferring to work full-time, or are not even counted as unemployed because they have given up looking for work.[1] In addition, there are about forty million more who have make-work jobs, jobs in sectors that are highly inefficient, or jobs in sectors that produce more goods or services than we need. They must be induced to leave their positions for more useful jobs that we need to create.

Some of the long-term unemployed, especially those who are members of the permanent underclass, will be difficult to place in *any* job because they have been out of the labor force for so long. In addition, even in really good economic times, about 4 percent of our labor force is unemployed.[2] Most of these folks are simply "between jobs" and will soon find work. So here's our bottom line: we need to create about fifty-five million jobs for people who will produce goods and services that improve our standard of living.

Millions of Americans are desperately seeking work—*any* kind of work. Tens of millions more have jobs that don't pay them enough to live on—or provide healthcare benefits. And still tens of millions of other Americans have jobs—some of which pay quite well—but produce nothing of any value. Let's see what needs to be done sector by sector.

We are now ready to talk about adding and subtracting millions of jobs in several large sectors of our economy. In each I will provide my estimate of how many jobs will need to be created and destroyed (or eliminated). Are these numbers arbitrary? Definitely. Please consider them as just my own very rough estimates. If somehow my plan is adopted, I would leave it to experts in each economic sector to determine which jobs, and how many, need to be created or destroyed.

THE BIG FOUR

Let us begin with the "Big Four"—the economic sectors that need to be vastly expanded, eventually accounting for about twenty million new jobs. We'll start by addressing the growing problem of global warming, and then consider manufacturing, innovation, and our nation's infrastructure.

Dealing with Global Warming

We haven't talked much about global warming and its consequences since chapter 6 because it has not yet had a great impact on our economy. But now that is changing. The effects of Hurricane Sandy, which struck the East Coast in 2012, shall long be remembered—especially in the scores of communities that were devastated by the storm. And yet, despite the likelihood of being hit by even bigger storms in the coming decades, most of the homeowners chose to rebuild.[3]

In reports issued in 2013 and 2014, the Nobel Prize–winning Intergovernmental Panel on Climate Change predicted continued rising global temperatures, and the consequent continued melting of hundreds of glaciers as well as the polar ice caps. Sea levels have been rising for decades, and at an accelerating rate. When large storms hit land, higher sea levels mean bigger, more powerful storm surges that can destroy virtually everything in their path. Oceans may rise between two and a half and six and a half feet over the rest of the century, putting much of the East Coast, West Coast, and Gulf Coast at great risk.[4]

What can all of these coastal communities do to protect themselves against "the next big one," and the even bigger one after that? They can build dikes, levies, and sea walls. But that would be very costly and extremely labor intensive, requiring millions of construction workers.

In the long run—looking beyond midcentury—unless we take very drastic measures very soon, the future of the human race will hang in the balance. It's imperative that we replace our great dependency on fossil fuels with renewable fuels. The short-sighted solution to our foreign oil dependency popularized by former Alaska governor and vice presidential nominee, Sarah Palin, "Drill, baby, drill," will not save the planet.[5]

We need to train and hire millions of STEM (science, technology, engineering, and math) workers from among our best and our brightest to develop the technology that enables us to vastly expand our use of renewable energy sources.

New jobs created: 8 million; old jobs destroyed: 0.

Manufacturing

To survive as a high-tech, high-wage nation, we have to rebuild our manufacturing base. Rust-belt jobs and factories should be replaced by manufacturing operations turning out electric cars, buses, and batteries. We must foster such industries as nanotechnology, wind and solar power, robotics, medical research and medical devices, computer chips, and oil and gas exploration, mining, and refining. But we still need to preserve millions of jobs in the production of vehicles, airplanes, chemicals, pharmaceuticals, and other manufactured goods.

The federal government must do whatever it takes to rebuild our manufacturing base. Its efforts should include giving private firms hundreds of billions of dollars in contracts, creating publicly owned venture capital firms, directly subsidizing certain industries, forming partnerships with firms in certain sectors, increasing funding for research and development, fostering education in STEM.

All of our global competitors—most notably China, Japan, and the European Union—heavily subsidize major industries. Our own best model for industrial policy is our massive defense spending, which subsidizes our major weapons programs. As part of our industrial policy, the federal government should determine which industries we cannot afford to lose, as well as which new industries we can help grow. Each of them could be subsidized, if necessary. These subsidies would help finance the hiring of millions of employees, ranging from blue-collar and white-collar workers to people working in research and development and other high-tech jobs.

New jobs created: 8 million; old jobs destroyed: 0.

Innovation

Few of our college students are majoring in science, technology, engineering, or mathematics, and hundreds of our largest corporations have been shifting their research and development operations to India, China, Eastern Europe, and elsewhere. The federal government has been lagging in its support for basic and applied research.

If we are to regain our technological preeminence we will need to reverse these trends. Every college student majoring in STEM must be guaranteed a good job in that field upon graduation. The government has got to substantially increase its funding of research, and must pour money into high-tech firms in the form of government contracts, direct investment, and subsidies. Publically held venture capital firms must fund tens of thousands of high-tech start-ups. And private and university research labs must be financed. All of these initiatives should ensure our regaining our technological edge.

New jobs created: 5 million; old jobs destroyed: 0.

Infrastructure

Our nation has an infrastructure deficit of clogged roads and highways, antiquated air traffic systems, and outdated levees built more than fifty years ago. We have inefficient electrical power grids, leaking water and sewer mains, aging railroad systems, and clogged seaports. Our rail network has such bad bottlenecks that it can take hours just to get through some of them. Our air traffic systems are so outdated and overloaded that the Federal Aviation Administration predicts that it will soon reach total gridlock.[6]

All of these need to be repaired and modernized. The last time such an extensive project was undertaken was during the New Deal in the 1930s. And like the New Deal programs, these too would be very labor intensive.

New jobs created: 6 million; old jobs destroyed: 0.

OTHER MAJOR ECONOMIC SECTORS

Transportation

We have to move more people by public transportation and fewer by car. For intermediate trips—longer than fifty miles and less than five hundred miles—we should get more people to take trains rather than planes or cars. We also need to haul more freight by train and less by truck.

There are about two million jobs that could be subtracted: truck drivers, auto mechanics, auto insurance brokers, car salespeople, gas station employees, highway construction and repair employees, auto assembly line workers, auto marketers, and advertisers.

Some three million jobs could be added: bus, streetcar and train builders, conductors, drivers, railroad builders, public transportation maintenance, and repair workers. The largest project will be to build a high-speed railroad system.

New jobs created: 3 million; old jobs destroyed: 2 million.

Education

Our entire public education system needs to be overhauled from top to bottom. There are a vast number of incompetent, underperforming people who earn their livelihoods in education from preschool through graduate school.[7] All of them need to find other work.

Here's a list of the first million who need to go:

- The entire federal, state, and local departments of education, boards of education, and local school boards.
- Every college and university school and department of education.
- Most public school administrators, school superintendents, and other bureaucrats.

Abolishing those positions and laying off the people who fill them would, in itself, immensely raise the quality of public education. But we're not nearly done. We also need to fire as many as one million incompetent teachers beginning with those who can't read at an eighth-grade level.

Then, starting with pre-kindergarten, and all the way up through high school, we need to hire the best and many of the brightest of our college graduates—and pay them accordingly. We will want the most motivated and skilled teachers we can hire. Over the next ten years we will probably need to replace more than half of the nation's public school teachers.

Because so many parents are working, we should keep all public schools open from 7:00 a.m. to 7:00 p.m. Similarly, our libraries must be kept open ten or twelve hours a day, seven days a week. After school, many children, especially from poorer neighborhoods, have no place to go. Some, happily, find their way to a local library, where often librarians help them with their homework. Children from poor families, who don't have computers at home, can use those in the library.

Hundreds of thousands of educational bureaucrats could be shifted to keeping schools open from 7:00 a.m. to 7:00 p.m. Hundreds of thousands of new daycare centers could provide jobs for those laid off from other jobs inside and outside of education. Keeping public libraries open seven days a week would also create hundreds of thousands of jobs.

The main reason so many children from poor families are unprepared to enter kindergarten is that no one reads to them—or even talks to them very much.[8] Most libraries have storytelling hours. These should be greatly expanded. A few years ago, there was a newspaper photo of dozens of preschoolers listening spellbound to a storyteller in a New York City public library. The accompanying article discussed budget cutbacks that would end this popular program.

Full-day preschool and childcare should be made available to every child. If possible, it should be free. A major activity should be storytelling, which is essential to making children reading-ready.

In poor neighborhoods, especially when the weather is warm, you'll see young children and teenagers just sitting around with nothing to do. Often that leads to their getting themselves into trouble, and sometimes a lot worse. Whoever thought up the idea of "midnight basketball" was clearly an original thinker. Why not expand upon that idea by building indoor and outdoor facilities, where kids could play ball, socialize, or just hang out? These could be staffed by athletic directors, counselors, and maybe vocational advisors.

Our nation has an excellent network of libraries, museums, parks, beaches, and other public facilities. Their widespread use makes our lives so much richer and more enjoyable. In terms of government-speak, they are often "understaffed," and must be kept closed during times when there would otherwise be heavy usage.

So what can we do about all of this understaffing? We can provide the needed funding to move one or two million people from jobs that produce no useful goods or services into much more useful work at these public facilities. The woman working at the doctor's office calling insurance companies all day seeking reimbursement can now work as a lifeguard at Coney Island. The guy who works at the insurance company denying reimbursement could be a librarian at the Omaha Public Library. And maybe your tax attorney could referee midnight basketball games.

All of these changes will require additional staffing of three million people. Once we tote up all the hires and firings, we'll probably end up with more and better qualified people educating our children.

New jobs created: 4.5 million; old jobs destroyed: 1 million.

Healthcare

Central to the gross inefficiency of our healthcare system is the way it is paid for. Employing three million people to literally argue over reimbursement adds hundreds of billions of dollars each year to our healthcare bill.[9] So at the top of our list is to dispense with these negotiations, which would obviate the need for all these employees.

Tens of millions of Americans have no primary care doctor, and of those who do, only one in four can get an appointment for the same day.[10] Primary care centers fill this need. Building thousands more of these clinics would increase the quality of medical care, while limiting its cost. Hundreds of thousands of people could be employed building and staffing these facilities, while encouraging more young doctors to enter this field of medicine.

If you've ever visited a friend or family member in a nursing home, then you know how short-staffed they are. Patients needing help often have to wait thirty minutes or more for someone to answer their help button. Hospitals and residential rehab facilities are also seriously understaffed. Think of all the patients often having to wait more than half an hour for someone to help them get to the restroom.

Millions of Americans suffer from severe mental illness. Some are cared for by their families, some are institutionalized, and many more are homeless. The best and the safest place for most of the mentally ill would be group homes in their own communities. We need hundreds of thousands of group homes for the mentally ill—including a large and growing number of autistic children and adults whose families can no longer provide the full-time care that they need. I estimate that this will require one million full-time workers.

To say that most hospitals and nearly all nursing homes are seriously understaffed would be quite an understatement. Almost no one—and certainly no child, very sick person, or very old person—can manage without a private nurse, a parent or relative, or at least an advocate. We all can tell horror stories of the treatment we, or a friend or relative, received during an extended hospital stay. Surely people formerly employed by doctors and by hospitals solely to seek reimbursement from insurance companies—and other people employed by insurance companies to deny claims—could find much more useful employment helping and comforting patients in hospitals and nursing homes.

As our population continues to age, we will need many more home health aides. Just a single elderly person living alone may need two—or even three—full-time aides. To fully meet the needs of all these patients, we'll have to hire well over one million healthcare workers.

Just imagine how much better our healthcare system would be if we could expand our primary care system and provide needed assistance to hospitals, nursing homes, and homebound patients. We could do that by switching to a single-payer healthcare system, which would avoid the need to three million people negotiating reimbursement.

New jobs created: 4.5 million; old jobs destroyed: 3.5 million.

Military-Industrial Complex

Cutting our defense spending by one-half would cause five million people to lose their jobs.[11] They would include members of our armed forces, civilian employees of the Defense Department, and employees of our military contractors, subcontractors, and the firms doing business with them.

The Department of Veterans Affairs is severely understaffed, and must hire tens of thousands of employees to reduce the long waiting times that disabled veterans must often endure. Still more workers are needed to help veterans return to civilian life, including finding jobs and getting all of the necessary social services.

New jobs created: 200,000 (0.2 million); old jobs destroyed: 5 million.

Criminal Justice System

This sector needs to be drastically downsized. We are locking up far too many people, and consequently employing too many people to watch them. Nearly all of those imprisoned for nonviolent drug offenses should instead be enrolled in residential or outpatient drug treatment programs. Most other nonviolent criminals could be punished in alternative ways, such as being placed under house arrest, doing community service, or forced to pay steep fines.

We must make a major effort to rehabilitate those prisoners who are scheduled for release. This could begin with a literacy program and vocational training. Once they are released, they should be provided with a place to live and a decent job. This will make it much easier for them to be reintegrated into our society, and much less likely to fall back into a life of crime.

Instead of building more prisons, we should be building and staffing more drug treatment facilities. Tens of thousands of these jobs could go to ex-convicts. Since virtually all drug treatment programs employ ex-addicts, this would be a particularly good fit.

Similarly, hundreds of thousands of prisoners, most of them nonviolent, have very serious mental health issues. Some have even committed so-called nuisance crimes just to be incarcerated in the hopes of getting treatment.[12] Wouldn't it make a lot more sense to be building more mental health treatment facilities that would be much better suited to help these people?

While hundreds of thousands of people employed in the criminal justice system would lose their jobs, hundreds of thousands of other jobs would be created to carry out these reforms.

New jobs created: 500,000 (0.5 million); old jobs destroyed: 1 million.

Financial Services

We lead the world in real estate brokers, financial planners, insurance claims adjusters, stockbrokers, check cashers, payday lenders, and hedge fund operators. We have at least twice as many financial services employees per capita as any other advanced economy.[13] Surely we could get by with half as many. We can cut three million of the jobs in the financial sector without any loss in the level of financial services.

Hundreds of thousands of laid-off financial workers could find gainful employment in the one area that has been largely neglected—where the poor live. Poor neighborhoods are extremely underserved by banks. In their stead we find payday lenders, check cashing services, and tax preparers offering "instant refunds" at exorbitant interest rates. A few thousand bank branches could give their customers most of the same services that other Americans enjoy—ATMs, debit and credit cards, and checking accounts. These banks should also extend personal and small business loans.

New jobs created: 200,000 (0.2 million); old jobs destroyed: 3 million.

THE MAKE-WORK SECTOR

The Internal Revenue Code and the Tax Preparation Industry

By far, our largest make-work project is our tax preparation industry, which was created by our growingly complex Internal Revenue Code. Simplifying the code would put over three million people—most of whom prepare income tax returns—out of work.

New jobs created: 0; old jobs destroyed: 3 million.

Telemarketers

Telemarketing is based on making hundreds or even thousands of cold calls, in the hope of making a single sale. The fact that they are bothering all of these people is not even a consideration to the owners of these businesses. There may well be as many as two million telemarketers making these annoying calls. If the operations would somehow be shut down, all of these folks would now be available to do useful work.

New jobs created: 0; old jobs destroyed: 2 million.

Telephone Solicitors

Hundreds of thousands of these folks spend their workdays and evenings "dialing for dollars." Many work for very worthy causes that range from colleges to cures for cancer. But their extremely labor-intensive efforts are not just intrusive, but take a very large slice out of the funds collected. I would suggest that these institutions find a more efficient way of gathering contributions.

New jobs created: 0; old jobs destroyed: 0.5 million.[14]

Attorneys

Largely because lawyers write our laws, they are so complex that only lawyers can understand them. If our laws were simplified, we could probably do with just half of our 1.3 million lawyers and another million people who work with them.[15] We certainly could do without the "ambulance chasers" whose advertisements promise high monetary rewards for their injured clients. If the states enacted meaningful medical malpractice reform, these lawyers would have to look for other work.

New jobs created: 0; old jobs destroyed: 1.5 million.

Sales Reps and Interns

We have far too many sales reps. How many is too many? There are probably one or two million people who are working entirely on commission and earning either nothing or less than the minimum hourly wage of $7.25 an hour. Among the worst offenders are insurance companies, whose new sales reps earn nothing for the first few months, and are asked to sell insurance to their friends and family, rather than being given legitimate sales leads.[16] If an employer cannot pay the minimum wage, then very possibly the work is not worth doing.

The minimum hourly wage should be extended to all jobs—not just to sales reps. It should also be extended to cover currently unpaid interns, except for work that is performed by high school or college students for which they get course credit. Otherwise their employers are getting free labor.

New jobs created: 0; old jobs destroyed: 3.5 million.

PRIVATE AND PUBLIC BUREAUCRATS

Automobile companies, pharmaceutical firms, large universities, and various governmental bureaus and departments all follow Parkinson's Law: "Work expands so as to fill the time available for its completion." Just picture all of those seemingly busy bureaucrats scurrying around, firing off memos, talking on the phone, and rushing off to meetings. But no discernible output results. C. Northcote Parkinson added a corollary: "Work expands to occupy the people available for its completion."[17] If Parkinson is right, then large government and private organizations are filled with important-looking people who appear very busy but are doing virtually no real work.

If the jobs of all these folks could somehow be eliminated, I would guess that ten million of them would be out of work.

New jobs created: 0; 10 million jobs destroyed.

PUTTING THE PERMANENT UNDERCLASS BACK TO WORK

Let's train hundreds of thousands of the unemployed poor to do construction work. They could rebuild the decaying urban and rural slums. In addition, millions of homeless Americans around the nation need roofs over their heads.[18]

There are vast numbers of abandoned houses in Detroit, Cleveland, Philadelphia, St. Louis, and scores of other large and mid-sized cities as well as large numbers of homeless people. If these homes were rehabilitated, they could be used to house the homeless. In fact, many of the homeless—as well as anyone else who needs a job—could be put to work making these homes once again habitable.

Many permanently poor families are so dysfunctional that they desperately need intense social services that only well-trained social workers, family counselors, and vocational counselors can provide. To bring these families back into the social mainstream, we will need to train and hire hundreds of thousands of people in these professions.

AmeriCorps VISTA should be expanded from the 80,000 young people who currently serve to at least 500,000.[19] By working on literacy, education, healthcare, and economic development projects in poor neighborhoods, they too can help reintegrate the poor within the rest of our society.

Many of the poor go into the military service, so why not provide them with alternative employment helping other poor people, whether through AmeriCorps or other social agencies that currently exist or can be created? More than anything, the poor need decent jobs. Not only are millions of poor people out of work, but millions more are holding such low-paying jobs that they don't earn enough to raise their families above the poverty line. It is essential, then, that we create enough decent jobs so that no one who is ready, willing, and able to work will have to live in poverty.

New jobs created: 4 million; old jobs destroyed: 0

MY PERSONAL WISH LIST OF JOBS

1. There is no reason why nearly all post offices need to close at 5:00 p.m. on weekdays, nor for there to be long lines. I would hire an additional 300,000 workers.
2. Let's hire one million people to keep every public and private museum, library, beach, park, and playground open twelve hours a day, seven days a week.
3. We could use about a million people to assist the blind, the disabled, and the aged to more fully participate in their communities.
4. How about a program to ensure that every American gets three meals a day?
5. How about a program to ensure that every American has a place to live?
6. How about a program to wipe out illiteracy?

I'm not sure how many additional people would be needed to staff the last three programs, but I'll guess that my entire list will require at least six million workers.

New jobs created: 6 million; old jobs destroyed: 0.

MATCHING JOB APPLICANTS WITH JOB OPENINGS

Most Americans would agree that our great shortage of decent jobs is our most pressing economic problem. So far, we identified tens of millions of jobs that we need to create. Now let's talk briefly about how we'll place job applicants in these jobs.

Every state has a free employment service that finds jobs for the unemployed. But their efforts are limited by the number of jobs available, and by the number of job counselors that they employ. If we are to move more than fifty million Americans into new jobs, then we're going to need a lot more job counselors and a lot more job listings.

So let us begin by hiring and training 100,000 job placement counselors. Then we'll need to list all the jobs we've created with the state employment services. The job counselors would compare the job requirements with each applicant's background to find the best possible matches. The state employment services would also need 200,000 vocational counselors and trainers to guide job seekers who are not employment-ready. This effort can be supplemented by giving these listings to private employment agencies and to high school and college job placement offices.

New jobs created: 0.3 million; old jobs destroyed: 0.

LET'S DO THE MATH

At the beginning of the chapter, we set out to create about fifty-five million new jobs. Let's add up all the new jobs we need to create, sector by sector. We've done that in the table in Fig. 26.1.

As you can see, the figures in the table fall short of what we need to do. I came up with about five million short of the fifty-five million jobs we need to create. No individual can possibly know how many jobs need to be created in each economic sector. Nor can any person know how many jobs need to be cut in each area of our economy. Those decisions would best be left to experts in each economic sector. What should be clear is that tens of millions of Americans need to be switched from unproductive work to jobs that create useful goods and services.

Sector	Number of Jobs (in millions)	
	Created	Destroyed
Global Warming	8	0
Manufacturing	8	0
Innovation	5	0
Infrastructure	6	0
Transportation	3	2
Education	4.5	1
Healthcare	4.5	3.5
Military-Industrial Complex	0.2	5
Criminal Justice	0.5	1
Financial Services	0.2	3
Tax Preparation Industry	0	3
Telemarketers	0	2
Telephone Solicitors	0	0.5
Attorneys and Employees	0	1.5
Unpaid Sales Reps and Interns	0	3.5
Public and Private Bureaucrats	0	10
Jobs for the Permanently Unemployed	4	0
State Employment Services	0.3	0
My Personal Wish List	6	0
Totals	50.2	36

Fig. 26.1. Total number of jobs created.

GETTING PEOPLE TO SWITCH JOBS

To carry out the Great Jobs Switch, we'll employ both the carrot and the stick approaches. Although most of the jobs will be with private employers, the wheels of change will be greased mainly by the federal government. And we'll require a few hundred billion dollars' worth of grease each year. Changes in public education, the military-industrial complex, and the Internal Revenue Code will illustrate the use of the carrot and the stick to carry out the Great Jobs Switch.

In education, by abolishing the entire bureaucracy—which includes the federal, state, and city departments of education, and all of the colleges, schools, and departments of education—we would lay off one million employees. In addition, hundreds of thousands of incompetent teachers would be fired. That's the stick. And the carrot? We would attract better teachers by easing the certification process and by paying higher salaries.

Millions of people who worked for defense contractors and subcontractors would be laid off when their employers lose their government contracts. Each would then find one of the fifty-five million jobs funded mainly by other government contracts, such as building high-speed rail systems, working for high-tech start-ups, or perhaps dealing with global warming.

Three million accountants, tax attorneys, tax preparers, and the people working with them would lose their jobs if the Internal Revenue Code were drastically simplified. These folks would find other work, perhaps as teachers, librarians, vocational counselors, social workers, or even as venture capitalists.

In sum, most of the people who leave their jobs will have been laid off, but a significant number will leave them voluntarily because they found better jobs among those that we've created. But most importantly, we will now have fifty-five million more people producing useful goods and services. *Think* about it: we'll move fifty-five million people from the unemployment rolls or from jobs in which they produced nothing of economic value, and put them to work creating goods and services that we actually want and need.

Will most of the jobs we create be government jobs? No! Perhaps 90 percent will be in the private sector.

WAR AND PEACE

Believe it or not, we actually did manage a couple of job switches on the scale that I'm proposing. But to remember them, you'd need to be at least in your middle to late eighties. In the early 1940s we quickly converted from a peacetime economy that was still recovering from the Great Depression to one that was on a full war-time footing. And then, at the close of World War II, we went almost seamlessly from a very prosperous wartime economy to a very prosperous peacetime economy. One-third of our labor force was smoothly shifted from jobs that produced or used military goods to jobs that produced "civilian" goods and services.[20]

Defense plants were reconverted to civilian production, and millions of workers—primarily married women—were let go. Twelve million veterans were discharged in 1945 alone, and most of them quickly found jobs.[21] Production shifted smoothly from making planes, tanks, jeeps, ships, bombs, and bullets to building streets, roads, highways, cars, appliances, and consumer electronics.

Of course we were a very different nation back then. As a people, we had survived back-to-back existential challenges—a depression and an all-out war. Our "greatest generation," a term coined decades later by TV news anchor Tom Brokaw, met the challenge of the war, when almost every American joined in this patriotic effort. And for the very few who somehow had not gotten the message, there was the popular reminder, "Hey, bub, don't yuh know there's a war goin' on?"

One of the big differences between those days and more recent times was the end of the military draft in the mid-1970s. Men—and women, who had volunteered—from all walks of life had served together. Another crucial difference was that our very national survival was threatened, and few Americans wanted to think about what their lives would be like if we had lost.

While I cannot claim that our economic demise threatens our survival as a nation—at least in the foreseeable future—it is surely changing our lives. And that change has not been good for most Americans.

I believe that a massive switch from jobs that produce no useful goods and services to jobs that do will restore our nation once again to economic preeminence. But even if most Americans could be convinced that this plan would save us, do we have the national will to follow through with it? Are we capable, as was our greatest generation, of making the necessary sacrifices?

A WORD ABOUT BERNIE SANDERS'S PRESIDENTIAL CAMPAIGN PLATFORM

More than any other major presidential candidate in decades, Bernie Sanders has addressed some of the same economic problems that we've talked about in this book. Indeed, five of the planks in his campaign platform are identical to the solutions that I have proposed in this book:

1. Put millions of Americans to work rebuilding our crumbling infrastructure.

2. Create a single-payer health insurance system that insures all Americans.
3. Downsize the bloated financial sector—especially the too-big-to-fail banks.
4. Overhaul the tax system, while redistributing income from the rich to the middle class and the poor.
5. Shrink the military-industrial complex.

The main objectives of the Sanders campaign are social justice, a more equitable income distribution, and a more democratic society. I fully support those objectives. But the primary objective of this book is to reverse the decline of the American economy and to restore its role as the greatest economy in the history of the world. To paraphrase a famous line spoken by Marc Antony in Shakespeare's *Julius Caesar*, "They say that *Sanders* was ambitious?"

Sanders's policies would move millions of Americans from nonproductive work—especially in the healthcare and financial services sectors—to productive work rebuilding the infrastructure and halting global warming. But if we are to reverse our economic decline, we need to solve *all* of our fundamental economic problems, while moving tens of millions of Americans into jobs producing needed goods and services. Had he been elected, perhaps he would have addressed the rest of these problems during his second term.

Full disclosure: Bernie and I ran track together at Brooklyn's James Madison High School in the 1950s, and were roommates for one semester at Brooklyn College. But since then we have been in touch just sporadically and have formulated our economic policy proposals independently over the decades.

Chapter 27

A LONG-TERM STRATEGY TO SAVE THE AMERICAN ECONOMY

Politics is the art of the possible.

—Otto von Bismarck

From the beginning of this book we have talked about our fundamental economic problems and how to solve them. Because of their overwhelming magnitude, only the federal government has the resources to do most of this. But if politics *is* the art of the possible, then what are the chances that Congress will pass the needed legislation? We all know the answer to *that* one!

Having read this far, you probably agree that our nation is in long-term economic decline. But we are in a tiny minority. While waiting for a national consensus that compels the federal government to take meaningful action to solve our fundamental economic problems, what can be done on the federal level?

Given the results of the 2016 election, the prospect for meaningful action by the federal government is highly unlikely in the near future. About the only major initiative that we can realistically hope for is a much-needed overhaul of our crumbling infrastructure.

During his election campaign Donald Trump proclaimed, "We are going to fix our inner cities and rebuild our highways, bridges, tunnels, airports, schools, hospitals."[1]

Although Mr. Trump often mentioned spending $1 trillion on this endeavor—while sharply reducing taxes—there is concern among Republicans in Congress that this major spending program will sharply increase the budget deficit. So, we have to wait to see if this trillion-dollar plan, or even a scaled down version of it, will ever come to be.

The outlook for positive change on the state and local levels is considerably better. Former New York City mayor Michael Bloomberg predicts that the nation's cities will continue to lead the way to find solutions to our fundamental economic problems. He cites initiatives in New Orleans "to connect students from low-income families to learn skills that can translate into jobs in growing industries."[2] He also notes that "cities from Seattle to Houston and Phoenix to Detroit have all been building extensions to their transit system."

During the last two decades, the states along with the cities have taken strong initiatives to deal with rising sea levels, expanding mass transit, switching to renewable energy sources, and reducing greenhouse gas emissions.[3]

Still, the cities and states can do only so much, especially without large infusions of money from the federal government. So, we may ask one question: What can we do in the meanwhile? The first thing would be to ask the experts what can be done, so that we will be ready to hit the ground running when the opportunity presents itself.

ASK THE EXPERTS

Throughout this book I've suggested solutions to our many economic problems. But who am *I* to be proposing solutions? I can hardly claim to be an expert in *all* these areas.

In political economy, like in medicine, there is a division of labor. Your family doctor, a general practitioner, can provide a diagnosis of your various ailments, but she may need to send you to specialists to get more expert treatment. As the author of an introductory economics textbook, I am basically an economic generalist. While I can come up with a list of our fundamental economic problems, it would take teams of experts to figure out how to solve them.

PRESIDENTIAL COMMISSIONS

A journey of a thousand miles begins with a single step.
—Lao-tzu, Chinese philosopher

Presidents appoint commissions of experts to study problems and recommend solutions. Sometimes these commissions are created mainly to provide the illusion of action. President Ronald Reagan occasionally resorted to his ploy, but he did appoint two commissions that did outstanding work.

The recommendations of one induced Congress to shore up the finances of the Social Security trust fund, and the other led to a very workable procedure for closing unneeded military bases. If the template created by the latter commission can be replicated, it may be used to solve some of our fundamental economic problems. Let's see how the Base Realignment and Closure Commission worked out.

BRAC

As the Cold War was finally winding down in the late 1980s, there was widespread agreement among Pentagon officials, congressional leaders, and military affairs experts that many of the hundreds of military bases scattered across our country were no longer needed. Working together, Sen. Barry Goldwater, the chair of the Senate Armed Services Committee, and Texas Republican congressman Dick Armey authored the landmark legislation that would enable the closing of excess bases.[4]

Since every military base was in someone's congressional district, representatives and senators from those states would band together to stop virtually every base from closing. The only way to close unneeded bases would be to remove the process from politics.

The plan, called BRAC (Base Realignment and Closure) was passed in 1988, and led to five rounds of base closings in 1988, 1991, 1993, 1995, and 2005, resulting in the closure of over one hundred major bases and several hundred minor facilities, and annual savings of about $7 billion.[5]

The genius of the plan, which was Armey's brainchild, was in the details. After the president appointed a commission of military experts that was confirmed by the Senate, the secretary of defense provided the commission with a list of bases to be closed. The commission, after visiting all the bases in question and doing a careful analysis of their military usefulness, then cut some bases from the list and added others. Its list of bases slated for closure was submitted to the president, who was to either accept or reject the list without modification. In each of the five rounds, the president accepted the commission's list and it was then sent to both houses of Congress.

It was up to Congress to accept the entire list without amendment or to reject it. Now comes the interesting part. If Congress accepted the list, it did nothing. To reject it, Congress would need to pass a joint resolution. This provision is the genius of the plan. Given our congressional gridlock, requiring Congress to act is a whole lot harder than just counting on Congress to do nothing. In all five rounds of base closings, while there was some debate in Congress, in no case was a joint resolution passed to reject the commission's list.

Professor Jerry Brito of George Mason University, who has done an excellent analysis of the workings of BRAC, describes what he considers the most important explanation for the success of the commission in closing military bases:

> [T]he structure of BRAC gives members of Congress political cover to act against their parochial interest. Members can vote for the popular budget-cutting measure and then deflect blame to the Commission if a base in their district is ultimately selected for closure.[6]

Sen. Phil Gramm, one of the originators of BRAC, made this point somewhat more picturesquely:

> The beauty of this proposal is that, if you have a military base in your district . . . under this proposal, I have 60 days. So, I come up here and say, "God have mercy. Don't close this base in Texas. We can get attacked from the South. The Russians are going to attack Texas. . . ." Then I can go out and lie in the street and the bulldozers are coming and I have a trusty aide . . . to drag me out of the way. All the people . . . will say, "You know, Phil Gramm got whipped, but it was like the Alamo. He was with us until the last second."[7]

Despite how well BRAC has worked, so far no one has been able to replicate its template. In recent years Senators Sam Brownback (R-KS), Kent Conrad (D-ND), and Judd Gregg (R-NH)—all of whom have retired from the Senate—introduced legislation to lower government spending based on BRAC, but despite repeated attempts, none has succeeded.[8]

Given our congressional gridlock, it will be exceedingly hard to get Republicans and Democrats to agree to pass an economic renewal plan as costly and as radical as the one that I've advocated over the last two chapters. BRAC may offer the only model under which my plan, if presented piecemeal, could succeed in the foreseeable future.

Would Congress vote for *any* of the proposals I've made? Or would we need to wait for the next economic crisis before any meaningful action is taken?

IN TIME OF ECONOMIC CRISIS

> *You never let a serious crisis go to waste . . . it's an opportunity to do things you think you could not do before.*
>
> —Rahm Emanuel, President Barack Obama's first chief of staff and later mayor of Chicago

When the nation demanded that its government take strong action to end the Great Depression, President Franklin Roosevelt was able to push much of his relief and recovery program through Congress during his first one hundred days in office. But in 2008, even with a possible financial meltdown staring us in the face, there was no great urgency for the government to act, nor was there widespread agreement on what should be done. Just two years later, many of those in Congress who voted for the $700 billion TARP bank rescue plan were unceremoniously voted out of office.[9] And despite the fact that fifteen million Americans were officially unemployed during the depths of the Great Recession, President Obama barely got his woefully inadequate $787 billion economic stimulus program through a Congress that had small Democratic majorities.[10]

SHOVEL-READY PROJECTS

During Depressions, John Maynard Keyes suggested that the unemployed be given shovels and paid to dig holes in the ground. But then, some people thought, why not have the unemployed carry out more useful projects? Hence someone coined the term "shovel-ready projects."

In 2009, when Congress passed the economic stimulus bill, we didn't have an up-to-date list of projects that could quickly put millions of the unemployed back to work. Just as we are well advised to always keep our résumés up-to-date—since we can never be sure when we might lose our jobs—we would do well to keep an up-to-date list of shovel-ready—or perhaps lab-ready—projects that could be set in motion at a moment's notice. Not only would we be ready to fight the next recession, but much more important, we would have a fully developed plan for economic renewal.

Now we come to a very interesting question: Who will carry out this extremely ambitious plan—the government or private business firms? While the federal government would provide the funding and the overall strategy, most of the direction would come from state, regional, and local government agencies. And private business firms under government contract would perform nearly all of the work.

Money provides a great incentive to get people to do all kinds of things. After all, isn't our economy based on the profit motive? And so, just as individuals flock to well-paying jobs, business owners line up to bid for lucrative government contracts. Some very large companies—such as military contractors—earn tens of billions of dollars a year by performing work for the government. So putting out contracts to bid—whether for high-speed rail lines, inner-city rehabilitation projects, or setting up child-care centers—would not be a departure from standard practice.

SUMMING UP OUR BASIC ECONOMIC PROBLEM

To sum up our basic economic problem in just a few words: we are not making efficient use of our labor force. Many of our best and our brightest—especially those with excellent academic credentials—are underemployed. Many of our semi-skilled and unskilled workers are underemployed or unemployed. And finally, at least a quarter of our labor force is engaged in basically unproductive work—that is work that produces no useful goods or services.

Putting the unemployed to work by offering them decently paying jobs is the easy part. Much more challenging is getting one-quarter of our labor force to shift from basically unproductive work to jobs in which they can actually produce useful goods and services.

LAST WORD

My grand strategy has three parts. First, let's begin a national discussion about our self-destructing economy. Second, we need several presidential commissions to analyze our fundamental economic problems and come up with a set of solutions. And third, when the next economic crisis strikes, we should be ready to put those plans into action.

Like most other practitioners of the dismal science, I am a pessimist. Will the American people and its political leaders ever be willing to make the sacrifices I'm calling for? What do *you* think?

Reversing our unsustainable economic course would obviously

require a monumental national effort. This cannot happen unless there is a radical change of attitude on the part of most Americans. No longer can we put ourselves first and our country second. In his 1961 inaugural address, President John F. Kennedy uttered this stirring call to arms: "Ask not what your country can do for you. Ask what you can do for your country."

During the long debate leading up to the passage of the Affordable Care Act of 2010, lobbyists spent one million dollars a day in an effort to persuade members of Congress to vote for provisions that their clients favored.[11] None was asking what she or he could do for our country. In the words of our poet laureate Charles Simic, "We have essentially squandered the wealth of this country and forgotten the whole idea of the common good."[12]

Can we subordinate our self-interest for the good of the country? Many, of course, have done this in time of war. Immediately after Pearl Harbor and 9/11, volunteers lined up outside military recruiting centers. But during peacetime, can we put aside our own economic interests for the national interest? How would *you* answer that question?

No plan for solving our nation's fundamental economic problems can succeed unless it has strong political support. Right now that support is sorely lacking. Today President Kennedy's appeal to American patriotism seems not just overly idealistic but quite naïve. Perhaps in the not too distant future another president will urge his or her fellow Americans to a very different call to arms: "Look out for numero uno!"

Despite my own pessimism, I do believe that there is still time for us to get our economy back on track. But as each year passes, the task will be that much harder. And if we are truly the exceptional nation we once believed we were, then just maybe we can roll up our sleeves and get our economy back on track. It is my hope that this book will begin a national discussion leading to the restoration of America's economic state of grace.

ACKNOWLEDGMENTS

It took many years to write this book and to find the right publisher. Steve Harris, of CSG Literary Partners, submitted my manuscript to Steven L. Mitchell, the editor in chief of Prometheus Books, and the rest is history. When we had a conference call, there was some confusion as to who was addressing whom since each of us was a Steve.

The editorial assistant Hanna Etu and copyeditor Jeff Curry I worked with at Prometheus made hundreds of suggestions, which greatly improved the book. Lisa Michalski and Jill Maxick were very helpful in getting the book reviewed and in accessing the college market.

Over the years, my fellow economist, Jim Watson, provided a great deal of feedback and encouragement. I also want to thank my old high school friend, Martha Weinstein Alpert, for proofreading the first draft.

Finally, I'd like to thank my first editor, Gary Nelson, who signed me to write an introductory economics textbook, now in its eleventh edition. Gary thought it would be a nice idea to publish a book that students could actually understand.

NOTES

Introduction

1. John J. Sweeney, *America Needs a Raise: Fighting for Economic Security and Social Justice* (New York: Houghton Mifflin, 1996).

2. John Bivens and Lawrence Mishel, "Understanding the Historic Divergence between Productivity and a Typical Worker's Pay," Economic Policy Institute, September 2, 2015, http://www.epi.org/publication/understanding-the-historic-divergence-between-productivity-and-a-typical-workers-pay-why-it-matters-and-why-its-real/ (accessed April 10, 2017).

3. Reuters, "More Than 1 in 5 US Children Poor, Census Says," November 18, 2011, http://www.reuters.com/article/us-usa-poverty-children-idUSTRE7AG2C920111118 (accessed March 31, 2017).

4. Pat Garofalo, "Report: US Has One of the Highest Child Poverty Rates in the Developed World," *ThinkProgress*, May 29, 2012, https://thinkprogress.org/report-us-has-one-of-the-highest-child-poverty-rates-in-the-developed-world-c43e3f4b5da1 (accessed March 31, 2017).

5. Associated Press, "Millennials Are Falling behind Their Boomer Parents," CNBC, January 13, 2017, http://www.cnbc.com/2017/01/13/millennials-are-falling-behind-their-boomer-parents.html (accessed February 7, 2017).

6. "US Military Spending vs the World," SPRI, National Priorities Project, https://www.nationalpriorities.org/campaigns/us-military-spending-vs-world/ (accessed September 30, 2016).

Chapter 1. Is Our Economy Fundamentally Sound?

1. Andrew Taylor and Julie Pace, "President Trump Proposes a $54 Billion Increase in Defense Spending," *Time*, February 27, 2017; Julie Hirschfeld Davis and Alan Rappeport, "Tax Overhaul Would Aid Wealthiest," *New York Times*, April 27, 2017, p. A1.

2. John Bentley, "McCain Says 'Fundamentals' of US Economy Are Strong," CBS News, September 15, 2008, http://www.cbsnews.com/news/mccain-says-fundamentals-of-us-economy-are-strong/ (accessed March 31, 2017).

3. Trent Hamm, "How the Average American Family Spends Their Income—and How to Trim It," Simple Dollar, August 27, 2014, http://www.thesimpledollar.com/how-the-average-American-family-spends-their-income

-and-how-to-trim-it/ (accessed September 30, 2016); Derek Thompson, "Where the Middle Class Spends 75 Percent of Its Income on Housing and Transport: A Fresh Look at the Most Expensive Cities from the Center for Housing Policy and the Center for Neighborhood Technology," *CityLab*, November 29, 2012, http://www.citylab.com/work/2012/11/cities-where-people-spend-75-percent-their-income-housng-and-transportation/4027/ (accessed September 30, 2016).

4. See chapter 12.

5. "United States per Capita Healthcare Spending is More Than Twice the Average of Other Developed Countries," Peter G. Peterson Foundation, May 3, 2016, http://www.pgpf.org/chart-archive/0006_health-care-oecd (accessed September 30, 2016).

6. "US Military Spending vs the World," SPRI, National Priorities Project, https://www.nationalpriorities.org/campaigns/us-military-spending-vs-world/ (accessed September 30, 2016).

7. "United States Incarceration Rate," *Wikipedia*, September 1, 2016, https://en.wikipedia.org/wiki/United_States_incarceration_rate (accessed September 30, 2016).

8. Stephen L. Slavin, *Microeconomics* (New York: McGraw-Hill, 2013), p. 398, Figure 8.

9. See chapter 17 and chapter 18.

10. See chapter 7.

11. Half of our eighteen-year-olds don't go to college. Two-thirds cannot function at an eight-grade level. Of the half that does go to college, 60 percent are placed in remedial classes in math, English, or both. Forty percent of freshmen are enrolled in community colleges, where 75 percent are placed in remedial courses. One half of these students are placed in the lowest level of remediation: learning reading, writing, and arithmetic. This will be further discussed in chapter 12. Also, see "The Gap between Enrolling in College and Being Ready for College," http://www.highereducation.org/reports/college_readiness/gap.shtml (accessed September 30, 2016). About half of incoming college freshmen are placed in remedial courses. "Beyond the Rhetoric: Improving College Readiness through Coherent State Policy," National Center for Public Policy and Higher Education and Southern Regional Education Board, June 2010, http://highereducation.org/reports/college_readiness/index.shtml (accessed September 30, 2016).

12. See chapter 10.

13. See chapter 9.

14. See chapter 22.

15. See chapter 23.

16. See chapter 20.

17. Since the turn of the new millennium, we have been running annual current account deficits of more than $365 billion. This figure, which comes out to more than $1 billion a day, represents the amount of money we borrow from

foreigners. Stephen L. Slavin, *Microeconomics* (New York: McGraw-Hill, 2013), p. 498; *Economic Report of the President: Together with the Annual Report of the Council of Economic Advisers* (Washington, DC: US Government Publishing Office, 2016).

Chapter 2. What Went Wrong?

1. Since the turn of the new millennium, we have been running annual current account deficits of more than $365 billion. This figure, which comes out to more than $1 billion a day, represents the amount of money we borrow from foreigners. Stephen L. Slavin, *Microeconomics* (New York: McGraw-Hill, 2013), p. 498; *Economic Report of the President: Together with the Annual Report of the Council of Economic Advisers* (Washington, DC: US Government Publishing Office, 2016).

2. Trent Hamm, "How the Average American Family Spends Their Income—and How to Trim It," Simple Dollar, August 27, 2014, http://www.thesimpledollar.com/how-the-average-American-family-spends-their-income-and-how-to-trim-it/ (accessed October 1, 2016); Derek Thompson, "Where the Middle Class Spends 75 Percent of Its Income on Housing and Transport: A Fresh Look at the Most Expensive Cities from the Center for Housing Policy and the Center for Neighborhood Technology," *CityLab*, November 29, 2012, http://www.citylab.com/work/2012/11/cities-where-people-spend-75-percent-their-income-housng-and-transportation/4027/ (accessed October 1, 2016).

3. About half of incoming college freshmen are placed in remedial courses. "Beyond the Rhetoric: Improving College Readiness through Coherent State Policy," National Center for Public Policy and Higher Education and Southern Regional Education Board, June 2010, http://highereducation.org/reports/college_readiness/index.shtml (accessed October 1, 2016).

4. See Robert Pear, "National Health Spending to Surpass $10,000 a Person in 2016," *New York Times*, July 13, 2016, p. A1.

5. "United States per Capita Healthcare Spending is More Than Twice the Average of Other Developed Countries," Peter G. Peterson Foundation, May 3 2016, http://www.pgpf.org/chart-archive/0006_health-care-oecd (accessed October 1, 2016).

6. *Economic Report of the President: Together with the Annual Report of the Council of Economic Advisers* (Washington, DC: US Government Publishing Office, 2016).

7. "United States Incarceration Rate," *Wikipedia*, September 1, 2016, https://en.wikipedia.org/wiki/United_States_incarceration_rate (accessed October 1, 2016).

8. See Benjamin Landy, "Graph: How the Financial Sector Consumed America's Economic Growth," Twentieth Century Fund, February 25, 2013, https://tcf.org/content/commentary/graph-how-the-financial-sector-consumed-americas-Economic-growth/ (accessed October 1, 2016).

9. See Marc Levinson, "US Manufacturing in International Perspective" (Congressional Research Service report prepared for members and committees of Congress, April 26, 2016), http://fas.org/sgp/crs/misc/R42135.pdf (accessed October 1, 2016).

10. "List of Countries by Motor Vehicle Production," *Wikipedia*, October 8, 2016, https://en.wikipedia.org/wiki/List_of_countries_by_motor_vehicle_production (accessed October 1, 2016); "List of Countries by Steel Production," *Wikipedia*, August 19, 2016, https://en.wikipedia.org/wiki/List_of_countries_by_steel_production (accessed October 1, 2016).

11. Bernie Sanders, *Our Revolution* (New York: St. Martin's Press, 2016), p. 89.

Chapter 3. Depression and War

1. "What Was the Unemployment Rate During the Great Depression?" Answers, http://www.answers.com/Q/What_was_the_unemployment_rate_during_the_Great_Depression (accessed October 1, 2016).

2. See Howard Rosen, "Public Works: The Legacy of the New Deal," SocialStudies.org, http://www.socialstudies.org/sites/default/files/publications/se/6005/600506.html (accessed October 1, 2016).

3. Jane Holtz Kay, *Asphalt Nation* (New York: Crown Publishers, 1997), p. 199.

4. Ibid., p. 199; Gavin Wright, "The New Deal and the Modernization of the South," *Federal History*, 2010, http://shfg.org/shfg/wp-content/uploads/2011/01/5-Wright-design5-_Layout-1.pdf (accessed October 1, 2016).

5. Kay, *Asphalt Nation*, p. 213.

6. FHA Underwriting Manual (August 1, 1935) section 309, section 310.

7. "Racial Restrictive Covenants," Seattle Civil Rights & Labor History Project, 2016, http://depts.washington.edu/civilr/covenants.htm (accessed October 1, 2016).

8. See United States Census Bureau, www.census.gov.

9. *Economic Report of the President: Together with the Annual Report of the Council of Economic Advisers* (Washington, DC: US Government Publishing Office, 1983).

10. US Government Spending, http://www.usgovernmentspending.com/defense_spending (accessed April 14, 2017).

11. Keith Miller, "How Important Was Oil in World War II?" History News Network, July 5, 2002, http://historynewsnetwork.org/article/339 (accessed October 1, 2016).

12. *Economic Report of the President* (1983).

13. See chapter 13.

14. Wright, "New Deal."

15. Kay, *Asphalt Nation*.

16. LaDavia S. Hatcher, "A Case for Reparations: The Plight of the African-American World War II Veteran Concerning Federal Discriminatory Housing Practices," *Modern American* 2, no. 2 (Summer 2006), pp. 18–23, http://digitalcommons.wcl.american.edu/cgi/viewcontent.cgi?article=1100&context=tma (accessed April 14, 2017).

17. "US Military Spending vs. the World," SPRI, National Priorities Project, https://www.nationalpriorities.org/campaigns/us-military-spending-vs-world/ (accessed October 1, 2016).

18. Oil is vital to our national defense. During the Cold War, we quickly became the world's largest oil importer. To insure an uninterrupted supply of oil to ourselves and our allies, we needed to devote as much as one-third of our defense spending to protecting the flow of oil. See chapter 14.

Chapter 4. Suburbanization

1. Colin Stief, "An Overview of Suburbs: The History and Development of Suburbs," About, http://geography.about.com/od/urbaneconomicgeography/a/suburbs.htm (accessed October 2, 2016).

2. Lewis Mumford, *The Culture of Cities* (Cambridge, MA: Harvard University Press, 1955), p. 82.

3. "Racial Restrictive Covenants," Seattle Civil Rights & Labor History Project, 2016, http://depts.washington.edu/civilr/covenants.htm (accessed October 1, 2016).

4. Richard F. Weingroff, "Origins of the Interstate Maintenance Program," Federal Highway Administration, November 18, 2015, https://www.fhwa.dot.gov/infrastructure/intmaint.cfm (accessed October 2, 2016).

5. Drew Desilver, "The Biggest US Tax Breaks," Pew Research Center, April 6, 2016, http://www.pewresearch.org/fact-tank/2016/04/06/the-biggest-u-s-tax-breaks/ (accessed October 2, 2016).

6. "White Flight," *Wikipedia*, September 15, 2016, https://en.wikipedia.org/wiki/White_flight (accessed October 2, 2016).

7. David Callahan "How the GI Bill Left Out African Americans," Demos, November 11, 2013, http://www.demos.org/blog/11/11/13/how-gi-bill-left-out-african-americans (accessed October 2, 2016); "Residential Segregation in the United States," *Wikipedia*, August 19, 2016, https://en.wikipedia.org/wiki/Residential_segregation_in_the_United_States (accessed October 2, 2016).

8. Andres Duany, Elizabeth Plate-Zyberk, and Jeff Speck, *Suburban Nation: The Rise of Sprawl and the Decline of the American Dream* (New York: North Point Press, 2001), pp. 5–7.

9. Ibid., p. 7.

10. Ibid., p. 10.

11. Rob Wile, "Just 5% of Americans Are Using Public Transportation to Get

to Work," Fusion, May 26, 2015, http://fusion.net/story/139743/just-5-percent-of-workers-in-americas-largest-cities-use-public-transit/ (accessed October 2, 2016).

12. Ibid.

13. Corey Kilgannon, "Change Blurs Memories in a Famous Suburb," *New York Times*, October 13, 2007, http://www.nytimes.com/2007/10/13/nyregion/13suburb.html (accessed October 2, 2016).

14. "Characteristics of New Housing," United States Census Bureau, https://www.census.gov/construction/chars/highlights.html (accessed April 5, 2017).

15. "McMansion," *Wikipedia*, August 24, 2016, https://en.wikipedia.org/wiki/McMansion (accessed October 2, 2016). See also, "McMansion Hell," http://www.mcmansionhell.com/ (accessed October 2, 2016).

16. Jonathan Martin and Mike Allen, "McCain Unsure How Many Houses He Owns," *Politico*, August 21, 2008, http://www.politico.com/story/2008/08/mccain-unsure-how-many-houses-he-owns-012685 (accessed October 2, 2016).

17. David Brooks, "The Real Romney," *New York Times*, August 28, 2012, p. A23.

18. "Number of Vehicles Registered in the United States from 1990 to 2014 (in 1,000s)," Statista, 2016, https://www.statista.com/statistics/183505/number-of-vehicles-in-the-united-states-since-1990/ (accessed October 2, 2016).

19. See chapter 23.

20. "Urbanization of America, Move to Suburbia," Countries Quest, http://countriesquest.com/north_america/usa/people/urbanization_of_america/move_to_suburbia.htm (accessed October 2, 2016).

21. "Oil Imports and Exports," US Energy Information Administration, November 28, 2016, https://www.eia.gov/energyexplained/index.cfm?page=oil_imports (accessed April 14, 2017).

22. "US Military Spending vs the World," SPRI, National Priorities Project, https://www.nationalpriorities.org/campaigns/us-military-spending-vs-world/ (accessed September 30, 2016).

23. "What is White Flight?" WiseGeek, 2016, http://www.wisegeek.org/what-is-white-flight.htm (accessed October 2, 2016).

24. See chapter 20.

25. See chapter 20.

26. "Frequently Asked Questions," American Road and Transportation Builders Association, http://www.artba.org/about/faq/ (accessed October 2, 2016).

Chapter 5. The Cold War

1. "Kennan and Containment, 1947," Office of the Historian, https://history.state.gov/milestones/1945-1952/kennan (accessed April 5, 2017).

2. Palash Ghosh, "Green, White and Lots of Red: How Italy Got the West's Biggest Communist Party," *International Business Times*, July 26, 2013, http://www.ibtimes.com/green-white-lots-red-how-italy-got-wests-biggest-communist-party-1360089 (accessed April 14, 2017).

3. "Marshall Plan," *Wikipedia*, October 19, 2016, https://en.wikipedia.org/wiki/Marshall_Plan (accessed October 4, 2016).

4. "We Will Bury You!" *Time*, November 26, 1956.

5. For the full story of how the Japanese took over this industry, see chapter 6 of Pat Choate's book, *Agents of Influence* (New York: Touchstone, 1990).

6. Barry C. Lynn, *End of the Line* (New York: Doubleday, 2003), p. 61.

7. Ronald Hilton, "The Collapse of the Soviet Union and Ronald Reagan," https://wais.standord.edu/History/history-ussrandreagan.htm (accessed April 15, 2017).

8. Richard Halloran, "The Sad, Dark End of the British Empire," *Politico*, August 26, 2014, http://www.politico.com/magazine/story/2014/08/the-sad-end-of-the-british-empire-110362 (accessed October 4, 2016); "Decolonization after 1945," Map as History, http://www.the-map-as-history.com/maps/11-decolonization_independence.php (accessed October 4, 2016).

9. *Economic Report of the President: Together with the Annual Report of the Council of Economic Advisers* (Washington, DC: US Government Publishing Office, 2016).

10. Robert Higgs, "The Cold War Economy: Opportunity Costs, Ideology, and the Politics of Crisis," Independent Institute, July 1, 1994, http://www.independent.org/publications/article.asp?id=1297 (accessed October 4, 2016).

11. These two points are fully discussed in chapter 14.

12. *Economic Report of the President: Together with the Annual Report of the Council of Economic Advisers* (Washington, DC: US Government Publishing Office, 1983).

13. This is fully discussed in chapter 14.

14. "US Government Spending," http://www.usgovernmentspending.com/defense_spending (accessed April 14, 2017).

15. *Economic Report of the President: Together with the Annual Report of the Council of Economic Advisers* (Washington, DC: US Government Publishing Office, 2016).

16. Choate, *Agents of Influence*.

Chapter 6. Globalization and Global Warming

1. "Automotive Industry in the United States: 1960s," *Wikipedia*, October 11, 2016, https://en.wikipedia.org/wiki/Automotive_industry_in_the_United_States#1960s (accessed October 4, 2016).

2. Thomas L. Friedman and Michael Mandelbaum, *That Used to Be Us* (New York: Farrar, Straus and Giroux, 2011), p. 311; Thomas L. Friedman, *The World Is Flat* (New York: Farrar, Straus and Giroux, 2005), p.218.

3. Russ Koesterich, "China Is Now the Largest Car Market in the World," Market Realist, January 23, 2015, http://marketrealist.com/2015/01/china-now-largest-market-world-cars/ (accessed October 4, 2016).

4. Richard White, "The Rise of Industrial America, 1877–1900," Gilder Lehrman Institute of American History, https://www.gilderlehrman.org/history-by-era/essays/rise-industrial-america-1877-1900 (accessed October 4, 2016).

5. Ron Hira and Anil Hira, *Outsourcing America* (New York: American Management Association, 2005), p. 70.

6. Heather Havenstein, "IT Feels the Squeeze: IT Salaries Are Down, the Job Market Is Still Soft, and the Term 'Expense Center' Has Returned," *InfoWorld*, June 13, 2003, http://www.infoworld.com/article/2681823/techology-business/it-feels-the-squeeze.html (accessed October 4, 2016); "The TPP: More Job Offshoring and Lower Wages," Citizen.org, http://citizen.org/documents/tpp-wages-jobs.pdf (accessed October 4, 2016).

7. Clyde Prestowitz, *The Billion New Capitalists* (New York: Basic Books, 2005), pp. 184–85, 204–205; Friedman, *World Is Flat*, p. 293; Louis Uchitelle, *The Disposable American* (New York: Alfred A. Knopf, 2006), pp. 68–69.

8. Prestowitz, *Billion New Capitalists*, p. 205.

9. United States Department of Labor, Bureau of Labor Statistics, http://www.bls.gov/ (accessed October 4, 2016).

10. Stephen L. Slavin, *Microeconomics*, 11th ed. (New York: McGraw-Hill, 2013), p. 394, Figure 8.

11. Tim Sharp, "What Is the Temperature on the Moon?" Space.com, October 22, 2012, http://www.space.com/18175-moon-temperature.html (accessed October 4, 2016).

12. "Carbon Dioxide in Earth's Atmosphere," *Wikipedia*, October 20, 2016, https://en.wikipedia.org/wiki/Carbon_dioxide_in_Earth%27s_atmosphere (accessed October 4, 2016).

13. Bernie Sanders, *Our Revolution* (New York: St. Martin's Press, 2016), p. 357.

14. Michael Drewniak and Kevin Roberts, "Christie Administration Releases Total Hurricane Sandy Damage Assessment of $36.9 Billion," State of New Jersey Governor Chris Christie, November 28, 2012, http://www.state.nj.us/governor/news/news/552012/approved/20121128e.html (accessed October 4, 2016); Matt

Sledge, "Hurricane Sandy Damage in New York By-the-Numbers," *Huffington Post*, December 3, 2012, http://www.huffingtonpost.com/2012/12/03/hurricane-sandy-damage-new-york_n_2234335.html (accessed October 4, 2016).

15. Michael Bastasch, "Poll: 53 Percent of Americans Don't Believe in Man-Made Global Warming," Daily Caller News Foundation, June 26, 2014, http://dailycaller.com/2014/06/26/poll-53-of-americans-dont-believe-in-man-made-global-warming/ (accessed October 4, 2016).

16. Scott Neuman, "1 in 4 Americans Thinks the Sun Goes around the Earth, Survey Says," NPR, February 14, 2014, http://www.npr.org/blogs/thetwo-way/1014/02/14/277058739 (accessed October 4, 2016).

17. Justin Gillis, "For Third Year, the Earth in 2016 Set Heat Record," *New York Times*, January 19, 2017, p. A1.

18. Helen Briggs, "Global Climate Deal: A Summary," BBC News, Science & Environment, December 12, 2015, http://www.bbc.com/news/science-environment-35073297 (accessed January 11, 2017).

19. Chris Mooney, "Steps to Address Climate Change Are 'Irreversible,' World Leaders Decline in Marrakech," *Washington Post*, November 18, 2016.

PART III. THE DEINDUSTRIALIZATION OF AMERICA

1. United States Department of Labor: Bureau of Labor Statistics, http://www.bls.gov/ (accessed October 5, 2016).

Chapter 7. The Rise and Fall of American Industrial Power

1. See Barry C. Lynn, *End of the Line* (New York: Doubleday, 2005), p. 4.

2. "Growing a Nation: The Story of American Agriculture: Historical Timeline: 17th–18th Centuries," National Institute of Food and Agriculture, http://agclassroom.org/gan/timeline/17_18.htm (accessed October 5, 2016).

3. Stephen L. Slavin, *Microeconomics*, 11th ed. (New York: McGraw-Hill, 2013), p. 5

4. Ibid.

5. See Fig. 15 in Gene Smiley, "The US Economy in the 1920s," *Economic History Association*, http://eh.net/encyclopedia/the-u.s.-economy-in-the-1920s/ (accessed October 5, 2016).

6. Edward L. Ayers, Lewis L. Gould, et al., *American Passages: A History of the United States, Volume II: Since 1865* (Boston: Wadsworth/Cengage Learning, 2010), p. 505.

7. Paul Kennedy, "The (Relative) Decline of America," *Atlantic*, August 1987.

8. In chapter 5, we described America's efforts to shore up the economies of Japan and Western Europe in an effort to win the Cold War.

9. "1950s TV Turns on America," *Advertising Age*, March 28, 2005, http://adage.com/article/75-years-of-ideas/1950s-tv-turns-america/102703/ (accessed October 5, 2016).

10. Ibid.

11. Pat Choate, *Agents of Influence* (New York: Touchstone, 1990).

12. Barry C. Lynn, *End of the Line* (New York: Doubleday, 2003), p. 61.

13. Bureau of Labor Statistics, http://www.bls.gov/ (accessed October 5, 2016).

14. Ibid.

15. Lynn, *End of the Line*, p. 5.

16. Hedrick Smith, *Who Stole the American Dream?* (New York: Random House, 2012), p. 252.

17. Kyle Pomerleau and Emily Potosky, "Corporate Income Tax Rates around the World, 2016," Tax Foundation, August 18, 2016, http://taxfoundation.org/article/corporate-income-tax-rates-around-world-2016 (accessed October 5, 2016).

18. Ibid.

19. Kevin Drawbaugh, "When Companies Flee U.S. Tax System, Investors Often Don't Reap Big Returns," Reuters, August 18, 2014, http://www.reuters.com/article/us-usa-tax-inversion-insight-idUSKBN0GI0AY20140818 (accessed April 17, 2017).

20. As we've seen in chapter 6, the process of globalization describes this great industrial transformation.

21. Kim Peterson, "The Big Three Aren't So Big Anymore," CBS News, December 19, 2014, http://www.cbsnews.com/news/the-big-three-arent-so-big-anymore/ (accessed October 5, 2016); "Passenger Vehicles in the United States," *Wikipedia*, October 4, 2016, https://en.wikipedia.org/wiki/Passenger_vehicles_in_the_United_States (accessed October 5, 2016).

22. "Cell Phones Made in the USA," Americans Working, http://americansworking.com/listing-category/cell-phones-made-in-the-usa/ (accessed October 5, 2016).

23. David Sims, "China Widens Lead as World's Largest Manufacturer," ThomasNet, March 14, 2013, http://news.thomasnet.com/imt/2013/03/14/china-widens-lead-as-worlds-largest-manufacturer (accessed October 5, 2016).

Chapter 8. Innovation, Infrastructure, and Industrial Policy

1. Stephen S. Cohen and John Zysman, *Manufacturing Matters: The Myth of the Post-Industrial Economy* (New York: Basic Books), p. 68; Jeremy Quittner, "Not Made in America: Where US Innovation Really Comes From: Many of the Country's Best and Brightest Ideas? Well, They're Not Exactly Home-Grown," *Inc.*, April 10, 2014, http://www.inc.com/jeremy-quittner/foreign-patents-and-united-states-innovation.html (accessed October 5, 2016).

2. Robert E. Scott, "The Consequences of Neglecting Manufacturing Compared with Other Nations: US Has More Import Competition in Leading Export Industries," Economic Policy Institute, April 20, 2015, http://www.epi.org/publication/the-consequences-of-neglecting-manufacturing-compared-with-other-nations-u-s-has-more-import-competition-in-leading-export-industries/ (accessed October 5, 2016); "Knowing Which Products Are Truly Made in America: How to Know Which Flag-Waving Products Are True Red, White, and Blue," *Consumer Reports*, February 2013, http://www.consumerreports.org/cro/magazine/2013/02/made-in-america/index.htm (accessed October 5, 2016).

3. Louis Uchitelle, "Goodbye, Production (and Maybe Innovation)," *New York Times*, December 24, 2006, Section 3, p. 4.

4. President's Council of Advisors on Science and Technology, *Sustaining the Nation's Innovation Ecosystems, Information Technology, Manufacturing, and Competitiveness* (Washington, DC: President's Council of Advisors on Science and Technology, 2004), p. 14.

5. Jon Gertner, "True Innovation," *New York Times*, February 20, 2012, Sunday Review, p.

6. "Amazon, Full-Time & Part-Time Employees: Worldwide," Nakono, https://fusion.nakono.com/data/amazon-full-time-part-time-employees-worldwide-annual; Bill Kutik, "Oracle Comes Out Swinging at HCM World," *Human Resources Executive Online*, March 30, 2015, http://www.hreonline.com/HRE/view/story.jhtml?id=534358554; Julie Bort, "Google's Hiring May Have Slowed, but It's Still Adding Thousands of New Employees," *Business Insider*, July 17, 2015, http://www.businessinsider.com/google-has-57000-employees-2015-7; Apple, "Creating Jobs through Innovation," https://www.apple.com/about/job-creation/; "Microsoft Corporation: Employee Count from 2005 to 2016," Statistica, https.www.statistica.com/number-of-employees-at-the-microsoft-corporation; "Number of Facebook Employees from 2004 to 2016 (full-time)," Statistica, https://www.statista.com/statistics/273563/number-of-facebook-employees/; "eBay Total Full-Time Employees Worldwide," Nakono, https://fusion.nakono.com/data/ebay-total-full-time-employees-worldwide-annual; Symantec, "Corporate Profile," https://www.symantec.com/about/corporate-profile; "Number of Twitter Employees from 2008 to 2016," Statistica, https://www.statista.com/statistics/272140/employees-of-twitter/ (all accessed April 24, 2016).

7. "Creating Jobs through Innovation," Apple, http://www.apple.com/about/job-creation/ (accessed October 5, 2016).

8. Ibid.

9. Robert D. Atkinson and Stephen Ezeli, *Innovation Economics: The Race for Global Advantage* (New Haven: Yale University Press, 2012), p. 164.

10. "List of Countries by Research and Development Spending," *Wikipedia*, September 7, 2016, https://en.wikipedia.org/wiki/List_of_countries_by_research_and_development_spending (accessed October 5, 2016); "Historical

Trends in Federal R & D," AAAS, last updated October 13, 2016, http://www.aaas.org/page/historical-trends-federal-rd (accessed October 5, 2016).

11. Allie Bidwell, "American Students Fall in International Academic Tests, Chinese Lead the Pack: Education Leaders Say the Results Are Disappointing and 'Lackluster,'" *US News & World Report*, December 3, 2013, http://www.usnews.com/news/articles/2013/12/03/american-students-fall-in-international-academic-tests-chinese-lead-the-pack (accessed October 10, 2016).

12. Jenny Ung, "International Students Earn More Than Half of Advanced STEM Degrees in the U.S.," *USA Today College*, July 8, 2015, http://college.usatoday.com/2015/07/08/international-students-stem-degrees/; Alison Herget, "Foreign-Born Faculty Face Challenges," HigherEd Jobs, August 18, 2016, https://www.higheredjobs.com/articles/articleDisplay.cfm?ID=1012 (accessed April 25, 2017).

13. Ibid.

14. "China Usually Doubles Its GDP Every 5–10 Years, Assuming It Overtakes US' GDP by 2019, Why Is There No Prediction Made That China's GDP Will Be Many Times Larger Compared to That of US in 2050?" Quora, https://www.quora.com/China-usually-doubles-its-GDP-every-5-10-years-assuming-it-overtakes-US-GDP-by-2019-why-is-there-no-prediction-made-that-Chinas-GDP-will-be-many-times-larger-compared-to-that-of-US-in-2050 (accessed October 5, 2016).

15. Barry B. LePatner, *Too Big to Fall* (New York: Forster Publishing and Hanover, NH: University Press of New England, 2010), p. xx.

16. We talked about this in chapter 6.

17. LePatner, *Too Big to Fall*, p. 7.

18. Tom Yam, "China's High-Speed-Rail Programme a Case of Too Far, Too Fast," *South China Morning Post*, August 25, 2013, http://www.scmp.com/lifestyle/technology/article/1299188/chinas-high-speed-rail-programme-case-too-far-too-fast (accessed October 5, 2016); Michael Fitzpatrick, "Did China Steal Japan's High-Speed Train?" *Fortune*, April 15, 2013, http://fortune.com/2013/04/15/did-china-steal-japans-high-speed-train/ (accessed October 5, 2016); "High-Speed Rail in China," *Wikipedia*, October 20, 2016, https://en.wikipedia.org/wiki/High-speed_rail_in_China (accessed October 5, 2016).

19. LePatner, *Too Big to Fall*, p. 5.

20. Ibid.

21. Ron Nixon, "Human Cost Rises as Infrastructure Withers," *New York Times*, November 6, 2015, p. A12.

22. Atkinson and Ezeli, *Innovation Economics*, p. 139.

23. Katie Hafner, "Does Industrial Policy Work? Lessons from Sematech," *New York Times*, November 7, 1993.

24. Dave Demerjian, "As Congress Stalls, Air Traffic Creeps Towards Gridlock," *Wired*, January 22, 2009, https://www.wired.com/2009/01/congress-fails (accessed October 5, 2016).

25. Sheryll Poe, "Fueling the Discussion on Infrastructure," US Chamber of Commerce, April 30, 2014, https://www.uschamber.com/fueling-discussion-infrastructure (accessed October 5, 2016).

26. "Infrastructure Grades for 2013," American Society of Civil Engineers, http://www.infrastructurereportcard.org/ (accessed October 5, 2016).

27. Ibid.

28. Ibid.

29. Peter Coy, "China Spends More on Infrastructure Than the US and Europe Combined: Western Countries Put Less Money into Roads and Bridges Than They Did Before the Global Financial Crisis," *Bloomberg Business Week*, June 15, 2016, http://www.bloomberg.com/news/articles/2016-06-15/china-spends-more-on-infrastructure-than-the-u-s-and-europe-combined (accessed October 5, 2016).

30. Angie Schmitt, "The State of American Infrastructure Spending in Four Charts," Streets Blog USA (blog), May 21, 2015, http://usa.streetsblog.org/2015/05/21/the-state-of-american-infrastructure-spending-in-four-graphics/ (accessed October 5, 2016).

31. Eduardo Porter, "In Shovels, a Remedy for Jobs and Growth," *New York Times*, February 12, 2013, p. B8.

32. Hedrick Smith, *Who Stole the American Dream?* (New York: Random House, 2012), p 384.

33. Richard Florida, "Which Countries Pay Blue Collar Workers the Most? Manufacturing Compensation Is Closely Related to Productivity, Global Economic Competitiveness, and Overall Human Development," *CityLab*, January 9, 2012, http://www.citylab.com/work/2012/01/which-countries-pay-blue-collar-workers-most/818/ (accessed October 5, 2016).

34. Michael Grabell, "How Not to Revive an Economy," *New York Times*, February 11, 2012, http://www.nytimes.com/2012/02/12/opinion/sunday/how-the-stimulus-fell-short.html.

35. Lauren Gardner, "Trump's $1 Trillion Plan Hits DC Speed Bumps: The President-Elect's Pitch for an Upgrade of the Nation's Roads, Bridges, Tunnels and Airports Is Already Running into Washington Reality," *Politico*, November 20, 2016, http://www.politico.com/story/2016/11/trump-infrastructure-plan-washington-reality-231649 (accessed January 11, 2017).

36. Tom Hals, "U.S. Solar Firm Solyndra Files for Bankruptcy," Reuters, September 6, 2011, http://www.reuters.com/article/us-solyndra-idUSTRE77U5K420110906 (accessed April 17, 2017).

37. "Sens. Brown and Blunt Introduce Bill to Revitalize American Manufacturing through Network of Public-Private 'Innovation Hubs,'" Sherrod Brown Senator for Ohio press release, https://www.brown.senate.gov/newsroom/press/release/sens-brown-and-blunt-introduce-bill-to-revitalize-american-manufacturing-through-network-of-public-private-innovation-hubs (accessed April 17, 2017).

PART IV. JOBS, WAGES, AND THE JOB SHORTAGE

1. United States Department of Labor, "Employment Characteristics of Families Summary," Bureau of Labor Statistics, April 22, 2016, https://www.bls.gov/news.release/famee.nr0.htm (April 11, 2017).

2. Stephen L. Slavin, *Microeconomics*, 11th ed. (New York: McGraw-Hill, 2013), p. 394, Fig. 8.

Chapter 9. Jobs and Wages

1. "Employment Discrimination," Leadership Conference on Civil & Human Rights, http://www.civilrights.org/publications/reports/long-road/discrimination.html? (accessed October 6, 2016); "Our History: An Overview 1920–2012," United States Department of Labor, https://www.dol.gov/wb/info_about_wb/interwb.htm (accessed October 6, 2016).

2. W. Michael Cox and Richard Alm, "Creative Destruction," *Concise Encyclopedia of Economics*, http://www.econlib.org/library/Enc/CreativeDestruction.html (accessed April 18, 2016).

3. James Hash, as quoted in *New York Times*, October 30, 2006, p. A16.

4. Bureau of Labor Statistics, http://www.bls.gov/ (accessed October 6, 2016).

5. Ibid.

6. See Clyde Prestowitz, *Three Billion New Capitalists* (New York: Basic Books, 2005), pp. 184–85; pp. 204–205; Thomas Friedman, *The World Is Flat* (New York: Farrar, Straus, and Giroux, 2005), p. 293; and Louis Uchitelle, *The Disposable American* (New York: Alfred A. Knopf, 2006), pp. 68–69.

7. Ibid.

8. Nelson Schwartz, "Trump to Announce Carrier Plant Will Keep Jobs in US," *New York Times*, November 30, 2016.

9. Katherine Peralta, "Outsourcing to China Cost US 3.2 Million Jobs Since 2001," *US News and World Report*, December 11, 2014, http://www.usnews.com/news/blogs/data-mine/2014/12/11/outsourcing-to-china-cost-us-32-million-jobs-since-2001 (accessed January 11, 2017).

10. Associated Press, "U.S. Factories Still Thriving, but Robots Mean Fewer Workers," *Boston Herald*, November 2, 2016; "Industrial Production Index," FRED, April 18, 2017, https://fred.stlouisfed.org/series/INDPRO (accessed April 24, 2017).

11. Alan Wolff, "How Trump Can Make Trade with Mexico and China Work for America," *Fortune*, December 19, 2016.

12. James Pethokoukis, "What the Story of ATMs and Bank Tellers Reveals about the 'Rise of the Robots' and Jobs," American Enterprise Institute, June 6, 2016, http://www.aei.org/publication/what-atms-bank-tellers-rise-robots-and-jobs/ (accessed January 11, 2017).

13. Bureau of Economic Analysis, https://www.bea.gov/ (accessed January 11, 2017).

14. David Rotman, "How Technology Is Destroying Jobs," *MIT Technology Review*, June 12, 2013, https://www.technologyreview.com/s/515926/how-technology-is-destroying-jobs/ (accessed January 11, 2017).

15. Ibid.; Erik Brynjolfsson and Andrew McAfee, *Race against the Machine: How the Digital Revolution Is Accelerating Innovation, Driving Productivity, and Irreversibly Transforming Employment and the Economy* (Cambridge, MA: Digital Frontier Press, 2011).

16. Prestowitz, *Three Billion New Capitalists*, p. 149.

17. Bureau of Labor Statistics, "Union Members: 2015," news release, January 28, 2016, http://www.bls.gov/news.release/pdf/union2.pdf (accessed October 6, 2016); Quoctrung Bui, "50 Years of Shrinking Union Membership, in One Map," NPR, February 23, 2015, http://www.npr.org/sections/money/2015/02/23/385843576/50-years-of-shrinking-union-membership-in-one-map (accessed October 6, 2016).

18. Shane Hall, "Union vs Nonunion Wages," eHow, http://www.ehow.com/info_7994766_union-vs-nonunion-wages.html (accessed October 6, 2016).

19. "Jobs across America," Services Coalition, http://servicescoalition.org/jobs/ (accessed October 6, 2016).

20. Jeremy Rifkin, *The End of Work* (New York: Penguin, 2014), pp. xx–xxi.

21. Ibid.

22. "About Us," Walmart, 2016, http://corporate.walmart.com/our-story (accessed October 6, 2016).

23. "Walmart Hourly Pay," Glass Door, October 17, 2016, https://www.glassdoor.com/Hourly-Pay/Walmart-Hourly-Pay-E715.htm (accessed October 6, 2016).

24. Julie Gutman Dickinson, "Wal-Mart's War against Unions—and the U.S. Laws That Make It Possible," *Huffington Post*, August 5, 2013, http://www.huffingtonpost.com/julie-b-gutman/walmart-labor-laws_b_3390994.html (accessed April 17, 2017).

25. Hiroko Tabuchi, "Walmart's Imports From China Displace 400,000 Jobs, a Study Says," *New York Times*, December 9, 2015.

26. Associated Press, "Mayor Vetoes Chicago's 'Living Wage' Ordinance Aimed at Big Retailers," *USA Today*, September 11, 2006, http://usatoday30.usatoday.com/money/economy/employment/2006-09-11-chicago-wage_x.htm (accessed October 6, 2016).

27. Shruti Date Singh, "Wal-Mart Gets 25,000 Applications for Evergreen Park Store," *Crain's Chicago Business*, January 25, 2006, http://www.chicagobusiness.com/article20060125/NEWS01/200019286/wal-mart-gets-25,000-applications-for-evergreen-park-store (accessed October 6, 2016).

28. Greg LeRoy, *The Great American Jobs Scam* (San Francisco: Berrett-Koehler Publishers, 2005), pp. 140–41.

29. Ibid., p. 141.

30. Jeremy Rifkin, *End of Work*, p. 194.

31. Carl Biers and Marsha Niemeijer, "'Vote No' Campaign Heats Up over East Coast Longshore Union Contract," Labor Notes, May 21, 2004, http://labornotes.org/2004/05/%E2%80%9Cvote-no%E2%80%9D-campaign-heats-over-east-coast-longshore-union-contract?language=es (accessed October 6, 2016).

32. Louis Uchitelle, "Two-Tier Wage Scales Gain Traction," *New York Times*, November 20, 2010.

33. David Barkholz, "Ending Tier 2 Will Put UAW-GM Deal over the Top," *New York Times*, November 4, 2015.

34. See uswlocal1055.org/news.detailphp?id=84 (accessed October 2016).

35. Hedrick Smith, *Who Stole the American Dream?* (New York: Random House), p. 74.

36. Louis Uchitelle, "Unions Yield Pay Scales to Keep Jobs," *New York Times*, November 28, 2010, pp. A1, B2. See also, Louis Uchitelle, "How Two-Tier Union Contracts Became Labor's Undoing," *Nation*, February 25, 2013. He argues that current workers agree to lower pay for entry workers as long as their own wages go untouched.

37. *Economic Report of the President: Together with the Annual Report of the Council of Economic Advisers* (Washington, DC: US Government Publishing Office, 2016).

38. David Wessel, "Big US Firms Shift Hiring Abroad: Work Forces Shrink at Home, Sharpening Debate on Economic Impact of Globalization," *Wall Street Journal*, April 16, 2011, http://www.wsj.com/articles/SB10001424052748704821704576270783611823972 (accessed October 6, 2016).

39. Adam Smith, *An Inquiry into the Nature and Causes of the Wealth of Nations, Volume 1* (London: Methuen, 1950), pp. 8–9.

40. Michael J. Hicks and Srikant Devaraj, "The Myth and the Reality of Manufacturing in America," Ball State University, 2016.

41. Claire Cain Miller, "What's Really Killing Jobs? It's Automation, Not China," *New York Times*, December 22, 2016, p. A3.

42. Michael Morgenstern, "Automation and Anxiety: Will Smarter Machines Cause Mass Unemployment?" *Economist*, June 25, 2016.

Chapter 10. The Job Shortage

1. Bureau of Labor Statistics, "Shifts in Auto Industry Employment, 1979–98," September 28, 1999, https://www.bls.gov/opub/ted/1999/sept/wk5/art02.htm (accessed October 25, 2016).

2. United States International Trade Commission, Usitc.gov/publications/332/employment-changes.pdf (accessed October 25, 2016).

3. Anna Quindlen, "A Changing World," *New York Times*, May 20, 1990, Section 4, p. 11.

4. "Fastest Growing Occupations," United States Department of Labor: Bureau of Labor Statistics, last modified April 18, 2016, http://www.bls.gov/emp/ep_table_103.htm (accessed October 7, 2016).

5. Ibid.

6. Susan Adams, "Half of College Grads Are Working Jobs That Don't Require a Degree," *Forbes*, May 28, 2013, http://www.forbes.com/sites/susanadams/2013/05/28/half-of-college-grads-are-working-jobs-that-dont-require-a-degree/#2a04708410bb (accessed October 7, 2016).

7. United States Department of Labor: Bureau of Labor Statistics, http://www.bls.gov/ (accessed October 7, 2016).

PART V. WASTING OUR RESOURCES BY USING THEM INEFFICIENTLY

1. "US Imports of Crude Oil," US Energy Information Administration, September 30, 2016, http://www.eia.gov/dnav/pet/hist/LeafHandler.ashx?n=PET&s=MCRIMUS2&f=A (accessed October 7, 2016).

2. This is discussed in chapter 13.

3. This is discussed in the next chapter.

4. "The Gap between Enrolling in College and Being Ready for College" in "Beyond the Rhetoric: Improving College Readiness through Coherent State Policy" (special report, National Center for Public Policy and Higher Education and Southern Regional Education Board, June 2010), http://www.highereducation.org/reports/college_readiness/gap.shtml (accessed October 7, 2016).

Chapter 11. Our Wasteful Transportation System

1. Trent Hamm, "How the Average American Family Spends Their Income—and How to Trim It," Simple Dollar, August 27, 2014, http://www.thesimpledollar.com/how-the-average-American-family-spends-their-income-and-how-to-trim-it/ (accessed September 30, 2016).

2. "How We Use Energy: Transportation," National Academy of Sciences, 2016, http://needtoknow.nas.edu/energy/energy-use/transportation/ (accessed October 8, 2016).

3. "Energy Use in the United States," *Wikipedia*, September 3, 2016, https://en.wikipedia.org/wiki/Energy_in_the_United_States (accessed October 8, 2016).

4. See Joe Gross, *Trolly and Interurban Lines of the United States and Canada*, revised ed. (Spencerport, NY: privately published by Joseph Gross, 1977).

5. Jane Holtz Kay, *Asphalt Nation* (New York: Crown Publishers, 1977), p. 213. A large city like Los Angeles had a few different streetcar systems, some of which had more than a dozen individual lines.

6. United States Census Bureau, http://www.census.gov (accessed October 8, 2016).

7. *Field of Dreams*, directed by Phil Alden Robinson (Boston, MA: Gordon Company, 1989).

8. Kay, *Asphalt Nation*, p. 199

9. Ibid.

10. Robert Caro, *The Power Broker* (New York: Vintage Books, 1975).

11. Ibid., p. 519.

12. This is attributed to Walter Kulash, a prominent traffic engineer. See "Congestion Toolbox," Kentucky Transportation Cabinet, http://transportation.ky.gov/Congestion-Toolbox/Pages/default.aspx (accessed October 8, 2016).

13. Caro, *Power Broker*.

14. For New York, see Robert Caro, *Power Broker*.

15. Kay, *Asphalt Nation*, p. 64.

16. Nilima Achwal, "Note on the 'Big Three' US Auto Producers," William Davidson Institute at the University of Michigan, February 16, 2010, http://nilimaachwal.com/wp-content/uploads/2014/04/Globalens-Decline-of-the-Big-3-Auto-Makers.pdf (accessed October 8, 2016).

17. "Auto Marketplace Sales Data: 2015 Sales," Alliance Automobile Manufacturers, http://www.autoalliance.org/index.cfm?furl=auto-marketplace/sales-data (accessed October 8, 2016).

18. Christopher MacKechnie, "What Is the Passenger Capacity of Different Modes of Transit?" About, July 19, 2015, http://publictransport.about.com/od/Transit_Planning/a/What-Is-The-Capacity-Of-Different-Modes-Of-Transit.htm (accessed October 8, 2016); Transit Cooperative Research Program, onlinepubs.trb.org/onlinepubs/tcrp_webdoc_6-b.pdf.

19. Kay, *Asphalt Nation*, p. 304.

20. Jeffrey M. Zupan, "Beyond the Open Road: Reinventing Transportation Policy for the 21st Century," (address to New York University Law School) quoted in Kay, *Asphalt Nation*, p. 304.

21. Bureau of Labor Statistics, "How Do US Expenditures Compare with Those of Other Countries?" *Focus on Prices and Spending* 2, no. 16 (March 2012), http://www.bls.gov/opub/btn/archive/how-do-us-expenditures-compare-with-those-of-other-countries.pdf (accessed October 8, 2016).

22. *Annie Hall*, directed by Woody Allen (Los Angeles, CA: Rollins-Joffe Productions, 1977).

23. "Petroleum and Other Liquids," US Energy Information Administration, September 30, 2016, http://www.eia.gov/dnav/pet/hist/LeafHandler.ashx?n=PET&S=MCRIMUS2&f=A (accessed October 8, 2016).

24. Kay, *Asphalt Nation*, p. 80.

25. "TGV: Passenger Usage," *Wikipedia*, October 20, 2016, https://en.wikipedia.org/wiki/TGV#Passenger_usage (accessed October 8, 2016); "Shink-

ansen," *Wikipedia*, October 3, 2016, https://en.wikipedia.org/wiki/Shinkansen (accessed October 8, 2016).

26. Marcus Bowman, "High-Speed Rail Speed Comparisons," slide show, Slide Share, February 18, 2010, http://www.slideshare.net/marcus.bowman.slides/high-speed-rail-speed-comparisons (accessed October 8, 2016).

27. Newt Gingrich with Vince Haley and Rick Taylor, *Real Change: From the World That Fails to the World That Works* (Wilmington, DE: Regnery, 2008), pp. 206–207.

28. Associated Press, "110 Mph Train Service Starts on Part of Chicago–St. Louis Route," *Crain's Chicago Business*, November 23, 2012, http://www.chicagobusiness.com/article/20121123/NEWS10/121129929/110-mph-train-service-starts-on-part-of-chicago-st-louis-route (accessed October 8, 2016).

29. "China GDP Per Capita," Trading Economics, http://www.tradingeconomics.com/china/gdp-per-capita (accessed April 28, 2017); "China High-Speed Rail Network Has Passed 20,000 Kilometers in Total Length," Next Big Future, September 12, 2016, http://www.nextbigfuture.com/2016/09/china-high-speed-rail-network-has.html (accessed October 8, 2016).

30. Joseph P. Schwieterman, Brian Antolin, et al., *The Remaking of the Motor Coach: 2015 Year in Review of Intercity Bus Services in the United States* (Chicago: Chaddick Institute for Metropolitan Development at De Paul University, 2016), p. 16.

31. "ATA: Trucks Move More Than Two-Thirds of U.S. Freight in 2012," *Rubber & Plastics News*, May 31, 2013, http://www.rubbernews.com/article/20130531/NEWS/130539983/ata-trucks-move-more-than-two-thirds-of-u-s-freight-in-2012 (accessed April 17, 2017).

32. Joe Cortright, "Trucking Industry Imposes Up to $128 Billion in Costs on Society Each Year," *Streetsblog USA*, June 2, 2015, http://usa.streetsblog.org/2015/06/02/trucking-industry-imposes-up-to-128-billion-in-costs-on-society-each-year/ (accessed April 17, 2017).

33. Author's estimate using these sources: "NADA Data," National Automobile Dealers Association, 2015, https://www.nada.org/nadadata/ (accessed October 8, 2016); Paul Ausick, "Why Are There 115,000 (or 150,000) Gas Stations in America?" 24/7 Wall St., May 22, 2014, http://247wallst.com/economy/2014/05/22/why-are-there-115000-or-150000-gas-stations-in-america/ (accessed October 8, 2016); Kantar Media, "US Measured Ad Expenditures Declined 3.9% in Q3 2015 to $36 Billion," press release, December 16, 2015, http://www.kantarmedia.com/us/newsroom/press-releases/us-measured-ad-expenditures-declined-3-9-q3-2015-36-billion (accessed October 8, 2016).

34. See "Your Driving Costs," AAA Exchange, http://exchange.aaa.com/automobiles-travel/automobiles/driving-costs/#.WApAOfkrK1s (accessed October 8, 2016).

35. "United States GDP from Transportation and Warehousing," *Trading Economics*, 2005–2016 data, http://www.tradingeconomics.com/united-states/gdp-from-transport (accessed October 8, 2016).

36. "Gasoline Tax," American Petroleum Institute, http://www.api.org/oil-and-natural-gas/consumer-information/motor-fuel-taxes/gasoline-tax (accessed October 8, 2016).

37. Patricia Chen and Waqas Rehman, *Gas Tax Overview* (Los Angeles: Los Angeles County Metropolitan Transportation Authority, 2015), https://media.metro.net/about_us/committees/sfs/images/sfs_presentation_2015_0416_gastax.pdf (accessed October 27, 2016).

38. Marianne Lavelle, "Fuel Efficiency Plan Aims for Big Savings," *US News*, April 22, 2008, https://www.usnews.com/news/national/articles/2008/04/22/fuel-efficiency-plan-aims-for-big-savings?context=amp (accessed April 17, 2017).

39. Bill Vlasic, "Obama Reveals Details of Gas Mileage Rules," *New York Times*, July 29, 2011, http://www.nytimes.com/2011/07/30/business/energy-environment/obama-reveals-details-of-gas-mileage-rules.html.

40. "The MTA Network," Metropolitan Transportation Authority, http://web.mta.info/mta/network.htm (accessed April 25, 2017).

41. Brian McKenzie and Melanie Rapino, *Commuting in the United States: 2009* (Washington, DC: United States Census Bureau), https://www.census.gov/prod/2011pubs/acs-15.pdf (accessed April 25, 2017).

42. See Kay, *Asphalt Nation*, p. 119.

43. See S. Handy, "History of Federal Transportation Policy," University of California, Davis, April 4, 2016, http://www.des.ucdavis.edu/faculty/handy/TTP220/TTP220_History2.pdf (accessed October 8, 2016).

44. Fiscal Federalism Initiative, "Funding Challenges in Highway and Transit: A Federal-State-Local Analysis," Pew Charitable Trusts, February 24, 2015, http://www.pewtrusts.org/en/research-and-analysis/analysis/2015/02/24/funding-challenges-in-highway-and-transit-a-federal-state-local-analysis (accessed October 8, 2016).

Chapter 12. Our Failing Public Schools

1. "The Gap between Enrolling in College and Being Ready for College" in "Beyond the Rhetoric: Improving College Readiness through Coherent State Policy" (special report, National Center for Public Policy and Higher Education and Southern Regional Education Board, June 2010), http://www.highereducation.org/reports/college_readiness/gap.shtml (accessed October 10, 2016).

2. Associated Press, "US Education Spending Tops Global List, Study Shows," CBS News, June 25, 2013, http://www.cbsnews.com/news/us-education-spending-tops-global-list-study-shows/ (accessed October 10, 2016).

3. Allie Bidwell, "American Students Fall in International Academic Tests, Chinese Lead the Pack: Education Leaders Say the Results Are Disappointing and 'Lackluster,'" *US News & World Report*, December 3, 2013, http://www.usnews.com/news/articles/2013/12/03/american-students-fall-in-international-academic-tests-chinese-lead-the-pack (accessed October 10, 2016).

4. Kavitha Cardoza, "Turning the Page on Illiteracy, Adults Go Back to Class," NPR, October 13, 2013, http://www.npr.org/2013/10/31/241862699/turning-the-page-on-illiteracy-adults-go-back-to-class (accessed October 10, 2016); "Understanding Illiteracy," Visually, September 3, 2011, http://visual.ly/understanding-illiteracy (accessed October 10, 2016).

5. Jason Koebler, "Many STEM Teachers Don't Hold Certifications: Shortages Force Educators to Teach Subjects Outside of Their Specialty Areas," *US News & World Report*, June 8, 2011, http://www.usnews.com/education/blogs/high-school-notes/2011/06/08/many-stem-teachers-dont-hold-certifications (accessed October 10, 2016).

6. Sonali Kohli, "Students in These Countries Spend the Most Time Doing Homework," Quartz, December 12, 2014, http://qz.com/311360/students-in-these-countries-spend-the-most-time-doing-homework/ (accessed October 10, 2016); Julia Ryan, "How Much Homework Do American Kids Do? Various Factors, from the Race of the Student to the Number of Years a Teacher Has Been in the Classroom, Affect a Child's Homework Load," *Atlantic*, September 19, 2013, http://www.theatlantic.com/education/archive/2013/09/how-much-homework-do-american-kids-do/279805/ (accessed October 10, 2016).

7. Steve Slavin and Ginny Crisonino, *Basic Mathematics*, 2nd ed. (New York: Pi R Squared Publishers, 2006).

8. Ibid.

9. "Gap between Enrolling in College." In California, at least 85 percent of community college students must take remedial courses. See Eloy Ortiz Oakley and Pamela Burdman, "Community Colleges Sending Too Many into Remedial Math," *San Francisco Chronicle*, May 29, 2015, http://www.sfchronicle.com/opinion/article/Community-colleges-sending-too-many-into-remedial-6293307.php (accessed October 10, 2016).

10. "Staggering Illiteracy Statistics," Literacy Project Foundation, 2016, http://literacyprojectfoundation.org/community/statistics/ (accessed October 10, 2016).

11. Jeff Nesbit, "A Quarter of Americans Think the Sun Orbits the Earth . . . Sigh," Live Science, February 22, 2014, http://www.livescience.com/43593-americans-ignorant-about-science.html (accessed October 10, 2016).

12. Scott Neuman, "1 in 4 Americans Thinks the Sun Goes around the Earth, Survey Says," NPR, February 14, 2014, http://www.npr.org/blogs/thetwo-way/1014/02/14/277058739 (accessed October 4, 2016).

13. Thomas E. Friedman and Michael Mandelbaum, *That Used to be Us* (New York: Farrar, Straus and Giroux, 2011), p. 222.

14. Clyde Prestowitz, *Three Billion New Capitalists* (New York: Basic Books, 2005), p. 133.

15. Susan Holloway, Yoko Yamamoto, et al., "Determinants of Parental Involvement in Early Schooling: Evidence from Japan," *Early Childhood Research & Practice* 10, no. 1 (2008); Miki Y. Ishikida, *Japanese Education in the 21st Century*

(Bloomington, IN: iUniverse, 2005), http://usjp.org/jpeducation_en/jpEd Primary_en.html (accessed April 25, 2017).

16. Paul Tough, "Education," *New York Times*, November 26, 2006, Section 6, pp. 47–48.

17. Ibid. See also Margaret Talbot, "The Talking Cure," *New Yorker*, January 12, 2015, p. 38.

18. *Brooklyn College Magazine*, 2012, p. 4.

19. Tough, "Education."

20. Sara Rimer, "Paterson Principal: A Man of Extremes," *New York Times*, January 14, 1988, http://www.nytimes.com/1988/01/14/nyregion/paterson-principal-a-man-of-extremes.html?pagewanted=all (accessed October 10, 2016).

21. Julia Isaacs, "Starting School at a Disadvantage: The School Readiness of Poor Children," *Brookings Institution*, March 2012, p. 3.

22. Isaacs, "Starting School," p. 6.

23. Quote attributed to Moshe Dayan.

24. Concord Coalition Report, *New York Times*, January 5, 2007.

25. Lynn O'Shaughnessy, "Here's the Nation's Easiest College Major," MarketWatch, June 21, 2011.

26. Walter Williams, "A Time for Truth," *Jewish World Review*, April 19, 1999, http://www.jewishworldreview.com/cols/williams041999.asp (accessed October 10, 2016).

27. E. Thomas Ewing and David Hicks, eds., *Education and the Great Depression* (New York: Peter Lang, 2006).

28. O'Shaughnessy, "Here's the Nation's."

29. G. Will, "John Silber is Refreshingly Tart," *Ashbury Park Press*, May 10, 1990, p. 14, https://www.newspapers.com/newspage/145478753/ (accessed October 10, 2016).

30. C. Emily Feistritzer, *Profile of the Teachers in the U.S. 2011* (Washington: National Center for Education Information, 2011), p. viii, http://www.edweek.org/media/pot2011final-blog.pdf (accessed April 18, 2017).

31. David Klein, "A Brief History of American K–12 Mathematics Education in the 20th Century," in *Mathematical Cognition*, ed. James Royer (Charlotte, NC: Information Age Publishing, 2003), http://www.csun.edu/~vcmth00m/AHistory.html (accessed October 10, 2016).

32. Mike Antonucci, "Teachers Unions and the War Within," *Education Next* 15, no. 1 (2015), http://educationnext.org/teachers-unions-war-within/ (accessed April 18, 2017).

33. Robin Waters, "Teachers' Unions and Collective Bargaining Agreements: Roadblocks to Student Achievement and Teacher Quality or Educational Policy Imperatives?" (Loyola University Chicago Child Law and Education Institute Forum, 2013), http://www.luc.edu/media/lucedu/law/centers/childlaw/childed/pdfs/2013studentpapers/waters.pdf (accessed April 25, 2017).

34. "Social Studies," Illinois Loop, 2012, http://www.illinoisloop.org/socstud.html (accessed October 10, 2016).

35. See Williams, "Time for Truth."

36. Emily Friedman, "Are Students Coddled? Schools Get Rid of 'F's," ABC News, December 5, 2008, http://abcnews.go.com/US/story?id=6395403&page=1 (accessed April 26, 2017).

37. Barry Garelick, "A New Kind of Problem: The Common Core Math Standards," *Atlantic*, November 20, 2012, https://www.theatlantic.com/national/archive/2012/11/a-new-kind-of-problem-the-common-core-math-standards/265444/ (accessed April 10, 2017).

38. Klein, "Brief History."

39. Stephanie Banchero, "US High-School Students Slip in Global Rankings," *Wall Street Journal*, December 3, 2013.

40. Joe Klein, "Learning What Works," *Time*, May 14, 2012, p. 36.

41. "Diane Ravitch, PhD—a Brief History of Teacher Professionalism," US Department of Education, August 23, 2003, https://www2.ed.gov/admins/tchrqual/learn/preparingteachersconference/ravitch.html (accessed April 25, 2017); Neal McCluskey, "A Thought Experiment Gone Terribly Wrong," *Cato at Liberty* (blog), January 17, 2008, https://www.cato.org/blog/thought-experiment-gone-terribly-wrong (accessed April 25, 2017).

42. O'Shaughnessy, "Here's the Nation's."

43. Peter Schrag, "Schoolhouse Crock," *Harper's Magazine*, September 2007, p. 42.

44. Ibid.

45. S. A. Reid, "Report: Poor the Majority in South's Public Schools," *Atlanta Journal-Constitution*, October 31, 2007.

46. Quoted by Edward Luce, *Time to Start Thinking: America in the Age of Descent* (New York: Atlantic Monthly Press, 2012), p. 84.

47. Bruce Fisher, "Bob Wilmers and Education," *Public*, March 25, 2015, http://www.dailypublic.com/articles/03252015/bob-wilmers-and-education (accessed October 10, 2016).

48. Richard Rothstein, "For Public Schools, Segregation Then, Segregation Since: Education and the Unfinished March," Economic Policy Institute, August 27, 2013, http://www.epi.org/publication/unfinished-march-public-school-segregation/ (accessed October 10, 2016).

49. Paul Tough, *Whatever It Takes: Geoffrey Canada's Quest to Change Harlem and America* (New York: Mariner Books, 2009), p. 71.

50. Elizabeth Warren and Amelia Tyagi, *The Two-Income Trap* (New York: Basic Books, 2003), p. 8.

51. "International Programs," *Lane Community College*, https://www.lanecc.edu/international (accessed October 10, 2016); "What Are the Admission Requirements for Junior and Community Colleges?" Learn.org, http://learn

.org/articles/What_are_the_Admission_Requirements_for_Junior_Colleges_and_Community_Colleges.html (accessed October 10, 2016).

52. Joanne Jacobs, "Remediate in High School, Not College," Joanne Jacobs, August 10, 2015, http://www.joannejacobs.com/archives/54518 (accessed February 7, 2017).

53. Maxine Joselow, "Algebra No More," Inside Higher Ed, July 6, 2016, https://www.insidehighered.com/news/2016/07/06/michigan-state-drops-college-algebra-requirement (accessed February 7, 2017).

54. Courteney Kauffmann, "Is Math Keeping You from Graduating? There's a Waiver for That," *The Cuestonian*, April 14, 2015.

55. Joselow, "Algebra No More."

56. Richard Bisk and Mike Winders, "Lowering Math Standards Not the Answer," CommonWealth, April 26, 2015.

57. "The Gap between Enrolling in College and Being Ready for College," in "Beyond the Rhetoric: Improving College Readiness through Coherent State Policy" (special report, National Center for Public Policy and Higher Education and Southern Regional Education Board, June 2010), http://www.highereducation.org/reports/college_readiness/gap.shtml (accessed October 10, 2016).

58. Ibid.

59. Associated Press, "US Education Spending Tops Global List, Study Shows," CBS News, June 25, 2013, http://www.cbsnews.com/news/us-education-spending-tops-global-list-study-shows/ (accessed October 10, 2016).

60. Associated Press, "US Education Spending."

61. O'Shaughnessy, "Here's the Nation's."

62. National Center for Education Statistics, "Fast Facts," 2016, https://nces.ed.gov/fastfacts/display.asp?id=66 (accessed April 11, 2017).

63. "International Programs," Lane Community College, https://www.lanecc.edu/international (accessed October 10, 2016).

64. United States Department of Labor, "Employment Characteristics of Families Summary," Bureau of Labor Statistics, April 22, 2016, https://www.bls.gov/news.release/famee.nr0.htm (April 11, 2017).

65. W. Steven Barnett and Donald J. Yarosz, "Who Goes to Preschool and Why Does it Matter?" *Preschool Policy Brief*, November 2007, http://nieer.org/wp-content/uploads/2016/08/15.pdf (accessed October 10, 2016).

66. Ibid.

67. Ibid.

68. James J. Heckman, "Lifelines for Poor Children," *New York Times*, September 15, 2014, Sunday Review, p. 5.

69. Ibid

70. Lillian Mongeau, "Why Oklahoma's Public Preschools Are Some of the Best in the Country: Oklahomans Trend Conservative, Yet They've Embraced Free, Universal Early Education," *Hechinger Report*, February 2, 2016, http://

hechingerreport.org/why-oklahomas-public-preschools-are-some-of-the-best-in-the-country/ (accessed October 10, 2016).

71. Chester E. Finn Jr., "Young, Gifted and Neglected," *New York Times*, September 19, 2012, p. A29.

72. Ibid.

73. "Educational Attainment," National Center for Education Statistics, 2016, http://nces.ed.gov/fastfacts/display.asp?id=27 (accessed October 10, 2016).

74. Patricia Cohen, "Without a College Degree, Young People Find Good Jobs Are Out of Reach: Recruiters Line Up for College Graduates; Outlook for Others Is a Challenge," *Star Tribune*, May 11, 2016, http://www.startribune.com/without-a-college-degree-young-people-find-good-jobs-are-out-of-reach/379053011/ (accessed October 10, 2016).

75. Eric Westervelt, "The Secret to Germany's Low Youth Unemployment," NPR, April 4, 2012, http://www.npr.org/2012/04/04/149927290/the-secret-to-germanys-low-youth-unemployment (accessed October 10, 2016).

76. Ibid.

77. Chaz Bolte, "Apprenticeship Totals Expected to Top 60K in CA for the First Time Since the Recession," We Party Patriots, March 8, 2016, http://wepartypatriots.com/wp/2016/03/08/apprenticeship-totals-expected-to-top-60k-in-ca-for-the-first-time-since-the-recession/ (accessed October 10, 2016).

78. Danielle Kurtzleben, "Apprenticeships a Little-Traveled Path to Jobs: Apprenticeships Can Mean High-Paying Jobs, Without Degrees or Heavy Student Loan Bills," *US News & World Report*, January 13, 2013, http://www.usnews.com/news/articles/2013/01/13/apprenticeships-a-little-traveled-path-to-jobs (accessed October 10, 2016).

79. Rana Foroohar, "The School That Will Get You a Job," *Time*, February 24, 2014.

80. Nina Rees, "Charter Schools: Expanding Educational Opportunity for All," Heritage Foundation, 2016, https://medium.com/2016-index-of-culture-and-opportunity/charter-schools-expanding-educational-opportunity-for-all-ef46c6b61bc6#.d40qpb40x (accessed October 10, 2016).

81. KIPP Foundation, "National Partners," kipp.org/about/national-partners (accessed April 25, 2017).

82. See "About KIPP," *About KIPP*, 2016, www.kipp.org/about-kipp (accessed October 10, 2016).

83. Ibid.

84. Ibid.

85. Teach for America, https://www.teachforamerica.org/ (accessed October 10, 2016).

86. Kayla Webley, "Reboot the School," *Time*, July 9, 2012, p. 40.

87. Ibid.

88. "Development Process," Common Core State Standards Initiative, http://www.corestandards.org/about-the-standards/development-process/ (accessed April 18, 2017).

89. Valerie Strauss, "Why the Movement to Opt Out of Common Core Tests Is a Big Deal," *Washington Post*, May 3, 2015, https://www.washingtonpost.com/news/answer-sheet/wp/2015/05/03/why-the-movement-to-opt-out-of-common-core-tests-is-a-big-deal/?utm_term=.39acd8ccef6b.

90. "The Gap between Enrolling in College and Being Ready for College" in "Beyond the Rhetoric: Improving College Readiness through Coherent State Policy," (special report, National Center for Public Policy and Higher Education and Southern Regional Education Board, June 2010), http://www.highereducation.org/reports/college_readiness/gap.shtml (accessed October 10, 2016). Having taught in a New Jersey community college for nineteen years, I have had talks with several math department faculty members about the success rate of students placed in remedial math courses. Although the college's institutional research department apparently had many more important tasks, there were no studies to determine the percentage of students who took and passed all three remedial math courses, and actually enrolled in a college-level math course. But the consensus of math professors was that it was less than 1 percent.

91. "US News Data: Law School Costs, J. D. Salaries: Learn Which School Charged the Most—More than $60,000—for Tuition and Fees in 2015–2016," *US News & World Report*, March 17, 2016, http://www.usnews.com/education/best-graduate-schools/top-law-schools/articles/2016-03-17/us-news-data-law-school-costs-jd-salaries (accessed October 10, 2016).

92. O'Shaughnessy, "Here's the Nation's."

93. Marc F. Bernstein, "Everyone Passes Teacher Certification Exams," *Huffington Post*, July 28, 2013, http://www.huffingtonpost.com/marc-f-bernstein/everyone-passes-teacher-c_b_3345539.html (accessed October 10, 2016).

94. Matt Barnum, "Fact-Check: Just How Many Tenured Teachers Are Fired Each Year Anyway? (Hint: Not Many)," The 74, September 8, 2015, https://www.the74million.org/article/fact-check-just-how-many-tenured-teachers-are-fired-each-year-anyway-hint-not-many (accessed October 10, 2016).

95. O'Shaughnessy, "Here's the Nation's."

96. Koebler, "Many STEM Teachers"; Luba Ostashevsky, "Elementary School Teachers Struggle with Common Core Math Standards: Here's How Some Education Programs Are Trying to Help," *Hechinger Report*, June 15, 2016, http://hechingerreport.org/elementary-school-teachers-struggle-with-common-core-math-standards/ (accessed October 10, 2016).

97. Lam Thuy Vo, "How Much Does the Government Spend to Send a Kid to Public School?" NPR, June 21, 2012, http://www.npr.org/sections/money/2012/06/21/155515613/how-much-does-the-government-spend-to-send-a-kid-to-school (accessed April 18, 2017).

Chapter 13. Our Sick Healthcare System

1. Eric Pianin, "US Health Care Costs Surge to 17 Percent of GDP," *Fiscal Times*, December 3, 2015, http://www.thefiscaltimes.com/2015/12/03/Federal-Health-Care-Costs-Surge-17-Percent-GDP (accessed October 11, 2016).

2. "Overweight and Obesity Statistics," National Institute of Diabetes and Digestive and Kidney Diseases, October 2012, https://www.niddk.nih.gov/health-information/health-statistics/Pages/overweight-obesity-statistics.aspx (accessed October 11, 2016).

3. The Patient Factor, http://thepatientfactor.com/ (accessed October 10, 2016).

4. Peter Sullivan, "17 Million Gained Coverage Under ObamaCare, Study Finds," *Hill*, May 6, 2015, http://thehill.com/policy/healthcare/241259-17m-gained-insurance-under-obamacare-study-finds (accessed April 21, 2017).

5. Jason Kane, "Health Costs: How the U.S. Compares with Other Countries," PBS Newshour, October 22, 2012, http://www.pbs.org/newshour/rundown/health-costs-how-the-us-compares-with-other-countries/ (accessed April 21, 2017).

6. "United States per Capita Healthcare Spending Is More Than Twice the Average of Other Developed Countries," Peter G. Peterson Foundation, May 3, 2016, http://www.pgpf.org/chart-archive/0006_health-care-oecd (accessed September 30, 2016).

7. Dan Munro, "US Healthcare Spending on Track to Hit $10,000 per Person This Year," *Forbes*, January 4, 2015, http://www.forbes.com/sites/danmunro/2015/01/04/u-s-healthcare-spending-on-track-to-hit-10000-per-person-this-year/#c1f9eaf294c9 (accessed October 11, 2016).

8. "Health Insurance: Premiums and Increases," National Conference of State Legislators, http://www.ncsl.org/research/health/health-insurance-premiums.aspx (accessed April 21, 2017).

9. Eric Planin, "US Health Care Costs Surge to 17 Percent of GDP," *Fiscal Times*, December 3, 2015, http://www.thefiscaltimes.com/2015/12/03/Federal-Health-Care-Costs-Surge-17-Percent-GDP (accessed March 30, 2017); Centers for Medicare & Medicaid Services, "Research, Statistics, Data & Systems," cms.gov/research-statistics-data-and-systems/statistics-trendsandreports (accessed March 30, 2017); Victor R. Fuchs, "Major Trends in the US Health Economy since 1950," *New England Journal of Medicine*, March 15, 2012, http://www.nejm.org/doi/full/10.1056/NEJMp1200478#t=article (accessed March 30, 2017).

10. Dana P. Goldman and Elizabeth A. McGlynn, "US Health Care: Facts about Cost, Access, and Quality," RAND Corporation, 2005, http://www.rand.org/content/dam/rand/pubs/corporate_pubs/2005/RAND_CP484.1.pdf (accessed October 11, 2016).

11. Robert H. Frank, "Giving Health Care a Chance to Evolve," *New York Times*, July 1, 2012, Sunday Business, p. 6.

12. David Lazarus, "Latest Sign of a Sick Healthcare System," *Los Angeles Times*, October 28, 2011, https://www.pressreader.com/usa/los-angeles-times/20111028/283815735400802 (accessed April 26, 2017).

13. "2015 Employer Health Benefits Survey," Henry J. Kaiser Family Foundation, September 22, 2015, http://kff.org/report-section/ehbs-2015-summary-of-findings/ (accessed October 11, 2016).

14. Laurence J. Kotlikoff and Scott Burns, *The Coming Generational Storm* (Cambridge, MA: MIT Press), pp. 164–165.

15. "Questions and Answers for the Additional Medicare Tax," Internal Revenue Service, June 14, 2016, https://www.irs.gov/businesses/small-businesses-self-employed/questions-and-answers-for-the-additional-medicare-tax (accessed October 11, 2016).

16. Reuters, "Medicare Is Going to Run Out of Money a Lot Sooner Than Expected," *Fortune*, June 22, 2016, http://fortune.com/2016/06/22/medicare-reserves-exhausted-soon/ (accessed April 21, 2017).

17. Kotlikoff and Burns, *Coming Generational Storm*, p. 170.

18. The federal government reimburses a greater percentage of funds spent in poorer states, like Mississippi and Alabama, than it does in richer states such as New York and California. "Policy Basics: Introduction to Medicaid," Center on Budget and Policy Priorities, http://www.cbpp.org/research/health/policy-basics-introduction-to-medicaid (accessed April 21, 2017).

19. "FFF: Older Americans Month: May 2016," United States Census Bureau, last revised: May 27, 2016, http://www.census.gov/newsroom/facts-for-features/2016/cb16-ff08.html (accessed October 11, 2016); "The Demographics of Aging . . ." Transgenerational, http://transgenerational.org/aging/demographics.htm (accessed October 11, 2016).

20. Martha M. Hamilton, "What Health Care Will Cost You Most of Your Retirement Savings May Be Going toward Your Medical Costs," AARP, January/February 2013, http://www.aarp.org/health/medicare-insurance/info-12-2012/health-care-costs.html (accessed October 11, 2016); "The State of Aging and Health in America," Centers for Disease Control and Prevention, June 6, 2016, http://www.cdc.gov/aging/data/stateofaging.htm (accessed October 11, 2016).

21. Alan B. Hubbard, "The Health of a Nation," *New York Times*, April 3, 2006, p. A17.

22. "Industry Overview," Insurance Information Institute, http://www.iii.org/fact-statistic/industry-overview (accessed April 20, 2017).

23. Joshua Rothman, "The Trillion-Dollar Health Care Mystery: What Really Happens When You Change the System? MIT Economist Amy Finkelstein Decided to Find Out," *Boston Globe*, May 6, 2012, https://www.bostonglobe.com/ideas/2012/05/05/economics-health-care-trillion-dollar-mystery/YM5x5YAKftC51yonYEoKRM/story.html (accessed October 11, 2016).

24. Howard Gleckman, "So That's Why It's So Expensive," *Businessweek*, August 14, 2005, p. 65.

25. Audrey J. Weiss and Anne Elixhauser, "Overview of Hospital Stays in the United States, 2012," Healthcare Cost and Utilization Project, October 2014, https://www.hcup-us.ahrq.gov/reports/statbriefs/sb180-Hospitalizations-United-States-2012.jsp (accessed October 11, 2016).

26. "Healthcare Infographic: How Much Does a Hospital Stay Cost?" Zane Benefits, November 21, 2013, https://www.zanebenefits.com/blog/bid/325996/Healthcare-infographic-How-much-does-a-hospital-stay-cost (accessed October 11, 2016).

27. Ibid.; Weiss and Elixhauser, "Overview of Hospital Stays."

28. Aaron Hankin, "U.S. Healthcare Costs Compared to Other Countries," *Investopedia*, July 21, 2016, http://www.investopedia.com/articles/personal-finance/072116/us-healthcare-costs-compared-other-countries.asp (accessed April 21, 2017).

29. Jeanne Pinder, "How Much Does a Colonoscopy Cost? From $600 to Over $5,400," Clear Health Costs (blog), July 20, 2014, http://clearhealthcosts.com/blog/2014/07/much-colonoscopy-cost/ (accessed October 11, 2016).

30. Tina Rosenberg, "A Cure for the $1,000 Toothbrush," *New York Times*, August 18, 2013, Sunday Review, p. 8.

31. Eduardo Porter, "Finding Ways to Ration Health Care More Fairly," *New York Times*, August 21, 2012, Business Section, p. B2.

32. "Role of Pharmaceuticals in US Healthcare Spending," Global Policy and International Public Affairs, Pfizer Inc., October 2015, http://www.pfizer.com/files/about/Position-Role-of-Pharmaceuticals-in-US-Healthcare-Spending.pdf (accessed October 11, 2016).

33. "Observations on Trends in Prescription Drug Spending," United States Department of Health and Human Services, Office of the Assistant Secretary for Planning and Evaluation, March 8, 2016, https://aspe.hhs.gov/pdf-report/observations-trends-prescription-drug-spending (accessed October 11, 2016).

34. Elisabeth Rosenthal, *An American Sickness: How Healthcare Became Big Business and How You Can Take It Back* (New York: Penguin Press, 2017), p. 305.

35. Ana Swanson, "Big Pharmaceutical Companies Are Spending Far More on Marketing Than Research," *Washington Post*, February 11, 2015, https://www.washingtonpost.com/news/wonk/wp/2015/02/11/big-pharmaceutical-companies-are-spending-far-more-on-marketing-than-research/ (accessed October 11, 2016).

36. Laura Snyder, "Medicaid Financing: How Does It Work and What Are the Implications?" Henry J. Kaiser Family Foundation, May 20, 2015, http://kff.org/medicaid/issue-brief/medicaid-financing-how-does-it-work-and-what-are-the-implications/ (accessed April 21, 2017).

37. Shefali Luthra, "Texans React to Health Care Ruling," *Texas Tribune*, June 28, 2012, https://www.texastribune.org/2012/06/28/texas-reacts-health-care-ruling/ (accessed October 11, 2016).

38. Adam Liptak, "Supreme Court Upholds Health Care Law, 5-4, in Victory

for Obama," June 28, 2012, http://www.nytimes.com/2012/06/29/us/supreme-court-lets-health-law-largely-stand.html.

39. "Key Facts about the Uninsured Population," Henry J. Kaiser Family Foundation, September 29, 2016, http://kff.org/uninsured/fact-sheet/key-facts-about-the-uninsured-population/ (accessed October 11, 2016).

40. Allan Detsky, "Why America Is Losing the Health Race," *New Yorker*, June 11, 2014, http://www.newyorker.com/tech/elements/why-america-is-losing-the-health-race (accessed October 11, 2016).

41. "Administrative Waste Consumes 31 Percent of Health Spending," Physicians for a National Health Program, 2010, http://www.pnhp.org/single_payer_resources/administrative_waste_consumes_31_percent_of_health_spending.php (accessed October 11, 2016).

42. Ibid.

43. "Medical Justice Founder Shines on Lou Dobbs' Show," Medical Justice, August 11, 2009, http://www.medicaljustice.com/medical-justice-founder-shines-on-lou-dobbs-show/ (accessed April 24, 2017).

44. Berkley Rice, "Malpractice Premiums: Soaring Again," *Medical Economics*, December 9, 2002, http://medicaleconomics.modernmedicine.com/medical-economics/content/malpractice-premiums-soaring-again (accessed October 11, 2016).

45. Richard Thaler, "Overcoming Obstacles to Better Health Care," *New York Times*, February 23, 2013, Business Section, p. 6.

46. Michelle M. Mello, Amitabh Chandra, et al., "National Costs of the Medical Liability System," https://www.ncbi.nlm.nih.gov/pmc/articles/PMC3048809/ (accessed April 21, 2017).

47. "Reform and Medical Costs," *New York Times* editorial, November 15, 2009.

48. Michael Fine and James W. Peters, *The Nature of Health Care* (New York: Radcliffe Publishing, 2007), pp. 188–89.

49. Kevin Sack, "For Bush, a Rise in Health Clinics Shapes a Legacy," *New York Times*, December 26, 2008, p. 1; Health and Human Services, "HHS Announces $101 Million in Affordable Care Act Funding to 164 New Community Health Centers," press release, May 15, 2015.

50. "Socialized Medicine Has a Good Side," *Newsweek*, August 24 and 31, 2009, p. 63.

51. Haley Sweetland Edwards, "Why the Doctor Takes Only Cash," *Time*, February 6, 2017.

52. Ibid.

53. Atul Gawande, "Overkill," *New Yorker*, May 11, 2015, p. 42.

54. Christopher Hogan, June Lunney, et al., "Medicare Beneficiaries' Costs of Care in the Last Year of Life," *Health Affairs* 20, no. 4 (July 2001), http://content.healthaffairs.org/content/20/4/188.full.html (accessed April 26, 2017).

55. Julie Appleby, "Debate Surrounds End-of-Life Health Care Costs,"

USA Today, October 19, 2006, http://www.usatoday.com/money/industries/health/2006-10-18-end-of-life-costs_x.htm (accessed October 11, 2016).

56. If Medicare for All sounds familiar, that's because it is something that 2016 presidential candidate Bernie Sanders has been advocating for many years.

57. "National Medicaid & CHIP Program Information," Medicaid.gov, https://www.medicaid.gov/medicaid/program-information/index.html (accessed October 11, 2016).

58. Ken Jacobs, Ian Perry, and Jenifer MacGillvary, "The High Public Cost of Low Wages: Poverty-Level Wages Cost US Taxpayers $152.8 Billion Each Year in Public Support for Working Families" (research brief, University of California Berkeley Center for Labor Research and Education, April 2015), http://laborcenter.berkeley.edu/pdf/2015/the-high-public-cost-of-low-wages.pdf (accessed October 11, 2016); "National Medicaid & CHIP Program Information," Medicaid.gov, https://www.medicaid.gov/medicaid/program-information/index.html (accessed October 11, 2016).

59. "Key Facts about the Uninsured Population," Henry J. Kaiser Family Foundation, September 29, 2016, http://kff.org/uninsured/fact-sheet/key-facts-about-the-uninsured-population/ (accessed October 11, 2016).

60. Bureau of Labor Statistics, "Employer Costs for Employee Compensation," March 17, 2017, https://www.bls.gov/news.release/pdf/ecec.pdf (accessed April 26, 2017).

61. See chapter 9.

PART VI. WASTING OUR RESOURCES BY OVERPRODUCING

1. *Economic Report of the President: Together with the Annual Report of the Council of Economic Advisers* (Washington, DC: US Government Publishing Office, 2016).

2. "Prisons, Jails, and People Arrested for Drugs," DrugWarFacts.org, 2016, http://www.drugwarfacts.org/cms/Prisons_and_Drugs (accessed October 12, 2016); Nicholas Kristof, "Inside a Mental Hospital Called Jail," *New York Times*, February 8, 2014, http://www.nytimes.com/2014/02/09/opinion/sunday/inside-a-mental-hospital-called-jail.html?_r=0 (accessed October 14, 2016).

3. Benjamin Landy, "Graph: How the Financial Sector Consumed America's Economic Growth," Century Foundation, February 25, 2013, https://tcf.org/content/commentary/graph-how-the-financial-sector-consumed-americas-economic-growth/ (accessed October 13, 2016).

Chapter 14. The Military-Industrial Complex

1. "US Military Spending vs the World," SPRI, National Priorities Project, https://www.nationalpriorities.org/campaigns/us-military-spending-vs-world/ (accessed October 1, 2016).

2. Paul Kennedy, *The Rise and Fall of Great Powers* (New York: Random House: 1987), p. 444.

3. Ibid., p. 515.

4. Ibid., p. 446.

5. Andrew J. Bacevich, *The Limits of Power: The End of American Exceptionalism* (New York: Henry Holt, 2008), p. 138.

6. Kathy Roth-Douquet and Frank Schaeffer, *AWOL: The Unexcused Absence of America's Upper Classes from Military Service—and How It Hurts Our Country* (New York: HarperCollins, 2007), p. 43.

7. "College Enrollment Hits All-Time High, Fueled by Community College Surge," Pew Research Center, October 29, 2009, http://www.pewsocialtrends.org/2009/10/29/college-enrollment-hits-all-time-high-fueled-by-community-college-surge/ (accessed October 11, 2016).

8. Tim Kane, "Who Are the Recruits? The Demographic Characteristics of US Military Enlistment, 2003–2005," Heritage Foundation, October 27, 2006, http://www.heritage.org/research/reports/2006/10/who-are-the-recruits-the-demographic-characteristics-of-us-military-enlistment-2003-2005 (accessed October 11, 2016).

9. See *Atlantic Monthly*, October 2006, p. 46.

10. Andrew Bacevich, "Thank You for Your Service, Sort Of," *New York Times*, May 22, 2012, Book Review, p. 14.

11. David Rothkopf, *Superclass: The Global Power Elite and the World They are Making* (New York: Farrar, Straus and Giroux, 2008), p. 206.

12. Defense Systems Staff, "Top 20 Defense Contractors, 2015," Defense Systems, November 2, 2015, https://defensesystems.com/articles/2015/11/02/top-20-defense-contractors-2015.aspx (accessed October 11, 2016).

13. Bob Herbert, "Ike Saw It Coming," *New York Times*, January 27, 2006, p. A19.

14. Chloe Fox, "The 15 Most Amazing Places Uncle Sam Could Send You," *Huffington Post*, April 29, 2014, http://www.huffingtonpost.com/2014/04/29/best-military-bases-around-the-world_n_5216682.html (accessed April 21, 2017).

15. David Vine, "The United States Probably Has More Foreign Military Bases Than Any Other People, Nation, or Empire in History: And It's Doing Us More Harm Than Good," *Nation*, September 14, 2015, https://www.thenation.com/article/the-united-states-probably-has-more-foreign-military-bases-than-any-other-people-nation-or-empire-in-history/ (accessed October 11, 2016).

16. Cullen Murphy, *Are We Rome?* (Boston: Houghton Mifflin, 2007), p. 20.

17. Jeanne Sahadi, "What the NSA Costs Taxpayers," CNN, June 7, 2013,

http://money.cnn.com/2013/06/07/news/economy/nsa-surveillance-cost (accessed October 11, 2016); *Fiscal Year 2017: Budget in Brief: Strengthening Health and Opportunity for All Americans* (Washington, DC: United States Department of Health and Human Services), https://www.hhs.gov/sites/default/files/fy2017-budget-in-brief.pdf (accessed October 11, 2016).

18. "Homeland Security Budget," Brown University Watson Institute of International & Public Affairs, September 2016, http://watson.brown.edu/costsofwar/costs/economic/budget/dhs (accessed October 11, 2016); Stephan Salisbury "The Cost of America's Police State: Hundreds of Billions Have Been Spent to Militarize Our Nation against a Terrorism Threat That Barely Exists," *Salon*, March 5, 2012, http://www.salon.com/2012/03/05/the_cost_of_americas_police_state/ (accessed October 11, 2016); ASIS International and Institute of Finance and Management, "Groundbreaking Study Finds US Security Industry to be $350 Billion Market: ASIS International and IOFM Release First Comprehensive Security Market Study Since 1990," news release, August 12, 2013, https://www.asisonline.org/News/Press-Room/Press-Releases/2013/Pages/Groundbreaking-Study-Finds-U.S.-Security-Industry-to-be-$350-Billion-Market.aspx (accessed October 11, 2016).

19. Gregg Easterbrook, "Searching for Safety in a Time of Terrorism," *New York Times*, June 22, 2004, Section 4, p. 4.

20. "US Military Spending vs the World," SPRI, National Priorities Project, https://www.nationalpriorities.org/campaigns/us-military-spending-vs-world/ (accessed October 11, 2016).

21. Council of Economic Advisers, *Economic Indicators* (Washington, DC: Government Publishing Office, February 2017), p. 1, https://www.gpo.gov/fdsys/pkg/ECONI-2017-02/pdf/ECONI-2017-02.pdf (accessed April 14, 2017).

22. Ibid.

23. Bacevich, "Thank You for Your Service," p. 173.

24. John Mueller, *Overblown: How Politicians and the Terrorism Industry Inflate National Security Threats* (Glencoe, IL: Free Press, 2006), p. 5.

Chapter 15. The Criminal Justice Establishment

1. Sidney Lupkin, "US Has More Guns—and Gun Deaths—Than Any Other Country, Study Finds," ABC News, September 19, 2013, http://abcnews.go.com/blogs/health/2013/09/19/u-s-has-more-guns-and-gun-deaths-than-any-other-country-study-finds/ (accessed October 12, 2016); Robert Preidt, "How US Gun Deaths Compare to Other Countries," CBS News, February 3, 2016, http://www.cbsnews.com/news/how-u-s-gun-deaths-compare-to-other-countries/ (accessed October 12, 2016).

2. Manning Marable, "Along the Color Line: the Crisis of Black Men in Prison," *AlterNet*, September 11, 2000, http://www.alternet.org/story/9769/

along_the_color_line%3A_the_crisis_of_black_men_in_prison (accessed April 20, 2017).

3. "Incarceration in the United States: Ethnicity," *Wikipedia*, October 23, 2016, https://en.wikipedia.org/wiki/Incarceration_in_the_United_States#Ethnicity (accessed October 12, 2016).

4. DKN Nielson, "2.2 Million Incarcerated Americans," Criminal Mindset, December 16, 2015, https://criminalmindset.com/2015/12/16/2-2-million-incarcerated-americans/ (accessed October 12, 2016).

5. "Q: Prison Expenditures," Google Answers, June 11, 2004, http://answers.google.com/answers/threadview?id=359684 (accessed October 12, 2016).

6. Ibid.

7. "Prisons, Jails, and People Arrested for Drugs," DrugWarFacts.org, 2016, http://www.drugwarfacts.org/cms/Prisons_and_Drugs (accessed October 12, 2016).

8. Linda Qiu, "Juan Williams: No. 1 Cause of Death for African-American Males 15–34 is Murder," PunditFact, August 24, 2014, http://www.politifact.com/punditfact/statements/2014/aug/24/juan-williams/juan-williams-no-1-cause-death-african-americans-1/ (accessed October 12, 2016).

9. "Prisoners and Prisoner Re-Entry," United States Department of Justice, https://www.justice.gov/archive/fbci/progmenu_reentry.html (accessed October 12, 2016).

10. Saki Knafo, "1 in 3 Black Males Will Go to Prison in Their Lifetime, Report Warns," *Huffington Post*, October 4, 2013, http://www.huffingtonpost.com/2013/10/04/racial-disparities-criminal-justice_n_4045144.html (accessed October 12, 2016).

11. Rob Karwath, "Study Links High Dropout Rate to State Prison Overcrowding," *Chicago Tribune*, September 15, 1991, http://articles.chicagotribune.com/1991-09-15/news/9103090883_1_incarceration-rate-dropout-rate-inmates (accessed October 12, 2016).

12. Emily Badger, "Young Black Men Face Daunting Odds in Life. These Programs Can Help," *Washington Post*, June 3, 2015, https://www.washingtonpost.com/news/wonk/wp/2015/06/03/young-black-men-face-daunting-odds-in-life-these-programs-can-help/ (accessed October 12, 2016).

13. Marvin Harris, *Why Nothing Works*, 2nd edition (New York: Simon and Schuster, 1987), p. 125.

14. Marable, "Along the Color Line."

15. Qiu, "Juan Williams: No. 1 Cause of Death."

16. Bruce Western, *Punishment and Inequality in America* (New York: Russell Sage Foundation, 2006), p. 3.

17. Newt Gingrich with Vince Haley and Rick Tyler, *Real Change: From the World That Fails to the World That Works* (Washington, DC: Regnery Publishing, 2008), p. 209.

18. Nicholas Kristof, "Inside a Mental Hospital Called Jail," *New York Times*, February 8, 2014, http://www.nytimes.com/2014/02/09/opinion/sunday/inside-a-mental-hospital-called-jail.html?_r=0 (accessed October 12, 2016).

19. Rita Rubin, "Mentally Ill People are Sent to Jail More Often Than Hospital," *USA Today*, May 13, 2010, http://usatoday30.usatoday.com/news/health/2010-05-12-Jail12_ST_N.htm (accessed October 12, 2016).

20. Associated Press, "US Report: 2.2 Million Now in Prisons, Jails," NBC News, May 21, 2006, http://www.nbcnews.com/id/12901873/ns/us_news-crime_and_courts/t/us-report-million-now-prisons-jails/#.WA51QPkrK1s (accessed October 12, 2016).

21. PEW Charitable Trusts Public Safety Performance Project, "One in 31 US Adults Are Behind Bars, on Parole or Probation" press release, http://www.pewtrusts.org/en/about/news-room/press-releases/0001/01/01/one-in-31-us-adults-are-behind-bars-on-parole-or-probation (accessed October 12, 2016).

22. Ezra Klein and Evan Soltas, "Wonkbook: 11 Facts about America's Prison Population," *Washington Post*, August 13, 2013, https://www.washingtonpost.com/news/wonk/wp/2013/08/13/wonkbook-11-facts-about-americas-prison-population/ (accessed October 12, 2016).

23. "Incarceration in the United States," *Wikipedia*, October 23, 2016, https://en.wikipedia.org/wiki/Incarceration_in_the_United_States (accessed October 12, 2016).

24. "Race and the War on Drugs," *Wikipedia*, September 24, 2016, https://en.wikipedia.org/wiki/Race_and_the_War_on_Drugs (accessed October 12, 2016).

25. Ibid.

26. Klein and Soltas, "Wonkbook."

27. "United States Incarceration Rate," *Wikipedia*, September 1, 2016, https://en.wikipedia.org/wiki/United_States_incarceration_rate (accessed October 12, 2016).

28. Arthur Benavie, *How the Drug War Ruins American Lives* (Santa Barbara, CA: Praeger, 2016), p. 108.

29. Olga Khazan, "Most Prisoners Are Mentally Ill: Can Mental-Health Courts, in Which People Are Sentenced to Therapy, Help?" *Atlantic*, April 7, 2015, http://www.theatlantic.com/health/archive/2015/04/more-than-half-of-prisoners-are-mentally-ill/389682/ (accessed October 12, 2016).

30. Ibid.

31. "Incarceration in the United States: Ethnicity."

32. Thomas P. Bonczar and Allen J. Beck, *Lifetime Likelihood of Going to State or Federal Prison* (Washington, DC: United States Department of Justice Bureau of Justice Statistics, 1997), https://bjs.gov/content/pub/pdf/Llgsfp.pdf (accessed October 12, 2016).

33. Dahlia Lithwick, "Our Real Prison Problem," *Newsweek*, June 15, 2009, p. 28.

34. First Focus, "New Report Finds Millions of Youth Unemployed and Not in School," August 6, 2009, https://firstfocus.org/news/press-release/new-report-finds-millions-youth-unemployed-school/ (accessed October 12, 2016).

35. Executive Office of the President of the United States, *Economic Perspectives on Incarceration and the Criminal Justice System* (Washington, DC: Executive Office of the President of the United States, April 2016), https://obamawhitehouse.archives.gov/sites/default/files/page/files/20160423_cea_incarceration_criminal_justice.pdf (accessed April 26, 2017).

36. Jim Dwyer, "Out of One Gram of Marijuana, a 'Manufactured Misdemeanor,'" *New York Times*, March 21, 2013, p. A20.

37. Western, *Punishment*, p. 20.

38. Ibid., p. 21.

39. "The Right Choices," *Economist*, June 20, 2015, p. 26.

40. US Department of Justice, *Profile of Nonviolent Offenders Exiting State Prisons* (Washington, DC: Office of Justice Programs, October 2004), https://www.bjs.gov/content/pub/pdf/pnoesp.pdf (accessed April 27, 2017); Wagdy Loza, "Predicting Violent and Nonviolent Recidivism of Incarcerated Male Offenders," *Aggression and Violent Behavior* 8, no. 2 (2003), http://www.sciencedirect.com/science/article/pii/S1359178901000556 (accessed April 27, 2017).

41. David Kennedy, "God, It's Got to Stop," *Newsweek*, October 3, 2011, p. 25.

42. Andrew Romano, "Jailbreak!" *Newsweek*, October 3, 2011, p. 23.

43. Begin to Read, http://begintoread.com/ (accessed October 12, 2016).

44. James Webb, "What We Can Learn from Japanese Prisons," James Webb, January 15, 1984, http://www.jameswebb.com/articles/economic-fairness-social-justice/what-we-can-learn-from-japanese-prisons (accessed October 12, 2016).

45. "Recidivism," National Institute of Justice, June 17, 2014, http://nij.gov/topics/corrections/recidivism/Pages/welcome.aspx (accessed October 12, 2016).

46. United States Department of Justice, "Prisoners and Prisoner Re-Entry," https://www.justice.gov/archive/fbci/progmenu_reentry.html (accessed April 13, 2017).

47. Editorial Board, "Halfway Back to Society," *New York Times*, March 29, 2014, http://www.nytimes.com/2014/03/30/opinion/sunday/halfway-back-to-society.html (accessed October 12, 2016).

48. Geoff Mulvihill, "Camden Police Warn Heroin Buyers to Stay in the Suburbs," Associated Press, February 10, 2012, http://www.pressofatlanticcity.com/news/press/new_jersey/camden-police-warn-heroin-buyers-to-stay-in-the-suburbs/article_af44b5ce-543c-11e1-bf90-0019bb2963f4.html (accessed April 20, 2017).

49. Jesse Wegman, "The Injustice of Marijuana Arrests," *New York Times*, July 28, 2014, http://www.nytimes.com/2014/07/29/opinion/high-time-the-injustice-of-marijuana-arrests.html (accessed October 12, 2016).

50. Chris Elkins, "Addicts Grow Frustrated by Wait Times for Addiction

Treatment," Drug Rehab, January 20, 2016, https://www.drugrehab.com/2016/01/20/addicts-grow-frustrated-wait-addiction-treatment/ (accessed October 12, 2016).

51. Editorial, "Drug Treatment Cheaper Than Filling More Prison Cells," *Tampa Bay Times*, October 9, 2011, http://www.tampabay.com/opinion/editorials/drug-treatment-cheaper-than-filling-more-prison-cells/1195753 (accessed October 12, 2016).

52. "Facts on Drug Courts," National Association of Drug Court Professionals, http://www.nadcp.org/sites/default/files/nadcp/Facts%20on%20Drug%20Courts.pdf (accessed October 12, 2016).

53. "Rehab Success Rates and Statistics," American Addiction Centers, 2016, http://americanaddictioncenters.org/rehab-guide/success-rates-and-statistics/ (accessed October 12, 2016).

54. National Institute on Drug Abuse, "Principles of Drug Addiction Treatment: A Research-Based Guide (Third Edition)," https://www.drugabuse.gov/publications/principles-drug-addiction-treatment-research-based-guide-third-edition/frequently-asked-questions/drug-addiction-treatment-worth-its-cost (accessed April 13, 2017).

55. Bill Quigley, "40 Reasons Why Our Jails Are Full of Black and Poor People," *Huffington Post*, June 2, 2015, http://www.huffingtonpost.com/bill-quigley/40-reasons-why-our-jails-are-full-of-black-and-poor-people_b_7492902.html (accessed October 12, 2016).

56. Nick Pinto, "The Bail Trap," *New York Times*, August 13, 2015, http://www.nytimes.com/2015/08/16/magazine/the-bail-trap.html (accessed October 12, 2016).

57. Nick Pinto, "The Bail Trap," *New York Times Magazine*, August 13, 2015, https://www.nytimes.com/2015/08/16/magazine/the-bail-trap.html (accessed April 21, 2017).

58. Michael Ollove, "Getting the Mentally Ill out of Jails," *Stateline* (blog), April 7, 2017, http://www.pewtrusts.org/en/research-and-analysis/blogs/stateline/2017/04/07/getting-the-mentally-ill-out-of-jails (accessed April 26, 2017).

59. Nicholas Kristof, "Is It a Crime to be Poor?" *New York Times*, June 12, 2016, Sunday Review, p. 1.

60. Mona Chalabi, "Gun Homicides and Gun Ownership Listed by Country: Where Are the World's Guns—and Which Countries Have the Highest Rates of Firearms Murders?" *Guardian*, July 22, 2012, https://www.theguardian.com/news/datablog/2012/jul/22/gun-homicides-ownership-world-list (accessed October 12, 2016).

61. Ibid.

62. Associated Press, "50-State Study: More Gun Laws, Fewer Deaths," CBS News, March 6, 2013, http://www.cbsnews.com/news/50-state-study-more-gun-laws-fewer-deaths (accessed October 12, 2016)/.

63. Daily Mail Reporter, "Almost HALF of US Households Have at Least

One Gun, New Poll Reveals—with a Sharp Increase in Domestic Weapon Ownership Over the Last Two Years," *Daily Mail*, August 29, 2016, http://www.dailymail.co.uk/news/article-3763576/Now-44-percent-households-one-gun-showing-sharp-increase-domestic-weapon-ownership-says-new-poll.html#ixzz4IlCdnLRf (accessed October 12, 2016).

Chapter 16. Our Bloated Financial Sector

1. Benjamin Landy, "Graph: How the Financial Sector Consumed America's Economic Growth," Century Foundation, February 25, 2013, https://tcf.org/content/commentary/graph-how-the-financial-sector-consumed-americas-economic-growth/ (accessed October 13, 2016).

2. Bureau of Labor Statistics, "Industries at a Glance," https://www.bls.gov/iag/tgs/iag50.htm (accessed April 26, 2017).

3. William Mills Agency, "The Changing Landscape of U.S. Financial Institutions," *William Mills Agency* (blog), July 30, 2015, https://www.williammills.com/blog/the-changing-landscape-of-u-s-financial-institutions/ (accessed April 26, 2017).

4. Dean Baker, "Glass-Steagall Now: Because the Banks Own Washington: The Glass-Steagall Act Provided Financial Security for Americans and Now Is the Time to Revive the Legislation," Aljazeera, August 5, 2013, http://www.aljazeera.com/indepth/opinion/2013/08/201384183347752450.html (accessed October 13, 2016).

5. "Stated Income Loan," *Wikipedia*, July 6, 2015, https://en.wikipedia.org/wiki/Stated_income_loan (accessed October 13, 2016); Robert Kuttner, "The Subprime Scandal," *American Prospect*, March 19, 2007, http://prospect.org/article/subprime-scandal (accessed October 13, 2016); Stephen L. Slavin, *Macroeconomics*, 11th ed. (New York: McGraw-Hill, 2013), p. 372.

6. United Nations, *World Economic Situation and Prospects 2008* (New York: United Nations, 2008).

7. Curtis Greco, *Valor in Prosperity* (Charleston, SC: Advantage Media Group, 2010); Robert Pozen, *Too Big to Save?* (Hoboken, NJ: John Wiley & Sons, 2009).

8. See DealBook, *New York Times*, January 8, 2014, p. B5.

9. Gerald Epstein, "Financialization, Rentier Interests and Central Bank Policy," manuscript, Department of Economics, University of Massachusetts, Amherst, MA, 2001, p. 1.

10. See Felix Salmon, "Chart of the Day: US Financial Profits," *Reuters* (blog), March 30, 2011, http://blogs.reuters.com/felix-salmon/2011/03/30/chart-of-the-day-us-financial-profits/ (accessed October 13, 2016); Evan Soltas, "5 More Graphs on Finance," Evan Soltas (blog), February 27, 2013, http://esoltas.blogspot.com/2013/02/5-more-graphs-on-finance.html (accessed October 13, 2016).

11. "Financial Manager: Salary Details," *US News & World Report*, http://money.usnews.com/careers/best-jobs/financial-manager/salary (accessed October 13, 2016); Stephen D. Simpson, "Which Financial Careers Pay the Most?" Investopedia, October 5, 2012, http://www.investopedia.com/financial-edge/1012/which-financial-careers-pay-the-most.aspx (accessed October 13, 2016).

12. Kevin Roose, interview by Ezra Klein, "How Wall Street Recruits So Many Insecure Ivy League Grads," *Vox*, May 15, 2014, http://www.vox.com/2014/5/15/5720596/how-wall-street-recruits-so-many-insecure-ivy-league-grads (accessed October 13, 2016).

13. Richard Escow, "The 'Bankization' of America," *Huff Post Politics*, August 15, 2013.

14. See Floyd Norris, "Off the Charts: Higher Profits Lower Wages," *New York Times*, August 9, 2013; US Bureau of Economic Analysis, http://www.bea.gov/ (accessed October 13, 2016).

15. Thomas Philippon, "Has the US Finance Industry Become Less Efficient? On the Theory and Measurement of Financial Intermediation," paper, Stern School of Business, New York University, September 2014, http://pages.stern.nyu.edu/~tphilipp/papers/Finance_Efficiency.pdf (accessed October 13, 2016).

16. Jeff Cox, "There Are More Payday Lenders in US Than McDonald's," NBC News, November 24, 2014, http://www.nbcnews.com/business/economy/there-are-more-payday-lenders-u-s-mcdonalds-n255156 (accessed October 13, 2016).

17. Matt Sena, "Real Estate Industry Analysis 2016: Cost & Trends," Franchise Help, 2016, https://www.franchisehelp.com/industry-reports/real-estate-franchise-industry-report/ (accessed October 13, 2016).

18. Ibid.

19. Robert P. Hartwig, "Insurance Industry Employment Trends: 1990–2015 (June 2015)," Insurance Information Institute, August 12, 2015, http://www.iii.org/presentation/insurance-industry-employment-trends-1990-2015-june-2015-081215 (accessed October 13, 2016).

20. Ibid.

21. Jared Bernstein, "The Case for a Tax on Financial Transactions," *New York Times*, July 22, 2015.

22. Douwe Miedema and Michael Flaherty, "New Fed Rule Tells 8 Biggest US Banks to Bump Up Capital," *Reuters*, July 20, 2015, http://www.reuters.com/article/us-banks-regulations-fed-idUSKCN0PU1UB20150720 (accessed October 13, 2016); Victoria McGrane and James Sterngold, "Fed Sets Tough New Capital Rule for Big Banks: JP Morgan Would Face $21 Billion Shortfall," *Wall Street Journal*, December 9, 2014, http://www.wsj.com/articles/fed-proposes-extra-capital-requirement-for-8-biggest-u-s-banks-1418154076 (accessed October 13, 2016).

23. Binyamin Applebaum, "When She Talks, Banks Shudder," *New York Times*, August 10, 2014, Sunday Business, p. 1.

24. "Case Study: The Collapse of Lehman Brothers," *Investopedia*, February 16, 2017, http://www.investopedia.com/articles/economics/09/lehman-brothers-collapse.asp (accessed April 26, 2017).

25. Landy, "Graph: How the Financial Sector."

PART VII. WASTING OUR RESOURCES BY PRODUCING USELESS GOODS AND SERVICES

1. United States History, "Unemployment Statistics during the Great Depression," http://www.u-s-history.com/pages/h1528.html (accessed May 5, 2017).

Chapter 17. The Internal Revenue Code and the Tax Preparation Industry

1. "IRS Official Admits He Doesn't Do His Own Taxes," *CBN News*, March 9, 2010, http://www.cbn.com/cbnnews/finance/2010/march/irs-official-admits-he-doesnt-do-his-own-taxes-/?mobile=false (accessed April 20, 2017).

2. Susan Johnston Taylor, "12 Times When It Makes Sense to Hire a Tax Preparer: If You've Started a New Business, Consider Hiring a Professional Instead of Self-Preparing Your Taxes," *US News & World Report*, March 2, 2016, http://money.usnews.com/money/personal-finance/articles/2016-03-02/12-times-when-it-makes-sense-to-hire-a-tax-preparer (accessed October 13, 2016).

3. "Key Facts and Trends in the Accountancy Profession," report, Financial Reporting Council, June 2016, https://www.frc.org.uk/Our-Work/Publications/Professional-Oversight/Key-Facts-and-Trends-2016.pdf (accessed October 13, 2016).

4. AccountingEDU, http://www.accountingedu.org/ (accessed October 13, 2016).

5. "The Tax Jobs Market, Explained in 4 Charts," *Indeed* (blog), April 12, 2016, http://blog.indeed.com/2016/04/12/tax-jobs-market-explained-in-4-charts/ (accessed October 13, 2016); Tax Attorneys Directory, http://tax-attorneys.regionaldirectory.us/ (accessed October 13, 2016).

6. Erin Scottberg, "Americans Spend 6 Billion Hours a Year Doing Their Taxes," Yahoo! News, February 4, 2013, https://www.yahoo.com/news/americans-spend-6-billion-hours-doing-taxes-133900708.html?ref=gs (accessed October 13, 2016).

7. AccountingEDU.

8. John D. McKinnon, "High-Earning Households Pay Growing Share of Taxes," *Wall Street Journal*, May 3, 2011, https://www.wsj.com/articles/SB10001424052748703703304576299560728821804 (accessed April 20, 2017).

9. "Reaganomics," *Wikipedia*, October 21, 2016, https://en.wikipedia.org/

wiki / Reaganomics (accessed October 13, 2016); Stephen L Slavin, *Macroeconomics*, 11th edition (New York: McGraw-Hill, 2013), p. 164, Fig. 4.

10. Warren E. Buffett, "Stop Coddling the Super-Rich," *New York Times*, Op-Ed, August 15, 2011, p. A21.

11. Michael Parisi and Michael Strudler, "SOI Tax Stats: Top 400 Individual Income Tax Returns with the Largest Adjusted Gross Incomes," Internal Revenue Service, July 12, 2016, https: / / www.irs.gov / uac / soi-tax-stats-top-400-individual -income-tax-returns-with-the-largest-adjusted-gross-incomes (accessed October 13, 2016).

12. "Household Income in the United States," *Wikipedia*, October 21, 2016, https: / / en.wikipedia.org / wiki / Household_income_in_the_United_States (accessed October 13, 2016).

13. Sreekar Jasthi, "How Much Do Americans Really Pay in Taxes?" Nerd-Wallet, April 8, 2015, https: / / www.nerdwallet.com / blog / taxes / how-much-do -americans-really-pay-taxes-2015 / (accessed April 26, 2017).

14. Only earned income—wages and salaries—are subject to the payroll tax of 7.65 percent; capital gains are not.

15. "Reaganomics," *Wikipedia*.

16. Tom Kertscher, Just How Wealthy Is the Wal-Mart Walton Family?" PolitiFact Wisconsin, December 8, 2013, http: / / www.politifact.com / wisconsin / statements / 2013 / dec / 08 / one-wisconsin-now / just-how-wealthy-wal-mart -walton-family / (accessed October 13, 2016).

17. "Key Elements of the US Tax System: How Many People Pay the Estate Tax?" Tax Policy Center Briefing Book, 2016, http: / / www.taxpolicycenter.org / briefing-book / how-many-people-pay-estate-tax (accessed October 13, 2016).

18. Juliegrace Brufke, "Feds Stumped by 158 Tax Expenditures Worth $1.2 Trillion," *Daily Caller*, July 11, 2016, http: / / dailycaller.com / 2016 / 07 / 11 / feds -stumped-by-158-tax-expenditures-worth-1-2-trillion / (accessed October 13, 2016).

19. "Some Background: What Are the Largest Tax Expenditures?" Tax Policy Center Briefing Book, 2016, http: / / www.taxpolicycenter.org / briefing-book / what-are-largest-tax-expenditures (accessed October 13, 2016).

20. Ibid.

21. Ibid.

22. "Steve Forbes on Tax Reform," OnTheIssues, http: / / www.ontheissues .org / celeb / Steve_Forbes_Tax_Reform.htm (accessed April 20, 2017).

Chapter 18. Telemarketers, Ambulance Chasers, and Other Make-Work Occupations

1. Jeff Jacoby, "US Legal Bubble Can't Pop Soon Enough," *Boston Globe*, May 9, 2014, https: / / www.bostonglobe.com / opinion / 2014 / 05 / 09 / the-lawyer

-bubble-pops-not-moment-too-soon/qAYzQ823qpfi4GQl2OiPZM/story.html (accessed October 14, 2016).

2. *Wall Street*, directed by Oliver Stone (New York: Twentieth Century Fox, 1987).

3. See Fig. 13.1 in chapter 13.

4. This was discussed in chapter 13.

5. Robert D. Reich, *The Next American Frontier* (New York: Penguin, 1983), p. 140.

6. Ibid., p. 145.

7. Adam Smith, *An Inquiry into the Nature and Causes of the Wealth of Nations*, Volume IV (London: Methuen, 1950), pp. 477–78.

8. United States Department of Labor: Bureau of Labor Statistics, http://www.bls.gov/ (accessed October 14, 2016); *Economic Indicators*, current issue.

9. Terence P. Jeffrey, "21,995,000 to 12,329,000: Government Employees Outnumber Manufacturing Employees 1.8 to 1," CNS News, September 8, 2015, http://www.cnsnews.com/news/article/terence-p-jeffrey/21955000-12329000-government-employees-outnumber-manufacturing (accessed October 14, 2016).

10. Michael R. Strain, "Has Government Employment Really Increased Under Obama?" AEIdeas, September 10, 2012, https://www.aei.org/publication/has-government-employment-really-increased-under-obama/ (accessed October 14, 2016).

11. Ibid.

12. Erin Scottberg, "Americans Spend 6 Billion Hours a Year Doing Their Taxes," Yahoo! News, February 4, 2013, https://www.yahoo.com/news/americans-spend-6-billion-hours-doing-taxes-133900708.html?ref=gs (accessed October 13, 2016).

13. Alan Farnham, "Fighting Telemarketers: When Do-Not-Call List Fails, These Strategies Work," http://abcnews.go.com/Business/best-ways-turn-tables-telemarketers/story?id=21534413 (accessed April 21, 2017).

14. "Minimum Wage," United States Department of Labor, https://www.dol.gov/general/topic/wages/minimumwage (accessed April 21, 2017).

Chapter 19. The Economic Consequences of Wasting Our Resources

1. Corey Kilgannon, "Change Blurs Memories in a Famous Suburb," *New York Times*, October 13, 2007, http://www.nytimes.com/2007/10/13/nyregion/13suburb.html (accessed October 2, 2016).

2. "Characteristics of New Housing," United States Census Bureau, https://www.census.gov/construction/chars/highlights.html (accessed April 5, 2017).

3. Martin V. Melosi, "The Automobile Shapes the City: The 'Footprint' of

the Automobile on the American City," Automobile in American Life and Society, 2010, http://www.autolife.umd.umich.edu/Environment/E_Casestudy/E_casestudy2.htm (accessed October 14, 2016); Jane Holtz Kay, *Asphalt Nation* (New York: Crown Publishers, 1977), p. 64.

4. US Bureau of Labor Statistics, "How Do U.S. Expenditures Compare with Those of Other Countries?" *Focus on Prices and Spending: Consumer Expenditure Survey* 2, no. 16 (March 2012), https://www.bls.gov/opub/btn/archive/how-do-us-expenditures-compare-with-those-of-other-countries.pdf (accessed April 24, 2017).

5. Reuters, "US Oil Settles at $45.34 a Barrel, Up $1.29, or 2.39%," CNBC, September 21, 2016, http://www.cnbc.com/2016/09/20/oil-prices-rise-on-reported-us-crude-stock-draw-firm-japan-imports.html (accessed October 15, 2016).

6. "United States GDP from Transportation and Warehousing," *Trading Economics*, 2016, http://www.tradingeconomics.com/united-states/gdp-from-transport (accessed October 14, 2016).

7. "Auto Marketplace Sales Data: 2015 Sales," Alliance Automobile Manufacturers, http://www.autoalliance.org/index.cfm?furl=auto-marketplace/sales-data (accessed October 14, 2016).

8. Eugene Robinson, "The Campaign Nonsense Du Jour," *Washington Post*, May 2, 2008, http://www.washingtonpost.com/wp-dyn/content/article/2008/05/01/AR2008050102858.html (accessed October 14, 2016).

9. Peter Schrag, "Schoolhouse Crock," *Harper's Magazine*, September 2007, p. 42.

10. Stephen L. Slavin, *Microeconomics*, 11th ed. (New York: McGraw-Hill, 2013), Figure 8, p. 394.

11. John Goodman, "How Much Should Health Insurance Cost?" National Center for Policy Analysis, March 7, 2012, http://healthblog.ncpa.org/how-much-should-health-insurance-cost/ (accessed October 14, 2016).

12. Ezra Klein and Evan Soltas, "Wonkbook: 11 Facts about America's Prison Population," *Washington Post*, August 13, 2013, https://www.washingtonpost.com/news/wonk/wp/2013/08/13/wonkbook-11-facts-about-americas-prison-population/ (accessed October 14, 2016).

13. "Prisons, Jails, and People Arrested for Drugs," DrugWarFacts.org, 2016, http://www.drugwarfacts.org/cms/Prisons_and_Drugs (accessed October 14, 2016); "Incarceration in the United States," *Wikipedia*, October 23, 2016, https://en.wikipedia.org/wiki/Incarceration_in_the_United_States (accessed October 14, 2016).

14. Prisoners and Prisoner Re-Entry," United States Department of Justice, https://www.justice.gov/archive/fbci/progmenu_reentry.html (accessed October 14, 2016).

15. Nicholas Kristof, "Inside a Mental Hospital Called Jail," *New York Times*, February 8, 2014, http://www.nytimes.com/2014/02/09/opinion/sunday/inside-a-mental-hospital-called-jail.html?_r=0 (accessed October 14, 2016).

16. "Incarceration in the United States: Ethnicity," *Wikipedia*, October 23, 2016, https://en.wikipedia.org/wiki/Incarceration_in_the_United_States#Ethnicity (accessed October 14, 2016).

17. Executive Office of the President of the United States, *Economic Perspectives on Incarceration and the Criminal Justice System* (Washington, DC: Executive Office of the President of the United States, April 2016), https://www.whitehouse.gov/sites/default/files/page/files/20160423_cea_incarceration_criminal_justice.pdf (accessed October 14, 2016).

18. Ibid.

19. Tim Ryan, "It Takes Americans 6.1 Billion Hours to Prepare Their Taxes, Says Virginia Fox," PolitiFact, April 15, 2014, http://www.politifact.com/truth-o-meter/statements/2014/apr/15/virginia-foxx/it-takes-americans-61-billion-hours-prepare-their-/ (accessed October 14, 2016).

20. Rande Spiegelman, "Taxes: What's New for 2016?" Charles Schwab & Co., January 12, 2016, https://www.schwab.com/public/schwab/nn/articles/taxes-whats-new (accessed October 14, 2016).

21. "Minimum Wage," United States Department of Labor, https://www.dol.gov/general/topic/wages/minimumwage (accessed April 21, 2017).

Chapter 20. Our Twin Deficits

1. "Twin Deficits Hypothesis," *Wikipedia*, May 14, 2016, https://en.wikipedia.org/wiki/Twin_deficits_hypothesis (accessed October 15, 2016).

2. Like most other Republicans, for most of his long political career, Dick Cheney was a deficit hawk. Big federal budget deficits were bad. But when the administration of George W. Bush began running very large deficits in 2002, suddenly deficits were not so bad.

3. Peter G. Peterson, *Running on Empty* (New York: Farrar, Straus and Giroux, 2004), pp. 22–23.

4. Ibid., p. 18. Peterson has certainly put his money where his mouth is. He used $1 billion of his Wall Street fortune to create a foundation whose sole purpose is to educate Americans about the dangers of the deficit and the national debt.

5. Ibid., p. 17.

6. United States Bureau of Economic Analysis, "Federal Government Current Transfer Payments: Government Social Benefits: To Persons," FRED, Federal Reserve Bank of St. Louis, September 29, 2016, https://fred.stlouisfed.org/series/B087RC1Q027SBEA (accessed October 15, 2016).

7. US Bureau of Economic Analysis, http://www.bea.gov/ (accessed October 15, 2016); Council of Economic Advisers, *Economic Indicators* (Washington, DC: Government Publishing Office, February 2017), https://www.gpo.gov/fdsys/pkg/ECONI-2017-02/pdf/ECONI-2017-02.pdf (accessed April 14, 2017).

8. How this figure was derived was discussed near the end of chapter 14.

9. See chapter 5.

10. Reuters, "US Oil Settles at $45.34 a Barrel, Up $1.29, or 2.39%," CNBC, September 21, 2016, http://www.cnbc.com/2016/09/20/oil-prices-rise-on-reported-us-crude-stock-draw-firm-japan-imports.html (accessed October 15, 2016).

11. Marcos Chamon, Kai Liu, and Eswar Prasad, "The Puzzle of China's Rising Household Saving Rate," *Vox*, January 18, 2011, http://voxeu.org/article/puzzle-china-s-rising-household-saving-rate (accessed October 15, 2016).

Chapter 21. Our Unraveling Social Contract

1. United States Department of Labor: Bureau of Labor Statistics, http://www.bls.gov/ (accessed October 15, 2016).

2. Charlie Wilson was the president of General Motors in 1953 when he made that statement. He believed that the nation's great industrial strength—best exemplified by his own company—was what made America great.

3. "Education and Training: History and Timeline," US Department of Veterans Affairs, last updated November 21, 2013, http://www.benefits.va.gov/gibill/history.asp (accessed October 15, 2016).

4. Ibid.; "G.I. Bill," *Wikipedia*, October 12, 2016, https://en.wikipedia.org/wiki/G.I._Bill (accessed October 15, 2016).

5. "120 Years of American Education Statistical Portrait," PBworks, http://web20kmg.pbworks.com/w/file/85968592/120%20years%20of%20american%20education%20statistical%20portrait%20nces.pdf (October 25, 2016).

6. Stephen L. Slavin, *Microeconomics* (New York: McGraw-Hill, 2013), Fig. 8, p. 394.

7. Steven Greenhouse, "Share of the Work Force in a Union Falls to a 97-Year Low, 11.3%," *New York Times*, January 23, 2013, http://www.nytimes.com/2013/01/24/business/union-membership-drops-despite-job-growth.html (accessed October 15, 2016).

8. Jeff Faux, *The Global Class War* (Hoboken, NJ: John Wiley and Sons, 2008), p. 89.

9. Steven Greenhouse, *The Big Squeeze: Tough Times for the American Worker* (New York: Alfred A. Knopf, 2008), p. 4.

Chapter 22. Growing Income Inequality and the Shrinking Middle Class

1. Claudia Goldin and Robert Margo, "The Great Compression: The Wage Structure in the United States at Mid-Century," *Quarterly Journal of Economics* 107, no. 1 (1992): 11–34.

2. Timothy Noah, *The Great Divergence* (New York: Bloomsbury Press 2012), p. 55.

3. "Federal Individual Income Tax Rates History, Income Years 1913–2013," Tax Foundation, http://taxfoundation.org/sites/default/files/docs/fed_individual_rate_history_nominal.pdf (accessed October 16, 2016).

4. Ibid.

5. Ibid.

6. Ibid.

7. "A Historical Look at Capital Gains Rates," Wolters Kluwer, 2015, https://www.cchgroup.com/news-and-insights/wbot2015/historical-capital-gain (accessed October 16, 2016).

8. Ibid.

9. Ibid.

10. Ibid.

11. Ibid.

12. "Minimum Wage," United States Department of Labor, https://www.dol.gov/general/topic/wages/minimumwage (accessed April 21, 2017).

13. "The Productivity-Pay Gap," Economic Policy Institute, August 2016, http://www.epi.org/productivity-pay-gap/ (accessed October 16, 2016).

14. "US Household Income," Department of Numbers, 2015, http://www.deptofnumbers.com/income/us/ (accessed October 16, 2016).

15. "Productivity-Pay Gap," Economic Policy Institute, http://www.epi.org/productivity-pay-gap/ (accessed October 16, 2016); "US Household Income," Department of Numbers, http://www.deptofnumbers.com/income/us/ (accessed October 16, 2016).

16. Stephen L. Slavin, 11th ed., *Microeconomics* (New York: McGraw-Hill, 2013), Fig. 8, p. 394.

17. See *Economic Report of the President: Together with the Annual Report of the Council of Economic Advisers* (Washington, DC: US Government Publishing Office, 1986); *Economic Report of the President: Together with the Annual Report of the Council of Economic Advisers* (Washington, DC: US Government Publishing Office, 1996); *Economic Report of the President: Together with the Annual Report of the Council of Economic Advisers* (Washington, DC: US Government Publishing Office, 2006); *Economic Report of the President: Together with the Annual Report of the Council of Economic Advisers* (Washington, DC: US Government Publishing Office, 2016).

18. *Economic Report of the President: Together with the Annual Report of the Council of Economic Advisers* (Washington, DC: US Government Publishing Office, 2010), p. 366.

19. Avi Feller and Chad Stone, "Top 1 Percent of Americans Reaped Two-Thirds of Income Gains in Last Economic Expansion: Income Concentration in 2007 Was at Highest Level Since 1928, New Analysis Shows," Center on Budget and Policy Priorities, September 9, 2009, http://www.cbpp.org/research/top-1-percent-of-americans-reaped-two-thirds-of-income-gains-in-last-economic-expansion (accessed October 16, 2016) (See Figure 2); G. William Domhoff, "Wealth, Income, and Power," Who Rules America? September 2005, February

2013, http://www2.ucsc.edu/whorulesamerica/power/wealth.html (accessed October 16, 2016).

20. Ibid.

21. Patricia Cohen, "A Bigger Pie, but Uneven Slices," *New York Times*, December 7, 2016, p. B1.

22. "Distribution of Wealth," *Wikipedia*, September 11, 2016, https://en.wikipedia.org/wiki/Distribution_of_wealth (accessed October 16, 2016).

23. "An Economic Cancer: The Top 1% Earns More Than the Bottom 50%," LiveLeak, https://www.liveleak.com/view?i=a67_1385392418 (October 25, 2016).

24. Pat Garofalo, "Walmart Heirs Have as Much Wealth as Bottom 40 Percent of Americans Combined," ThinkProgress, July 17, 2012, https://thinkprogress.org/walmart-heirs-have-as-much-wealth-as-bottom-40-percent-of-americans-combined-7fe778936a32#.8711z3maq (accessed October 16, 2016).

25. "The Top 0.1 Percent Earns Half of American Capital Gains," RT, November 21, 2011, https://www.rt.com/usa/percent-half-capital-gains-887/ (accessed October 16, 2016).

26. Tami Luhby, "What It Takes to Get into the Top 1%," CNN Money, December 29, 2015, money.cnn.com/2015/12/29/news/economy/top-1-income (accessed April 26, 2017).

27. Robert Gebloff and Shaila Dewan, "Measuring the Top 1% by Wealth, Not Income," *New York Times*, January 1, 2012.

28. "Executive Compensation," *Wikipedia*, October 13, 2016, https://en.wikipedia.org/wiki/Executive_compensation (accessed October 16, 2016).

29. Steven Rattner, "Inequality, Unbelievably, Gets Worse," *New York Times*, November 17, 2014, p. A25.

30. Erik Sherman, "America Is the Richest, and Most Unequal, Country," *Fortune*, September 30, 2015, http://fortune.com/2015/09/30/america-wealth-inequality/ (accessed October 16, 2016).

31. Andrew G. Berg and Jonathan D. Ostry, "Equality and Efficiency," *Finance and Development* 48, no. 3 (September 2011), http://www.imf.org/external/pubs/ft/fandd/2011/09/berg.htm (accessed October 16, 2016).

32. Ibid.

33. Walter Isaacson, "Don't Run Out the Clock," *Time*, August 15, 2014, p. 20.

34. Christopher Lash, *The Revolt of the Elites and the Betrayal of Democracy* (New York: Norton, 1994), p. 45.

35. Robert Frank, *Richistan: A Journey through the American Wealth Boom and the Lives of the New Rich* (New York: Crown, 2007), pp. 3–4.

36. Hedrick Smith, *Who Stole the American Dream?* (New York: Random House), p. 109.

Chapter 23. Poverty and the Growing Permanent Underclass

1. "Federal Poverty Guidelines," Families USA, February 2016, http://familiesusa.org/product/federal-poverty-guidelines (accessed October 16, 2016).

2. "Poverty," United States Census Bureau, http://census.gov/topics/income-poverty/poverty.html (accessed October 16, 2016).

3. Stephen L. Slavin, *Microeconomics*, 11th ed. (New York: McGraw-Hill, 2013), p. 453

4. See chapter 15.

5. See chapter 15.

6. "About Homelessness," National Alliance to End Homelessness, 2016, http://www.endhomelessness.org/pages/about_homelessness (accessed October 16, 2016).

7. "Drug and Alcohol Abuse and the Homelessness," AddictionBlog, January 7, 2011, http://alcohol.addictionblog.org/drug-and-alcohol-abuse-and-the-homeless/ (accessed October 16, 2016).

8. See chapter 15.

9. Chana Joffe-Walt, "Unfit for Work: The Startling Rise of Disability in America," NPR, 2013, http://apps.npr.org/unfit-for-work/ (accessed October 16, 2016).

10. Maureen Callahan, "Almost Half of America Could Become the New Permanent Underclass," *New York Post*, September 17, 2016, http://nypost.com/2016/09/17/almost-half-of-america-could-become-the-new-permanent-underclass/ (accessed October 16, 2016); "Underclass," *Wikipedia*, October 7, 2016, https://en.wikipedia.org/wiki/Underclass (accessed October 16, 2016); Jeff Minick, "Putting a Face on the Growing White Underclass," *Smoky Mountain News*, September 14, 2016, http://www.smokymountainnews.com/news/item/18421-putting-a-face-on-the-growing-white-underclass (accessed October 16, 2016).

11. Nicholas D. Kristof, "The White Underclass," *New York Times*, February 9, 2012, p. A23.

12. Patrick F. Fagan, "The Real Root Causes of Violent Crime: The Breakdown of Marriage, Family, and Community," Heritage Foundation, March 17, 1995, http://www.heritage.org/research/reports/1995/03/bg1026nbsp-the-real-root-causes-of-violent-crime (accessed October 16, 2016); Daniel Weinberger, "The Causes of Homelessness in America" (paper, Stanford University, July 26, 1999), https://web.stanford.edu/class/e297c/poverty_prejudice/soc_sec/hcauses.htm (accessed October 16, 2016).

13. Nicola A. Conners et al., "Children of Mothers with Serious Substance Abuse Problems: An Accumulation of Risks," *American Journal of Drug and Alcohol Abuse* 29, no. 4 (2003): 743–758, http://www.womenstreatmentcenter.org/_files/sidebars/pdfs/childrenofmotherswithseriousssu_20120130125846815 8.pdf (accessed October 16, 2016); L. Margolin, "Child Abuse by Mothers' Boyfriends:

Why the Overrepresentation?" *Child Abuse and Neglect* 16, no. 4 (July–August 1992): 541–551, https://www.ncbi.nlm.nih.gov/pubmed/1393717 (accessed October 16, 2016).

14. Sasha Abramsky, "Toxic Persons: New Research Shows Precisely How the Prison-to-Poverty Cycle Does Its Damage," *Slate*, October 8, 2010, http://www.slate.com/articles/news_and_politics/jurisprudence/2010/10/toxic_persons.html (accessed October 16, 2016); "Poverty and Crime: Breaking the Vicious Cycle," Poverties.org, September 25, 2015, http://www.poverties.org/blog/poverty-and-crime (accessed October 16, 2016).

15. "Poverty," United States Census Bureau, http://census.gov/topics/income-poverty/poverty.html (accessed October 16, 2016).

16. "Ending Child Poverty Now," Children's Defense Fund, 2016, http://www.childrensdefense.org/library/PovertyReport/EndingChildPovertyNow.html (accessed October 16, 2016).

17. Kathryn J. Eden and H. Luke Schaefer, *$2 a Day: Living on Almost Nothing in America* (Boston: Houghton Mifflin Harcourt, 2015).

18. Nicholas Kristof, "Why I Was Wrong about Welfare Reform," *New York Times*, Sunday Review, June 19, 2016, p. 11.

19. Robert Wood Johnson Foundation, *Annual Report*, 1984.

20. Lisabeth B. Schorr and Daniel Schorr, *Within Our Reach* (New York: Doubleday, 1989), p. 151.

Chapter 24. How We Are Wasting Our Resources: The Big Picture

1. See chapter 12.

2. Vivienne Sanders, *Access to History: The American Dream: Reality and Illusion, 1945–1980* (London: Hodder Education, 2015).

3. United States Bureau of Labor Statistics, http://www.bls.gov/ (accessed October 17, 2016).

4. Newt Gingrich, Vince Haley, and Rick Tyler, *Real Change: From the World That Fails to the World That Works* (New York: Regnery, 2008), p. 210.

5. See chapter 11.

6. See chapter 11.

7. See chapter 11.

8. Concord Coalition Report, *New York Times*, January 5, 2007.

9. See chapter 12.

10. See chapter 12.

11. See chapter 12.

12. See chapter 13.

13. See chapter 13.

14. Kathryn M. O'Neill, "Measuring Health Care: Amy Finkelstein Spotted an Opportunity to Bring the Gold Standard in Scientific Research to One of the Most

Pressing Questions of the Day," *MIT News*, March 18, 2015, http://news.mit.edu/2015/measuring-health-care-amy-finkelstein-0318 (accessed October 17, 2016).

15. See chapter 14.
16. See chapter 14.
17. See chapter 15.
18. See chapter 15.
19. See chapter 15.
20. See chapter 15.
21. See chapter 15.
22. See chapter 15.
23. See chapter 16.
24. See chapter 16.
25. See chapter 17.
26. See chapter 5.
27. Bureau of Labor Statistics, http://www.bls.gov/ (accessed October 17, 2016).
28. "Intro to Criminal Justice ch 1–6," Quizlet, https://quizlet.com/24470626/intro-to-criminal-justice-ch1-6-flash-cards/ (accessed April 26, 2017).
29. See chapter 13.
30. See chapter 15.

Chapter 25. Solving Our Economic Problems and Saving the American Economy

1. See chapter 11.
2. See chapter 11.
3. See chapter 11.
4. *Field of Dreams*, directed by Phil Alden Robinson (Boston, MA: Gordon Company, 1989).
5. See chapter 12.
6. See chapter 12.
7. See chapter 12.
8. See chapter 13.
9. See chapter 13.
10. See chapter 14.
11. For this information and the following, see chapter 15.

Chapter 26: The Great Jobs Switch: Placing Tens of Millions of Americans in Useful Jobs

1. Bureau of Labor Statistics, "Employment Situation Summary," March 2017, https://www.bls.gov/news.release/empsit.nr0.htm (accessed April 27,

2017). The Bureau of Labor Statistics listed 7,200,000 people unemployed in February 2017. In addition, there were 5,600,000 part-time workers who would have preferred to work full-time, and 1,600,000 people without jobs who were considered marginally attached to the labor force because they had not looked for work for at least four weeks. Therefore, there were 14,400 people who wanted full-time jobs. My estimate of fifteen million people who would thankfully fill full-time jobs may actually be on the low side if we consider the small sample size (60,000 families) of the monthly employment survey.

2. Ibid.

3. Hurricane Katrina, which struck New Orleans and the surrounding Gulf Coast communities in 2005, was considered a local disaster rather than an effect of global warming.

4. See chapter 6.

5. Sarah Palin, in Biden-Palin Vice Presidential Debate, October 2, 2008, transcript, Commission on Presidential Debates, http://www.debates.org/index.php?page=2008-debate-transcript-2 (accessed April 19, 2017).

6. See chapter 11.

7. See chapter 12.

8. See chapter 12.

9. See chapter 13.

10. "Why Is It Difficult to Get Doctor's Appointment in US?" Quora, https://www.quora.com/Why-is-it-difficult-to-get-doctors-appointment-in-US (accessed October 18, 2016).

11. Heather Long, "Trump's Big Challenge: Cutting Federal Workers," CNN Money, January 12, 2017, http://money.cnn.com/2017/01/12/news/economy/trump-federal-worker-freeze-promise/ (accessed April 26, 2017); Jennifer Rizzo, "Defense Cuts: The Jobs Numbers Game," *Security Clearance* (blog), September 22, 2011, http://security.blogs.cnn.com/2011/09/22/defense-cuts-the-jobs-numbers-game/ (accessed April 26, 2017).

12. Mark Thoma, "Poor People Are Intentionally Getting Arrested to Access Mental Health Treatment," *AMERICAblog*, January 22, 2014, http://americablog.com/2014/01/poor-people-intentionally-getting-arrested-get-mental-health-treatment.html (accessed April 24, 2017).

13. See chapter 16.

14. Sarah Perez, "Callblock's New IOS App Will Block Calls from Over 2 Million Telemarketers," TechCrunch, September 7, 2016, https://techcrunch.com/2016/09/07/callblocks-new-ios-app-will-block-calls-from-over-2-million-telemarketers/?ncid=rss (accessed April 26, 2017).

15. See chapter 18.

16. See chapter 18.

17. "Parkinson's Law: Definition," Business Dictionary, 2016, http://www.businessdictionary.com/definition/Parkinson-s-Law.html (accessed October 18, 2016).

18. See Chapter 23.

19. "AmeriCorps," Corporation for National & Community Service, http://www.nationalservice.gov/programs/americorps (accessed October 18, 2016).

20. Doris Goodwin, "The Way We Won: America's Economic Breakthrough during World War II," *American Prospect*, Fall 1992, http://prospect.org/article/way-we-won-americas-economic-breakthrough-during-world-war-ii (accessed October 18, 2016).

21. "Demobilization of United States Armed Forces after World War II," *Wikipedia*, September 13, 2016, https://en.wikipedia.org/wiki/Demobilization_of_United_States_armed_forces_after_World_War_II (accessed October 18, 2016).

Chapter 27. A Long-Term Strategy to Save the American Economy

1. Emma G. Fitzsimmons, "Infrastructure Emerges As a Winner in Elections," *New York Times*, November 10, 2016, p. A12.

2. "Where Washington Fails to Drive Progress, Cities Will Act," *Time*, December 18, 2016.

3. Tatiana Schlossberg, "Unchartered Paths on Global Health and Climate," *New York Times*, December 20, 2016, p. D1.

4. Barry Goldwater, a long-serving Arizona Republican senator, ran for president in 1964 and lost to President Lyndon Johnson. Dick Armey went on to become the Republican House majority leader in 1995 and founded Freedom Works, a political organization that has funneled tens of millions of dollars to Tea Party groups.

5. Lawrence J. Korb, "BRAC Failed Capacity, Financial Goals," Center for American Progress, September 26, 2005, https://www.americanprogress.org/issues/security/news/2005/09/26/1638/brac-failed-capacity-financial-goals/ (accessed October 17, 2016).

6. Jerry Brito, "Running for Cover: The BRAC Commission as a Model for Federal Spending Reform" (working paper, George Mason University, no. 10–23, May 2010), p. 13.

7. *Hearings on Base Closures, Before the US Senate Comm. on Armed Services*, 99th Cong. 17 (1985) (statement of Senator Phil Gramm).

8. Brito, "Running for Cover."

9. "Troubled Asset Relief Program," *Wikipedia*, October 13, 2016, https://en.wikipedia.org/wiki/Troubled_Asset_Relief_Program (accessed October 17, 2016).

10. *Economic Report of the President: Together with the Annual Report of the Council of Economic Advisers* (Washington, DC: US Government Publishing Office, 2011).

11. Robert Steinbrook, "Lobbying, Campaign Contributions, and Health

Care Reform," *New England Journal of Medicine*, November 18, 2009, http://www.nejm.org/doi/full/10.1056/NEJMp0910879 (accessed October 17, 2016).

12. Charles Simic, interview by Deborah Solomon, February 3, 2008, "In-Verse Thinking," *New York Times Magazine*, http://www.nytimes.com/2008/02/03/magazine/03wwln-q4-t.html (accessed April 19, 2017).

INDEX

accountants, 219, 220
Affordable Care Act (ACA), 159, 173
  interest of lobbyists and, 331
  Medicaid and, 162, 167, 175
  Medicare for All and, 302
  provisions, 167
  repealing and replacing, 19–20
  Supreme Court ruling on, 167–68
African Americans
  confined to the cities during postwar suburbanization, 35, 42, 43
  drug use/arrests/imprisonments and, 192
  employment discrimination of, 99
  federally insured mortgage loans and, 34–35
  home mortgage loans denied to, 39, 42
  in prison, 189, 190, 192, 239
  social contract and, 256–57
  suburbanization and, 273, 274
  unable to rise out of poverty in the cities, 48, 49
age of the industrial capitalist, 74
AIG (American International Group, company), 93, 213
air pollution, 47, 127
air traffic systems, 90, 91, 310
air travel, 128
Allentown, Pennsylvania, 121
All-Volunteer Army, 182–83
al Qaeda, 187
alternate energy sources, 68, 186
Amazon (company), 81, 84
ambulance chasers, 227, 316
"American Century, The" (Luce), 13
American colonies, British manufacturing and, 59, 73
American Dream
  African Americans and, 48, 257
  attainment of, 255, 261
  end of, 266
  poor and, 273
  World War II, at close of, 41, 255
American economy
  eight fundamental problems with, 20–21, 284–92
  election of 2016 and, 13
  predictions on, 14
  six additional problems of, 22
  soundness of, 17
  unsustainable course of current, 22
  See also economic problems
American exceptionalism, 14
American Federation of Teachers (AFT), 140, 156, 286
American International Group. *See* AIG
American Revolution, 73
American Society of Civil Engineers, 91
"America the Beautiful" hymn, 14
AmeriCorps VISTA (company), 318
Amtrak (railroad service), 128, 129
Anti-Drug Abuse Act (1986), 192
Apple (company), 81, 84
apprenticeship programs, 149–50
Armey, Dick, 327
arms race, 55, 181
Asia, containment of Communism in, 53
Asphalt Nation (Kay), 122
AT&T (company), 92
ATMs (automated teller machines), 102, 202
attorneys
  decreasing people employed as, 316

getting by with less, 226–27
specializing in medical malpractice, 227
tax attorneys, 219, 220–21, 226
Australia, 173
automation
decline of organized labor and, 105
expanding employment, 111
explained, 110
manufacturing job loss and, 101, 102–103, 110–11
automobile industry
American industrial power and, 75
employment from, 115
federal government investment in, 93
Henry Ford, under, 74
Japan and, 60, 78, 80
large vehicles built by, 125, 296
automobiles
air pollution/global warming and, 127
alternate energy sources for fueling, 186
America's dependence on, 21, 44, 45, 284
America's land dedicated to, 125
dependence on oil and, 45, 50
electric, 131
gasoline tax and, 130–31
government spending on roads in 1930s and, 34, 39
incentives for not using, 130–31
as inefficient, 49–50
suburbanization and dependence on, 46, 49
wastefulness of resources and, 236

baby boom/baby boomers, 40, 42, 46, 160, 163, 245, 259, 260
Bacevich, Andrew, 182–83
Bacon, Francis, 16
bail money, 198
Baker, Dean, 204
Bangladesh, 78, 88, 102
bank employment, 102, 111
Banking Act (1980), 205
Banking Act (1999), 203–204, 205
Bank of America, 204, 213
Bank of China, 248
Bank of Japan, 248
banks and banking
bailout of, 206, 208
breaking up big, 213–14
changes in, 1970s and 1980s, 203
deregulation and, 203–204
Dodd-Frank Wall Street Reform and Consumer Protection Act (2010), 207, 213
economic role of, 201–202
higher capital requirements of, 212
Barbor, Sir Michael, 138, 286
Barnett, W. Steven, 147
Bell Labs (company), 93
Berg, Andrew, 268–69
Bernanke, Ben, 22, 205
big-box retailers, 48, 49, 78, 106
bin Laden, Osama, 303
birthrates, 35, 40, 42, 46
Bloomberg, Michael, 325–26
blue-collar jobs, 63, 97, 109, 150–51, 306
Blunt, Roy, 96
Bok, Derek, 133
borrowing from foreigners, 22, 25. *See also* foreign trade deficit
Boston, Massachusetts, 66, 196, 296
BRAC (Base Realignment and Closure, plan), 327–28
Brezhnev, Leonid, 55
bridges, 90
Briggs, Helen, 68
Brito, Jerry, 328
Brokaw, Tom, 322
Brooklyn College, 323
Brooks, David, 47
Brown, H. Rap, 189

Brown, Sherrod, 96
Brownback, Sam, 328
Brown v. the Topeka Board of Education, 143
Brynjolfsson, Erik, 103
budget deficit. *See* federal budget deficit
Buffet, Warren, 222
bureaucrats, destroying jobs of, 155, 300, 311–12, 317, 320–21
Burns, Scott, 161
Bush, George W., 170, 205, 245, 246
business firms
 benefits cut by, 255–56
 foreign, in China, 60–61
 government's investment in private, 93–94
 Medicare for All's effect on, 176
 prosperity of postwar, 254–55
 See also names of individual companies; offshoring
bus transportation, 129, 131

calculators, 141, 157, 286, 299
 banning from elementary schools, 157, 299
campaign contributions, 262, 270
Canada, 121, 173
Cantwell, Maria, 213
capital gains tax, 222, 240, 263, 264
capitalism, 29, 62, 80
carbon dioxide, 65, 68, 127
Carnegie, Andrew, 74
Caro, Robert, 124
Carrier, Willis, 75
Carter, Jimmy, 205
"Ceasefire" strategy, 196
CEOs. *See* chief executive officers
Charles Atlas cartoon, 21
Charlotte, North Carolina, 132
charter schools, 151–52
Cheney, Dick, 243
Chiang Kai-shek, 53
Chicago, Illinois, 295
chief executive officers (CEOs), 267
children
 entertainment of, 137
 in inner-city schools, 137–38
 in poverty, 15, 277, 278
 school readiness of poor, 138, 143
 See also students
Children's Health Insurance Plan. *See* CHIP
China
 America's loss of technologic edge and, 82
 America's shrinking manufacturing base and, 21
 communism and, 53
 economic growth in, 87
 electronics production in, 60
 foreign companies in, 88–89
 foreign companies sharing technology with, 61
 growth of manufacturing in, 60–61
 industrial policy and, 92, 96, 309
 Nixon's visit to, 55
 offshoring and, 78, 102, 258
 Paris Agreement and, 68
 public transportation in, 89, 128, 131, 284–85
 railway system in, 284–85
 research and development facilities in, 81, 83, 87
 selling in the American market, 248
 spending on infrastructure, 91
 STEM students in, 86
 Taiwanese production moved to, 54, 57, 60, 62, 77, 291
 Wal-Mart and, 78, 106
 as world's largest manufacturer, 29, 80
"Chinese buses," 129
CHIP (Children's Health Insurance Plan), 175
chronically poor, 275
Chrysler (company), 78, 80, 93, 125
Cincinnati, Ohio, 132, 196

Cisco (company), 84
Citicorp/Citigroup (company), 93, 204, 213
cities
  African Americans confined to neighborhoods in, 35, 42, 43
  downtowns of, 45, 47, 49
  efforts to solve economic problems by, 325–26
  suburbanization and the abandonment of, 42, 47–49, 273, 292
  at turn of the century, 41
  urban ghettoes, 190, 274
civic institutions, sprawl and, 44
Clark, Joe, 138
Clay, Henry, 21
Cleveland, Ohio, 317
Clinton, Bill, 205, 257
Clinton, Hillary Rodham, 13
Cohen, Stephen S., 83
Cold War, 14, 27, 31, 51–57
  America's aid to foreign countries during, 52–53, 54, 57, 77, 291
  containment of Communism and, 51–52
  costs of America's victory in, 55–56
  de-escalation of, 55
  economic competition and, 53
  economic costs of, 55–56, 57
  Marshall Plan and, 52, 57
  military-industrial complex and, 56
  Nixon's visit to China during, 55
  post-WWII Soviet threat and, 51–52
  Soviet Communist expansion and, 51–52
  United States sharing technology with Asia during, 54, 60
collateralized debt obligations (CDOs), 205, 206
college
  alternatives to, 149–50
  armed forces volunteers and, 183
  career colleges, 145–46
  community colleges, 134, 145–46
  denying admission to students who cannot read, write, or do simple arithmetic, 155, 300
  dropping out of, 134, 145, 146
  education majors in, 138–39, 140, 142, 157, 286, 311
  GI Bill of Rights, 256
  high school graduates not prepared for, 133, 134
  loans, 145–46
  math education/textbook for, 134, 146
  remedial courses and, 133, 287
  students in STEM subjects, 85–86
  volunteer army and, 182, 183
college graduates
  drawn to jobs in the financial sector, 209
  job prospects for, 116
  in make-work sector, 229–30
  moving in with parents, 262
  one in three twenty-five-year-olds as, 149
  Teach for America for, 152–53
  in teaching, 138–39, 142, 147
commercial banks, 203, 204
Common Core/core curriculum, 154, 298
Communism, 51–52, 53. *See also* Cold War
community college, 134, 145–46
community health centers, 170
computers
  automation and, 110
  banking and, 202
  entertainment of students from, 137
  in public libraries, 311
  technological innovations and, 86
Conrad, Kent, 328
consumption
  foreign trade deficit and, 250

mass production and mass, 74, 255
rising, stagnant wages and, 265
trade deficit and, 250
containment policy, 52, 53
Coolidge, Calvin, 75
copayments, 161, 164, 288
Corinthian College, 145
corporate pension plans, 255
corporations. *See* business firms; multinational corporations, operations set up in developing countries by; offshoring
"corrections," 193. *See also* criminal justice system
Costco (retailer), 48, 78, 104
courts, legal, 193
"creative destruction," 100, 176
crime
drug-related, 191–92, 197–98, 239, 314
high cost of, 193–94
nonviolent crime and criminals, 27–28, 195–96, 200, 303–304, 314–15
community service for, 195–96
poverty and, 194–95
punishing criminals for violent, 195
solutions to minimizing, 304
young black and Hispanic males and, 190
criminal justice system, 179
characteristics of prison inmates in, 191–93
economic consequences of wastefulness in, 239
facts on, 189
as a fundamental problem of American economy, 21
high cost of, 193
jobs created and destroyed in, 314–15
permanent American underclass and, 276
solutions to inefficiencies in, 194–200, 303–304
wastefulness of resources and, 27–28, 289
See also prisons
Cross Bronx Expressway, 124
Cuban Missile Crisis (1962), 51
Cutler, David, 166

DARPA (Defense Advanced Research Projects Agency), 92
Dart, Thomas, 191
Dayan, Moshe, 138
daycare programs, 147, 149, 311–12
deductions, tax, 223–24
defense contractors, 56, 92–93, 183–84, 321
defense spending, 179
arms race, 55, 181
cost of wasting resources on, 186
economic costs of the Cold War and, 55–56, 57
federal budget deficit and, 245–46
foreign trade deficit and, 250
industrial policy and, 96
influencing other economic issues, 292
since 2010, 186
suburbanization's influence on, 50
Trump on, 20
war on terror and, 185–86
wastefulness of resources and, 27, 181–82
World War II and, 37–38, 40
defensive medicine, 163, 168–69, 287–88, 301
deindustrialization of America, 60–61, 71, 76–80
Dell (company), 83, 84
democracy, income inequality and, 270–71
Democratic-Republican stalemate, 262
Democrats, 244, 254
Denmark, 173

Denver, Colorado, 132
Department of Homeland Security, 185
Department of Veterans Affairs, 174, 314
Depository Institutions Deregulation and Monetary Control Act (1980), 203
deregulation, 202–204
Detroit, Michigan, 317, 326
Detroit Regional Workforce, 135
Devaraj, Srikant, 110
DeVry University, 145
discrimination
  employment, 99, 139
  housing, 39, 42, 43
  sentencing disparities and, 192
disposable workers, 107–108
divorce lawyers, 227
doctors
  Americans waiting longer to see, compared with other countries, 170
  malpractice suits and, 168–69, 300–301, 305
  Medicare for All, under, 174, 302
  unneeded services by, 163–64, 288
Dodd-Frank Wall Street Reform and Consumer Protection Act (2010), 207, 213, 214
domino theory, 53
Downs, Anthony, 41
draft, military, 182, 183, 322
drug treatment, 197–98, 303, 304, 314
Duany, Andres, 44, 45
DuPont (company), 79
Durocher, Leo "the Lip," 101
Dwyer, Jim, 193–94

earned income tax credit. *See under* taxes
Easterbrook, Gregg, 185–86
Eastern Europe, 51, 81, 83, 87, 237, 291, 309
East Germany, 51
eBay, 84
economic consequences
  of financialization, 208–210
  of global warming, 66
  of income inequality, 268–69
  of suburbanization, 47–48, 235
  of technological change, 103
  of wastefulness in criminal justice sector, 239
  of wastefulness in financial sector, 239–40
  of wastefulness in healthcare, 237–38
  of wastefulness in make-work sector, 240
  of wastefulness in military-industrial complex, 238–39
  of wastefulness in public education, 236–37
  of wastefulness in US transportation sector, 235–36
  See also federal budget deficit
economic problems
  American attitude about reversing, 330–31
  cities and states initiatives in solving, 325–26
  events contributing to, 14, 31 (*see also* Cold War; globalization; global warming; Great Depression; suburbanization: postwar; World War II)
  experts used for solving, 326
  impacting each other, 292–93
  indicators of, 15
  origins of, 14, 23
  past events influencing, 14–15
  presidential commissions recommending solutions for, 326–27
  summing up America's basic, 330
  See also wastefulness of resources
economics
  definition, 26
  "efficiency" and "scarcity" in, 25–26

Eden, Kathryn J., 278
Edison, Thomas, 75
education
  beginning at home, 136
  bureaucracy, 140–42, 154
  Core Curriculum in, 154, 298
  efforts to find a decent, 144–45
  as a fundamental problem of American economy, 20, 21
  government jobs in, 230–31
  imprisonment and, 192–93
  inequities in, 143–44
  leaders of, 140–42
  poverty and, 142–43, 144
  technological innovation and, 85–86
  at turn of twentieth century, 13
  universal preschool, 147–48
  vocational, 141–42
  See also college; public education system; schools
educational establishment, 140–42, 155, 286–87, 300
education vouchers, 158
efficiency
  comparing, 26
  in definition of economics, 25–26
  in transportation, healthcare, and education, 119
  using resources inefficiently and, 27
  See also wastefulness of resources
Einstein, Albert, 95, 142, 220
Eisenhower, Dwight D., 39, 181
electricity, 75
electric trolley system, 121–22, 123
electronics industry
  Japanese television manufacturing, 54, 57, 60, 76–77
  research and development and, 249
  Taiwanese, 54, 57, 60, 77, 291
Emanuel, Rahm, 329
emergency room visits, 165, 301
employment
  discrimination in, 99, 139
  lack of growth in, 15
  rise and fall of industries and, 100
  two-tier wage system in, 107–108
  World War II, during, 37–38, 254
  See also jobs; make-work sector
England, 73, 291
entitlement spending, 244, 245, 259–60. *See also* Medicaid; Medicare; Social Security
Eskow, Richard, 209
Europe
  America's Cold War aid to, 54, 291
  containment of Communism in, 51–52
  foreign trade and, 248, 255
  gas taxes in, 130
  intercity trains in, 128
  Marshall Plan and, 57, 291
  postwar economic recovery in, 59
  public transportation in, 128, 131, 284, 285
  See also Eastern Europe; *individual country names*
European Union (EU), 96, 125, 212, 236, 309
express lanes, 131, 297
exurbs, 46, 124

FAA. *See* Federal Aviation Administration
Facebook, 81, 84, 85
Faux, Jeff, 258
Federal Aviation Administration (FAA), 91
federal budget deficit, 22, 50, 233
  defense spending and, 181, 245–46
  economic problems impacting, 292
  entitlement spending and, 245, 259
  Franklin D. Roosevelt, under, 36
  Great Depression and, 35–36, 40
  Great Recession and, 246
  main contributing factors to, 246

political and historical perspective of, 244–45
size of, 243–44
suburbanization adding to America's, 50
as symptom of economic decline, 251
2000–2017, 244
World War II and, 36–37, 40
Federal Deposit Insurance Corporation (FDIC), 204, 205, 207, 254
Federal Housing Administration (FHA), 34–35, 39, 42, 43
Federal Reserve, 203, 205, 207, 248
federal sentencing mandates, 192
federal spending. *See* government spending
Feinberg, Michael, 152
FDIC. *See* Federal Deposit Insurance Corporation
FHA. *See* Federal Housing Administration
Field of Dreams (film), 123, 296
financial crisis (2008), 28, 93, 204, 205–207, 214, 246
financialization, 208–10
financial predators, 210–11
financial sector, 179
college grads drawn to jobs in, 209
creating jobs in, 315
deregulation and, 203–204
Dodd-Frank Wall Street Reform and Consumer Protection Act (2010), 207, 213
economic consequences of wastefulness in, 239–40
economic role of banking, 201–202
financial crisis of 2008 and, 205–207
financialization and, 208–10
as a fundamental problem of American economy, 21
insurance industry, 211
jobs destroyed and created in, 315
real estate industry, 211
solutions to inefficiencies in, 212–14, 304–305
wastefulness of resources and, 28, 214–15, 290
Fine, Michael, 170
Finkelstein, Amy, 164–65, 288
First Focus (organization), 193
Fitzgerald, F. Scott, 266
flooding, 66, 67
Florida, 148, 198
food stamp program, 257, 259, 263, 278
Forbes, Steve, 224
Ford, Henry, 74, 75
Ford Motor Company, 78, 79, 80, 125
foreign countries
aid to, 52–53, 54
borrowing from, 22, 25, 50
businesses in China, 88–89
oil from, 38, 39, 40, 49
See also individual countries
foreign trade, 255
foreign trade deficit, 22, 50, 246–50, 251, 292
Fort Wayne, Indiana, 121
fossil fuels, 65, 68, 308
France, 52, 87, 128, 291
Frank, Robert, 269
Franklin, Benjamin, 94
free-enterprise economy, 30, 52
free parking, 131, 297
Friedman, Thomas, 103, 135

gang violence, 196
Gary, Indiana, 121
gasoline, 68, 130–31
tax, 130–31, 296
Gawande, Atul, 171–72
GE. *See* General Electric
Gekko, Gordon, 205
General Electric (GE, company), 54, 76, 79, 83, 84, 87
General Electric Capital Group, 213
General Motors (GM, company), 115

big autos built by, 125
building plants in China, 78
decline in manufacturing by, 80
decline in public transportation and, 34, 39, 121–22, 123
large vehicles built by, 125
streetcar system and, 122
wage system, 108
Georgia, 148, 256
Germany
America's shrinking manufacturing base and, 291
apprenticeship programs in, 150
Cold War and, 51
industrial policy and, 92
as industrial rival, 76
Marshall Plan and, 52, 291
oil shortage in, 37
postwar economic recovery in, 76, 87, 291
ghettoes, urban, 190, 274
GI Bill of Rights, 256
gifted, schools created for the, 149
Gingrich, Newt, 128, 190
Glass-Steagall Act (1933), 203–204, 207, 213
Gleckman, Howard, 165
globalization, 14, 31
corporate power and, 263
fall of American industrial power, 60–61
history of, 59
unraveling of the social contract and, 258–59
See also offshoring
global warming, 31
adding jobs to deal with, 308–309
automobiles and, 127
combating in the long run, 68
deniers and skeptics of, 67
economic consequences of, 66
explained, 64–66
hurricanes and, 66
mitigating effects of, 67
Paris Agreement and, 68
public transportation and, 126, 127
solutions to, 67–69
years with the hottest temperatures since 1880s, 68
GM. *See* General Motors
Goddard, Robert H., 75
Goldfarb, Janice, 137
Goldin, Claudia, 263
Goldman Sachs (company), 213
Goldwater, Barry, 257, 327
Google, 81, 84
government employees, 230–31
government spending
cuts in entitlement spending, 259–60
Democrats vs. Republicans, under, 244–45
on education, 133
entitlement programs and, 245, 259
funding shovel-ready projects, 329–30
in high-tech firms, 93–94
income inequality and, 266, 268
on infrastructure, 91
investment in private firms, 93–94
on Medicare and Medicaid, 162
on public transportation, 131–32
See also defense spending; subsidies, government
government subsidies. *See* subsidies, government
Gramm, Phil, 328
Great Depression, 14, 23
banking during, 204
birthrate during, 35, 36, 42
by-products of nation's effort to meet challenges of, 39–40
federal budget deficit and, 36
Federal Deposit Insurance Corporation and, 204
federally insured mortgage loans during, 34–35

home construction and, 35–36
New Deal spending on transportation and, 33–34
recovery from, 31
unemployment during, 217
Great Divergence, 263–64
Great Jobs Switch, 306, 307–22
Bernie Sanders's policies and, 323
in criminal justice system, 314–15
in education, 311–12
in financial services, 315
getting people to switch, 320–21
global warming and, 308–309
in healthcare system, 313–14
in infrastructure, 310
in make-work sector, 315–16
in manufacturing, 309
in military-industrial complex, 314
in 1940s, 321–22
overview, 307–308
placing jobs applicants in new jobs and, 319
in putting the permanent underclass back to work, 317–18
in technological innovation, 309–10
total jobs created, 319–20
in transportation, 310–11
Great Recession (2007–2009), 93, 103, 238, 243, 246, 329. *See also* financial crisis (2008)
Great Society program, 254, 257
Greenhouse, Steven, 258–59
greenhouse gases, 65, 68, 326
Greenspan, Alan, 22, 205, 207
Gregg, Judd, 328
Gulf Wars, 53, 289
gun control laws, 199
gun violence, 198–99

halfway houses, 197, 200, 304
Hamilton, Alexander, 73
Harley-Davidson (manufacturer), 108
Harris, Marvin, 190
Hart, Betty, 136
Hash, James, 100
healthcare insurance
administrative costs associated with, 164, 168, 173, 228, 238, 288
"Cadillac" plans, 174, 302
corporate income taxes and, 79
creating a standardized medical insurance form for, 169–70
emergency room visits and, 165
employer-based, 38, 160–61, 301–302
foreign governments providing, 79
inefficient use of labor in, 28
origin of employer-based healthcare, 38, 40
pay-as-you-go payments and, 164–65, 288
premiums
employer compensation for, 161, 237–38
employer-sponsored, 237–38
malpractice, 169
manufacturing and, 79
Medicare for All and, 174, 176, 301–302
tax deductions and, 224
single-payer system, 173, 174–77, 301–302, 305, 314
unneeded medical services and, 163–64, 288
See also Affordable Care Act
healthcare system
administrative costs for, 164, 168, 173, 228, 288
economic consequences of wastefulness in, 237–38
employer-based healthcare insurance and, 38, 40
factors influencing rising costs of, 163–66, 287–88
as a fundamental problem of American economy, 20
impacting other economic problems, 23

increased spending on, 159–60
inefficient use of labor in, 28
influencing other economic issues, 292–93
job prospects in, 116
jobs created and destroyed in, 313–14
make-work jobs in, 227–28, 238, 305
per capita healthcare spending on, 27
reducing costs associated with, 168
solutions to inefficiencies in, 300–302
sources of financing, 160–62
spending on in America vs. other wealthy nations, 119
steps to decreasing inefficiency in, 168–73
wastefulness of resources in, 28, 168, 237–38
See also Affordable Care Act
Heckman, James, 148
hedge fund operators, 267
Helmsley, Leona, 222
Hemingway, Ernest, 266
Herbert, Bob, 184
Hewitt, Peter Cooper, 75
Hewlett-Packard (HP, company), 83, 84, 87
Hicks, Michael J., 110
High Point, North Carolina, 196
high school
graduates
job prospects for, 115–16
math abilities of, 141
unprepared for college, 133
vocational and apprenticeship programs in, 141–42, 149–51
high-speed rail system, 89, 128–29, 236, 284–85, 295–96, 297, 311
high-tech industry. *See* technological innovation
highway mileage standards, 131
highways
building, 33–34, 42, 123, 296, 297
federal budget deficit and, 50
government ending subsidization of, 296
origins of federal system of, 123
traffic congestion and, 123–25
Hira, Anil, 62
Hira, Ron, 62
Hispanic Americans
dropping out of school, 193
in prison, 189, 190, 239
suburbanization and, 42, 43, 137, 273, 274
home construction, 35–36, 39–40, 46
Home Depot (retailer), 48
home health aides, 116, 313–14
homeless, 276, 317
home mortgages. *See* mortgage
Home Owners' Loan Corporation, 34
homework, 136, 285
Honda (company), 78
Hong Kong, China, 248
Hoover, Herbert, 17, 19, 36
hospital care costs, 165, 171
hospital jobs, 313–14
"hot wars," 51
housing
African Americans being denied to buy, 35
postwar home construction, 35–36, 39–40, 42
See also mortgage; suburbanization: postwar
housing subdivisions, 44, 274, 284
Houston, Texas, 125, 132, 326
Hubbard, Alan, 164
Hurricane Katrina (2005), 31, 67
Hurricane Sandy (2012), 31, 66, 67, 308
Hussein, Saddam, 47

IBM (International Business Machines), 79, 81, 83, 84, 87, 92, 151

illegal immigrants, 19–20, 97, 276
illiteracy, 135, 196, 303, 318
immigrants, 19–20, 41, 48, 97, 274, 276
"imperial overstretch," 182
incarceration rate, 27–28
income distribution
  consequences of inequality of, 268–71
  equality in (1930s–1970s), 261, 262–63
  Great Compression, 262–63
  Great Divergence, 263–64
  inequality in, 22, 261
  taxes and, 266, 268
income tax. *See* personal income tax; taxes
India, 81, 83, 86, 87, 237, 309
individualism, 14
Indonesia, 37, 63, 102, 109
industrial policy, 71, 91–93, 95–96
Industrial Revolution, 65, 73
industry
  America as leader in, 74–75
  American interdependence with other countries, 77–78
  America's rivals in, 60, 76, 77
  electricity and, 75
  fall of American power in, 60–61, 71, 76–80
  first two decades of twentieth century, during, 75
  mass production in, 74
  rise of America's power in, 73
  at turn of twentieth century, 13
  World War II and, 75–76
  See also manufacturing; technological innovation
industry innovation. *See* technological innovation
inefficient use of resources. *See* wastefulness of resources
infrastructure
  collapse of I-35W bridge, Minneapolis, 90
  decline in, 71
  deterioration of American, 71, 90–91
  explained, 89
  jobs created for repairing and modernizing, 310
  repairing America's crumbling, 94–95
inheritance tax. *See under* taxes
inner-city neighborhoods, 35, 137, 197, 274
inner-city schools, 137
innovation. *See* technological innovation
insurance. *See* healthcare insurance
insurance companies
  Medicare for All and, 176–77
  sales reps in, 228–29, 316–17
Intel (company), 81, 84, 87, 92
Intergovernmental Panel on Climate Change, 308
intermittently poor, 275
Internal Revenue Code, 28, 97
  costs of complying to, 219–20, 223
  cutting jobs in, 315
  economic consequences of wastefulness in, 240
  eliminating make-work jobs and, 231
  length of, 219
  loopholes in, 221
  people benefiting from, 220–21
  simplifying, 305
  solutions to reforming, 224
  tax breaks for the wealthy in, 222–23
  tax expenditures/deductions in, 223–24
Internal Revenue Service (IRS), 160, 219, 290
internships, 116, 228, 317
IRS. *See* Internal Revenue Service
Isaacson, Walter, 269
Italy, 52, 76, 173, 199, 291
I-35W bridge (Minneapolis, Minnesota), 90

Jackson, Michael, 15
Jacobson, Louis, 67
Japan
America's Cold War aid to, 52, 54, 60, 291
America's loss of technological edge and, 82
America's shrinking manufacturing base and, 21
automobile industry, 60, 78, 80, 125
China's high-speed rail system and, 89
competition with American manufacturing, 59, 76
industrial policy and, 92, 96, 309
as industrial rival, 76
parental involvement in education in, 136
Pearl Harbor (1941), 37, 331
postwar economic recovery in, 59
public transportation in, 128, 131, 284–85
railway system in, 128, 285
release of convicts in, 196
semiconductor industry and, 92
targeting American market, 54, 76, 248, 255
television manufacturing by, 54, 57, 60, 76–77, 281
trade wars with, 60
World War II and, 37
Jefferson, Thomas, 73
Jim Crow laws, 256
job placement counselors, 319
jobs
from American high-tech corporations, 84–85
Americans competing with foreign workers for, 103–104
author's personal wish list of, 318
automation's effect on, 110–11
in the city, suburbanization's influence on, 48, 49
for college grads, 116
created through New Deal public works projects, 33–34
in criminal justice sector, 239, 314–15
difficulties of young Americans getting, 241
for high school graduates, 115–16
in insurance industry, 211
involving compliance to tax code, 219–20, 223
lack of good, 105
manufacturing, loss of, 71, 100–103
offshoring of. *See* offshoring
for permanent underclass, 277–78, 317–18
postwar employment discrimination and, 99
in real estate, 211
shortage of, 22
shovel-ready projects, 329–30
unionized, 104–105, 140
Wal-Mart's influence on, 105–107
for working class, 105, 115–16
See also employment; Great Jobs Switch; make-work sector
Johnson, Lyndon B., 53, 161, 170, 254, 257
JPMorgan Chase (firm), 213
Julius Caesar (Shakespeare), 323
Jumpstart (program), 137

Katz, Lawrence, 111
Kawasaki (company), 89
Kay, Jane Holtz, 34, 122, 123, 126
Keillor, Garrison, 158
Kennan, George, 53
Kennedy, David M., 183, 196
Kennedy, John F., 267, 331
Kennedy, Paul, 181–82
Kentucky, 150
Keyes, John Maynard, 329
Khan, Salman, 153
Khan Academy, 153–54
Khrushchev, Nikita, 53

King, Angus, 213
King, Martin Luther, Jr., 111, 275
KIPP (Knowledge Is Power Program) schools, 151, 152, 153
Klein, Joe, 141–42
Kohler (manufacturer), 108
Kopp, Wendy, 152
Korean War (1950–1953), 53
Kotlikoff, Lawrence, 161
Kristof, Nicholas, 198, 277
Kurtz, David L., 115

labor
- comparing efficiency and, 26
- inefficient use of, 27, 117
- strikes, 105, 254
- unions
  - decline of, 104–105
  - postwar social contract with management, 254–55
  - service sector jobs, 104
  - strikes and, 105
  - teachers, 140, 286
  - wages and, 104
- women in labor market, 262, 263, 265
- *See also* employment; jobs; make-work sector

Lancaster, Pennsylvania, 121
Lao-tzu, 326
Lash, Christopher, 269
Lehman Brothers (firm), bankruptcy, 20, 205, 214
LePatner, Barry B., 90
LeRoy, Greg, 106–107
Levin, David, 152
Levittown (Long Island, New York), 46, 235
libraries, 260, 311, 312
Lincoln, Abraham, 270, 274
literacy programs, 196, 303, 314
Lithwick, Dahlia, 193
local zoning authorities, 42, 45
long-term poverty, 275
Los Angeles, California, 125
Luce, Henry, 13
Lynn, Barry, 54, 78

Madoff, Bernard, 195
magnet schools, 144
"Make America great again" slogan, 19
make-work sector
- adding nothing to American economy and standard of living, 225
- attorneys, 226–27
- cutting jobs in, 315–17
- economic consequences of wastefulness in, 240
- as a fundamental problem of American economy, 21, 290–91
- government jobs and, 230–31
- Great Jobs Switch and, 307
- in healthcare, 227–28, 238, 305
- number of Americans holding jobs in, 21, 97, 290
- overview, 97, 217
- sales reps, 228–29
- solutions to inefficiencies in, 231–32, 305
- tax preparation industry, 224, 231, 240, 290, 315
- telemarketers, 226
- telephone solicitors, 226
- waste of the best and the brightest in, 229–30
- *See also* Internal Revenue Code

malpractice
- insurance, 169, 227
- suits, 163, 168–69, 287–88, 300–301, 305

Mandelbaum, Michael, 135
Manhattan (New York City), 66
Manhattan Project, 186
manufacturing
- Alexander Hamilton on, 73
- America's decline in, 21, 29, 60–62, 71, 283, 291–92

China's growth in, 60–61, 88–89
Cold War competition with Japan, 54
corporate income tax rate influencing, 79
foreign trade deficit and, 249, 250
as a fundamental problem of American economy, 21
Japanese television, 54, 57, 60
jobs for rebuilding, 309
labor unions and, 104–105
loss of jobs in, 71, 100–103, 110–11
mass production as standard mode of, 74
offshoring and, 61–62
peak of employment from, 100
research and development and, 83–85, 249
solutions to inefficiencies in, 306
technological innovation and, 82–83
US aid to Asia and, 54, 60
Wal-Mart and, 78–79
World War II, immediately following, 59
See also industry; technological innovation

Margo, Robert, 263
marijuana, legalizing, 197, 199, 304
Marshall, George C., 52
Marshall Plan, 52, 57, 291
Marx, Karl, 55, 63
mass consumption, 74, 255
mass production, 74, 77, 255
mass transit. *See* transportation: public
math education, 134, 136, 140, 141, 146, 157–58, 285, 300. *See also* STEM education
McAfee, Andrew, 103
McCain, John, 17, 20, 21, 47, 213
McMansions, 46, 235
Medicaid
Affordable Care Act (ACA) and, 167, 175
constituency of, 163, 245
entitlement spending and, 245, 259
explained, 162
Medicare for All and, 175
opposition to growth of, 259
start of, 253, 257, 263
medical procedures and services
altering the pricing of, 171
high cost of, 165–66
last year of life, during, 172
unnecessary, 163–64, 169, 171–72, 176, 288, 292–93, 301
medical records, 163
Medicare, 168
Affordable Care Act (ACA) and, 168
drug prescription plan (2005), 257
entitlement spending and, 245, 259
expenses for last year of life, 172
explained, 161–62
extending to all Americans choosing to join, 174–77, 301–302
government spending on, 245
growing senior citizen population and, 163
hospital benefits through, 162
opposition to growth of, 259
prescription benefit program, 171
schedule of reimbursement payments, 173
start of, 253, 257, 263
unnecessary drugs, operations, and procedures under, 171–72
Medicare for All, 174–77, 301–302, 305
Megabus (transportation service), 129
mentally ill, 191, 192, 199, 200, 239, 276, 313, 315
Mercury Marine (manufacturer), 108
Mexico, 20, 21, 63, 78, 258
Miami-Dade County (Florida), 198
Microsoft (company), 81, 84, 87
middle class
consequences of technological change effecting, 103

consumption by, 265
decline of, 261, 262
educational options for, 143, 144
GI Bill of Rights and, 256
offshoring and "hollowing out" of, 103
redistribution of income to the rich from, 209
shrinking of, 261
stagnant wages and, 264–65
suburbanization and, 42, 43, 48, 274
tax rate for, 240
temporarily poor, 275
Middle East, 50, 127, 184
military (United States)
draft, 182, 183, 322
leaving ghetto environment for, 195
at turn of twentieth century, 13–14
volunteer service in, 182–83
military-industrial complex
BRAC (Base Realignment and Closure), 327–28
Cold War's influence on, 56, 57
components of, 92
defense contractors, 183–84
economic consequences of wastefulness in, 238–39
energy independence and, 186
as a fundamental problem of American economy, 20
industrial policy and, 92–93
jobs destroyed and created for, 314
oil supply and, 184–85
solutions to inefficiencies in, 186–87, 302–303
wastefulness of resources in, 27
See also defense spending
millennials, 15, 97, 99
minimum wage, 241, 254, 264, 305
Morgan Stanley (firm), 213
mortgage
deduction, 224
interest on tax returns, 42
loans
African Americans denied, 39, 42
collateralized debt obligations (CDOs) and, 206
Dodd-Frank Wall Street Reform and Consumer Protection Act and, 207
federally insured during Great Depression, 34–35, 39
for returning veterans, 42, 256
redlining, 35, 39, 43
Moses, Robert, 123–25
Motorola (company), 87
Mueller, John, 187
multinational corporations, operations set up in developing countries by, 61, 77, 78, 81, 88–89. *See also* offshoring
Murphy, Cullen, 185

National City Lines (company), 34
national curriculum. *See* Common Core/core curriculum
National Educational Association (NEA), 140, 156, 286
National Housing Act (1934), 34
National Institute of Education, 138
national railway network. *See* railway system
National Rifle Association (NRA), 199
New Deal
income equality and, 263
increase in employment from, 217
job creation through public works projects under, 33–34
major parts of, 254
roads and highway building under, 123, 310
spending on construction, 33
New Orleans, Louisiana, 121, 325–26
New York (state), 41, 123–24
New York City, 295
"Chinese buses" based in, 129
ending gang violence in, 196

flooding and subway tunnels in, 66
Levittown suburb, 46, 235
public transportation in, 132
subway system, Hurricane Sandy and, 66
tax rates, 222
Nissan (company), 78
Nixon, Richard, 55
Noah, Timothy, 263
No Child Left Behind Act, 158
Nomorobo (call-blocking service), 231
North Korea, 53
NRA. *See* National Rifle Association
nuclear arms race, 55
nuclear power, 68
nursing homes, 172, 196, 313

Obama, Barack, 91–92, 95, 96, 131, 207, 329
Obamacare. *See* Affordable Care Act
office parks, 44, 45, 46
offshoring
corporate income tax rates and, 79
loss of good jobs and, 105
manufacturing job loss and, 63–64, 101–102, 110–11
outsourcing vs., 108–109
overview, 61–62
permanent underclass and, 277
research and development facilities, 83–84, 87
solutions to problems related to, 306
wages and, 62–63, 64, 101, 109
by Wal-Mart, 78–79, 105–106
oil
defense spending and, 186
dependence on foreign, 38, 39, 40, 45, 49, 127, 236, 308
investing in a rail system and, 129
military establishment and, 184–85
suburbanization and dependence on foreign, 50
World War II and, 37, 38, 40
Oklahoma, 148
Olson, Nina E., 219
Oracle (company), 84
organized labor. *See* labor: unions
O'Shaughnessy, Lynn, 138
Ostry, Jonathan, 268–69
Our Revolution (Sanders), 30
outsourcing, 107, 108–109
Outsourcing America (Hira and Hira), 62

parents
America's educational decline and, 135–36, 285
children enjoying higher standard of living than their, 14, 15, 241
searching for good schools, 144
universal preschool and, 148
Paris Agreement, 68
Parker, Dorothy, 43
parking/parking lots, 44, 125, 131, 297
Parkinson, C. Northcote, 317
Parkinson's Law, 317
patents, 81
Paterson, New Jersey, 138
pay-as-you-go insurance payments, 164–65, 288
payroll tax, 162, 222
Pearl Harbor (1941), 37, 181, 331
pensions, 245, 253, 254, 255
permanent American underclass, 48, 50, 275–78
personal income tax, 20, 224, 263–64, 305
personal injury lawyers, 227
Peterson, Pete, 244
Pew Research Center poll on global climate, 67
pharmaceutical companies, 79, 166, 171, 176–77
Philadelphia, Pennsylvania, 66, 295, 317
Philippines, 78, 102
Phoenix, Arizona, 132, 326
Phoenix House (drug treatment program), 198

Plater-Zyberk, Elizabeth, 44, 45
plutocracy, 270
policing, 193, 303
political consequences of income inequality, 270–71
political left, solutions to economic problems proposed by, 19
political right, solutions to economic problems proposed by, 19
poor, the
  armed forces staffed by, 182, 183
  bail and, 198
  banking and, 202
  chronically, 275
  in the cities after suburbanization, 42, 43, 48
  community health centers for, 170
  creating jobs in financial sector for, 315
  financial predators and, 210–11
  Great Society program for, 257
  imprisonment of, 190
  intermittently, 275
  jobs created for helping, 317–18
  Medicaid for, 162
  national sales tax and, 224
  personal income tax and, 224
  public libraries for, 311
  redlined neighborhoods and, 35, 39
  temporarily, 275
  wages of, 264
Portland, Oregon, 121, 132, 295
postwar suburbanization. *See* suburbanization: postwar
poverty
  child, 15, 278
  crime and, 194–95
  education and, 142–44
  growing permanent American underclass, 275–78
  hopelessness and despair of those in, 278–79
  inner-city schools and, 137–38
  long-term, 275
  number of Americans living in, 274, 276–77
  school readiness and, 136–37, 138
  suburbanization and urban, 273–74
  See also poor, the
poverty line, 274
predators, financial, 210–11
preschool/preschoolers, 137, 147–48, 278, 312
prescription drugs
  eliminating unnecessary, 171–72
  high cost of, 166
  lowering the costs of, 171
  Medicare and, 162, 257
  Medicare for All and, 175, 176–77
presidential campaign (2008), 20
presidential campaign and election (2016), 22, 30, 325
presidential commissions, 326–27, 330
presidential election (1932), 33
President's Council of Advisors on Science and Technology, 85
Prestowitz, Clyde, 63, 101, 103–104, 135
primary medical care, population-based, 170, 313
prisons
  costs associated with, 189
  as counterproductive, 194–95
  for drug-related crimes, 189, 197–98, 314
  incarceration rate, 27–28
  inmates
    African American and Hispanic males, 190
    characteristics of, 191–93, 239
    facts about, 189, 289
    job training for, 303–304
    mentally ill, 179, 191, 315
    number of, 189
  job training in, 303–304
  literacy programs in, 196, 303
  for nonviolent crimes, 179, 192, 195–96

reasons for putting and keeping so many people in, 191–92
for violent crimes, 195
vocational training in, 197
productivity
automation and, 110
wages and, 112, 237, 265
"progressive education," 140–41
public education system, 283
charter schools and, 151–52
cost of America's wasteful, 146–47, 236–37
decline in American, 133–35
fixing America's, 147–58
inefficient use of labor and, 27
influencing other economic issues, 292
inner-city schools, 137–38
jobs created and destroyed in, 311–12
problem related to decline in, 135–42, 285–87
solutions to inefficiencies in, 298–300
See also education; schools
public libraries, 206, 260, 311, 312
public works projects, 33–34, 95

Quindlen, Anna, 25, 115

railway system
age of industrial capitalist and, 74
decrease in use of American, 121–22, 128
deterioration of, 236, 284–85
in Europe, China, and Japan, 128, 131–32, 284–85
high-speed, 89, 127–28, 132, 236, 294, 295–96, 311
refurbishing, 296–97
subsidization of, 131
suburbanization and, 48, 284
trucking and, 129
Rattner, Steven, 266, 268
Ravitch, Diane, 141
RCA (company), 54, 76
Reagan, Ronald, 55, 56, 77–78, 92, 181, 222, 326
real estate
brokers/agents, 35, 290
industry, 211
prices, 206
recidivism, 196–97
redlined neighborhoods, 35, 39, 43
Reich, Robert, 229–30
remedial courses, 27, 119, 133, 134, 145, 146, 155, 287
renewable sources of energy, 68, 309
Report Card (American Society of Civil Engineers), 91
Report on Manufactures (Hamilton), 73
Republican Party, 223, 245
research and development (R&D)
America's lagging support for, 86–87
bolstering, 93–94
high-wage jobs and, 249
industrial policy and, 96
manufacturing base and, 83–85, 249
for military-industrial complex, 92–93
offshoring, 83–84, 87
technological innovation and, 93–94
tying to the actual manufacturing, 249
resources, wasting. *See* wastefulness of resources
rich, the. *See* wealthy, the
Richistan (Frank), 269
Rifkin, Jeremy, 104, 107
Rise and Fall of Great Powers, The (Kennedy), 181
Risley, Todd R., 136
roads/roadways, 33–34, 39, 44. *See also* highways
Roaring Twenties, 75
Roberts, John, 167, 168
Robinson, Jackie, 256

Rochester, New York, 121
Rogers, David, 278
Romano, Andrew, 196
Romney, Mitt, 47
Roosevelt, Franklin D., 261
  federal budget deficit under, 36
  federal highway program under, 123
  New Deal spending on transportation under, 33
  public works projects under, 95
  relief and recovery program, 329
Rosenberg, Tina, 166
Rothkopf, David, 184
Rothstein, Richard, 143
Rotman, David, 103
Ryan, Paul, 20

sales reps, 228–29, 231–32, 305, 316–17
Salt Lake City, Utah, 132
Sanders, Bernie, 29, 30, 159, 322–23
San Diego, California, 121
Sandy Hook Elementary School (Newtown, Connecticut), 199
San Francisco, California, 66, 121, 296
Santa, John, 173
Santayana, George, 77
scarcity, in definition of economics, 25–26
schools
  banning calculators from elementary, 157, 299
  charter, 151–52
  for gifted, 149
  inner-city, 137
  magnet, 144
  open from 7:00 a.m. to 7:00 p.m. all year long, 148–49, 298, 311
  preschool, 137, 147–48, 278, 312
  segregated, 143
  shelter drills in, 51
  and vouchers, 158
Schorr, Daniel, 278–79
Schorr, Lisbeth, 278–79
Schrag, Peter, 142
Schumpeter, Joseph, 100
science education, 134, 140. *See also* STEM education
Sclar, Elliott, 46
Scranton, Pennsylvania, 121
Seattle, Washington, 132
SEMATECH (Semiconductor Manufacturing Technology), 92, 96
semiconductor industry, 91, 92, 96
senior citizen population, increase in, 163, 259, 287
September 11th terrorist attack, 331
service sector jobs, 63, 71, 101, 103, 110
Shaefer, H. Luke, 278
Shakespeare, William, 323
Shaw, George Bernard, 139
Shelby, Richard, 159
shopping centers / malls, 44, 46, 47–48, 49
shovel-ready projects, 95, 329–30
Shulman, Douglas, 219
Siemens (company), 150
Silber, John, 139
Simic, Charles, 331
Singapore, 87
Smith, Adam, 29, 110, 230
Smith, Hedrick, 108, 270
social consequences of inequality, 269–70
social contract, 253–60
  for African Americans, 256–57
  GI Bill of Rights, 256
  Great Society program, 257
  postwar labor-management, 254–56
  unraveling of, 253, 258–60
  See also Medicaid; Medicare; Social Security
socialized medicine, 302
social safety net. *See* social contract
Social Security, 45, 245, 253, 254, 259, 263
social services, jobs in the, 317–18

solar power, 68
solutions
  to economic problems and inefficiencies
    by Bernie Sanders, 322–23
    in criminal justice system, 194–200, 300–304
    in education, 298–300
    in financial sector, 212–14, 304–305
    in healthcare system, 168–77, 300–302
    Internal Revenue Code and, 224
    lack of support for, 331
    in make-work sector, 231–32, 305
    in manufacturing, 306
    in military-industrial complex, 186–88, 302–303
    by political left and right, 19
    presidential commissions recommending, 326–27
    public education, 147–58
    in transportation, 130–32, 295–97
    Trump, proposed by, 19–20
    See also Great Jobs Switch
  to global warming, 67–69
  for technological innovation, 93–96, 309–10
Solyndra (manufacturer), 96
South Carolina, 150
Southern Education Foundation, 143
South Korea, 21, 53, 77, 82, 87, 92, 236
Soviet Union, 27, 37, 51–52, 55, 57, 59, 181, 291
Sowell, Thomas, 141
Spain, 173
Speck, Jeff, 44, 45
sprawl, suburban, 43–45
standardized medical insurance form, 169–70
Stanley Kaplan University, 145
"Star Wars" missile defense system, 184
steel production, 29, 74
Stein, Herbert, 22
STEM education, 85–86, 151, 309, 310
Stevenson, Bryon, 194
St. Louis, Missouri, 317
stock market crash of 1929, 75, 204, 261
Stockton, California, 196
streetcars, 121–22, 132
student loans, 145–46
students
  academic abilities, 119, 134
  low-income, 142–43
  removing disruptive, 154–55, 299
  as a source of America's educational decline, 137–38, 286
subprime loans, 206
subsidies, government, 96
  cuts in, 260
  for highways, 48, 123, 129, 285, 296
  industrial policy and, 96
  for public transportation, 131–32
  for rebuilding manufacturing base, 306, 309
suburbanization
  four centuries ago, 41
  postwar, 14, 31, 41–50
    abandonment of American cities and, 47–49, 273, 292
    demise of American education and, 137
    economic consequences of wastefulness in, 235
    effects of, 284
    federally insured mortgage loans and, 34–35
    foreign trade deficit and, 250
    housing for veterans and, 35–36, 42
    New Deal investment in transportation and, 34
    oil dependence and, 40
    public to private transportation and, 122

public transportation and, 42–43, 45, 49–50
short-term success of, 47, 49
sprawl and, 43–45
urban ghettoes before and after, 274
urban poverty and, 273–74
wastefulness of resources and, 46–47, 49–50
Suburban Nation: The Rise of Sprawl and the Decline of the American Dream (Duany, Plater-Zyberk, and Speck), 44
Summers, Lawrence, 95
Sweden, 173
Sweeney, John J., 15, 99
swimming pools, 47
Sylvania (company), 76
Symantec (company), 84
Syracuse, New York, 121

Taiwan, 92, 236
America's Cold War aid to, 54, 57, 77, 291
electronics production in China, 60, 62, 291
industrial policy and, 92
rising living standards in, 87
Target (retailer), 48, 78, 104
tax attorneys. *See under* attorneys
tax code. *See* Internal Revenue Code
tax cuts, 246, 261
taxes
on bank assets over $500 billion, 214
corporate income tax, 20, 79
rates, 20, 79
earned income tax credit, 257, 261, 263
federal income tax, 38, 221, 222, 224
flat personal, 224
on financial transactions, 212
fossil fuel, 68
gasoline, 130–31, 296
income inequality and, 266, 268
inheritance, 20, 222–23, 224, 262
treatment of the rich, 222–23, 263–64
See also Internal Revenue Code
tax preparers, 221
teachers
certification process of, 142, 156, 299, 321
declining quality of, 138–40
incompetent, getting rid of, 156–57, 286, 298–99
for low-income students, 144
math, 157–58
raising wages of, 156, 299
replaced with best and brightest of college graduates, 311
Teach for America and, 152–53
unions, 140, 286
Teach for America (TFA), 152–53
Tea Party, 19
technological advances. *See* automation; technological innovation
technological innovation
America's loss of industrial innovation and, 81, 82–85
creating jobs for, 309–10
East catching up with West in, 87
education system and, 85–86
industrial policy and, 92
loss of America's lead in, 71, 81–82
manufacturing and, 82–83
patents and, 82
research and development and, 83–85, 86–87, 93–94, 249
solutions for regaining lead in, 93–96, 309–10
technology
America's Cold War aid to foreign countries and, 54, 57, 60, 77
growth in Chinese, 60–61
job loss and change in, 101, 102–103
need for high-tech manufacturing base, 249

United States losing innovative lead in, 81–82
See also automation; research and development
telemarketers, 226, 231, 316
telephone operators, 105
telephone solicitors, 226, 316
television
manufacturing, 54, 57, 60, 76–77
public education and, 137
tellers, bank, 105, 111
tenure for teachers, 156, 157, 299
terrorism/terrorists, 185–86, 187, 303
Texas Instruments (company), 92
Thaler, Richard, 169
Three Billion Capitalists (Prestowitz), 103
"three strikes and you're out" laws, 192
thrift institutions, 203
Toledo, Ohio, 121
Too Big to Fall (LePatner), 90
Tough, Paul, 136
"toxic assets," 205
Toynbee, Arnold, 270
Toyota (company), 78, 150
trade deficit, 20, 50, 246–50, 251, 292
trade wars, United States–Japan, 60
traffic congestion, 123–24
trains, transportation by, 128, 284. *See also* railway system
transportation, 283
average American family expenditure on, 130
economic consequences of wastefulness in, 235–36
federal budget deficit and, 292
as a fundamental problem of American economy, 20, 21
influencing other economic issues, 292
jobs created and destroyed for, 310–11
New Deal spending on, 33–34, 39
public
advantages of, 125–27
bus transportation, 129, 131
high-speed rail lines, 89, 127–28, 236, 284, 295–96, 297, 311
incentives for using, 130–31
neglected during the 1930s, 34, 39
prevalence of American, 132
shift to private transportation from, 122–25
streetcars, 34, 39, 121–22, 132
subsidizing, 131–32
suburbanization's influence on, 42–43, 45, 49–50
See also railway system
solutions to inefficiencies in, 130–32, 295–97
spending on in America vs. other wealthy nations, 119
suburbanization and, 41, 42–43, 45, 49
traffic congestion and, 123–24, 123–25
by trucking, 129
at turn of twentieth century, 13
wastefulness and inefficiencies in, 27, 121, 129–30, 284–85
See also automobiles; highways
Troubled Assets Relief Program (TARP), 205, 329
trucking, 129, 130, 284, 285
Truman, Harry, 39, 52, 77–78
Trump, Donald J.
campaign slogan (2016), 13, 19
rebuilding infrastructure proposed by, 95
solutions to fixing the economy, 19–20
tax plan by, 20
trillion-dollar plan of, 325
United Technology offshoring and, 101–102
Twain, Mark, 201

Twitter, 84, 85
two-tier wage system, 107–108
typists, 105, 110

Uchetelle, Louis, 108
UN. *See* United Nations
underclass. *See* permanent American underclass
unemployment/unemployed
    among permanent underclass, 307, 317
    federal budget deficit and, 36
    Great Depression, during, 217
    Great Recession, since the, 103
    healthcare coverage and, 238
    in mid-2017, 117
    in 1933, 33
    in 1943, 38
    offshoring and, 63, 101
    repairing infrastructure and, 94–95
    shovel-ready projects for, 329–30
    World War II, during, 254
unemployment insurance, 246, 253, 254, 263
Union County College, 115
United Auto Workers, 160–61
United Kingdom, 173
United Nations (UN), 187
United Parcel Service (UPS), 107
United States Patents Office, 81
United Steel Workers, 160–61
United Technology (Carrier division), 101–102
universal healthcare, 159
    Medicare for All, 174–77
    single-payer system of, 173, 174–77, 301–302, 305, 314
    See also Affordable Care Act
universal preschool and childcare programs, 147–48, 278
universities, research and development at, 96
University of Phoenix, 145
UPS. *See* United Parcel Service
US Department of Agriculture, 274
US Department of Health and Human Services, 171, 276
US Navy SEALs, 303
US Postal Service, 230
US Steel (company), 79
US Treasury, 205, 207

VA. *See* Veterans Administration
Vargo, Franklyn J., 83
venture capital firms, 62, 94, 310
Vermont, 148
veterans
    free medical care for, 174
    GI Bill of Rights, 256
    housing and, 36, 42
    jobs created by help, 314
    mortgage loans to, 35
    post-WWII housing shortage and, 35–36
    refusing home mortgages to African American, 39
Veterans Administration (VA), 35, 39, 42
Veterans Affairs, 174, 314
Vietnam, 78, 88, 102
Vietnam War, 51, 53, 55
violence
    dealing with gun violence, 198–99
    ending gang violence, 196
    in lives of young black and Hispanic males, 190
violent crime, 194–96, 195–96, 303–304, 314
vocational counselors, 319
vocational education, 141–42, 149–51
vocational training in prisons, 197, 239
Volcker, Paul, 201, 214
"Volcker Rule," 214
Volkswagen (company), 150
von Bismarck, Otto, 325

wages
    between 1947 and 1973, 112
    between 1973 and 2015, 112

factors depressing, 112–13
in healthcare, 116
high-tech manufacturing and, 249
increase in for the rich, 263
of jobs found by laid-off workers, 101, 104
mass production and, 74
minimum, 241, 254, 264, 305
money vs. real, 111–12
offshoring and, 62–63, 64, 101, 109
paid by Wal-Mart, 106, 107
of poor, 264
productivity and, 112, 237, 265
raising teachers', 156, 299
real, 111–12, 255, 258
decline in after 1973, 258
stagnation of, 15, 22, 97, 111–12, 237, 264–65
taxation and, 222
two-tier system, 107–108
of unionized workers, 104
of working poor, 264, 276
World War II, during, 254
Wall Street (film), 227
Wal-Mart
basic facts about, 105–106
contracting out jobs to other firms, 108
influence on jobs and wages, 105–107
labor unions and, 104
offshoring and, 78–79
suburbanization and, 48
wages paid by, 106, 107
Walton, Sam, 267
Walton family, 223, 267
war on terror, 185–86, 245–46, 303
"war profiteers," 254
Warren, Elizabeth, 213
Washington, DC, 66, 295
Washington, George, 73
wastefulness of resources, 15–16
as cause of economic decline, 25–26
in criminal justice system, 239
defense spending and, 181–82
in education, 27, 146–47, 236–37
in financial sector, 28, 214–15, 239–40
in healthcare system, 28, 168, 237–38
Internal Revenue Code and, 240
in make-work sector, 28, 229–30, 231–32, 240
in military-industrial complex, 238–39
by overproducing in some economic sectors, 27–28
overview, 283
suburban lifestyle and, 46–47, 49–50, 235
in transportation, 27, 121, 129–30, 235–36, 284–85
by using them inefficiently, 27
See also solutions: to economic problems and inefficiencies
Wealth of Nations, The (Smith), 29, 230
wealthy, the
benefiting from a complicated tax code, 221
campaign contributions by, 270
definition of, 266
distancing themselves from the American mainstream, 269–70
income inequality and, 263
political consequences of, 270–71
social consequences of, 269–70
income of, 266, 267
increase in income of, 263
inheritance tax and, 222–23, 262–63
as 1 percent, 266, 267
redistribution of income from working and middle class to, 209, 240
tax treatment of, 220, 221, 222–24, 263–64

"We Are the World" (song), 15
Webb, James, 191
Webley, Kayla, 153
welfare benefits, 48, 136, 257, 266, 268, 276
Welfare Reform Act (1996), 257
Wells Fargo (company), 213
Western, Bruce, 190, 194
Westinghouse (company), 54, 76
West Virginia, 148
"white underclass," 277
WHO. *See* World Health Organization
Wilkes-Barre, Pennsylvania, 121
Wilson, Charles, 79, 253, 255
wind power, 68
Within Our Reach (Schorr and Schorr), 278–79
women
  employed as tellers, typists, and telephone operators, 105
  employment discrimination of, 99, 139
  in labor market, 262, 263, 265
women's liberation movement, 107, 139
Worcester State University, 146
working class
  armed forces staffed by, 182
  educational options for, 143, 144
  GI Bill of Rights and, 256
  jobs for, 105, 115–16
  redistribution of income to the rich from, 209
  suburbanization and, 42, 43, 48, 274
  temporarily poor and, 275
working poor, 264, 274, 276
World Health Organization (WHO), 159
World Is Flat, The (Friedman), 103
World War II, 14, 31, 33
  American industrial power and, 75–76
  birthrate and, 35, 40
  by-products of nation's effort to meet challenges of, 39–40
  defense spending during, 37–38, 40
  employer-based healthcare insurance and, 38
  federal budget deficit and, 36–37
  full-out national effort to win, 295
  home construction and, 35–36, 39–40
  lessons of, 38
  oil and, 40
  wage and price controls during, 254
  See also suburbanization: postwar
Wright brothers, 75

Yarosz, Donald J., 147

zoning authorities, 42, 43, 45
Zupan, Jeffrey M., 126
Zysman, John, 83